George Long

The Decline of the Roman Republic

Volume IV.

George Long

The Decline of the Roman Republic
Volume IV.

ISBN/EAN: 9783742821850

Manufactured in Europe, USA, Canada, Australia, Japa

Cover: Foto ©Thomas Meinert / pixelio.de

Manufactured and distributed by brebook publishing software (www.brebook.com)

George Long

The Decline of the Roman Republic

THE DECLINE

OF

THE ROMAN REPUBLIC.

BY

GEORGE LONG.

VOL. IV.

LONDON:
BELL & DALDY, YORK STREET, COVENT GARDEN.
CAMBRIDGE: DEIGHTON, BELL, & CO.
1872.

PREFACE.

This volume contains the History of Caesar's Gallic campaigns, and of the contemporaneous events at Rome. With the exception of Cicero's orations and letters, the Commentaries on the Gallic and the Civil wars, and we may add the books on the Alexandrine, African and Spanish wars, are the only extant contemporary history of the Republic. The value of Caesar's military histories is well known to those who have studied them, but those who have read them carefully are very few. Parts of the Gallic war and of the Civil war are read by boys, and if the teacher does his duty, the pupil may learn some Latin and something else too.

It is strange that one of the best Roman writers, perhaps the best of all Roman writers, is generally read only by schoolboys and to a small extent. One reason may be that the language is supposed to be so simple and easy that older students will be better employed on other writers, and that a military history is not so instructive as other antient books. But Thucydides is a political and military history, and it is read most diligently, and it is worth the labour. The scene of Caesar's campaigns is so near to us and the events resemble so much those of more recent times that perhaps the matter seems common and familiar, and we care less for it than for that which is more remote both in time and place. But there is no country in Europe the history of which is so closely connected with that of our own country as the history of France, and no history is more instructive to Englishmen than French history; which ought to be a sufficient reason for studying the book from which we learn most about the antient nations of Gallia.

This country has undergone many changes and revolutions since Caesar's time. The history of the Galli may be traced much farther back than the date of Caesar's first appearance in Gallia, but the history of France as a political community begins with Caesar's Commentaries. The country was conquered by the Romans and received from them a new language, a social organization, a system of law and many useful improvements. France still contains some of the noblest monuments of Roman architecture and innumerable traces of the skill of the Romans in the magnificent works which supplied the towns with water. The invasion of the Franks subjected a large part of this country to foreign invaders, and the effects of the conquest remain to the present day, particularly in the northern and eastern parts of Caesar's Gallia. But notwithstanding invasions, conquests and the mixture of races, a large part of the population of France retain the characteristics of the nations which Caesar brought under Roman dominion. The Gaul sticks to his native soil and is most tenacious of national habits, though he is also, as Caesar says, ingenious and capable of learning from others. His impetuous temper and want of reflection have made him in all ages the prey of greedy and cunning men, and he has paid dearly for his want of prudence and his political ignorance. In fact the elements which compose French society have not yet attained a condition of stability and never will so long as the nation remains so ignorant. The mass of the people in other countries are ignorant also, but ignorance combined with the excitability of the Gallic temperament, and the numerous civil disorders and revolutions which have agitated the country, make the prospect of permanent tranquillity very uncertain. The French are still disturbed by their own passions, and the love of military glory, and so they are liable to be misled by adventurers and sacrificed to the cupidity of governors, who draw from an industrious people the fruits of their hard labour and squander the money in luxury and expensive wars. Gallia was the country of revolutions in Caesar's time, and so it is still.

There are many editions of Caesar and many Commentaries on his writings. The latest and in some respects the best Commentary on the Gallic war is the "Histoire de César" (vol. ii.) written, as the publisher informs us, by the Emperor Napoleon III., who has also put his name at the end of the book and dated it from the Tuilleries (March 20, 1866). The volume contains both the history of the Gallic campaigns and the contemporary events at Rome. The history of the war is written after Caesar in a plain, simple and clear style, and the remarks and notes are useful for the explanation of Caesar's text. The work is accompanied by a very cheap atlas of thirty-two plates, well engraved, which will assist a reader who wishes to understand Caesar's campaigns. The author had the means of doing what no other person could have done. Excavations were made on the sites of Caesar's battle-fields and sieges, and excellent officers, among whom was Stoffel, furnished the author with valuable information. But the aid which he received diminishes in no degree the merit of the author's design, which may be assumed to be his own; and he has produced a book which will be a lasting memorial of his reign.

The work of Goeler (Cäsar's Gallischer Krieg, 1858) is also very useful, and I have often referred to it. I have not always agreed with the opinions and conclusions either of the author of the "Histoire" or of the German soldier; and I do not expect that those who have studied Caesar will always agree with me. The matter contained in the eight books of the Gallic war is so varied and extensive that no man who handles it can avoid error. I have spared no pains, and I have done my best to make the history of the conquest of Gallia intelligible to any person who will read carefully and consult good maps.

Cicero's letters, the letters written by him to Atticus, and the collection[1] of letters written by him to other persons and by other persons to him, form a valuable part of the evidence for the facts stated in this volume. Those who would form a just estimate of Cicero's character will find these letters both instructive and entertaining. They are often very difficult to understand in the original and I do not know that there is any translation which is completely sufficient. There is an English translation with notes by William Melmoth of the "Letters of Marcus Tullius Cicero to several of his Friends;" and an English translation of the sixteen books of letters to Titus Pomponius Atticus by William Heberden. There is also a French translation with notes of the letters to Atticus (1773), by the Abbé Mongault. I have not seen the German translation which Wieland began. It was finished and published after his death.

G. L.

[1] They are entitled "Ad Familiares," or "Ad Diversos," and I have often referred to them under both titles.

ROMAN CONSULS

From b.c. 57 to b.c. 40.

(CLINTON'S FASTI)

B.C.
- 57. P. Cornelius Lentulus Spinther.
  Q. Caecilius Metellus Nepos.
- 56. Cn. Cornelius Lentulus Marcellinus.
  L. Marcius Philippus.
- 55. Cn. Pompeius Magnus II.
  M. Licinius Crassus II.
- 54. L. Domitius Ahenobarbus.
  Appius Claudius Pulcher.
- 53. Cn. Domitius Calvinus.
  M. Valerius Messalla.

B.C.
- 52. Cn. Pompeius Magnus III. sole consul.
  Q. Caecilius Metellus Pius Scipio. The colleague of Pompeius during the last five months of the year.
- 51. Ser. Sulpicius Rufus.
  M. Claudius Marcellus [1].
- 50. L. Aemilius Paulus.
  C. Claudius Marcellus.
- 49. C. Claudius Marcellus.
  L. Cornelius Lentulus Crus.

---

[1] M. Claudius Marcellus, consul 51, and C. Claudius Marcellus, consul 49, were brothers, and the cousins of C. Claudius Marcellus, consul 50.

CONTENTS.

CHAPTER I.

THE HELVETII.

B.C. 58.

Livy, Epit. 103; *Caesar, B. G.* I. 1—29; *Dion Cassius,* 38. c. 31—33; *Strabo,* p. 205. 190; *Plutarch, Caesar; Suetonius, Caesar,* 24—26; *Florus*[1], iii. 10.

Caesar arrives at Geneva and raises troops in the Provincia—He constructs a wall and ditch along the south bank of the Rhone from Geneva to the Montagne du Vuache to stop the passage of the Helvetii through the Provincia—The design of the Helvetii and the other emigrants is to reach the country of the Santones near the Lower Garonne—Caesar leaves T. Labienus in command of his lines on the Rhone, and crosses the Alps into Cisalpine Gallia to bring fresh troops—His return and march from Ocelum over the Alps into Gallia Transalpina, and his passage over the Rhone above its junction with the Saône—The slow journey of the Helvetii through the defiles of the Jura to the Saône—They plunder the country—Caesar attacks one division of the Helvetii at the Saône after the main body had crossed the river, and thus destroys and disperses one fourth of the Helvetii—He crosses the Saône and follows the Helvetii—Caesar's Gallic cavalry put to flight by the enemy—Caesar's allies the Aedui do not keep their promise to furnish supplies for his army—He is informed of the treachery of Dumnorix, the Aeduan chief who commanded the Aeduan cavalry, and is only prevented from punishing him by the intercession of Divitiacus, the brother of Dumnorix—The pursuit of the Helvetii continued—Caesar's plans spoiled by the cowardice of P. Considius, one of his officers—Caesar leaves the pursuit of the

---

[1] Florus has written the history of the first seven years' campaign in a single chapter, which is worthy of this wretched compiler and rhetorician.

enemy in order to advance to Bibracte, the capital of the Aedui, and get supplies—The enemy turn round to follow Caesar, who is compelled to fight—The Helvetii are defeated and the survivors retreat in the night to the territory of the Lingones—After three days Caesar follows and compels the enemy to surrender unconditionally—Six thousand men of one of the Helvetic cantons escape in the night, are brought back and "treated as enemies"—The survivors of the emigrants are sent back to their several homes, except the Roii—The muster rolls found in the Helvetic camp show the numbers of the emigrants to have been 368,000—The number of those who returned home was 110,000 . . . 1

CHAPTER II.

ARIOVISTUS AND THE GERMANS.

B.C. 58.

Livy, Epit. 104; *Caesar, B. G.* l. 30—54; *Dion Cassius,* 38, c. 34—50; *Justinus,* xxxii. 3; *Tacitus, Germania,* c. 18; *Plutarch, Caesar*; *Orosius,* vi. 7; *Cicero, De Provinciis Consularibus,* c. 13.

Caesar is thanked by the Celtic states for defeating the Helvetii—The complaints of the Celtae about the cruelty of the German king Ariovistus, who had settled in Gallia—The parts occupied by the Germans—Caesar promises to look after the interests of the Galli—Caesar's reasons for dealing with Ariovistus—Caesar's description of the country of the Germans—The Suevi and their character and customs—The religion of the Germans, and their public economy—Caesar proposes a conference with Ariovistus—The answer of the German, and Caesar's second message to him—Caesar's demands, and the answer of Ariovistus—Caesar marches to meet Ariovistus and seizes the town of Vesontio (Besançon)—The panic of Caesar's army at the prospect of a battle with the Germans, and their mutiny—Caesar's address to his officers—The army recover their courage, and Caesar leads them from Vesontio towards the Rhine—The course of his march to the great plain—The conference between Caesar and the German king, and his answer to Caesar's demands—The conference interrupted by the Germans—Ariovistus proposes to renew the conference, which Caesar refuses, but sends two commissioners to him—The king seizes the two men and puts them in chains—The movement of the king by which he places himself in the rear of Caesar and cuts off his communications with the Aedui and Sequani—The German manner of fighting—Caesar makes a second camp in the rear of the Germans—The German attack on the second camp—Caesar compels the Germans to fight at Cernay near Mühlhausen—The battle and defeat of the Germans, who fly to the Rhine—The escape of Ariovistus with the loss of his two wives—The supposition that the river Ill was then a branch of the Rhine—The Suevi who had advanced to the Rhine retreat when they hear the news of Ariovistus' defeat—Caesar puts his troops into winter quarters, and crosses the Alps into North Italy 20

CHAPTER III.

THE BELGAE.

B.C. 57.

Livy, Epit. 104; *Caesar, B. G.* II. III. 1—6; *Strabo,* p. 206; *Dion Cassius,* 39, c. 1—5; *Plutarch, Caesar.*

Caesar in Gallia Citerior hears of the combination of the Belgae—He raises two new legions and sends them over the Alps under Q. Pedius—He crosses the Alps and marches with eight legions from the winter quarters among the Sequani to the borders of the Remi, who submit to him—The report of the Remi about the Belgian confederates; and the estimate of the forces of the several Belgian states—The geographical position of these states—Caesar places his camp on the north bank of the Axona (Aisne)—The Belgae attack Bibrax; their way of assaulting towns—They place themselves about two miles from Caesar's camp—Description of the ground of Caesar's camp, and his defences—The Belgae attempt to cross the Aisne and are defeated—The Belgian army disperses, is pursued by the Romans and slaughtered—Caesar takes Noviodunum a town of the Suessiones, and Bratuspantium a town of the Bellovaci—The leaders of the Bellovaci in this war run off to Britain—Surrender of the Ambiani—Caesar advances into the territory of the Nervii—The thick hedges in this country—Caesar prepares to make his camp on the Sabis (Sambre)—Description of the place which is identified with Neuf-Mesnil on the left bank of the Sambre—Caesar's troops are attacked while they are making their camp by the Nervii and their confederates—The great battle on the Sambre—The Belgae are defeated, and the Nervii are almost annihilated—The Aduatuci who are coming to aid the Belgae return to their country and retire to their stronghold—The position of this stronghold at the hill of Falhize, opposite to Huy on the Maas—Caesar forms a contravallation round this hill fort, which surrenders—The Aduatuci attack Caesar's lines after the surrender and are repulsed—He breaks into the town and sells all the people in the place, 53,000 in number—P. Crassus with one legion reduces the Armoric states to subjection—The position of Caesar's legions during the winter—On the arrival of Caesar's despatches at Rome a thanksgiving (supplicatio) for fifteen days is decreed—Before setting out for Italy Caesar sends Galba with one legion into the Valais to open the passage over the Alps—Galba takes possession of Octodurus (Martigny)—Galba is attacked in his quarters by the Veragri and Seduni—He defends himself with difficulty, sallies from the camp and completely routs the enemy—Galba retreats into the country of the Allobroges and winters there 44

CHAPTER IV.

P. CLODIUS, POMPEIUS AND CICERO.

B.C. 58.

Livy, Epit. 103; *Plutarch, Cicero, Pompeius, Cato Minor; Dion Cassius,* 38, c. 30; *Cicero's Letters and Orations; Josephus, Antiq.* 14, 5, 1; *Plinius, H. N.* 36, c. 2, and c. 15, 24, § 7.

PAGE

Cicero's house demolished after he fled from Rome—P. Clodius destroys the Porticus of Catulus and dedicates part of the ground on which Cicero's house stood—The story of Tigranes who was a prisoner at Rome—Gabinius and Clodius quarrel—Cicero's brother Quintus returns to Rome from Asia—Pompeius comes no more into public during the tribunate of Clodius—He does what he can to restore Cicero from exile—An effort is made to recall Cicero—The Roman attempts to prevent the repeal of enactments by prohibitive clauses—The mode of fixing the allowance for the outfit of the consuls when they took a province—Piso and Gabinius leave Rome for their respective provinces—Ptolemaeus the king of Cyprus was on friendly terms with the Romans—His wealth and kingdom are coveted by the Romans, and a bill is passed for the annexation of Cyprus—M. Cato is appointed to take possession of the island and the king's money—Cato stays at Rhodes on his voyage and advises king Ptolemaeus of Egypt, who calls there on his voyage to Rome, to return to Egypt—Cato first goes to Byzantium to settle affairs there and then visits Cyprus—The king of Cyprus commits suicide—Cato sells the king's property in Cyprus, and brings the money to Rome—Cyprus is annexed to the provincial government of Cilicia—The magnificent shows of the curule aedile M. Aemilius Scaurus—His great temporary theatre at Rome 71

CHAPTER V.

CICERO'S RESTORATION.

B.C. 57.

Livy, Epit. 104; *Dion Cassius,* 30, c. 6—11; *Cicero, Pro P. Sestio,* c. 33, &c.; *Pro Milone,* c. 14; *Pro Plancio,* c. 32; *Plutarch, Cicero, Pompeius; Appian, B. C.* ii. 16; *Schol. Bob. in Orat. Pro P. Sestio.*

On the first of January Cicero's restoration is proposed by the consul Lentulus—On the day when the bill for his restoration is proposed, there is a great fight in the Forum—The tribune P. Sestius is nearly killed in Castor's temple—Sestius now collects a force for his defence—Milo attempts to bring

CONTENTS.   xiii

                                                                        PAGE

Clodius to trial for disturbing the public peace, but his attempt is frustrated—The Senate undertake Cicero's case—The popular feeling in Cicero's favour displayed—Pompeius exerts himself in favour of Cicero—The vote of the Senate in favour of Cicero, and the consequent fall in the price of grain—The people meet on the fourth of August to vote on the question of Cicero's restoration, and the bill for his return is carried—On the fifth of August Cicero arrives at Brundisium, where he is met by his daughter—His triumphant progress to Rome, where he arrives on the fourth of September—He thanks the Senate on the fifth of September—The character of the extant speech supposed to have been delivered on this occasion, and of an extant speech in which he thanks the people—On the fourth and fifth of September there is again scarcity in Rome—Pompeius is appointed to look after the supply of grain—The story of Cicero writing a book in defence of his political conduct—Cicero speaks before the Pontifices about his house—The character of the extant speech attributed to him—The nature of the question before this ecclesiastical court—The judgment is in favour of Cicero—The resolution of the Senate upon the judgment of the Pontifices—The valuation of the damage done to Cicero's property—Rome is disturbed by the riots of Clodius—Milo resolutely opposes Clodius—The matter of the Campanian land is again stirred in the Senate in the absence of Pompeius—The discussion on the trials for the late disturbances—Clodius escapes being put on his trial—Remarks on the Roman police of corn, and the poor in Rome . . . 84

CHAPTER VI.

CAESAR AND THE VENETI.

B.C. 56.

Livy, Epit. 104; *Caesar, B. G.* III.; *Dion Cassius*, 39, c. 40—43 and 44—48; *Strabo,* 194, 195; *Orosius,* vi. 8.

Caesar in North Italy—The winter quarters of P. Crassus—Commissioners are sent by Crassus to make requisitions on the Seuusii, Curiosolitae and the Venetii—The position of these several states—The Veneti had many ships and traded with Britannia; they make prisoners of the commissioners who are sent to them—All the coast people combine against the Romans—Caesar sends orders to P. Crassus to build ships, and leaves Italy for Gallia after the congress of Luca—Description of the country of the Veneti, and their preparation for war—The allies who join them—The country to which Caesar's operations were limited—Caesar sends Labienus with some cavalry to the country of the Treviri, and P. Crassus with a force into Aquitania—Sabinus with three legions is sent against the Unelli, Curiosolitae and Lexovii—Caesar's fleet—The position of the towns of the Veneti, and Caesar's way of attacking them—The ships of the Veneti; they use iron chains as cables—The only advantage which the Romans

had over the Veneti was in the speed of their ships and the use of oars—
Caesar waits for the arrival of all his fleet, and fights a battle with the
Veneti in the bay of Quiberon—Dion's description of the battle and
Caesar's—The contrivance of the Romans for disabling the tackle of the
Venetian ships—The battle is fought in the presence of Caesar and his
army, who look down from the heights—The wind suddenly drops and
the Romans take nearly all the enemy's ships—The great loss of the
Armoric States—They surrender to Caesar, who puts to death the Vene-
tian Senate and sells the rest of the people by auction—The campaign of
Q. Titurius Sabinus in the country of the Unelli—Many idle and desperate
men in Gallia—The prudence of Sabinus—The Galli attack his camp
and are completely defeated—The remarks of Caesar and Livy on the
character of the Galli—P. Crassus enters Aquitania and increases his
force by drawing men from the western towns of the Roman Provincia
—He leads his troops against the Sotiates and takes their chief town—
Adcantuannus and his soldurii—Crassus advances to the west parts of
Aquitania—The leagues among the Aquitani, and the aid that they receive from Hispania—The old soldiers of Sertorius—Crassus attacks and
takes the camp of the Aquitani, who attempt to escape—Great slaughter
of the Aquitani and Cantabri—The submission of the greater part of
Aquitania—The names and positions of the nations which submit—Caesar
leads his forces against the Morini and Menapii—He cuts a road through
the forest—He is compelled to retire by the heavy rains—He wastes the
enemy's country, and takes his troops back to the country south of the
Seine 106

CHAPTER VII.

P. CLODIUS.

B.C. 58.

Livy, Epit. 104; *Dion,* 39, c. 12—16, and c. 18—21; *Cicero, De Pro-
vinciis Consularibus; Ad Q. Fr.* ll. 2, 3, 4; *Ad Div.* i. 1—9; *Cicero,
Pro P. Sestio,* c. 44, and *Schol. Bob.; Pro Rabirio Postumo; Pro
L. Cornelio Balbo; Strabo,* 798. 641; *Plutarch, Pompeius, Caesar,
Cicero, Cato Minor; Appian, B. C.* ii. 17.

P. Clodius elected curule aedile—A Roman public meeting—Clodius
unsuccessfully attempts to prosecute Milo—The street brawls in Rome—
Cicero defends L. Calpurnius Bestia—The trial of P. Sestius for a breach
of the peace; he is defended by Cicero in an extant speech—Cicero's speech
against P. Vatinius, who gave evidence against Sestius—Ptolemaeus
Auletes king of Egypt borrowed money at Rome—He leaves Egypt
and his daughter Berenice is made queen of Egypt—C. Rabirius a loan
contractor lends more money to Ptolemaeus at Rome—A deputation is

sent from Alexandria to Rome to complain of the king—The question
of the restoration of Ptolemaeus, who goes to Ephesus and takes asylum
in the temple of Diana—The allowance to Pompeius for the purchase of
grain—The conference at Luca—Caesar goes to the Venetian war, and
Pompeius to Sardinia—Cicero's apology to Lentulus for his submission to
Caesar and Pompeius—Cicero's books—He urges L. Lucceius to write
the history of his acts from the conspiracy of Catilina to his return from
exile—The reconciliation of Pompeius and P. Clodius—The speech De
Haruspicum Responsis—The squabbles of P. Clodius and Cicero—
Cicero's speech in defence of M. Caelius—The question of the Consular
Provinces and Cicero's extant speech—Cicero's submission to Caesar—
Cicero's extant speech in defence of L. Cornelius Balbus, a native of
Gades, who had been made a Roman citizen—A Roman citizen could
be admitted a citizen of another state, but he lost his Roman citizen-
ship—A man cannot owe absolute obedience to two sovereign powers—
The English Naturalization Act of 1870—The policy of Pompeius ac-
cording to Dion 123

CHAPTER VIII.

CAESAR AND THE GERMANS.

B.C. 55.

Livy, Epit. 105 ; *Caesar, B. G.* iv. 1—19 ; *Dion Cassius*, 39, c. 47, 48 ;
Plutarch, Caesar, Cato Minor, c. 51.

The Usipetes and Tencteri cross the Rhine from Germany, and occupy
the country of the Menapii—The position of the Menapii and Eburones
—Caesar leads his troops against the German invaders—The conference
between Caesar and a deputation from the Germans—Caesar's cavalry is
attacked and defeated by the Germans, whom he charges with treachery
—He seizes a great number of Germans and all the chiefs, who came to
his camp after the attack on his cavalry—Caesar suddenly falls on the
camp of the Germans, who are put to flight and driven into the Rhine—
The confluence of the Mosa and the Rhenus, where the Germans were
routed—Caesar's description of the course of the Rhine—Caesar determines to cross the Rhine—His description of the wooden bridge which
he built—The bridge made over the Scheldt by the Duke of Parma—
Caesar crosses the river and advances into the country of the Sigambri—
He burns the villages and buildings and cuts the corn—The Sueci retire
into the great forests—Caesar passes eighteen days on German soil, and
returns to Gallia 150

CHAPTER IX.

THE FIRST INVASION OF BRITANNIA.

B.C. 55.

PAGE

Livy, Epit. 105; *Caesar,* iv. 20—38; *Dion Cassius,* 39, c. 50—53; *Strabo,* p. 200.

Caesar's reason for invading Britannia—He marches with his forces from the Rhine to the coast of the Morini—He is visited by commissioners from the island, who are sent back accompanied by Commius, king of the Atrebates—He gets together vessels enough to carry two legions, and sails for the British coast—Description of the coast which he reached, and of the place where he landed—He is opposed at his landing by the Britons—The Britons submit to Caesar and give hostages—The full moon after Caesar's landing, and the damage done to his ships by the spring tide—The Britons resolve to attack Caesar again—Caesar brings corn daily from the country into his camp and repairs his ships—The seventh legion goes out to forage and is attacked by the Britons—Description of the British mode of fighting in war chariots—The Britons attempt to take the Roman camp and are repulsed—They are pursued by the Romans, who burn all the buildings within their reach—The Britons sue for peace and give the hostages which Caesar demanded—Caesar leaves Britain and reaches the Gallic coast safely—Two of the transports are carried further south than the other ships, and the men after landing are attacked by the Morini—The cavalry come to the relief of the men—The next day Caesar sends Labienus to attack the Morini—Titurius and Cotta waste the country of the Menapii, cut the corn, and burn the houses—Caesar's despatches reach Rome, and a thanksgiving (supplicatio) of twenty days is ordered by the Senate 162

CHAPTER X.

THE SECOND CONSULSHIP OF POMPEIUS.

B.C. 55.

Livy, Epit. 105; *Dion Cassius,* 39, c. 31—39. 55—65; *Plutarch, Pompeius, Cato Minor, Antonius; Suetonius, Caesar,* c. 24; *Tacitus, Ann.* xiv. 20; *Plinius,* 30, c. 13, 24, 7; 8, c. 7; *Cicero, ad Div.* vii. 1; *Appianus, Syriaca,* 51; *Josephus, Antiq.* xiv. c. 4, 5, 6; *Wars,* i. c. 8; *Strabo,* p. 688. 700.

CONTENTS.   xvii

PAGE

Cn. Pompeius and M. Crassus are elected consuls—The new consuls by fraud and bribery exclude M. Cato from the praetorship and P. Vatinius is elected—Disturbances at the election of the curule aediles—The bill of C. Trebonius about the consular provinces is carried by violence—Another bill of C. Trebonius gives to C. Caesar another term of five years in his provinces—The Lex Licinia de Sodalitiis—The Lex Pompeia Judiciaria—The return of Calpurnius Piso from his province Macedonia—Cicero's extant speech against Piso—Pompeius dedicates his theatre—Cicero is present at the games exhibited by Pompeius—The elephant fights—The state of Spain—Gabinius in his province Syria—Alexander, the son of Aristobulus, makes disturbance in Judaea—Gabinius settles the affairs of Judaea and divides the country into five parts or conventus—Josephus affirms that Gabinius did good service in Judaea—Pompeius writes to Gabinius and urges him to restore Ptolemaeus Auletes to his throne—The king promises large sums of money to Gabinius—Berenice, queen of Egypt, strangles her first husband and marries Archelaus, the high priest of Comana—Gabinius advances to Egypt through the desert, occupies Pelusium, and defeats the Egyptian troops and Archelaus, who is killed—Ptolemaeus takes possession of Egypt, and puts to death his daughter Berenice—Gabinius leaves some Gauls and Germans in Egypt to protect Ptolemaeus—Alexander, the son of Aristobulus, again stirs the Jews to revolt—Gabinius, the Publicani, and Cicero—Cicero is reconciled to M. Crassus, who sets out for his province Syria—The tribune Ateius curses Crassus as he leaves Rome 175

CHAPTER XI.

BRITANNIA.

B.C. 55.

Livy, Epit. 105; *Caesar, B. G.* v. 12—14; *Strabo,* iv. p. 199; *Diodorus,* v. 21, 22; *Ptolemaeus,* II. 3.

The coast of Britannia is occupied by people, who had crossed over from Belgium—The population is large, and there is much cattle—The metals, and timber trees, and the climate—The form of the island, and the dimensions—Strabo's notions about the dimensions of Britannia; his opinion of Pytheas—The inhabitants of Cantium are the most civilized; the habits of the Britanni differ little from those of the Galli—The usage of the Britanni as to women—Gold, silver, iron, skins, slaves, and hunting dogs exported from Britannia, according to Strabo—The bad character of the British climate—Strabo knows nothing exact about Ierne (Hibernia or Ireland)—Pomponius Mela and Plinius add nothing to our knowledge of Britannia 190

VOL. IV.   B

CHAPTER XII

THE SECOND INVASION OF BRITANNIA.

B.C. 54.

PAGE

Livy, Epit. 105; *Caesar, B. G.* v. 1—23; *Dion Cassius,* 40, c. 1—4;
Cicero, ad Q. Fratrem, ii. 15; *Ad Fam.* vii. 5—9.

Caesar does not leave Gallia for Italy before the commencement of B.C. 54—His preparation of a fleet for a second invasion of Britannia—Caesar crosses the Alps, and visits Illyricum—He is in Gallia Cisalpina to the end of May of the unreformed calendar—Quintus Cicero joins Caesar, to whom M. Cicero recommends the lawyer Trebatius—Correspondence between Caesar and M. Cicero in B.C. 54—Caesar joins his troops in the country of the Belgae, and orders all the vessels to assemble at Portus Itius or Itium—Caesar makes an expedition to the country of the Treviri, and settles their disputes—He returns to Itius and finds his ships ready—Dumnorix intrigues with the Gallic chiefs, and attempts to go home without Caesar's permission—He is overtaken and killed by Caesar's orders—Computation of the time between Caesar's leaving North Italy and landing in Britain—Caesar's activity—The voyage to Britain and the landing—Caesar takes a strong place belonging to the Britons—Conjecture about the site of this place—The Roman ships are damaged by a storm—The loss is repaired, the ships are hauled upon the land, and connected with the camp by one line of defence—Caesar advances into the interior, where he finds a large force under Cassivellaunus—The narrative is interrupted by three chapters of the description of Britannia—The fights between Caesar and the natives—He reaches the Tamesis (Thames) and crosses the river into the territory of Cassivellaunus—Cassivellaunus watches the march of the Roman army with his essedarii—The position of the British people named Trinobantes—The British tribes which submit to Caesar—He takes the town (oppidum) of Cassivellaunus—The four kings of Kent (Cantium), on the suggestion of Cassivellaunus, attack Caesar's camp and are repulsed—Cassivellaunus sends ambassadors to treat about submission—Caesar receives hostages and fixes an annual tribute—He returns to the coast with his hostages, and takes his men back to Gallia in two divisions—The letters sent by Caesar and Quintus Cicero from Britain to M. Cicero—The probable conclusion from these letters about the time of Caesar's landing in Britain and the time of his return to Gallia 108

CHAPTER XIII.

THE WINTER OF B.C. 54.

Livy, Epit. 105; *Caesar, B. G.* v. 24—58; *Dion Cassius,* 40, c. 4—11, and 31.

A meeting of the Gallic States held by Cæsar at Samarobriva—The distribution of Cæsar's troops in winter quarters—The number of Cæsar's legions—Tasgetius, whom Cæsar had made King of the Carnutes, is murdered—Soon after the arrival of Sabinus and Cotta at their winter quarters among the Eburones an insurrection breaks out under Ambiorix and Cativolcus, kings of the Eburones—The interview between two men on the side of the Romans and Ambiorix, who tells them that all the Galli are rising against the Romans and advises them to retreat—Sabinus and Cotta are perplexed at the report of the two men—The debate on the question whether the Romans should stay in their camp and resist any attack, or attempt a retreat, Ambiorix having promised to allow them a safe passage—After much contention it is decided that they will leave the camp and try to reach the nearest winter quarters—The site of the camp of Sabinus and Cotta—The Romans leave the camp at daybreak, and enter a long defile, where the enemy fall upon them—They resist a long time, and finally the greater part are massacred—The remainder retreat to the camp and resist to nightfall when they kill one another—A few of the Romans make their way through the forests to the winter quarters of Labienus and report the disaster—Cæsar's judgment on Sabinus—He expresses neither indignation nor sorrow at the loss which he had sustained—Ambiorix stirs up the Aduatuci and Nervii, and persuades them to attack the quarters of Q. Cicero—The confederates attack Cicero's camp, but are repelled—Cicero writes letters to Cæsar, but the letter-carriers are intercepted—He strengthens his camp, and resists the attacks of the enemy—A conference between Cicero and the chiefs of the enemy, who inform him of the death of Sabinus, and offer him a free passage if he will leave the country—Cicero refuses the proposal, and the enemy surround the Roman camp with a rampart and ditch—The brave resistance of the Romans—Cicero succeeds in sending a message to Cæsar, who immediately sets out with two legions to relieve him—Cæsar by forced marches reaches the country of the Nervii—Conjecture about the site of Cicero's camp—Cæsar sends a letter to Cicero by a Gallic horseman, and announces his approach by the burning of the houses of the natives—The enemy give up the blockade of Cicero's camp, and go to meet Cæsar with about sixty thousand men—Cæsar makes a camp of small dimensions to induce the enemy to believe that his force is still less than it was—The enemy are deceived, and attack the camp—The Romans sally out, and put the enemy to flight—On the same day Cæsar arrives at the camp of Cicero—He commends Cicero and his men for their brave defence—The news of Cæsar's victory is carried to Labienus with wonderful speed—The Treviri, who were intending to attack Labienus, retire to their own country—Cæsar stays near Samarobriva with three legions, and remains all the winter in Gallia—He receives continually intelligence of the Galli intending to rise—By various means he keeps a great part of the country in obedience—The Senones attempt to put to death Cavarinus, whom Cæsar had set over them as king—Cavarinus escapes from his subjects—The Senones send commissioners to Cæsar to explain their behaviour, but when he summons the Senate they refuse to come—With the exception of the Aedui and the Remi, there is hardly a single people whom Cæsar does not suspect—Indutiomarus, the

Treviri, unsuccessfully attempts to persuade the Germans over the Rhine to help him—He collects men, disciplines them, and invites exiles and criminals to join him—The Gallic fashion of summoning men to arms—Indutiomarus comes up to the camp of Labienus, who deceives him into a belief that the Romans are afraid—Labienus makes a sally from his camp, and puts the enemy to flight—Indutiomarus is caught as he is fording a river, and his head is brought to Labienus—Conjectures as to the name of the river—The Gallic forces disperse, and Caesar finds Gallia somewhat more tranquil 215

CHAPTER XIV.

THE TREVIRI AND THE EBURONES.

B.C. 53.

Livy, Epit. 107; Caesar, B. G. vi.; Dion Cassius, 40, c. 32.

Caesar prepares for his sixth campaign—He raises fresh troops in North Italy, and Cn. Pompeius sends him one legion—His whole force is now ten legions—The Treviri make an alliance with some Germans and with Ambiorix. Caesar during the winter enters the territory of the Nervii, and compels them to submit—In spring the States of Gallia are summoned to meet, and all come except the Senones, Carnutes, and Treviri—Caesar transfers the place of meeting from Samarobriva to Lutetia (Paris), the chief town of the Parisii—He suddenly enters the country of the Senones, who are compelled to submit—The submission of the Carnutes—Caesar now turns against the Treviri and Ambiorix—He sends the baggage of the whole army and two legions to Labienus, who was in the country of the Treviri—With five legions Caesar falls on the Menapii, the only people who had never sent deputies to him about peace—He burns the houses and villages of the Menapii, who sue for peace—Caesar takes hostages from the Menapii, and leaves Commius, king of the Atrebates, to look after the Menapii—Caesar sets out for the country of the Treviri—The Treviri prepare to attack Labienus, who had wintered in their country—Labienus deceives the Treviri by pretending to retreat before them—The Treviri attack the Romans and are defeated—The Treviri again acknowledge the Roman supremacy—Caesar resolves to cross the Rhine a second time—He makes a bridge a little higher up than the first bridge and crosses the Rhine—The Ubii protest to Caesar that they had given no help to the Treviri—Caesar finds that the help had been sent by the Suevi, and he makes inquiry about them—He learns that the Suevi had retired to the remotest part of their territory—Caesar's reasons for not following them—He destroys part of the bridge over the Rhine, and leaves twelve cohorts to protect it—Caesar marches through the great forest

Arduenna against Ambiorix and the Eburones—The extent of this forest—Caesar's cavalry surprise Ambiorix in a forest, but he escapes—The flight of the Eburones from the Romans—Cativolcus, king of one-half of the Eburones, an old man, poisons himself with yew—Caesar divides his force into three parts, and takes all the baggage to Aduatuca—Q. Cicero is left there with the fourteenth legion and two hundred horsemen—Caesar with nine legions in three divisions advances towards the sea, to the parts adjacent to the Aduatuci and to the Scaldis (Schelde)—He promises to return to Aduatuca on the seventh day—Caesar's purpose was to destroy the Eburones: and we hear no more of them—The difficulties of the Roman troops in the country of the Eburones—Caesar invites the neighbouring peoples to plunder them—The news of the invitation reaches the Sigambri, who cross the Rhine, and plunder the Eburones—One of the Eburones being made a prisoner suggests to the Sigambri an attack on Aduatuca—On the seventh day Caesar had not returned, and Q. Cicero, moved by the clamour of his men, sends five cohorts and about three hundred veteran soldiers to cut the nearest corn—A great number of camp servants and beasts of burden are also allowed to go—The German horsemen arrive at this time, and attempt to break into the camp—The traders, who are outside the camp, have no time to escape—The alarm and confusion within the camp—The foragers returning see the danger, but the officers are stupified by the sudden surprise—The veterans break through the enemy, and reach the camp without loss; and the camp servants and horsemen follow them, and are also saved—Two cohorts out of the five are destroyed by the Germans, who retreat across the Rhine with their booty—Caesar returns to the camp—His narrative contains no direct censure of Cicero or his men, but it is a severe condemnation of both—Caesar's remarks on Fortune—He again sets out to vex the enemy—He burns the villages and wastes the country—Ambiorix is hunted, but he escapes in the forests—Caesar leads his troops to Durocortorum (Reims), and inquires into the conspiracy of the Senones and Carnutes—Acco, the chief mover in the rebellion, is whipped to death—The legions are placed in winter quarters, and Caesar goes to North Italy—Modern warfare compared with Caesar's warfare 236

CHAPTER XV.

M. CRASSUS.

B.C. 54, 53.

Livy, Epit. 106; Dion Cassius, 40, c. 12—27; Plutarch, Crassus; Strabo, p. 514; Justinus, 41, c. 1; 42, c. 4; Josephus, Antiq. xiv. 7. 1. B. J. i. 8. 8.

In B.C. 54 M. Crassus begins his attack on the Parthians—He crosses the Euphrates, plunders part of Mesopotamia, takes some towns, and

xxii   CONTENTS.

PAGE

returns to spend the winter in Syria—He does nothing in the winter to strengthen his forces, or to exercise his men for the next campaign—Strabo's remarks on the country of the Parthians, and those of Dion Cassius on their mode of war—During the winter Crassus is busy with getting money—He plunders a Syrian temple, and takes from the temple at Jerusalem all the gold which Pompeius had left—His almost incredible greediness—The gold in Jerusalem was the gift of Jews who were in foreign countries—The message of the Parthian Orodes to Crassus—Some of the Roman soldiers who were in garrison in Mesopotamia and had escaped from Surenas, the general of Orodes, bring reports of the great numbers of the enemy—The chief officers advise Crassus to hold a council of war, and the soothsayers declare the signs to be unfavourable, but Crassus pays no attention to them—The Armenian king Artavasdes visits Crassus—The Romans cross the Euphrates in a hurricane—The dangerous hurricanes on this river—The force of Crassus—The advice of the Quaestor Cassius to Crassus—Crassus is deceived by an Arab chief, who advises him to meet Surenas and not to march to Seleuceia, as he intended—The wealth and pomp of Surenas—The scouts announce the approach of the Parthian army, and Crassus prepares for battle—He crosses the river Balissus (Belik), and is attacked by the Parthian mounted bowmen—Publius, the son of Crassus, attempts to force the enemy to a battle—He has some Gallic horsemen—Publius being wounded orders his shield-bearer to kill him—The destruction of the troops of Publius—The Parthians again attack Crassus and show him his son's head on a spear—The Parthians retire when the darkness comes and the Romans pass the night among their dead and wounded—The Romans leave their camp and move slowly—The place of the defeat is not far from Carrhae—The Parthians do not pursue the Romans by night—They massacre those who were left in the camp—Crassus reaches Carrhae and leaves it by night with his troops—He is deceived by a Greek guide, overtaken by the Parthians and killed—The reported loss of the Romans—The head and hand of Crassus are sent to the Parthian king—The mock triumph of the Parthians at Seleuceia—The reconciliation of Orodes and the Armenian king, who marries his sister to Pacorus, the son of Orodes—Banquets on this occasion and Greek plays—Orodes settles the Roman prisoners in Antiochia Margiana   251

CHAPTER XVI.

ROME.

B.C. 54, 53.

Livy, Epit. 106; *Dion Cassius*, 30, c. 59—65; *Strabo*, p. 609; *Cicero's Letters*; *Cicero, Pro Plancio, and Pro Rabirio Postumo.*

Cicero finishes his treatise De Oratore—His poem in three books on his own times, and his treatise De Re Publica—The copying of Latin and

Greek books—Cicero withdraws from public affairs; his complaints—The contest for the consulship—Oppius and Cicero buy ground at Rome on Caesar's account for a new Forum—Caesar's way of getting money—The month of February at Rome—Canvassing and bribery active at Rome—Cicero is busy in the courts during a very hot July—He defends P. Vatinius, whom he had formerly abused—The trial of M. Aemilius Scaurus on the charge of Repetundae—Cicero is one of his advocates—Cicero's defence of his friend Cn. Plancius who was prosecuted for bribery—The Lex Licinia de Sodalitiis, and the purpose of this Lex—Wunder's opinion about this Lex—Cicero says that the Roman people like the voting by ballot—Remarks on this mode of voting at elections—The peroration of Cicero's speech for Plancius—Cicero writes a long news-letter to his brother Quintus—The return of Gabinius to Rome—He receives notice of a prosecution for Majestas—He is acquitted—Gabinius is tried again on the charge of Repetundae—Cicero is reconciled to Gabinius and defends him—Gabinius is convicted and goes into exile—The trial of C. Rabirius Postumus, a loan contractor and money lender—Rabirius had accompanied Gabinius to Egypt to look after his debtor king Ptolemaeus—The nature of the charge against Rabirius—Caesar's liberality to Rabirius, whom Cicero defends—The long delayed triumph of C. Pomptinus for his victory over the Allobroges—The death of Julia, the daughter of Caesar, and the wife of Cn. Pompeius—Caesar's marriage proposals—The Roman Interregnum and Interreges—At the end of B.C. 53 neither praetors nor consuls had been elected for the following year—Cicero supports Milo in his canvas for the consulship—M. Antonius, the grandson of the great orator, who was in Gallia with Caesar, comes to Rome with letters from Caesar to Cicero—Antonius is a candidate for a quaestorship, and Cicero helps him—Antonius returns to Caesar—The death of Crassus' son Publius makes a vacancy in the college of augurs—Cicero is elected an augur, and consecrated by Hortensius 202

CHAPTER XVII.

THE REVOLT OF GALLIA.

B.C. 52.

Livy, Epit. 107; Caesar, B. G. vii. 1—34; Dion Cassius, 40,' c. 33, 34.

The death of P. Clodius—Troops are raised in Italy by order of the Senate—Caesar also raises troops—The troubled state of Italy is reported in Gallia, and the Galli resolve to revolt—Massacre of the Romans at Genabum (Orléans)—The importance of the position of Genabum—Vercingetorix, an Arvernian, heads the revolt; he is elected commander-in-chief of the Galli; his activity and severity—Lucterius invades the country of the Ruteni: the Bituriges join the Arverni—Caesar leaves Gallia Cisalpina and crosses the Alps—Lucterius brings over the Ruteni to the Arverni—Caesar provides for the defence of the Provincia, and crosses the Cévennes which are covered with snow six feet deep—He terrifies the Arverni, and Vercingetorix returns from the country of the Bituriges—Caesar leaves Decimus Brutus in the country of the Arverni, and again crosses the Cévennes and arrives at Vienna (Vienne) on the Rhone—He travels day and night and reaches the Lingones, among whom two legions were wintering—He collects all his legions at Agendicum (Sens), and thus accomplishes his purpose of uniting his forces after having drawn Vercingetorix southwards—Caesar leaves two legions at Agendicum, and advances to Velaunodunum, which surrenders—He appears before Genabum, enters the town, plunders it, and sets it on fire—Vercingetorix advances to meet Caesar, who takes Noviodunum of the Bituriges—Caesar's German horsemen defeat the Gallic cavalry—Caesar continues his march to Avaricum (Bourges) the chief town of the Bituriges—Vercingetorix persuades the Bituriges and other peoples to burn their towns—At the entreaty of the Bituriges Avaricum is spared contrary to the judgment of Vercingetorix, and it is determined to defend the town—The position of Avaricum and of Caesar's camp—His works before the town, and the sufferings of his men—He leaves the town to attack the enemy's camp which Vercingetorix had left—Caesar will not attack the enemy in his strong position, and returns to Avaricum to continue the siege—Vercingetorix is charged by his army with treachery for leaving them without a general—His defence is accepted by his men—The deception which he practises—The sources of Caesar's information—The ingenuity of the Galli in defending Avaricum —The Bituriges are skilled in mining—Description of the way in which Gallic town walls were constructed—The defenders of Avaricum fire the wood in the Roman embankment—Caesar's record of the courage of the Galli—The enemy prepare to leave the town in the night, but are prevented by the cries of the women which are heard by the besiegers—Caesar makes a sudden assault and takes Avaricum—All the people within the town are massacred to the number of near forty thousand—Vercingetorix comforts his men after the capture of Avaricum, and advises them to fortify their camps in Roman fashion—The influence of Vercingetorix increases after the capture of Avaricum, which was defended contrary to his advice—He repairs his losses—Caesar finds great stores in Avaricum—The civil troubles among the Aedui—Caesar goes to Decetia on the Loire and settles the disputes by delivering judgment in favour of Convictolitanis—He divides his forces into two parts—Labienus with four legions is ordered to march against the Senones and Parisii—With the other six legions Caesar marches southwards into the country of the Arverni . 237

CHAPTER XVIII.

GERGOVIA.

B.C. 52.

Livy, Epit. 107; Caesar, B. G., vii. 35—56; Dion Cassius, 40, c. 35—33.

Caesar marches south on the east bank of the Elaver (Allier)—Vercingetorix marches on the west bank in the same direction, after breaking down the bridges over the river—Caesar crosses the Elaver by a stratagem, and Vercingetorix hurries to Gergovia—Position and description of Gergovia—The camp of Vercingetorix on the hill of Gergovia—Caesar seizes a strong position—His two camps—The treachery of the Aedness Convictolitanis, who is bribed to desert Caesar—Convictolitanis gains Litaviccus, who has the command of ten thousand Aedui, who were going to Gergovia to Caesar—Litaviccus deceives the men by lying, and persuades them to join the Arverni—Caesar is informed of the defection, and sets out soon after midnight with a large force to meet the insurgents—He meets the ten thousand Aedui, terrifies them into submission, and returns to his camp, which had been attacked in his absence—The rapidity of his march to meet the Aedui, and his rapid march back to his camp—The Aedui fall on the Romans in their country, whom they rob and massacre—On hearing of the ten thousand being in Caesar's power, they change their behaviour, and send commissioners to Caesar to clear themselves of blame—Caesar's prudence and foresight; he says that he does not condemn the state for the folly of a few—The reasons of his policy—Caesar's design on Gergovia, and the plan for the execution—He seizes three of the enemy's camps on the hill side—Part of the force disobey his orders, and attempt to break into the town of Gergovia, which is on the summit of the hill—His men are driven down the hill with great loss—He rebukes his men for not following his orders, tells them that he requires obedience as well as courage, and that he is the judge of the means to victory—He twice offers Vercingetorix battle in the plain, and the offer not being accepted he leaves Gergovia and crosses the Elaver—The author of the "Histoire" condemns Caesar—The answer to his censure—Caesar allows two of the chief men of the Aedui to leave him on the pretence of confirming the fidelity of their countrymen to the Romans, though he suspects that they will hasten the revolt—The reasons for his conduct—The Aedui plunder and destroy Caesar's stores at Noviodunum (Nevers)—Caesar reaches the Loire, which is swollen by the melted snows—His reasons for crossing the river, which he passes in safety—He supplies his men with corn and cattle in the country of the Aedui, and joins Labienus—He is now ready to resist the combination of the Galli, which he had foreseen—Caesar's conduct during the difficult campaign of 52 207

CHAPTER XIX.

ALESIA.

B.C. 52.

Livy, Epit. 108; *Caesar, B. G.*, 57—90; *Dion Cassius*, 40, c. 39—11; *Plutarch, Caesar.*

Labienus advances from Agendicum (Sens) against Lutetia (Paris)—His march along the left bank of the Yonne and the Seine—The enemy collect their forces under Camulogenus, who determines to stop Labienus at a marsh—Labienus, being unable to pass the marsh, retreats to Melodunum (Melun), where he crosses the Seine on boats—He leads his forces along the right bank of the river to Lutetia, which is burnt by order of Camulogenus—Opinion of the author of the "Histoire" on the position of the marsh where Labienus was stopped—The news spreads that Caesar had retired from Gergovia, and that Gallia is rising—Labienus is threatened by the Galli on the north and on the south, and determines to leave his position on the north bank of the Seine opposite to the island of Lutetia—He crosses to the south side of the Seine in the night by a skilful stratagem, defeats Camulogenus, retreats to Agendicum, and joins Caesar—The defection of the Aedui is a signal for the general rising of the Galli—Vercingetorix is elected commander-in-chief of the united Gallic forces—His declaration as to the way of conducting the war against Caesar—The danger to the Provincia; men are raised there by L. Caesar, a kinsman of C. Caesar—Caesar gets cavalry and light infantry from the Germans east of the Rhine—The number of his legions—Caesar marches from the Loire to the country of the Lingones in order to reach the Provincia—Vercingetorix opposes Caesar's march, and is totally defeated—Caesar follows Vercingetorix, who takes refuge in Alesia (Alise), a town of the Mandubii—He sees on his arrival that the place can only be taken by blockade—The site of Alesia, and the site of the battle field where Vercingetorix was defeated—Caesar's description of Alesia corresponds to the site of Alise—The camps of Caesar round Alesia—The cavalry fight on the plain of Les Laumes, and the superiority of Caesar's German cavalry—Vercingetorix sends off his cavalry with instructions to summon the Gallic nations to his relief—He takes possession of all the provisions in Alesia—Caesar forms his contravallation; description of his works—The line of circumvallation is fourteen Roman miles in circuit—The Gallic States summon a large force for the relief of Alesia—The force is estimated at 240,000 men—The commanders who are appointed—Want of food in Alesia—Critognatus, an Arvernian, recommends resistance, and eating those who are too young or too old to fight—The Mandubii, with their wives and children, are turned out of their own town by Vercingetorix—They intreat the Romans to be taken as slaves and fed, but Caesar refuses to receive them—The confederate Galli arrive in front of Alesia—The cavalry fight between the relieving army and Cæsar's cavalry—The victory is determined in favour of Cæsar by his German cavalry—The Galli of the relieving army attempt to assault the Roman lines just after midnight—Vercingetorix leads his men out of Alesia to attack the Roman lines from the inside—No part of the Roman lines is forced—The attack made by a detachment of the relieving army on the north-west side of the Roman lines at Mont Réa—Other parts of the outer and inner lines are attacked at the same time—Cæsar's position on the north-west side of the hill of Flavigny—Labienus is ordered to support the troops at Réa, and is instructed to sally out if he cannot resist the enemy—The Galli assault Cæsar's position on the hill of Flavigny, but are repulsed—Cæsar hurries towards the camp on Réa, being informed by Labienus of his intention to sally out on the enemy—Cæsar is followed by part of the cavalry, and he sends part round the external lines to attack the enemy on the rear—Conspicuous by his scarlet cloak he is seen approaching by the Galli and the Romans—On both sides there are loud shouts—The sally is made; the cavalry appear on the rear of the Galli, who turn their backs, and the victory is won—The surrender of Vercingetorix to Cæsar—The veracity of Cæsar is justified by the evidence of the localities—He puts his troops in winter quarters—When Cæsar's despatches reach Rome, a thanksgiving of twenty days is proclaimed . 320

CHAPTER XX.

MILO AND CLODIUS.

B.C. 52.

Livy, Epit. 107; Asconius in Orationem Pro Milone, ed. Orelli, p. 40—55; Cicero's speech for Milo; Dion Cassius, 40, c. 44—57.

Clodius and Milo meet on the twentieth of January on the Appian road, and Clodius is killed by Milo's men—The body of Clodius is carried to Rome, to his house, and finally to the Curia Hostilia, which is burnt with the body—The mob break into the house of the Interrex Lepidus—Milo returns to Rome—Great disturbance in the city—The Senate issue the usual commission for the protection of the State—Pompeius is empowered to raise troops in Italy—Pompeius is afraid, or pretends to be afraid, of Milo—The historian Sallustius and Milo's wife Fausta—Pompeius' supposed fear of Milo—The nephews of P. Clodius demand the slaves of Milo and Fausta to get evidence from them—Pompeius is appointed sole consul—He promulgates two bills, one de vi, the other about bribery at elections—The new regulations about trials—The reference of Asconius to the journals of the Senate (acta)—Milo is falsely charged with having a dagger in the Senate—Some of the tribunes keep up the popular excitement against Milo—The quaesitor L. Domitius allows Appius to take and examine some of Milo's slaves—Some of the slaves of P. Clodius are put to the torture to extract evidence from them—The trial of Milo—Cicero speaks in Milo's defence under great trepidation—The nature of Cicero's defence—Milo is convicted and goes to Massilia (Marseille)—The sale of his property—The suspicion against Cicero of buying some of Milo's property—Cicero's explanation of this transaction—The opinion of some modern writers on this matter—Cicero's extant speech for Milo—The trials which followed Milo's trial—Scipio, the father-in-law of Pompeius, escapes trial—On the first of August Scipio becomes the colleague of Pompeius in the consulship—The law which requires candidates for a magistracy to be present at the Comitia—Caesar is excepted from the law—After the tenth of December the tribunes Pompeius Rufus, and Munatius Plancus are tried for burning the Curia Hostilia and convicted—Cicero prosecutes Plancus and rejoices over his conviction—M. Cato an unsuccessful candidate for the consulship—Cato will not shake hands with the Roman electors—The gold which is said to have disappeared from the seat of Jupiter Capitolinus 352

CHAPTER XXI.

THE STATE OF GALLIA.

B.C. 51.

Livy, Epit. 108; B. G. viii. 1—48.

The eighth book of the Commentaries was not written by Caesar—Some of the Gallic States plan an insurrection—Caesar with his forces enters the country of the Bituriges on the last day of the year 52—The Bituriges submit—Caesar rewards the two legions who went on this winter expedition—The Bituriges ask for aid against the Carnutes, whom Caesar quickly disperses—He is informed by the Remi that the Bellovaci are in arms—He advances against the Bellovaci and their allies with four legions—The enemy occupy an elevated position at Mont St. Marc in the forest of Compiègne above the junction of the rivers Aisne and Oise—Caesar makes and fortifies a camp separated from the enemy by a marsh—Skirmishes with the enemy—Caesar sends for three more legions—The enemy fearing a blockade like that of Alesia send off by night those who were feeble and unarmed—Caesar occupies a height, Mont Collet, separated by a small depression from the height on which the enemy are encamped—The enemy make a great fire in front of their camp and retreat covered by the smoke—They encamp again in a strong position and do great damage to Caesar's foragers—Caesar learns that Correus, the commander of the Gallic forces, had formed an ambuscade in a place which he expected the Romans to visit for corn and forage—Caesar sends his cavalry to protect the foragers and follows with his legions—The place of ambuscade—The fight between the Roman cavalry and the enemy—Caesar approaches and the enemy fly—Correus is killed, and the Bellovaci with their allies submit to Caesar—The attempt of Labienus in the previous year to assassinate Comm, who now seeks refuge among the Germans, from whom he had got some help for this war—Caesar sends C. Fabius to the south-west of Gallia to support C. Caninius Rebilus against some of the Galli who are in arms—He also sends a legion into Gallia Cisalpina to protect the Roman colonies there—Caesar sets out to ravage the territory of Ambiorix—The reason for this invasion—He burns the houses and plunders and kills the people—Caninius goes to relieve Duratius, an ally of the Romans, who is besieged in Lemonum (Poitiers) by the Galli under Dumnacus—Fabius comes to relieve Duratius—Dumnacus retreats towards the Loire, is overtaken by Fabius, and is defeated with great loss—Some men who escape from the slaughter under Drappes move towards the Roman Provincia—Drappes is joined by Lucterius, and they are pursued by Caninius—Fabius marches against the Carnutes, who submit—Dumnacus seeks refuge in the remotest parts of Gallia—Drappes and Lucterius occupy the strong position of Uxellodunum in the country of the Cadurci—Caninius makes three camps and begins to invest the place—Drappes and Lucterius with a force leave Uxellodunum to collect provisions—Some troops remain to defend the town—Lucterius attempts to introduce provisions into Uxellodunum, but the attempt fails—Caninius hearing from his prisoners where Drappes is falls upon his troops and defeats them—Drappes is made prisoner—Caesar leaves M. Antonius with fifteen cohorts among the Bellovaci—He comes to the Carnutes and flogs to death Gutruatus, the leader in the insurrection—Hirtius' apology for Caesar—The character of the Galli—Caesar comes to Uxellodunum, and the siege is continued—He diverts a spring of water which supplies the town, and the place surrenders—He cuts off the hands of all the men who had defended Uxellodunum—The apology of Hirtius—Drappes dies in chains—Lucterius is delivered up to Caesar by Epasnactus, an Arvernian—The site of Uxellodunum at Puy d'Issolu—Description of this strong place—The excavations which have been made there—Labienus defeats the Treviri and the Germans—Caesar visits Aquitania and comes to Narbo (Narbonne)—The disposition of ten legions during the winter—Caesar visits the Provincia, and then goes to Nemetocenna (Arras) where he spends the winter—Comm annoys the Romans in the country of the Atrebates—M. Antonius sends C. Volusenus Quadratus in pursuit of Comm—A cavalry fight between Comm and Volusenus, who is wounded by Comm—Comm escapes—Comm sends a message to Antonius, and informs him that he will stay in any place where he is ordered to remain and will give hostages—Antonius accepts Comm's offer 569

CHAPTER XXII.

CAESAR AND THE SENATE.

B.C. 51.

Livy, Epit. 108; *B. G.* viii. 49; *Dion Cassius*, 40, c. 58, 59; *Plutarch, Caesar,* and *Pompeius.*

Cicero leaves Rome for Cilicia; and Bibulus for Syria—Cicero's correspondence with Atticus and M. Caelius—Reports at Rome about Caesar's campaign with the Bellovaci—Cicero visits Pompeius at Tarentum—Caelius' opinion of Pompeius—In July C. Claudius Marcellus and L. Aemilius Paulus are elected consuls—C. Curio is elected tribune, and M. Caelius curule aedile—Pompeius' statement in the Senate about the legion which he had sent to Caesar—C. Claudius Marcellus tried for bribery and acquitted—Resolutions of the Senate; and the form in which they were drawn up—The number of provinces at this time—Pompeius declares that he cannot give his opinion about Caesar's provinces before the first of March B.C. 50—Caelius' opinion that Pompeius will not allow Caesar to be elected consul, unless he gives up his army and his provinces—The consul M. Marcellus flogs a man of Novum Comum—Remarks on this story—Caesar in the winter of 51 and 50 endeavours to keep the Galli quiet by gentle means—The results of his Gallic campaigns—Caesar's policy from the time that he entered Gallia—He never allows passion or resentment to prevail over his interest—Caesar's opportunities for making money in Gallia—He congratulates Cicero on his exploits in Cilicia . . . 391

CHAPTER XXIII.

CICERO IN CILICIA.

B.C. 50.

Livy, Epit. 109; *B. G.* viii. 50—54; *Dion Cassius*, 40, c. 60—63; *Appian, B. C.* ii. 27—29; *Plutarch, Pompeius.*

Appius Claudius, Cicero's predecessor in Cilicia, is tried twice at Rome on two charges and acquitted—Appius Claudius and L. Piso censors—The severity of Appius in his office and Caelius' opinion of him—Appius ejects from the Senate all the freedmen, and others, among whom is the historian Sallustius—Curio proposes to intercalate a month in this year—Censorinus on the practice of intercalation—Other proposals of Curio, which fail—Meeting of the Senate probably on the first of March—Discussion about superseding Caesar, and the results—Plutarch's narrative—Death of Hortensius, which causes a vacancy in the college of Augurs—M. Antonius is elected in his place—Caesar visits Cisalpine Gallia and is received with unbounded demonstrations of honour and affection—He returns to his army at Nemetocenna in Transalpine Gallia, and summons all his legions to meet him in the country of the Treviri—He sets Labienus over Cisalpine Gallia to secure the votes for his election—He puts the affairs of Gallia in order—He hears reports of the attempts of his enemies to seduce Labienus, but does not believe them 399

CHAPTER XXIV.

CICERO IN CILICIA.

B.C. 51, 50.

Livy, Epit. 109; *B. G.* viii. 52—54; *Appian, B. C.* ii. 28—31; *Dion Cassius,* 40, c. 65, 66; *Cicero's Letters to Atticus,* v. vi.

The letter of Pompeius from Campania to the Senate—He falls sick at Naples—Rejoicings on his recovery, and Cicero's subsequent remarks on them—Appian's opinion of Pompeius' insincerity—Curio's proposal about Caesar and Pompeius—The affairs of Syria—L. Cassius, formerly the quaestor of Crassus, defeats the Parthians in Syria—Cicero at Tarsus on the fifth of October, 50—He kills a great number of mountaineers of the Amanus—He besieges and takes Pindenissus, and sells the people—Cicero informs Atticus that the report of his approach to Cilicia frightened the Parthians, and enabled Cassius to gain a victory over them—Cicero congratulates Cassius on his victory—The report of Cassius to the Senate, and Cicero's letters to the Senate—The falsehood of Cicero's statement to Atticus about the victory of Cassius proved by his own letters—Cicero in his letter to M. Cato does not repeat the falsehood—Cicero intreats Cato to use his interest to secure Cicero's triumph—Cato's answer to him—Cicero complains to Atticus of Cato's behaviour—The Senate deprive Caesar of two legions on pretence of sending them to Syria—Caesar places the thirteenth legion in Gallia Cisalpina, and eight legions in winter quarters in Gallia Transalpina—He goes to Italy—Caesar gives money to the legion of Pompeius, which he sent to Italy in obedience to the order of the Senate—False report of Appius Claudius about Caesar's troops—The consul C. Marcellus gives the two legions to Pompeius—The confidence of Pompeius—Curio's proposal about Caesar and Pompeius—False report that Caesar was marching on Rome—Pompeius is empowered to resist Caesar—Curio, on the expiration of his office, goes to Ravenna to Caesar—Cicero arrives at Brundisium from Cilicia—He tells Atticus his opinion of Caesar, and says that Caesar had not been as liberal to him as to others—He sees Pompeius on his road to Rome—Pompeius speaks of war as certain—Cicero's perplexity at this time—Cicero thinks it would be

hesi to grant Cæsar's demands, and that it was too late to resist him—
Both Cæsar and Pompeius express friendship towards him—Cicero owes
Cæsar money—He is annoyed about paying his debt to Cæsar, because
the money would be useful for his triumph—Another meeting between
Cicero and Pompeius, who expresses the greatest contempt for Cæsar, and
confidence in his own troops—Cicero appears before Rome on the fourth of
January, 49, but does not enter the city—He is satisfied with his reception
by the people, but says that he has fallen into the flames of civil discord
or rather of war—Cæsar's force at Ravenna—Curio's advice to Cæsar,
who sends Curio with a letter to the Senate—Cæsar's demands . . 405

CHAPTER XXV.

CICERO IN CILICIA.

B.C. 51, 50.

*Cicero's Letters to Atticus, v. 9—21, vi., and vii. 1—9 ; Letters to Appius
Claudius Pulcher, ad Div., iii. 1—13 ; Savigny, Vermischte Schriften,
Erster Band.* xiii.

Cicero's voyage and journey from Brundisium to Athens—He leaves
Athens, calls at Samos, and reaches Ephesus, where he is well received—
He arrives at Laodicea on the thirty-first of July, 51—The extent of the
province Cilicia—The præfecti—Cicero's legati and attendants—The
letters of Cicero to his predecessor Appius Claudius Pulcher—The Roman
Permutatio or bills of exchange—The behaviour of Appius to Cicero after
Cicero's arrival in his province—Cicero's answer to Appius' complaints—
Appius' treatise on Augury—Cicero's servility—Cicero, in his letters to
Atticus, gives his real opinion of the maladministration of Appius—
Cicero's good administration—The story of the money-lending of M.
Brutus to the town of Salamis in Cyprus—The Lex Gabinia, and Savigny's
exposition of this affair of M. Brutus—Ariobarzanes III., King of Cappadocia, a debtor to Cn. Pompeius and M. Brutus—Cicero is employed by
these two Romans to dun the beggarly King of Cappadocia—Cicero quits
his province on the thirtieth of July, 50—He visits Rhodes on his homeward voyage, calls at Ephesus and Athens—He sails from Patræ, where
he leaves Tiro sick—His affectionate letters to Tiro—A letter to Tiro contains Cicero's journal till his arrival at Brundisium—The book of Cicero's
letters to Tiro 416

APPENDIX I.—On the two Invasions of Britannia . . 430

    ,,   II.—Cæsar's Provinces 412

    ,,   III.—Cato and Marcia 447

THE DECLINE

OF

THE ROMAN REPUBLIC.

CHAPTER I.

THE HELVETII.

B.C. 58.

On his arrival at Geneva Caesar ordered the bridge over the Rhone to be destroyed (vol. iii. 482). There was only one legion[1] in the Provincia, and we assume that it was either stationed near Geneva or Caesar took it there. He also ordered a levy of men to be raised. Muster-rolls were kept in the provincial towns of those who were liable to service (B. G. iii. 20), and Caesar now required all the men in the Provincia who were able to bear arms. As soon as the Helvetii heard of Caesar's arrival they sent their chief men, at the head of whom were Nameius and Verodoctius, to inform him of their intention to pass through the Provincia, for they had no other road, to declare that they would do no damage, and to ask for his consent. Caesar remembering what had happened to L. Cassius (vol. ii. p. 1) and his army, had no disposition to grant this request, and he did not believe that

---

[1] There is no evidence about the normal or complete strength of a legion in Caesar's time. We only find statements about the actual numbers of a legion on the occasion of some battle or military movement. Rüstow assumes the average strength of one of Caesar's legions to be 3000, or at the highest 3600 men. (Heerwesen und Kriegführung C. Julius Cäsars). In B. G. v. 49, two legions hardly contain 7000 men.

the Helvetii would pass through the Provincia without plundering. However with the view of gaining time until the arrival of the provincial troops, he answered the deputation that he must have time for deliberation, and if they wished to see him again they must return on the thirteenth of April.

It is probable that the Helvetii were not yet assembled on the opposite bank of the Rhone; for before the thirteenth of April Caesar had time to construct, with the legion which he had with him and the soldiers collected from the Provincia, a rampart of earth and a ditch along the south side of the Rhone, from the point, where the Leman lake flows into the river, to the Montagne du Vuache, which is opposite to the Pas-de-l'Écluse. The length of his earthworks was nineteen Roman miles measured along the river[1]. The height of the earth-wall from the bottom of the ditch in front of it was sixteen feet. When the works were finished, Caesar posted his men at convenient places along the line, and strengthened it at intervals with forts or redoubts. When the deputation came again on the thirteenth of April, Caesar refused to allow

[1] A note in the Histoire de César (II. 49) contains a report of the commandant d'artillerie Baron Stoffel on the Rhone between Geneva and the Pas-de-l'Écluse. The note states "that the general character of the river from Geneva to the Pas-de-l'Écluse is that of an immense trench from one hundred to one hundred and twenty mètres in width, with scarp and counter-scarp abrupt and very high. The parts where it has not this character are few and of comparatively small extent. These are the only places where a passage could be attempted, and consequently the only places which it was necessary for Caesar to fortify on the left bank." This long note with the plate (Planche 3) gives a clear view of the character of the river banks along which Caesar constructed his lines. The author remarks that "Caesar, who was pressed for time, had no need to make intrenchments except on the weakest points of the line, where the river was easy to cross, and this is in fact what Dion Cassius (38, c. 31) says." But Dion does not exactly say this; and what he does say, shows that he had a very imperfect conception of the matter. Caesar states that his rampart was continuous, and though there would be no occasion to make it so strong in some parts as in others, still we must assume that he has told the truth; and besides this, it is plain that a continuous line would be a much better defence against the enemy than a line of defence at certain parts only. The enemy crossed the river by bridges of boats, by rafts and at the fords. They could therefore cross at any part, and notwithstanding the steepness of the river-banks in most places, they might have made their way up, if they had not been checked by Caesar's continuous lines.

the Helvetii to pass through the Roman province, and told them that if they attempted to force a passage he should resist. The fighting-men of the Helvetii and their allies, who had joined them, being thus disappointed crossed the river by bridges of boats and rafts, and some by the fords where the Rhone was shallowest. They made a series of attacks on Caesar's earthworks, sometimes in the day, more frequently by night, and attempted to break through the lines, but the strength of the works and the activity of the Roman soldiers who opposed the enemy at every point compelled the enemy to desist from the enterprise.

There remained only the road through the defile on the north bank of the river, and this was in possession of the Sequani, who were separated from the Helvetii by the range of the Jura. As the Helvetii had not been able to obtain permission of the Sequani to take this road, they employed as their agent the Aeduan Dumnorix (vol. iii. 470, 481), whose popularity and liberality had gained him many friends among the Sequani. He was also a son-in-law of Orgetorix, and for this reason well disposed towards the Helvetii; and it was with the view of forwarding his own ambitious schemes that he endeavoured to lay different states under obligations to him. Dumnorix undertook the negotiation with the Sequani, who consented to allow the Helvetii to pass through their territory on condition that they did no damage. Hostages were given on both sides as a security.

Caesar now learned that it was the purpose of the Helvetii to pass through the territory of the Sequani and Aedui in order to reach the country of the Santones, a people who, as he expresses it, were not far distant from the Tolosates (people of Toulouse), a nation in the upper basin of the Garonne, and comprehended within the Roman Provincia. The Santones or Santoni were north of the lower Garonne, on the coast of the Atlantic, in the country named Saintonge before the division of France into departments. Caesar saw that the warlike Helvetii would be very dangerous neighbours to the Provincia, if they planted themselves so near to the wide and fertile plains of Toulouse. Accordingly he placed T. Labienus in command of the lines which he had constructed, and hurrying into North Italy he raised[a] two fresh legions and drew out of their winter camp the three legions (vol. iii. p. 492) which were near Aquileia, a Roman colony at the head of the Gulf of Venice. With these five legions Caesar took the shortest road over the Alps into Transalpine Gallia. On his way he was opposed by the Alpine tribes, the Centrones, Graioceli and Caturiges, who had occupied the higher positions and attempted to stop the march of the Roman army. After defeating these mountaineers in several battles Caesar secured his passage over the Alps. The most western position in North Italy, where he began to enter the mountain region, was Ocelum; and after fighting his way through the defiles he reached on the seventh day the territory of the Vocontii who were in the Roman Provincia. From the Vocontii he marched into the country of the Allobroges, and then crossed the Rhone into the territory of the Segusiani, who occupied the angle between the junction of the Rhone and Saône.

The narrative of the journey from Geneva into Italy, of the return over the mountains with the new troops, and their arrival in the territory of the Segusiani, is contained in eleven lines (B. G. i. 10); an example of brevity which it would be difficult to find in any other writer, and most characteristic of the man. In this short compass Caesar has really said all that is necessary for the purpose of his military history, but modern taste is not satisfied with a narrative which supposes in the reader some knowledge and some imagination, and modern fashion requires the bare facts to be dressed up. It is one of the great difficulties in reading Caesar's history of the Gallic War that his simple narrative can only be duly appreciated by those who have read him often and can supply what he has not said. Indeed a great deal must be supplied, and much of what he has said must be explained in order to make his narrative intelligible. But this can only be done completely by an ample commentary, which would fill several volumes. It is not only impossible to do this in what is called a history, but such an attempt is inconsistent with any exact notion of an historical narrative. I shall therefore in this

---

[a] Perhaps he raised these legions without any authority, as Suetonius (Caesar, c. 24) charges him with doing after the conference at Luca.

volume frequently state facts as Caesar states them, and where
explanation is added, I shall sometimes simply give results
without the reasons and the evidence on which the results depend.
To show the reader that such a method of handling
the matter is necessary in a work of this kind, and also to
show him how much must be added to Caesar's narrative, if
we would fully understand it, I shall briefly examine what is
contained in these eleven lines.

Caesar does not say by what road he crossed the Alps into
Italy from Geneva, nor what force he had with him. I conclude
that he did not go by the pass by which he returned,
that he had only a few men, and that by good luck he crossed
the mountains without being stopped, or perhaps he even
bought a free passage (B. G. iii. 1). It was his fashion to run
great hazards when it was necessary (B. G. vii. 9). When he
reached Cisalpine Gallia, he might send a messenger to the
camp at Aquileia with orders to the officers to lead the men
to Ocelum (probably Uxeau) in the valley of Fenestrelles, near
the base of the Cottian Alps. The march of the three legions
from Aquileia to Ocelum would be nearly in a straight line
and a direct distance of more than three hundred miles. The
other two legions would be raised from the muster-rolls kept
in the towns of Cisalpine Gallia, and the recruits would be
ordered to Ocelum, which was plainly the place of rendezvous
for all the legions. When all were ready, Caesar led his troops
from Ocelum across the Alps by the shortest road, which
means the shortest road to that part of Transalpine Gallia to
which he was going; and the position of Ocelum and his
march to the territory of the Vocontii show that he led his
men by the pass of the Mont Genèvre. It was full six days'
march from Ocelum to the territory of the Vocontii, and as
Caesar could not feed his men in the mountains, he must
have carried his supplies with him on beasts. The men themselves
probably carried something, and some of the native
peoples near the Alps may have been pressed into the carrying
service, as was done by Roman generals on other occasions
(vol. iii. p. 21). The Alpine tribes of the Centrones,'

* De Saulcy (Les Campagnes de Jules César, p. 291) names them Centrones

Graioceli and Caturiges attempted to stop the passage of the Romans, but with what view they resisted so large a force it is not easy to conjecture, unless their object was plunder. These mountaineers were not repelled without several fights[1]. The position of the Caturiges is ascertained to be on the road over the Alps by the pass of the Mont Genèvre, and in the valley of the Durance between Embrun and Gap. The Centrones, as far as we can learn, were north of the Caturiges and in the valley of the Tarentaise: the situation of the Graioceli is unknown. The Centrones must have come some distance and by a difficult road to join in the attack on the Roman army, for they lived on the road over the Little St. Bernard. It is generally assumed that Caesar after reaching Briançon (Brigantium) on the route over the Mont Genèvre led his men to Grenoble on the Isère; but we may doubt if there was at that time a practicable road from Briançon to Grenoble, and if there was, it is nearly certain that it went through no part of the territory of the Vocontii. I conclude that Caesar took the comparatively easy road through Embrun, Gap, Die (Dea), to Valence (Valentia) on the Rhone. We do not know what means of communication he had with Labienus, nor whether he was yet informed about the movements of the Helvetii, but by reaching the lower regions of the Provincia he would obtain supplies, and he would meet his vessels on the Rhone which contained provisions for his men (B. G. i. 16). From the territory of the Vocontii Caesar crossed the Isère into the territory of the Allobroges, and from the territory of the Allobroges he crossed the Rhone above the junction with the Saône, probably making use of his vessels for the transit of the army. Here he would learn, if he did not already know, the position of the Helvetii, and here we may assume that he was joined by Labienus and his legion, a fact which he does not mention.

The Helvetii had now passed through the defile of the Jura and through the territories of the Sequani, and they had

on the authority of antient inscriptions; but he does not say what inscriptions. Many of the best MSS. have Centrones (Schneider).

[1] Polyaenus (Strat. viii. 23. 2) records a stratagem of Caesar, who took advantage of a morning fog to escape from the mountaineers; but his story is not worth much.

reached the country of the Aedui, which they were plundering. Caesar says nothing of the time which he employed in visiting Italy and leading his troops to the junction of the Rhone and the Saône. A modern writer[6] thinks that it could not be done in less than sixty days, and no objection can be made to this estimate. This time had been employed by the Helvetii in negociating with the Sequani and making their way to the Saône. The season of the year would be now early in June. As the emigrants took with them only three months' ground corn, they must have exhausted a large part of the stock during the journey to Geneva, the delay in that neighbourhood, and on their tedious road to the Saône. After passing the defile of the Jura the track of the Helvetii was through the modern department of the Ain, the eastern part of which is hilly, then through the plain of Ambérieux, across the river Ain, and over the plateau of Dombes, probably to Trévoux on the Saône or some point a little north of Trévoux in this fertile district. The Helvetii had not well calculated the obstacles to their journey. The slowness of the march is easily explained by the want of roads, the enormous number of waggons which they had, the necessity in many parts of moving in single file and the impossibility of making their way, whenever the rain fell and the track was deep cut with the wheels of many thousand vehicles[7].

[6] Histoire de Jules César, ii. 57.
[7] An estimate is made in the Histoire de César (p. 58) of the weight of three months' provisions for 368,000 persons, which was the number of the emigrants. It is founded on the assumption that ⅔ of a kilogramme a day was the allowance of each person for the three months (vol. iii. p. 480). A kilogramme is 2.2 English pounds avoirdupois. The reader may calculate the necessary number of waggons, when he has ascertained how much a waggon with two horses, or four horses, if he prefers four, can draw besides the weight of the waggon. But we must add something for the weight of other baggage, which would increase the number of waggons and beasts. The author by his assumptions attains a result of 8500 waggons, drawn by 34,000 beasts of some kind; and this estimate does not include any food for the draft beasts, the beasts of burden, and the cavalry horses, of which the emigrants had at least 500 (B. G. i. 15). Such a column of 8500 waggons, moving in single file, would not occupy less than thirty-two leagues in length, as the writer estimates, if we allow 15 mètres (49 feet) for each team and carriage. The waggons must certainly have passed in single file along the gap in the Jura, and perhaps in certain parts east

The Aedui being unable to defend themselves against the Helvetii sent to implore the aid of Caesar. Some Aedui, named also Ambarri, who seem to have been on the east side of the river Saône, probably in the neighbourhood of Ambérieux* informed Caesar that their lands were ravaged and their towns were in danger. Some of the Allobroges also, who had lands and villages between the Rhone and the Saône, fled to Caesar and told him that the Helvetii had stripped them of every thing except the very soil. Caesar promptly determined what he would do. The Helvetii were now engaged in crossing the Saône probably a little north of Trévoux. This river, the current of which is very slow, as Caesar observes, flowed partly through the territory of the Aedui and partly through the territory of the Sequani, and the emigrants were crossing it on rafts and bridges of boats. When Caesar was informed by his scouts that three fourths of the enemy had crossed the Saône, he left his camp after the beginning of the third* watch with three legions and surprised the remaining fourth of the emigrants who had not crossed the river. A great part of this division was destroyed, and those who escaped hid themselves in the neighbouring woods. This unfortunate divison was the Pagus of the Tigurini, which had defeated the consul L. Cassius. Caesar, who seldom makes reflections, observes that either through chance or through the interposition of the gods, this part of the Helvetic nation, which had inflicted a signal calamity on the Roman state, was the first that suffered for it; and he adds that by this attack on the enemy he had avenged not only the Roman state, but his own wrongs too, for the Tigurini had killed in the same battle, in which L. Cassius perished, L. Piso also, who was the grandfather of L. Piso, one of the consuls of this year and Caesar's father-in-law.

of the river Ain, but we cannot suppose that in the open plains they would move in single file.

* Their country was the parts of anterevolutionary France which were named le Bugey and la Bresse. The railroad from Geneva now passes by Ambéricus.

* The night was reckoned from sunset to sunrise on the following morning and divided into four equal parts named 'vigiliae,' 'watches.' The length of a 'vigilia' would of course vary with the season of the year.

After this slaughter of the enemy Caesar made a bridge, or perhaps more than one, over the Saône, and took his army to the other side in one day (c. 11). This bridge was probably a bridge of boats formed of the vessels which carried his provisions. The Helvetii alarmed by his unexpected appearance on the west side of the river, which only three fourths of their number had been able to cross in twenty days, sent commissioners to him, the chief of whom was Divico, who had commanded in the war against Cassius forty-nine years before. Divico promised that if Caesar would make peace with the Helvetii, they would settle in any part of Gallia that he would name; but if he should resolve to continue the war, he ought not to forget the former defeat of the Romans and the old valour of the Helvetic nation. Caesar replied that he had not forgotten the past, nor could he forget the recent wrongs which the Helvetii had done to the Aedui, Ambarri and Allobroges; but if the Helvetii would give him hostages as a security for their promise, and make satisfaction to the Aedui for the wrongs done to them and their allies, and would also do the same for the Allobroges, he would come to terms with them. Divico replied that it was the antient usage of the Helvetii to receive, not to give hostages, as the Romans well knew. Thus ended the conference.

On the following day the Helvetii began their march northward with the Saône on their right and the hills of the Beaujolais and Charolais on the left. Caesar followed them, and in order to ascertain what road they were taking he sent forward all his cavalry four thousand in number, which was furnished by the Roman Provincia, and the Aedui and their allies. Caesar's cavalry pressing onwards with too much ardour were attacked at a disadvantage by five hundred horsemen of the Helvetii and lost a few men. The enemy encouraged by this success sometimes made a halt and with their rear even ventured to attack the Romans. Caesar would not let his men fight, and he limited himself to checking the enemy in plundering and foraging. The march and the pursuit were continued for about fifteen days in such manner that between the rear of the enemy and the head of the Roman army the interval was not more than five or six miles.

It is remarked (Histoire de Jules César, p. 63), that the easiest way by which you can go from the lower Saône to Saintonge (Santones) is by taking a north-west course towards the source of the Bourbince, a small branch of the Loire, and then marching to the west. In this north-west direction lies the greatest depression in the mountains which separate the basins of the Saône and the Loire, and Caesar was compelled to follow the Helvetii without attacking them, because there was no place in which he could overtake them or execute any military movement. This road which the Helvetii took followed, as the author observes, the old Gallic route through the mountains of the Charolais, along which line was afterwards constructed the Roman road from Lugdunum (Lyon) to Augustodunum (Autun). This route followed the Saône to Belleville, where it turned off to the north-west over the pass of Avenas, and thence ran on to Cluny, and St. Vallier on the Bourbince. From St. Vallier the emigrants would have turned to the Loire and crossed it at Decise (Decetia). This remark leads us to observe that the Helvetii could not pass direct from the place where they crossed the Saône to Roanne on the Loire, which would be the shortest road. The rugged country between the basins of the Saône and the Loire could not have been crossed in this direction by their waggons; and west of the Loire there is the high range of the Forez, which is seen from the noble modern bridge at Roanne. In fact the Helvetii were now taking the best route to Saintonge; and when they originally intended to pass through the Provincia, it was either because they were ill informed, or because they could not at first obtain permission to pass through the territory of the Sequani and the Aedui.

The author of the Histoire (p. 61) conjectures that a detachment of Caesar's force was stationed at the site of Lyon on the right bank of the Saône, after Caesar had passed that river, to prevent the Helvetii from turning southwards through the Provincia; and yet he says that the easiest road to Saintonge from the lower Saône was that which the Helvetii did take. Goeler (Gallischer Krieg, p. 14) also supposes that it was the intention of the Helvetii after crossing the Saône to pass to the south-west through the country of the Vellavi or

Vellauni, Gabali, and Petrocorii to Saintonge. But any one who knows this part of France will also know that the Helvetii could not have passed in the direction which Goeler supposes; nor could they have gone due south along the west bank of the Rhone. Both writers refer to Livy's Epitome, 103, which even with their reading proves only that the original intention of the Helvetii was to go through the Provincia, which Caesar himself tells us; and he also tells us that it was reported to him after he had barred the Rhone against the Helvetii, that their intention was to reach Saintonge through the country of the Sequani and the Aedui (c. 10).

The Aedui had promised to supply Caesar with corn, for the grain in the fields was not yet ripe and the army therefore could not help themselves, nor was there even sufficient forage. When the Helvetii turned inland and Caesar followed them, he left behind him the grain which his vessels had brought up the Saône, and if he made any use of this supply, it must have been carried after the army from the river on boats, or he may have also used some of the waggons of the Tigurini who were dispersed on the east side of the Saône. The Aedui did not keep their promise to Caesar, who discovering the treachery of his allies called together their chief men of whom he had a large number in his camp, and among them Divitiacus (vol. iii. p. 477) and Liscus, the Vergobret or chief magistrate of the Aedui, who was elected annually. Caesar complained bitterly of the Aedui not furnishing him with corn, especially as it was in a great measure through their entreaty that he had begun the war. Liscus then told him that there were some men among the Aedui who had more influence with the people than the magistrates, that these men prevented the Aedui from bringing the corn, reported to the enemy Caesar's plans, and could not be checked: he ran great risk, as he said, in giving Caesar this information, and this was the reason why he had kept the truth from him so long. Caesar saw that Liscus pointed to Dumnorix[1], the brother of Divitiacus, and as he did not wish these matters to be discussed before

[1] The name is Dubnorex or Dubnoreix on the Gallic medals. The reverse of one medal is a soldier with a human head in each hand. (Communicated by Mr. Lindsay).

the meeting, he dismissed all the chiefs except Liscus, who then being alone with Caesar spoke more freely. Caesar also inquired from others severally, and he discovered that Dumnorix was the guilty man: his audacity was unbounded, his influence with the common sort was great owing to his liberality, and his designs were revolutionary: he had farmed for many years the tolls and all the other taxes of the Aedui at a low rent, for these taxes were let by auction and no one dared to bid against Dumnorix: thus the man grew rich; he maintained at his own cost and kept about him a large body of cavalry. His influence was great both at home and in the neighbouring states, and he increased it abroad by marrying his mother to a man of the highest rank and power among the Bituriges, a people west of the Loire; his wife was an Helvetian woman, and he had found husbands for his half-sister on the mother's side and for others of his kinswomen in other states. Through his Helvetic wife he was a friend of that nation, and he hated Caesar and the Romans because their coming diminished his power and restored his brother Divitiacus to his former influence. If the Romans should be defeated, he expected to make himself king of the Aedui with the aid of the Helvetii; but if the Romans obtained the supremacy, he would lose his present power. Caesar discovered also that in the late cavalry fight Dumnorix and his horsemen were the first who fled, for Dumnorix commanded the Aeduan cavalry in Caesar's service, and their flight was the cause of the rest being seized with a panic.

For all these reasons, and because Dumnorix had negotiated with the Sequani for the passage of the Helvetii through their country, Caesar thought he could justly punish him, or ask the Aedui to do so. The only thing that prevented him was the fear of offending Divitiacus, who was a good friend to the Romans and himself, and an honourable man. Accordingly Caesar summoned Divitiacus, and sending away the interpreters whom he usually employed, he made use of C. Valerius Procillus, one of the chief men of the Roman Provincia, in whom Caesar had the greatest confidence. Procillus was a young Gaul, whose father had been made a Roman citizen by C. Valerius Flaccus the governor of the Provincia in B. C. 53, and he was well acquainted with the Gallic language, and also of course with Latin.

Caesar reminding Divitiacus of his brother's crimes expressed a hope that he would not take it amiss if he brought his brother to trial and passed judgment on him, or asked the Aedui to do it. Divitiacus earnestly entreated Caesar to spare his brother, though he admitted that the charges were true. Dumnorix owed his influence to Divitiacus his elder brother, but he had ungratefully used his power towards impairing the popularity of Divitiacus and almost to his ruin. Still Divitiacus was moved by affection for Dumnorix, and also by regard to public opinion, and if Caesar should inflict any severe punishment on Dumnorix, he being Caesar's intimate friend would be supposed to have assented to it, and he should become odious to all the people of Gallia. Divitiacus was a Druid (vol. iii. p. 477), a fact which may explain his fear of becoming unpopular all through Gallia. Caesar pretended to yield to the prayers of the Druid, but in fact he yielded to necessity. He was in great straits, with a warlike enemy in front and doubtful allies around him, on whom his army was dependent for food. A later passage in the Commentaries (v. 6) may perhaps explain why Caesar has said so much of the treachery of Dumnorix and his own generosity. He now sent for the man and in his brother's presence told him what he was charged with, and advising him for the future to give no cause for suspicion, pardoned the past out of regard to Divitiacus. But he took care that Dumnorix was well watched.

On the same day on which Dumnorix was detected and pardoned, Caesar, being informed by his scouts that the enemy had halted at the foot of a mountain eight miles from the Roman camp, sent some men to ascertain if it was possible to ascend the mountain on the side turned from the enemy. The report was that the ascent was easy. At the beginning of the third watch of the night Caesar sent T. Labienus with two legions, and the men as guides who had examined the road. Labienus was ordered to make his way to the summit of the mountain. At the beginning of the fourth watch Caesar set out on the track of the enemy and ordered all the cavalry to advance before him. P. Considius, who had a very great reputation as a soldier and had served under L. Cornelius Sulla and afterwards under M. Crassus, was sent ahead with the scouts.

At daybreak Labienus had occupied the summit of the mountain, and Caesar was not more than a mile and a half from the enemy, who, as it was afterwards known from some prisoners, were not aware of the Roman general's approach or of the position of Labienus, when Considius returned at full gallop and reported that the mountain, which Labienus had been ordered to occupy, was in the possession of the Helvetii whom he recognized by their armour and standards. Caesar immediately led his troops up the nearest hill and prepared for battle. In the meantime Labienus following his instructions not to begin the battle until Caesar's troops were seen near the enemy's encampment, in order that both attacks might be made at the same time, was waiting for the other division. At last when it was broad daylight, Caesar was informed that the summit of the mountain was occupied by his men, that the Helvetii had moved from their place, and that Considius in his fright had reported that he saw what he did not see. On that day Caesar followed the enemy at the usual distance, and encamped three miles from them.

On the next day instead of pursuing the Helvetii Caesar turned in another direction and began to move towards Bibracte (Autun), which was about eighteen miles distant, and the largest and richest town of the Aedui. The army had only two days' provision of corn on hand, and the proconsul thought it prudent to secure a further supply. This movement was reported to the enemy by some deserters from L. Aemilius, one of the commanders (decurio) of a company of Gallic cavalry. The Helvetii, either supposing that the Romans were discontinuing the pursuit through fear, especially as they had not made an attack the day before when they were in possession of the higher ground, or expecting to cut them off from the supply of corn, turned round and began to harass the Roman rear. It was now necessary to fight, and Caesar led his forces to the nearest hill, while he sent his cavalry to check the advance of the enemy. In the meantime he placed

on the slope, half-way up the hill, his four veteran legions in
three lines, and above them on the summit all his auxiliary
troops and the two legions, which he had lately raised in North
Italy. Thus the summit and the whole side of the hill half-
way down were covered with the Roman troops. The baggage and the soldiers' kits[a] (sarcinae) were brought together
to one place, and those who were on the summit of the hill
were ordered to throw up earthworks about them. The Helvetii, who had followed Caesar with all their waggons, put
them together on one spot, and made of them a kind of fortified camp. This operation must have occupied the enemy
some time, and it gave Caesar the opportunity of providing
for the safety of his baggage and securing a place of retreat
on the hill top if he should be defeated. The Helvetii now
closed their ranks, drove back Caesar's cavalry[b], and forming
what he calls a phalanx advanced up the hill to attack the
first line of the Romans.

Caesar dismounted from his horse and sent it to the rear:
all the mounted officers followed his example. This was done
to show the soldiers that they and their commanders would
share the danger, and that no man had the chance of saving
himself by flight. The general encouraged his troops and
gave the signal for the onset. The Romans being on the
higher ground easily broke the phalanx of the enemy by a
discharge of their javelins (pila[c]), and then fell upon them with

---

[a] 'Sarcina' generally means only what the soldiers carried. Virgil (Georg.
iii. 347) names it 'fascis.' It may perhaps include beasts of burden here, if
Caesar had any with him on the hill. Goeler assumes that Caesar had already
sent on his heavy baggage towards Bibracte, because he has only spoken of
securing what the soldiers carried. See vol. ii. p. 24, on the "sarcina."

[b] Nothing more is said of the cavalry, and the true conclusion is that there
was nothing more to say. They may have retired to the rear of the four
legions. Goeler (p. 81) supposes that part of the cavalry may have protected
the third line in forming a new front, when the Boii and Tulingi fell on the
Roman flank. This may be so, but there is no evidence of it. He also assumes
(Plan der Schlacht bei Autun) that Caesar's cavalry after being repulsed may
have protected Caesar's baggage on the road to Bibracte.

[c] As to the 'pilum,' see vol. ii. p. 23. The author of the Histoire (ii. 60)
says "that the pilum was 1·70 to 2 mètres long. The iron was thin and
flexible, 0·60 to 1 mètre in length, weighing from 300 to 600 grammes, ter-
minating in a part slightly wider, which formed a point sometimes barbed.
The shaft, sometimes round, sometimes square, was in diameter from 25 to 32

the sword[1]. As the same javelin pierced several of the shields of the enemy and nailed them together, in consequence of the way in which the phalanx was formed, and the iron head of the javelin was bent in the shields, the Helvetii could neither tear it out nor fight with the left arm thus encumbered. At last after many fruitless efforts to rid themselves of this intolerable burden, they threw away the shield and fought with the body exposed. After a long struggle the Helvetii drew back still facing the Romans to a hill a mile distant.

When the Helvetii had reached the hill and the four legions were following up after them, the Boii and Tulingi to the number of fifteen thousand men, who formed the enemy's rear and were just making their appearance on the field, fell without a moment's delay on the flank and rear of the Romans. The Helvetii who had retreated to the hill now again advanced upon the legions and renewed the contest. Upon this Caesar ordered the first and second lines to oppose the Helvetii who had been repulsed, and the third to make a movement by which they presented another front to the Boii and Tulingi. The battle was thus renewed on two lines, and the struggle was long and obstinate[2]. When they could no

millimètres. It was fastened to the iron by a collar, or pin, or a groove. Such are the characters of the fragments of pila found in the excavations at Alise. Some pila made after the model of those found at Alise, and weighing with the shaft from 700 grammes to 1 kilog. 200, have been thrown from 30 to 40 mètres. Accordingly we may fix the mean range of a pilum at 25 mètres, or near it (82 feet)." 25 should be 35.

[1] The sword was short and used for pushing, not cutting. See vol. II. p. 23; and Machiavelli, Dell' Arte della Guerra, lib. II.; Goeler, Gallischer Krieg, p. 53, n. 6.

[2] Dion Cassius, 38, c. 33, says, "When the main body of the Helvetii were put to flight, some of those who were not fighting, for owing to the numbers and the hurry they were not all on the field at once, suddenly fell on the rear of the pursuing Romans, and threw them into confusion; but this was all the advantage that they gained, for Caesar ordering his cavalry to pursue the fugitives, himself with the legions attacked and routed the new assailants, and then followed both divisions of the enemy who had fled to the waggons, and after a hard fight defeated them." I do not remember that Dion cites Caesar's Commentaries, but he used them. It is impossible to say whether he had any other authorities for the Gallic war. If he had, he showed his want of sense in following them, if he did follow them, instead of following Caesar. If he had not, he showed his want of sense still more by not strictly following Caesar. I am inclined to think that Caesar was Dion's only authority, and that after his

longer resist the impetuosity of the Roman soldiers, the Helvetii retired to the hill which they had before begun to ascend, and the Boii and Tulingi retreated to the waggons. During this long fight, which lasted from the seventh hour of the day to evening, not a single man in the enemy's ranks was seen to turn his back. The contest was continued far into the night around the waggons, from which the enemy discharged their missiles on the assailants, and some by pushing pikes and javelins between the waggons and the wheels wounded the Roman soldiers. After an obstinate resistance Caesar's men at last got possession of the waggons and the baggage. A daughter of Orgetorix and one of his sons were found there. About one hundred and thirty thousand persons who survived the fight retreated from the bloody field in a north-east direction, and continued their journey all that night. On the fourth day they reached the territory of the Lingones, the plateau of Langres. Caesar was unable to follow them immediately, being detained three days in looking after his wounded and burying the dead[7]; but he sent messengers forward with letters to the Lingones, in which he gave them orders not to aid the enemy with food or any thing else; if they did, he would treat them like the Helvetii. After an interval of three days he set out with all his forces to follow the fugitives.

The site of this great battle cannot be determined. The author of the " Histoire" (p. 71, note) thinks that the place which he has marked (Planche 5), between Luzy and Chides, satisfies "all the exigencies of the text of the Commentaries." Luzy is on the small river Alène and near Mont Beuvray, which the author supposes to be the site of Caesar's Bibracte. Beuvray is about thirteen kilomètres[8] west of Autun, which is generally believed to be the site of Bibracte. There is no

---

fashion of writing history, he invented and altered facts. I shall seldom take any notice of his history of the Gallic campaigns. He had a very imperfect conception of the facts, and none at all of the geography of Gallia.

[7] This, I think, is the only occasion in his history of the Gallic war in which he speaks of burying those who had fallen. He says nothing of his loss in this great battle, but it could not be small.

[8] A kilomètre is about 1093 English yards.

doubt that there was a Gallo-Roman town on the hill Beuvray, as the remains found there clearly prove. M. de Saulcy (Les Campagnes de Jules César, p. 340) has fixed the site of the battle at Cussy-la-Colonne, E.N.E. of Autun, but I agree with the author of the "Histoire" that this position cannot be accepted. The Helvetii on their way to the Loire would pass south of Bibracte, whether it is Beuvray or Autun, and it is impossible that Caesar and the enemy could have met at Cussy-la-Colonne.

The Helvetii being reduced to the greatest straits sent to Caesar to offer unconditional surrender. The commissioners meeting the proconsul on the road threw themselves at his feet and humbly prayed for peace. The answer was that the Helvetii must stay where they were and wait for his arrival. When Caesar came, he demanded of them hostages, their arms and all the slaves who had escaped to them. While both sides were employed in executing these orders, night came on, when about six thousand men of the Helvetian Pagus named Verbigenus, either fearing that they would be massacred after giving up their arms, or hoping that among so great a number of prisoners their flight would not be observed, left the Helvetian camp as soon as it was dark and marched towards the Rhine and the country of the Germans. When their escape was discovered, Caesar sent orders to the people through whose country the fugitives had passed, to stop them and bring them back, if they wished to be clear of all blame. The men were brought back, and in Caesar's simple language "were treated as enemies," which means that they were all massacred, or to take the mildest sense of the words, they were sold as slaves. All the rest after delivering hostages, arms, and runaway slaves, were treated as "dediticii," a term which implies unconditional surrender. The Helvetii, Tulingi, and Latobrigi, were commanded to return to their homes, and as they would find no means of subsistence there, orders were given to the Allobroges to supply them with corn. The emigrants were also commanded to rebuild the towns and villages which they had burnt. Caesar would not allow the parts which the Helvetii had left to lie unoccupied, for fear that the fertility of the soil might invite the Germans to cross the Rhine and become neighbours to the Roman Provincia and the Allobroges. It was easy to give such orders, but we are not informed how they were executed. After a few months the winter would come, and many of these unfortunate people would perish of hunger and cold. It is probable that the Germans did cross the Rhine and occupy some of the vacant lands, for there would be more than sufficient for the few who returned out of so great a number. The Boii, who were famed for their courage, were allowed at the request of the Aedui to settle in their country. The Aedui gave them lands, and afterwards admitted them to the condition of perfect equality with themselves. Nothing is here said of the Rauraci (B. G. i. 5), but as they occupied a territory on the left bank of the Rhine and bordered on the Helvetii, we may assume that they were treated like them.

There were found in the Helvetian camp and brought to Caesar tablets or muster-rolls made out in Greek characters. These rolls contained a list of all the fighting men who had emigrated, and separate lists of the children, women, and old men. The whole number of the Helvetii was 263,000, of the Tulingi 36,000, of the Latobrigi 14,000, of the Rauraci 23,000, of the Boii 32,000. The number of fighting men was 92,000. The sum total was 368,000. A census was taken pursuant to Caesar's order of those who returned home, and the number was found to be 110,000. Perhaps a few of those Tigurini, who took shelter in the woods when they were surprised on the east bank of the Saône (c. 12), may have joined their countrymen after they were sent home[*]. The time of the year when this great battle was fought may have been the month of June. The corn was not ripe when Caesar was pursuing the Helvetii after he had crossed the Saône. Two months probably passed between his leaving Geneva for Italy and his return over the Alps to the Rhone. The Roman calendar was in disorder at the time, and the dates which Caesar gives (i. 6, 7) are not the true dates.

[*] Plutarch, Appian (De Rebus Gallicis, iii.), Polyaenus, and even Strabo (p. 193), report the numbers of the Helvetii differently from Caesar, a sufficient proof of the carelessness of antient compilers; for they could have no better authority than Caesar.

CHAPTER II.

ARIOVISTUS AND THE GERMANS.

B. C. 58.

The war with the Helvetii being ended, the chief men of nearly all the states of Gallia Celtica came to congratulate Caesar. It is not said where Caesar was when these commissioners came, but he was in the country of the Lingones when he received the submission of the Helvetii, and he does not say that he had left it. Another passage seems to show that he was not now in the country of the Aedui (B. G. i. 37). The commissioners told him that he had done the Celtic states a great service by defeating the Helvetii, whose design was to establish their dominion over the Celtic country, to seize the best part of it and to make the rest tributary. They asked Caesar's permission to summon a meeting (concilium) of all the Celtic states in order to agree about certain things which they intended to propose to him. Permission being granted, the meeting was held, and all the members were bound by oath not to divulge what was done, except those who received instructions to that effect by the general resolution of the assembly.

When the meeting separated, the same men who had first come to Caesar, came again and asked for an interview in some place where they would not be observed, which was granted. They told Caesar, they were as anxious that what they should say to him should not be reported as they were to obtain what they wanted, for they well knew what they would suffer, if their petition were made known. Diviciacus spoke for all of them. He told Caesar the story of the quarrels between the Arverni and the Aedui, which ended in the

Germans being invited into Gallia by the Arverni and the Sequani (vol. iii. p. 476); the defeat of the Aedui and their dependents by the Germans, their forced submission to the Sequani; and finally, the tyranny exercised over the Sequani by their German allies, whose king Ariovistus had taken possession of one third of their territory, which was the best land in all Gallia, and he was demanding another third, which he intended to give to the Harudes, a body of Germans, twenty-four thousand in number, who had arrived a few months before this interview with Caesar. In a short time all the Galli would be driven out of their territories, and all the Germans would cross the Rhine, for the land on the Gallic side of the river was much better than that on the German side, and the Gallic way of living much superior. Ariovistus was a cruel tyrant who demanded their children as hostages from all the Gallic nobles, and tortured them if his arbitrary commands were not obeyed. The dominion of this barbarian was intolerable, and if Caesar and the Roman people did not help them, the Galli must follow the example of the Helvetii: they must leave their country, and at all risks seek new homes far away from the Germans. If what was said to Caesar should be reported to Ariovistus, it was certain that he would take vengeance on all the hostages who were in his hands. Caesar either by using his influence supported by his army, or by availing himself of his recent victory, or by employing the name of the Roman people could prevent any more Germans from being brought across the Rhine, and could protect Gallia against the tyranny of Ariovistus.

When Divitiacus had finished his speech, all who were present with tears implored Caesar's aid. Caesar observing that the Sequani alone did not act like the others, but kept their eyes sorrowfully fixed on the ground, asked them the reason of this behaviour. The Sequani gave no answer, but persisted in their mournful silence. As Caesar put the same question to them several times without being able to draw a word from them, Divitiacus said, that the Sequani were so far in a worse condition than the rest that they dared not complain even in secret or pray for help, and they dreaded the cruel German king as much as if he were present: the rest of the Galli had still the power of escape, but the Sequani having received Ariovistus within their territory, and all their towns being in his possession, must submit to his tyranny.

If these statements of Divitiacus were true, there was at that time danger of the Germans occupying a large part of Gallia, and chiefly in consequence of the disunion among the Gallic nations. If the Galli could have acted together, they might have driven out the Germans and confined the Romans to the limits of their Provincia; but disunion was their ruin.

The country of the Sequani, in which Ariovistus had planted himself, lay between the Saône, the Jura, the Rhone and the Rhine, for it is described by Caesar (B. G. i. 1, iv. 10), as bordering on the Rhine, and it therefore included some part of the fertile plain between the Vosges and the river. If the position of the Rauraci is rightly fixed about Bâle, where the river turns to the north, the Sequani on the Rhine may have been the neighbours of the Rauraci. But there was also a people named Tribocci on the left bank of the Rhine, and they were Germans; and it is a fair conclusion from Caesar that he supposed these Tribocci to have settled on the left bank of the river before he entered Gallia. These Tribocci fought with Ariovistus in the great battle near the Rhine. It seems probable then that the Germans had fixed themselves between the Vosges and the river, and driven the Sequani from part of their territory, which in former days may have extended as far north as Strasburg.

Caesar encouraged the Gallic chieftains after hearing the story of their sufferings from the Germans, promised that he would look after their interests, and expressed a strong hope that he could induce Ariovistus to put a stop to his cruelties. With these words he dismissed the meeting. Caesar tells us his reasons for resolving to deal with Ariovistus. The Roman Senate had often conferred on the Aedui the title of brothers and kinsmen, and yet they were now enslaved by the Germans, and their hostages were in the hands of Ariovistus and the Sequani; which Caesar considered a great disgrace to himself and to the power and dominion of the Roman state. If the Germans should be accustomed to cross the Rhine and to enter Gallia in large numbers, the danger was manifest.

After taking possession of Gallia, as the Cimbri and Teutoni had done, they would invade the Provincia and enter Italy, for the Rhone alone separated the Sequani from the Provincia. This danger ought to be met immediately; and the pride and arrogance of Ariovistus were become intolerable.—Caesar's reasons were sufficient, but he had other reasons also. His design was to penetrate farther into Gallia and to subjugate all the country; and he could not safely advance northwards with Ariovistus and his Germans in the rear.

Caesar in several parts of his "Commentaries" has spoken of the Germans. The name "Germani," under which he comprehends many peoples, was the name which the Galli gave to these formidable invaders, and the Romans accepted the name from the Galli. The Germans had probably no general name for all the Germanic tribes (vol. ii. p. 46). The Rhine was the boundary between the Germanic and the Celtic nations, though there were Germans settled west of the Rhine even in Caesar's age. There was a time (B. G. vi. 24) when the Galli surpassed the Germans in valour, invaded the German country, and settled colonies there. The most fertile parts of Germany about the Hercynian forest were occupied by some Volcae Tectosages, a people who in Caesar's time possessed the western parts of the Provincia about Toulouse. These Tectosages, who settled in Germany, must have been a body of adventurers, who wanting room at home sought it in the countries east of the Rhine. The emigrants, as Caesar reports, occupied their German lands even in his time, and had a high reputation for justice and a warlike spirit. They lived the same hardy life as the Germans, using the same kind of food and dress. There was also a tradition (Justin. xxxii. 3) that a remnant of the army of Brennus settled at the confluence of the Danube and the Save under the name of Scordisci. (Compare Livy, v. 34.)

The Hercynian forest was known by report to Eratosthenes and some other Greeks, under the name Orcynia. The width of this forest, as Caesar says (B. G. vi. 25), was nine days' journey to a man without any incumbrance. It commenced at the territory of the Helvetii, Nemetes[1], and Rauraci, and

[1] We cannot exactly conclude what was the position of the Nemetes in

following the straight course of the Danube reached to the country of the Daci and the Anartes. Here it turned to the left in different directions from the river, and extended to the territory of many nations. No man of western Germany could affirm that he had reached the eastern termination of this forest even after a journey of sixty days, nor that he had heard where it did terminate. This is all that Caesar knew of this great forest, which in his time covered the high lands and probably part of the level country also north of the Danube. The nine days' journey, which measures the width of the Hercynian forest, is the width from south to north; and if we assume this width to be estimated at the western end of the Hercynia, which part would be the best known, it will correspond to the Schwarzwald and Odenwald, which extend on the east side of the Rhine from the neighbourhood of Bâle nearly as far north as Frankfort on the Main. The eastern parts of the forest would extend on the north side of the Danube along the Raube Alp and the Boehmerwald and still farther east. Caesar mentions another German forest named Bacenis (B. G. vi. 10), but all that he could say of it is this: it was a forest of boundless extent, and it separated the Suevi and the Cherusci; from which we may conclude that it is represented by the Thüringerwald, Erzgebirge, Riesengebirge, and the mountain ranges farther east, which separate the basin of the Danube from the basins of the Oder and the Vistula. Caesar's information about the German forests was probably derived from traders (mercatores), who visited the Germans on the Rhine. Caesar describes the reindeer (bos cervus), the elk (alces), and the huge urus (bos urus) in his sixth book (c. 26, 27, 28), but only from hearsay.

The Suevi were the largest and most warlike of the German nations (B. G. iv. 1); but Caesar did not exactly know the position of the Suevi; at least he has not told us. Ariovistus was a Sueve, if one passage (B. G. i. 53) justifies this conclusion. Caesar was informed that the Suevi had one hundred Pagi or divisions, out of each of which a thousand men went

Caesar's time. They are not mentioned in B. G. iv. 10 among the Germans on the left bank of the Rhine, though they were afterwards settled there, and their chief town was Noviomagus (Speyer).

annually to war beyond the limits of the Suevian territory. The rest who stayed at home raised food for themselves and the fighters, who next year stayed at home while the others took the field. Each Pagus then contained two thousand men able to bear arms; but perhaps we must not take Caesar's words literally. The Suevi were like those modern European nations some of whose men learn the business of war, while others work in the fields. Tacitus (Germ. c. 15) reports that all the great German fighters did no work. The care of the house and the field labour was put on the women, the old men and the weakest persons in the family. In the European countries alluded to the women now bear the great burden of labour. Thus modern civilization and antient barbarism produce the same result.

The Suevi had no private property in land, and the same persons were not allowed to cultivate the same spot more than one year. They did not produce much grain, but lived chiefly on milk, flesh, and game. This kind of food, their daily exercise, and the perfect freedom which they enjoyed from boyhood made them grow large and strong. Though the country was very cold, habit enabled them to do without any other clothing than skins, which were so scanty that a great part of the body was exposed; and they bathed in the rivers. Traders were allowed to go among the Suevi rather because they were ready to purchase what the Suevi got in war than because these people had any desire for foreign articles. The Galli took great pleasure in horses and would buy them at a large price, but the Germans did not import horses. Their own animals, which were ill-made, attained very great powers of endurance by daily exercise. In battle the Suevi often got down from their horses and fought on foot, their beasts being trained to stand still, and when it was necessary, the riders quickly retired and mounted again. The Suevi thought nothing more disgraceful or unmanly than the use of saddles, and a small number of their horsemen would attack any number of saddle-men. The Gallic cavalry could not stand the attack of Caesar's German cavalry (B. G. vii. 12). The Germans did not allow wine[2] to be imported, because they thought that

[2] Posidonius in his thirtieth book (ap. Athen. iv. 153) stated that the Ger-

it made men unfit to endure fatigue. The Suevi were therefore water-drinkers, unless they made beer. Like the Germans generally (B. G. vi. 21) the Suevi bestowed the highest commendation on those young men who retained their chastity the longest, it being their opinion that this abstinence increased the growth and strength. To know a woman before a man attained his twentieth year was considered most disgraceful. It is sometimes useful to contrast what we call civilization with that which we call barbarism[a].

The Suevi thought it glorious for the lands which bordered on their territory to be desolate as far as possible, for this was a proof of their power. Accordingly in one direction from the territory of the Suevi the country was said to be uninhabited for six hundred miles, which is no doubt a monstrous exaggeration. The direction of which Caesar speaks must be the east. On the other side, as he says, the Ubii were next to the Suevi, and formed a large and flourishing community for a German state. They were more civilized, in the Roman sense, than the other Germans, because their territory extended to the Rhine and they were visited by traders, and familiar with the habits of the Galli on the opposite side of the river (B. G. iv 3). The Suevi had often attacked the Ubii, and though they had not been able to expel them from the country, they had made them tributary and weakened their power.

In Caesar's time the Ubii were only on the east side of the Rhine. Their territory extended southward from the parts opposite Bonn and from the Westerwald at least as far as to the parts opposite to the Treviri, who were on the river Mosel, but there is no evidence that they extended farther south[c].

---

mans ate roasted meat and drank with it milk and pure wine. Posidonius is a good authority, but we do not know if Athenaeus understood him right. Posidonius may have spoken of those Germani who had been improved or corrupted by their proximity to Gallic civilization. The Galli were great drinkers.

[b] See Machiavelli's opinion of Germany (Discorsi, l. c. 55) and the simple habits of the Germans in those days, when they were not corrupted by intercourse with foreigners: "Perchè non hanno praesto pigliare i costumi nè Francesi, nè Spagnuoli nè Italiani, le quali nazioni tutte insieme sono la corruttela del mondo."

[c] Gorler argues that the Ubii could not have been civilized by their proximity to the Treviri, who were themselves a savage people (B. G. viii. 25). But Caesar did

North of the Ubii on the east side of the Rhine were the
Sigambri. Some tribes on the west side of the Rhine, and
north of the Treviri, were said to be Germans. The Vangiones,
Nemetes and Tribocci, German tribes, occupied the plain between
the Vosges and the Rhine in the imperial period, and Caesar
(B. G. iv. 10), as it has been observed, means to say that the
Tribocci were on the Gallic side of the river in his time. This
silence about the position of the Vangiones does not allow us
to make any conclusion about them. We have seen what he
says of the Nemetes.

In another passage (B. G. vi. 21) after describing the customs
of the Galli (vol. iii. p. 468, &c.) Caesar reports a few other
matters about the Germans. They have no priests like the
Druids to look after the affairs of religion, nor do they sacrifice [a]. They consider only those powers to be gods which they
can see, and from which they receive advantage, the sun, fire,
and the moon. The other gods they have not even heard of.
Instead of being much given to religious ceremonies like the
Galli, the Germani were eminently practical. They acknowledged only as gods those whom experience showed to be
useful. An extract from Appian [b] attributes the German
contempt of death to the belief that they would live again, but
Caesar says nothing of this kind. He repeats (B. G. vi. 22)
what he had said before about the land of the Suevi. The
magistrates and chief men of the Germans assigned annually
to persons, who were akin to one another and who associated
themselves together, as much land as they thought proper
and in such place as they chose, and in the next year they
compelled them to go to another place. The following
reasons were assigned for this usage: that the people might
not by becoming attached to one place give up military pur-
suits for agriculture; that men might not attempt to acquire

not write the eighth book of the Gallic war, and so far Oeler's argument is not
worth much. He concludes that Caesar (B. G. iv. 8) alludes to the Harudes,
who possessed Alsace or part of it, and to their neighbours the Leuci and Lingones, and that consequently the country of the Ubii must have extended to the
Upper Rhine and probably to the Breisgau.

[a] Or " they pay no great attention to sacrifices." Caesar, vi. 21.

[b] De Rebus Gallicis, III. What his history of Caesar's wars against the Celtae
was worth is shown by the fragments.

large estates and the more powerful expel the weaker from their possessions; that they might not take more pains to build houses which would protect them against the heat and cold; that greediness after wealth might not be engendered, which greediness is the cause of factions and dissensions; that the common sort might be kept in order by being contented when every man saw that his own means were as great as those of the men who had the chief authority. If the Germans accomplished all that they designed, they did more than our civilization has done or ever will do. Among them all men lived alike: they were all equally poor. The distinctions between the powerful and the rest must therefore have been founded on something else than wealth, perhaps on birth or descent, and we may certainly conclude on military prowess.

When a German state either prepared to repel an attack or to make an attack, men were chosen (by the people, probably) to direct the operations of war with power to decide on matters that affected a man's life. In time of peace there was no person who had general authority, but the chief men of the districts and Pagi administered justice and settled disputes. The administration was local, as we call it. Plunder, or robbery, as Caesar names it, beyond the limits of each man's state, was not infamous: and it was practised for the purpose of exercising the young men and preventing idleness. When any chief at a meeting gave notice that "he was ready to lead; let those who would follow, give in their names;" they who liked the proposed venture and the men rose at once, promised their aid and were commended by the multitude; those who did not were considered deserters and traitors, and were never trusted afterwards. The Germans thought it wrong to do any violence to strangers; they protected all who came among them: every man's house was open to them, and every man's food was shared with them.

For the reasons stated above (p. 23) Caesar sent messengers to Ariovistus to ask him to name a place half way between Caesar and himself for a conference on matters which were of the greatest importance to both. The answer of the German was, that if he had wanted any thing from Caesar, he would have come to Caesar: if Caesar wished to see him, he must come himself: further, he could not venture without an army into those parts where Caesar was, nor could he bring his men together without much trouble and cost; indeed he wondered what either Caesar or the Roman people had to do in that part of Gallia which he had conquered.

On receiving this answer Caesar sent a second message to this effect: since Ariovistus after being honoured with the title of king and friend by the Senate in Caesar's consulship refused a conference when he was invited, he should now be informed of Caesar's demands; first that he must not bring any more Germans into Gallia; next, that he should restore their hostages to the Aedui and allow the Sequani also to restore to them those whom they held, and that he should not do any wrong to the Aedui nor make war on them and their allies: on these terms there should be perpetual friendship between Ariovistus and Caesar and the Roman people. If Ariovistus would not do what was required, he was told that Caesar would not overlook the wrongs of the Aedui, for the Senate had passed a resolution in the consulship of M. Messala and M. Piso (B.C. 61), that the governor of the Provincia, so far as he could do it consistently with the interests of the Roman State, should protect the Aedui and the other friends of the Romans.—Caesar was therefore acting directly under the authority of the Senate, when he resolved to protect the Roman allies; and Cicero said in the Senate, in B.C. 56, that his design was to conquer all Gallia, which he could safely infer from what Caesar had then done[f]. (De Prov. Cons. c. 13.)

To this message the German answered. It was the law of war that the victor should treat the vanquished as he pleased; and this was what the Romans did. If he did not tell the Romans how they ought to use their power, he ought not to be interfered with in the exercise of his power. The Aedui had tried the fortune of war, and they had been defeated and made tributary by him. Caesar did him great wrong in impairing his revenues by coming among the Aedui. He would

---

[f] The Lex Julia (vol. III. p. 412) forbade a magistrate from going beyond the limits of his province. Whether the Lex Julia applied to Caesar's case or not, such an enactment would not stop him.

not restore their hostages, but he also would not make war on
the Aedui nor their allies so long as they observed the agreement
with him and paid their tribute annually: if they did not do
that, the name of brothers of the Roman people would be of
no use to them. As to Caesar's threats, he said that no man
had ever come to a contest with him without being ruined.
Caesar might try a fight, when he liked: he would then find
out what his invincible Germans could do, men who were well
inured to arms and for fourteen years had never been under
the roof of a house.

At the time when this answer was returned to Caesar, messengers came from the Aedui and the Treviri. The Aedui
complained that the Harudes who had lately crossed over into
Gallia were wasting their country, and that they could not
purchase quiet from Ariovistus even by giving hostages[a].
The Treviri reported that the hundred Pagi of the Suevi had
fixed themselves on the Rhine under the brothers Nasua and
Cimberius for the purpose of passing the river. Caesar now
saw that he must be quick in his movements, for if this fresh
body of Suevi joined the troops of Ariovistus, it would be
less easy to oppose the united force. Accordingly having provided for his supplies he went to meet Ariovistus. After
three days' march Caesar was informed that Ariovistus had
advanced with all his forces three days' march from his own
territory for the purpose of seizing Vesontio; but Caesar
neither tells us from what point he made his own advance nor
from what point Ariovistus advanced. Vesontio (Besançon)
the largest town of the Sequani was on the river Aklunsdubis
or Doubas (Doubs). This town contained a great supply of
military stores, and was naturally so strong that it offered
great facilities for conducting a war, being almost surrounded
by the river. The space of six hundred feet, says Caesar,
where the river does not flow, is occupied by a high hill, the
base of which extends on both sides to the banks of the river.
A wall which runs round this hill converts it into a citadel and
joins it to the town[b]. Caesar advanced to this place by forced

---

[a] We must conclude that Caesar was not now in the country of the Aedui.
[b] This description of Besançon is exact, but the width of the isthmus is 1030

marches day and night¹, took possession of it, and put a garrison in the town (B. G. i. 38).

While Caesar was staying a few days at Vesontio for the purpose of getting ready his supplies and means of transport, the soldiers heard a good deal from the Galli and the traders about the huge size of the Germans, and their wonderful courage and practice in arms: they were told by those who had often fought with them that it was impossible to stand even the look and fierce eyes of these warriors. In consequence of this talk a general panic seized the army. It began with the tribunes, the praefecti (commanders of the auxiliaries) and others, who had followed Caesar from the city through friendship, as he says, and had not much military experience. We know that it would have been difficult for Caesar to refuse places to many of the young Romans, if he wished to keep on good terms with his partisans at Rome, and that he had officers forced upon him whom he would gladly have refused. At a later period Cicero recommended to Caesar for promotion several persons, and one of them at least, the lawyer Trebatius, was unfit for any other military service than receiving his pay. These men, with whom the panic began, urging various reasons asked for leave of absence: some, who were ashamed to ask, kept quiet to avoid the suspicion of being afraid; but they could not put on a bold face, nor could they refrain from shedding tears sometimes. Skulking in their tents, they deplored their sad condition, or with their friends they lamented over the danger of the army. All through the camp the men were making their wills. The alarm spread even to those who had great military

Roman feet, from which fact the author of the "Histoire" makes the probable conclusion that 'DC' in Caesar's text should be 'MDC.'

¹ Forced marches are named great marches by Caesar. The Roman soldiers were trained to march well, and good marching is an essential quality of a good soldier; and for this purpose the soldier must be well shod. Vegetius (l. 9) says that soldiers must be trained to march twenty Roman miles in military step in five summer hours, and at full marching speed (pleno gradu) twenty-four miles in the same time. The twenty miles make a regular day's march: the twenty-four or more are a forced march (magnum iter). The five summer hours are near seven hours in our reckoning. But it is probable, as Hostow observes (p. 93), that the ordinary day's march would not exceed fifteen Roman miles. See B. G. vii. 40, for an example of hard marching.

experience, soldiers and centurions, and those at the head of
the cavalry. Those of them who wished to pass for being
less cowardly than the rest, said they were not afraid of the
enemy, but of the narrow defiles through which they must
march, and of the extent of the forests between them and
Ariovistus, or that the supplies could not be safely brought
up after them. Some even reported to Caesar that when he
should give orders to march, the soldiers would not obey.

Caesar has reported this shameful panic in his homely style
without disguising any thing, and he has recorded the disgrace of the army. In speaking of the origin of the panic
he mentions the tribunes first, who were the superior officers
in a legion; and as they were without doubt men who were
not of his own choice, he takes this opportunity of showing
what they were. In fact we read little of the tribunes in
Caesar: in his description of the bloody battle on the Sambre
(ii. 25) and the resistance of the twelfth legion, he only just
mentions the tribunes; and when he speaks of brave officers,
it is generally the centurions; a brave tribune is mentioned
in iii. 5. His practice was to place his legati at the head of
the legions, because he could trust them. The tribunes were
reduced to insignificance; and indeed with such officers as
his centurions were, he did not want tribunes, at least such as
he had (vol. ii. p. 26).

In these difficult circumstances Caesar's ability and courage
were equal to the danger. He summoned a meeting of his
officers, and called all the centurions. He began by scolding
them well for troubling themselves about the direction in
which he was going to take them or about his plans. 'Why
should they suppose that Ariovistus, who had so eagerly
sought the friendship of the Roman people in his consulship,
would now forget his obligations? For his part he was persuaded that when Ariovistus was well acquainted with his
demands and the fairness of the proposed terms, he would not
reject Caesar's friendship and that of the Roman people. But if
in his madness he should prefer war, what had they to fear or
why should they distrust their own valour or their general's
vigilance? They had tried the enemy within the remembrance
of their fathers, and by the defeat of the Cimbri and Teutoni

under C. Marius the Roman soldiers had gained equal glory with the commander; and they had tried him again in the late servile insurrection[1], in which the enemy had the advantage of the military experience and discipline which he had learned from the Romans. These Germans were the men whom the Helvetii in their contests with them generally defeated, and yet the Helvetii were no match for the Roman army. If any of them were troubled because Ariovistus had beaten the Galli in battle, they would find, if they inquired, that after the Galli were worn out by the protracted war and had given up all hope of a fight, Ariovistus, who had kept in his camp and the marshes for months without giving the Galli an opportunity of fighting, suddenly attacked them and gained a victory by superior prudence rather than by valour. Now though Ariovistus found an opportunity of practising such a stratagem against inexperienced barbarians, not even the German himself expected that the Roman troops could be caught in that way. Those who made the pretext about the supplies and the narrow defiles on the march an excuse for their panic acted presumptuously, since they must be considered either to doubt about the general doing his duty or to be telling him what he should do. It was his business to look after these matters: the Sequani, Leuci[2], Lingones would furnish supplies, and the corn was now ripe in the fields. As to the march they would soon judge about that themselves. He had been told that the men would not obey his orders, but this did not disturb him at all: he knew that those generals who had not been able to secure their soldiers' obedience, had either been deficient in good fortune as proved by want of success, or the discovery of some scandalous act

---

[1] The war in which the slaves rose under Spartacus B.C. 73. There were Germans (vol. iii. 49) among these insurgents, and they may have been the sons of some of the Germans who were captured in Italy by C. Marius. It is hardly possible that they were the captured prisoners themselves, for the great battle in North Italy was fought B.C. 101 (vol. ii. 73) and few slaves would live seven and twenty years in Italian bondage and still be able to fight.

[2] The Leuci lived on the upper Mosel north of the Lingones, and their chief place was Tullum (Toul). They are not mentioned again in the Commentaries. Caesar, if he had not visited their country, had been near enough to make them submit to his orders.

had convicted them of greediness: his own integrity was
shown in the whole course of his life, and his good fortune
in the Helvetic war. If no others would follow him, he
would go with the tenth legion alone, which he could trust,
and that should be his praetorian cohort[1].—Caesar had shown
the greatest favour to this legion, and by reason of the men's
courage had the greatest confidence in it.

This speech produced a wonderful effect[2]. The men were
now eager to meet the Germans. The tenth legion through
their tribunes first thanked Caesar for his good opinion of
them, and declared that they were ready to fight. The other
legions apologized through their tribunes and the centurions
of the first rank. Caesar accepted the apology as a prudent
man would do, and set out at the fourth watch. The season
was now harvest time. In order to reach the valley of the
Rhine where Ariovistus would be found, Caesar's direct course
would be along the river Doubs for some distance, through a
hilly country covered with forests, and this was the road that
the army feared. But Caesar following the information of
Divitiacus, in whom he had perfect confidence, led his men
northwards from Vesontio, crossed the river Oignon, and then
passed by a north-east and eastern circuitous course through
an open country round the hilly tract which, lying between
Besançon and Montbéliard on the Doubs, occupies the country
between the Doubs and the Oignon, and extends north of the
Oignon also. The length of this circuitous part of the march
from Besançon to Arcey was above fifty miles. From Arcey
he advanced north-east past Belfort, or near to that place, and
thence to Cernay on the Thur, a branch of the Ill[3]. He was now

[1] "Praetorian cohort:" the commander's "comites," his guard or staff, which
consisted of the chief persons about him, such as the young men for instance who
accompanied him from Rome, or were sent to him to see what war was and get
promotion. Cicero, ad. Q. Fr. L 1, 8.

[2] Dion instead of copying Caesar's speech has written one himself in eleven
tiresome chapters; a fact from which we may form a just estimate of his capacity as an historian. He says that Ariovistus was an Allobrogian (38. c. 43),
and he names his men Celtae, by which however he means Germans (38. c. 34).

[3] The author of the "Histoire" estimates this road distance from Besançon to
Cernay to be 140 kilomètres; and if we suppose the Roman army to have
marched twenty kilomètres (near twelve and a half English miles) a day, Caesar
would be near Cernay on the seventh day. Rüstow (Heerwesen, p. 175)

in the great plain of the Rhine. On the seventh day, while he was still on his march, Caesar was informed by the scouts that Ariovistus was only twenty-four Roman miles distant. The German now sent Caesar notice that he was ready for an interview, and Caesar accepted the proposal in the hope, as he says, that Ariovistus after having considered the terms offered to him would not persist in his obstinacy. The day named for the conference was the fifth day from the day of the message.

During these few days messengers passed backwards and forwards between the two camps. Ariovistus sent word that Caesar must not bring any infantry to the interview: he pretended that he was afraid of treachery: both he and Caesar must have cavalry only: on no other terms would he come. Caesar did not wish the conference to be dropped in consequence of any objection, nor could he venture to trust himself to his Gallic horsemen. Accordingly he took all the horses of the Gallic cavalry and mounted on them the soldiers of the tenth legion, in whom he had perfect confidence (c. 42).

The two armies were in a great plain, in which there rose a natural mound of earth of some extent. The spot was nearly equidistant from the camps of Ariovistus and Caesar, and this was the place where the conference was held. It is probable that the camps of Ariovistus and Caesar were now nearer to one another than the twenty-four miles mentioned above; and one or both of the armies had moved. Caesar placed his men two hundred paces from the mound, and the horsemen of Ariovistus were at the same distance. Ariovistus insisted that the conference should be held on horseback, and that he and Caesar should each bring ten men besides themselves. Caesar began by reminding Ariovistus of the great favours which he had received from himself and from the Senate, that he had been intitled king and friend by the Senate, who sent him magnificent presents. He spoke of the old and friendly relations between the Romans and the Aedui, and of the many resolutions passed by the Senate in honour of

_{supposes that Caesar's course from Besançon was towards the upper Saône, over the plateau of Langres into the valley of the Meas, and from Toul past Nancy. This great mistake has been made chiefly in consequence of the writer trusting to the false reading "quinquaginta" (B. G. L. 89).}

the Aedui, who had always held the first place among the nations of Gallia, even before they sought the friendship of the Romans. It was the custom of the Roman people not to allow their allies to lose any thing that they had, and even to raise them to a more honourable condition. Caesar then repeated the demands which he had already made, that Ariovistus must not make war on the Aedui or their allies, and must restore the hostages: if he could not send a part of the Germans back, he must at least not allow any more to cross the Rhine.

The German made a short answer to Caesar's demands: he said a good deal on his own merits: he had crossed the Rhine at the invitation of the Galli, and he had been induced to leave his home and kinsmen by great expectations and great offers. The Galli gave him lands in Gallia, they gave him hostages; and he took tribute by the law of war. He did not attack the Galli: they attacked him: all the states of Gallia came against him, and he defeated all of them in one battle. If they were ready for another fight, he was ready also: if they wished to enjoy peace, it was not fair that they should refuse the tribute, which they had hitherto voluntarily paid. The friendship of the Romans ought to bring him honour and protection, not harm, and with the expectation of these advantages he had asked for their friendship. If through the Roman people his tribute was not paid and his subjects were taken from him, he would reject the friendship of the Romans as readily as he had sought it. He was bringing over a number of Germans for the purpose of protecting himself, not attacking Gallia, which was proved by the fact that he had not come without being asked, and that he did not attack but only defended himself. He came into Gallia before the Roman people. Never before this time had a Roman army gone beyond the limits of the Provincia. What reason had Caesar for entering the possessions of Ariovistus? The country which Caesar had entered was the Provincia of Ariovistus, as the other Provincia was the Provincia of the Romans. As Ariovistus ought not to be allowed to attack the Roman possessions, so the Romans were unjust in disturbing him in his rights. It was urged that the Aedui had been named brothers by the Romans, but he was not such a barbarian or so ignorant as not to know that neither did the Aedui help the Romans in the last war with the Allobroges, nor had the Aedui in their contests with him and the Sequani received aid from the Roman people. He had reason for suspecting that Caesar only pretended friendship, and having an army in Gallia intended to use it for crushing him. Now if Caesar did not retire and take his army from these parts, he would consider him not as a friend, but as an enemy; and if he killed Caesar, he would do what was agreeable to many of the Roman nobles and leading men: he knew this from their own messengers, and he could purchase the favour and friendship of these men by Caesar's death. But if Caesar would retire and give up to him the possession of Gallia, he would repay him well; and if Caesar had any wars that he wished to undertake, Ariovistus would do the business without any labour and danger on Caesar's part (c. 44).

Caesar said a good deal to show why he could not desist from his purpose: it was not his practice nor the usage of the Roman people to desert deserving allies, nor could he allow that Gallia belonged to Ariovistus rather than to the Roman people. The Arverni and Ruteni, both of them Gallic nations, had been defeated (B.C. 121) by Q. Fabius Maximus (vol. i. p. 315); but the Romans pardoned them, and neither reduced their country to the form of a province nor imposed tribute on the people. If priority of time was to be considered, the Romans had the best title to sovereignty in Gallia; if the judgment of the Senate ought to be respected, then Gallia should be free, for after it had been conquered, the Senate still left it independent.

While the conference was going on, Caesar was informed that the horsemen of Ariovistus were approaching the mound and riding up to the Roman soldiers, at the same time discharging stones and missiles at them. Caesar stopped the conference, and retiring to his men commanded them not to return a single missile. Though he knew[7] that there would

---

[7] We cannot suppose that Caesar means that his mounted legionary soldiers would have been a match for the German cavalry. Goeler (p. 47) explains the matter by assuming that the "tumulus" was near Niederaspach on the north side of the Little Doller, which flows into the Doller; and he says that the land

not be the least risk in his legion fighting with the German cavalry, he did not choose by repulsing the enemy to let it be said that they were surprised in the conference by his breach of faith. When the Roman army heard of the arrogance of Ariovistus and of the attack which had put an end to the conference, their eagerness to fight the enemy was greatly increased.

Within the next two days Ariovistus sent to propose a renewal of the conference, or if Caesar refused, then he asked him to send one of his legati. Caesar would not consent to renew the conference, and particularly because the day before the Germans could not be prevented from throwing missiles at his men; nor did he think that he could safely send one of his own people. He therefore determined to send C. Valerius Procillus who was trustworthy and well acquainted with the Gallic language, which Ariovistus also from long practice spoke with ease. Besides these reasons for sending Procillus, the Germans, as Caesar supposed, would have no reason for ill-treating him. Procillus was accompanied by M. Mettius who was on friendly terms with Ariovistus. Their instructions were to hear what Ariovistus had to say, and to report. As soon as Ariovistus saw the men in his camp, he broke out into furious exclamations before his army: Why were they coming to him? were they spies? The men attempted to explain, but the king stopped them and put them in chains.

On the same day the king advanced and pitched his camp under the mountains, six miles from Caesar's camp. Caesar does not name the mountains, but they were the Vosges (Vosegus). On the following day the king made a flank march, passed Caesar's camp, and planted himself two Roman miles in the rear of Caesar with the view of intercepting any

on the south side of the brook was hilly and favourable to the Romans, who would have fought on foot after detaching part of the legion to look after the horses.

The author of the "Histoire" (p. 86) contends that the place selected by Goeler is a hill, not a "tumulus," and that it is not in the plain, which only begins at the north slope of this hill. I think that these two objections are sufficient. The author adds that the plain which extends north of the Doller and between the Vosges and the Rhine contains several small rounded eminences, to which the term "tumulus" may be applied; and that the most remarkable are one near Feldkirch, due west of Knelsheim, and the other between Wittenheim and Knelsheim.

supplies brought up from the country of the Aedui and the Sequani. Nothing is said about the communication with the Leuci and Lingones being interrupted (B. G. i. 40)¹. During five successive days from that day Caesar placed his troops in front of the Roman camp and offered the German battle, for the position of Ariovistus on Caesar's line of supply made it necessary to fight the enemy. Ariovistus kept his infantry in their camp, but his cavalry skirmished every day. The manner of their fighting was this. There were six thousand horsemen, and as many foot soldiers, the most active and bravest of the army, one of whom every horseman had selected for his protection. The horsemen were accompanied in battle by the foot soldiers, and to them the cavalry would retire: if there was any danger, the foot soldiers hurried to the aid of the horsemen: if any man fell from his horse in consequence of a severe wound, they protected him: if the horsemen had occasion to advance a great distance or to retreat quickly, such was the activity of the foot soldiers produced by practice that they kept up with the cavalry by hanging on the manes of the horses (c. 48).

When Caesar saw that the German maintained his position in the camp, and that his own communications with the supplies were still interrupted, he selected a convenient² spot in the rear of the place, in which the Germans had planted themselves, and about six hundred paces (passus) from it, and marched thither with his army drawn up in three lines or divisions. The first and second division remained under arms: the third worked at making a camp. Upon this Ariovistus sent about sixteen thousand light armed men with all his cavalry to prevent the formation of this new camp, but Caesar kept the third division at work, and the two other divisions kept the

---

¹ The author of the "Histoire" (p. 88) describes the movements of the German king as minutely as if he had seen them. Goeler also (p. 48) describes them, and explains why Caesar did not attack Ariovistus on his flank march. Caesar had some good reason for it, though he has not told us. Both Goeler and the author of the "Histoire" place Caesar's camp at Cernay, and that may be the true place.

² The same spot, as Goeler assumes (p. 50), on which the conference had taken place. Such a spot would be very convenient, but the assumption without any evidence is not a satisfactory way of making matters convenient.

enemy from disturbing them. When the new camp was
ready, Caesar left there two legions and part of the auxiliary
troops, and led the other four legions back to his camp.

Caesar does not say that he left any defence for his larger
camp, while he was forming this new camp, and it does not
seem to have been necessary. Ariovistus could gain no advantage by taking the larger camp, and if he had moved
towards it, he would have done the very thing that Caesar
wished, and he would have been attacked by the Romans.
By this manœuvre Caesar again opened his communications
with Vesontio, and by placing Ariovistus between two camps
had shut him out from any communication with his own
country. On the next day Caesar, persisting in his plan of
forcing the Germans to fight, drew his troops out of both
camps, and advancing a little from the large camp he offered
the enemy battle. When the enemy declined even this invitation, Caesar led back his army into camp about mid-day.
He does not say that the two legions, which had come out of
the smaller camp, retired into it when the four legions retired
into the larger camp; but we may assume that they did. On
the retirement of the four legions Ariovistus sent part of his
force to attack the smaller camp, and there was a furious
fight up to evening, when Ariovistus led his troops away.
There were many wounded on both sides. Goeler (p. 51)
raises the question why Caesar's four legions did not fall on
the Germans in flank and rear while they were attacking the
smaller camp. He suggests that men who had been kept
under arms until mid-day would be tired, which is a good
reason, and much better than the assumption that Caesar
might not have heard of the fight for some time, owing to the
assumed peculiar nature of the ground, and so would not
choose to bring on a general engagement so late in the day.
Ariovistus, as Caesar says, sent only part of his force to
attack the smaller camp, from which it is plain that if Caesar
had advanced with his four legions, the assailants of the
smaller camp would have retired to the German camp, and
there would have been no general battle. Caesar found out
from some prisoners that it was the German custom for the
married women by a peculiar kind of divination to ascertain

whether a battle should be fought or not, and they had declared that the Germans could not conquer if they fought before new moon. (Comp. Frontinus, Strat. ii. 1. 16.)

On the next day Caesar left a force in each camp sufficient to protect it: he placed all the auxiliary troops in sight of the enemy in front of the smaller camp to make a show, on account of his inferiority in force of legionary soldiers compared with the numbers of the enemy[1]. With his six legions he advanced in a triple line right up to the enemy's camp. Then the Germans not being able to avoid a fight led their forces out of the camp and placed them in battle order, each nation by itself with equal intervals between, Harudes[2], Marcomani, Tribocci, Vangiones, Nemetes, Sedusii, Suevi. They put the waggons and carts on the flanks and rear, that there might be no possibility of flying. On the waggons and carts were placed the women, who with outstretched hands intreated the men as they went out to battle not to deliver them up to Roman slavery.

Both the modern authorities, whom I have often quoted, place the battle-field near Cernay and about five Roman miles west of Mühlhausen; but the author of the "Histoire" (p. 91) supposes that the Germans faced the west and the Romans the east. Goeler makes the Romans face the west and the Germans the east. Caesar had five legati and a quaestor, each of whom he set over a legion, that every soldier might feel that his conduct was under the eyes of an inspector. The legati therefore were appointed to witness the fight, as Caesar expresses it, and not to direct it. Caesar was on the right wing and he began the battle by attacking the enemy's left, which he had observed not to be strong. When the signal

---

[1] The author of the "Histoire" (p. 91) and Goeler (p. 52) assume that Ariovistus took three auxiliaries to be the two legions of the smaller camp, and that these two legions leaving their camp by the rear gate (porta decumana) joined Caesar's four legions without being seen by Ariovistus. This supposition is not supported by any thing in Caesar's text. Ariovistus was sharp enough to see how many legions Caesar had when he came up to the German camp, and to distinguish between auxiliaries and Romans.

[2] The Harudes, it is said (c. 37), were ravaging the lands of the Aedui. Caesar does not explain how they were present at the battle. Both facts may be true; and if they are, Caesar might state both without troubling himself to remove the apparent discrepancy.

was given, the Romans made so furious an onset, and the
enemy advanced so quick that there was no time for the Romans
to discharge their pila, which they threw down and
fought hand to hand with the sword. The Germans according
to their custom immediately formed the phalanx, as Caesar
names it, and received the attack of the Romans. This phalanx
was formed by the men of the first rank standing close
together with their shields in front, while their heads were
protected by the shields of the rear rank, and so on. Many
of the Roman soldiers were bold and active enough to leap on
the shields of the Germans, tear them up with their hands and
pierce the men from above, for which their short pointed
sword was well adapted. The enemy's left wing was at last
repulsed and put to flight; but the right, which was stronger,
was pressing the Romans hard, when young P. Crassus, who
commanded Caesar's cavalry and saw what was going on better
than those who were engaged in the fight, ordered the third
division to advance in support of the other two. This movement
decided the battle. All the Germans turned their backs
in flight, and did not stop until they reached the Rhine,
which was about five miles from the field of battle[1]. A very
small number trusting to their strength attempted to swim
the river, or saved themselves in the boats which they found
there. Among them was Ariovistus, who seized a little vessel
which was fastened to the river bank and escaped in it. All
the rest were overtaken by Caesar's cavalry and massacred.
The women and children perished too or were sold as slaves,
but Caesar says nothing about them. The two wives of
Ariovistus perished in the flight: one was a Sueve whom he
brought with him from home, and the other was a Noric
woman, a sister of King Voctio, who sent her to Gallia to

[1] "Millia passuum circiter quinque" (c. 53). "Quinquaginta," which is in
some editions, is an emendation founded on Plutarch (Caesar, c. 19), and Orosius,
vi. 7. All the MSS. have " quinque " except one, which has "duo," but the numerals
II and V are often confounded (Schneider). The author of the "Histoire,"
who follows the emendation "quinquaginta" has a very bad note on this passage.
It is certain that Caesar did not ride "fifty miles," for he says that the flight
of the Germans was uninterrupted. The description of the battle in Dion
Cassius (38, c. 48—50), is founded on Caesar, but the author has invented much,
and invented badly.

marry Ariovistus. There were two daughters of these women: one was killed and the other was made prisoner.

The routed Germans fled along the Doller to the site of Mühlhausen on the Ill. Goeler affirms[4], and he gives some reasons for what he says, that the Ill was at that time an arm of the Rhine. This hypothesis or assumption settles all difficulties, and makes Caesar's narrative perfectly intelligible.

Caesar himself, who rode with the cavalry in pursuit of the fugitives, fell in with C. Valerius Procillus and rescued him from his keepers, who were dragging him with them in their flight bound in a triple chain. The general was as much pleased with saving his friend as with his victory. Procillus reported that three trials were made in his presence by the German mode of divination to ascertain whether he should be immediately burnt or reserved to another time: fortunately the result was in his favour. M. Mettius was also found and brought back to Caesar.

When the news of the battle was carried over the Rhine, the Suevi who had advanced to the banks of the river began their retreat homeward. Those[5] who dwelt on the banks of the Rhine, seeing the alarm of the Suevi, pursued them and killed a great number. Caesar having destroyed two great armies in one campaign put his troops into winter quarters among the Sequani somewhat earlier than was required by the time of the year. Labienus had the command in the winter quarters, which were probably at Vesontio, for no other place would be so convenient. The proconsul crossed the Alps into his province of Gallia Citerior to make his circuits and hold the courts. He would also have the opportunity of knowing what was going on in Rome.

[4] Goeler (p. 54).
[5] Some texts have, "The Ubii who dwell nearest to the Rhine." The true reading is uncertain.

CHAPTER III.

THE BELGAE.

B.C. 57.

When Caesar was in Gallia Citerior or Cisalpina in winter quarters, frequent reports were brought to him, and he was also informed by the letters of Labienus, that all the Belgae (B. G. i. 1) were combining against the Roman people and exchanging hostages as a pledge of mutual fidelity. This is the Roman proconsul's way of viewing the matter (B. G. ii. 1). The causes of the combination, as he says, were these: first, the Belgae were afraid that if all Gallia Celtica were reduced to submission, the Roman army might be led against them; second, they were stirred up by some of the Galli, part of whom had wished to rid Gallia of the Germans, and now were vexed to see the Romans wintering in their country; while others with the native fickleness of temper were bent on making some revolution. There was also another class of the Galli who roused the Belgae against the Romans, the powerful and those who were rich enough to keep armed men in their pay; for they saw that if the Roman dominion were established, there would be an end of those attempts which were often successfully made to seize royal power.

On receiving this intelligence Caesar raised two new legions in Gallia Citerior, and at the commencement of the season for military operations he sent Q. Pedius, his nephew probably, to lead them over the Alps into Transalpine Gallia. Pedius may have taken his men over the Pennine pass, the Great St. Bernard, one of the two roads which led across the mountains from the country of the Salassi (Val d'Aosta). As soon as the grass began to grow, Caesar joined his army in the country of the Sequani. By his agents he engaged the Senones, a Celtic people in the valley of the Yonne, a branch of the Seine, and the other Galli who bordered on the Belgae, to inquire about the Belgae and let him know what they were doing. The reports were always the same: the Belgae were collecting their forces, and bringing them together. The proconsul immediately formed his resolution. He provided supplies for his army, left his quarters in the country of the Sequani, and in about fifteen days he and his eight legions were on the borders of the Belgae, and probably at Châlons-sur-Marne, for this river was the southern boundary of the territory of the Belgae. The direct distance from Besançon in the country of the Sequani to Châlons is about 140 miles.

Caesar appeared before he was expected on the borders of the Remi, a people who were north of the Marne and the nearest of the Belgic nations to the Galli in those parts. The Remi sent to him two commissioners to make their humble submission, and to declare that they had not joined the other Belgae, nor in any way combined against the Romans: they were ready to give hostages, to obey Caesar's orders, to receive him in their towns, to supply him with food and every thing else. The Remi played a cunning and cowardly part now and all through the war. They told Caesar that all the rest of the Belgae were in arms, that the Germans on the west side of the Rhine had joined them, and that they had been unable to prevent their own neighbours, the Suessiones, who formed with the Remi one political community, from siding with the confederation[1]. The Remi further informed Caesar that most of the Belgae were the descendants of Germans, who in former days crossed the Rhine and settled in the parts west of that river because the soil was fertile: they expelled the Gallic cultivators, and they were the only people who prevented the Cimbri and Teutoni

[1] It is difficult to understand the connexion between the Remi and the Suessiones as it is stated in B. G. II. 8. Caesar afterwards says that the Suessiones had at this time a king.

from entering their territory when these invaders harassed all Gallia one generation before the present time (vol. ii. c. 4); the remembrance of these things made the Belgae proud and confident in their military superiority. The Remi being connected with the confederates by kinship and marriage could tell Caesar how many men each nation had promised in the general council of the Belgae. The most numerous, most courageous and most powerful were the Bellovaci: they could raise one hundred thousand armed men, they promised sixty thousand picked fighters, and demanded the general conduct of the war. The Suessiones had a large and very fertile territory: within the memory of some living persons they had a king Divitiacus, the most powerful man in all Gallia, who held dominion over a large part of the country of the Belgae and even in Britannia: they had now a king Galba, on whom on account of his justice and prudence the supreme command in the campaign was conferred by general consent: the Suessiones had twelve towns, and they promised fifty thousand fighters. The Nervii, who were considered the most savage among the Belgae and were the most distant, promised the same number. The Atrebates promised fifteen thousand; the Ambiani, ten thousand; the Morini, twenty-five thousand; the Menapii, seven thousand; the Caleti, ten thousand; the Velocasses and Veromandui, ten thousand; the Aduatuci, nineteen thousand; the Condrusi, Eburones, Caeroesi, and Paemani, who are all included by Caesar in the name Germani, were supposed to be able to bring forty thousand men. The sum total was 296,000 fighting men (ii. 4).

This Belgian confederation included the people of all the country north of the Seine and Marne, bounded by the Atlantic on the west, and the Rhine on the north and east, except the Mediomatrici and Treviri, who, whatever may have been their nationality, did not join the confederation. The Remi, as we have seen, were Belgae; they went over to Caesar, put their country in his power, furnished him with supplies, and enabled him to make their territory the basis of his operations.

The old divisions of France before the great revolution of 1789 corresponded in some degree to the divisions of the country in the time of Caesar, and the names of the people are still retained with little alteration in the names of the chief towns or the names of the anterevolutionary divisions of France. In the country of the Remi between the Marne and the Aisne there is the town of Reims. In the territory of the Suessiones between the Marne and the Aisne there is Soissons on the Aisne. The Bellovaci were west of the Oise (Isara) a branch of the Seine: their chief town, which at some time received the name Caesaromagus, is now Beauvais. The Nervii were between and on the Sambre and the Schelde. The Atrebates were north of the Bellovaci between the Somme and the upper Schelde: their chief place was Nemetacum or Nemetocenna, now Arras in the old division of Artois. The Ambiani were on the Somme (Samara) : their name is represented by Amiens (Samarobriva). The Morini, or sea-coast men, extended from Boulogne towards Dunkerque. The Menapii bordered on the northern Morini and were on both sides of the lower Rhine (B. G. iv. 4). The Caleti were north of the lower Seine along the coast in the Pays de Caux. The Velocasses were east of the Caleti on the north side of the Seine as far as the Oise; their chief town was Rotomagus (Rouen), and their country was afterwards Vexin Normand and Vexin Français. The Veromandui were north of the Suessiones: their chief town under the Roman dominion, Augusta Veromanduorum, is now St. Quentin. The Aduatuci were on the lower Maas. The Condrusi and the others included under the name of Germani were on the Maas, or between the Maas and the Rhine. The Eburones had the country about Tongern and Spa, and were the immediate neighbours of the Menapii on the Rhine. The name of the Condrusi is preserved in the country of Condroz or Condrost in the Pays de Liège, and that of the Paemani in the Pays de Famenne, of which country Durburg, Laroche on the Ourthe, and Rochefort on the Homme are the chief towns. These are two signal instances of the permanence of historical evidence. A mound of earth, or the name of an insignificant tribe often survives the proudest monuments. The estimate of the Belgian force which the Remi gave to Caesar cannot be taken as the true amount of the troops which the Belgae brought into the field, though there is no doubt that the force was very large. To oppose them Caesar had his eight legions, besides his auxiliary troops; and he had also some Cretan archers, light armed Numidians, and Balearic slingers.

After thanking the commissioners of the Remi for their offers and the information, Caesar summoned the council or senate, as he names it, to meet him, and ordered the children of the chief men to be brought as hostages. His orders were obeyed to the day. For the purpose of diverting part of the enemy's force he sent Divitiacus with the troops of the Aedui to waste the country of the Bellovaci. Being now informed that the Belgian army was advancing he crossed the Axona (Aisne), a river which runs from east to west through the northern part of the country of the Remi, and enters the Oise near Compiègne. He placed himself on the north side of the river, a position which secured one side of his camp and all his rear, and also a safe passage for his supplies from the Remi and other states. There was a bridge over the Aisne near the Roman camp. Caesar strengthened the bridge by a "praesidium" (tête de pont), on the left bank of the river, and placed Q. Titurius Sabinus in it with six cohorts[1]. The camp was protected by a rampart twelve feet high, including the breastwork, and a ditch eighteen feet wide. The place where Caesar crossed the Aisne was Berry-au-Bac, and his camp was on the high ground immediately north of the bridge, about eighty feet above the Aisne and between it and the small stream of the Miette, which joins the Aisne on the right bank about two miles below Berry-au-Bac.

About eight miles from Caesar's camp and on the north side of the Aisne there was a town of the Remi, named Bibrax[2]. This place was furiously assaulted by the Belgae

[1] The author of the "Histoire" (p. 100), and Goeler (p. 60) agree in fixing the position of Caesar's camp on the hill between the Aisne and the Miette; and there is no other place so probable.

[2] Bibrax was north of the Aisne, eight miles from Caesar's camp and on the road by which the Belgae were approaching. Bibrax has been generally identified with Bièvre. Goeler fixes the place at Beaurieux on the north bank of the Aisne; and the author of the "Histoire" puts it at the hill of Vieux Laon. I do not agree with either of them or accept their reasons. Both of them assume that Caesar's light troops entered Bibrax, which is not distinctly said by Caesar,

on their march, and the inhabitants defended themselves with great difficulty. The Gallic and Belgic way of attacking towns was to surround them with men, who cleared the walls of the defenders by throwing stones, and then forming a tortoise[1] (testudo) by locking the shields over their heads came up to the gates and undermined the walls. The men of Bibrax could not keep their place on the walls against the stones and missiles discharged by such a host, and when night stopped the assault, Iccius, who commanded in the town, a man of the highest rank among the Remi, and one of the commissioners who had come to Caesar, informed him by a message, that he could not hold out any longer, if relief was not sent. Immediately after midnight, Caesar employing as guides the messengers from Iccius, sent Numidian light infantry, Cretan archers, and Balearic slingers to aid the people of Bibrax. The arrival of this force encouraged the townsmen to resist and deprived the enemy of all expectation of taking the place. Accordingly after staying before the town a short time, ravaging the lands of the Remi and firing all the villages and buildings within their reach, they approached Caesar's camp with all their forces and placed themselves less than two miles from him on the west side of the Miette. The Romans saw from their intrenchments the smoke and flame of the Belgian-camp extending along a front of more than eight miles, and around these fires there were above two hundred thousand men in arms.

The great number of the enemy and their reputation for valour determined Caesar to defer an engagement, but he tried his Gallic cavalry daily in skirmishes with the Belgian horse. Finding that his cavalry was not inferior, he prepared for a battle. The ground in front of the Romans was well adapted for placing the troops in order. The hill, on which the camp was made, rising a little above the flat below extended in

---

though they ought to have entered, if they were intended to be of any use. If they did enter, it was by night, and we must assume that the town was not surrounded by the enemy at that time, as it had been during the day.

[4] "Tortoise." See Livy, 34. c. 39; Lucan, lil. 474. "Testudo facta" is a different thing from "testudinem agere," B. G. v. 43, where the "testudo" is a machine of war. In Virgil, Aen. ix. 505, the poet should have written "facta testudine."

width on the side opposite to the enemy as much as the Roman order of battle could occupy, and on both flanks it had a descent, while the front gently sloping upwards terminated again in a flat. At each flank of this hill Caesar formed a ditch at right angles to the front and about four hundred paces in length, and at the ends of the ditches[1] he made towers and placed there his military engines, to prevent the enemy's superior numbers from attacking his men in flank after he had formed his order of battle. The two new legions were left in the camp to be employed as a reserve, if it should be necessary. Caesar drew up in order of battle the six other legions in front of the camp. The enemy also brought out their forces and set their battle in order.

A small marsh formed by the Miette lay between the Romans and the Belgians. The enemy were waiting to see if the Romans would cross this marsh, and the Romans were ready to attack if the enemy should attempt it. In the meantime there was a cavalry skirmish in the space between the two armies. As neither side would cross the marsh, and Caesar's cavalry had the advantage in the skirmish, he led his men back to their camp. Upon this the enemy immediately advanced to the Aisne, which was in the rear of the Roman encampment, and having found the ford, attempted to take part of their force across the river with the intention of

---

[1] The author of the "Histoire de César" (p. 100) says "that the excavations made in 1862 showed all the ditches of the camp to be eighteen feet wide and nine or ten deep. If then we allow ten feet for the width of the platform of the parapet, it would measure eight feet high, which with the palisade of four feet would give to the crest of the parapet an elevation of twenty-one or twenty-two feet above the bottom of the ditch."

Plate 9 of this work shows the plan of the camp, which has been discovered complete; it also marks the castella and the ditches, such as the excavations have exhibited them; but the author adds, "it has not been possible for us to explain the outline of the castella."

In his plan the author makes one of the ditches run from the left side of the camp towards the Miette, and the other from the right side of the camp to the Aisne; but this direction of the ditch on the right side of the camp does not agree with the Latin text. Caesar's ditches were cut on each flank of the hill for the purpose which he mentions. If the ditch on the right had been cut as Plate 9 shows, it would not have been of much use. Goeler's plan (Taf. 6) is better.

storming the fort^a commanded by Q. Titurius and destroying the bridge: if they could not do this, their design was to waste the lands of the Remi which furnished the Romans, and to cut them off from their supplies. Titurius was better placed than Caesar for seeing the movement of the enemies, for he informed him of it, and Caesar led all the cavalry, the light armed Numidians, the slingers and archers over the bridge and advanced towards the enemy, who were crossing the river below it.

Caesar's force attacked the Belgae in the river, and killed a great number of them. The survivors, who courageously attempted to pass over the bodies of the slain, were repulsed by the numerous missiles; and those who had already crossed the river were surrounded by Caesar's cavalry and massacred. The enemy had now failed in all their attempts; the Romans would not fight them on unfavourable ground, and the supplies of the confederates began to fall short, upon which they determined in council that it was best to return to their several homes, and if the Romans attacked any of them, the rest should come to their aid. They were led to this resolution in addition to other reasons by the fact that they had heard of the approach of Divitiacus and the Aedui to the territory of the Bellovaci, who could not be persuaded to stay any longer with the confederates.

During the second watch the enemy began to quit their encampment with great noise and in no order, for all of them wished to be first on the road home, and the consequence was that the retreat was like a flight. Caesar was immediately informed by his scouts, but he kept his legions and the cavalry

^a The author of the "Histoire" (Planche 9) places the "praesidium" of Sabinus on the north side of the Aisne, and he says "the intrenchments of this tête de pont, particularly the side parallel to the Aisne, are still visible at Berry-au-Bac. The gardens of several inhabitants are placed on the rampart itself, and the ditch appears outside of the village in the form of a large basin. The excavations have clearly disclosed the profile of the ditch." But this tête de pont would be of little or no use on the north side of the river; and if the "praesidium" of c. 5 and the "castellum" of c. 9 are the same, as I think they are, Caesar placed the tête de pont on the south side of the Aisne. Goeler in his plan (Taf. 6.) places the tête de pont on the south side, and he indicates also some defences on the north side, which may be the ditches mentioned by the author of the "Histoire."

in the camp, for he did not yet know the reason of the enemy's movement, and he feared some ambuscade. At daybreak the intelligence being confirmed by the scouts, he sent all the cavalry under the legati Q. Pedius and L. Aurunculeius to check the march of the enemy's rear. The legatus T. Labienus with three legions was ordered to follow the cavalry. The infantry and the cavalry coming up with the enemy's rear and following them for many miles made a great slaughter of the fugitives; for those in the rear when they were overtaken made a stand and resolutely received the attack of the Romans, while those who were in advance believing that they were out of danger and not being under any necessity to halt or under any control, hearing the distant shouts and falling into disorder, thought that their only safety was in flight. Thus the Romans without any risk slaughtered the flying Belgians all day long till sunset, when they returned to the camp pursuant to Caesar's orders. The formidable confederation was now dispersed, and the proconsul had the opportunity of dealing with his enemies separately. On the next day before the enemy had time to recover from their alarm, Caesar led his forces into the country of the Suessiones, who were the neighbours of the Remi on the west, and after a long day's march he reached the town Noviodunum'. Without any delay he attempted to take the place, for he was informed that it was undefended, but though the number of men in it was small, the width of the ditch and the height of the wall saved it from this sudden attack. After

---

' "Noviodunum" is generally supposed to be Soissons on the south side of the Aisne, about twenty-eight Roman miles west of Berry-au-Bac, direct distance. If there was a bridge over the river, we may assume that the fugitives entered the town by it from the north. There is a difficulty about this long day's march, which is much increased by the supposition, which has been made by M. Paigné-Delacourt, that Noviodunum is Noyon west of the Oise, for Noyon is much farther distant from Caesar's camp at Berry-au-Bac. This chapter contains difficulties, which a careful reader may discover. For instance, Caesar must have constructed his "vineas" on the spot, and according to his narrative there was no time to do this. But we may suppose that in his rapid style, when he speaks of pushing up the vineae before the arrival of the fugitives on the next night, he may have neglected the order of events, and we must conclude the vineae were brought up after preparation had been made for the siege.

making the intrenchments for his camp Caesar began to push up the "vineae*" towards the town and to make other preparations for a siege. In the meantime all the fugitive Suessiones entered the city during the next night. The "vineae" being quickly brought up, the "agger" or earth thrown into the ditch, and the towers planted, the Galli terrified at the magnitude of the works, such as they had neither seen nor heard of, and at the rapidity with which they were executed, proposed an unconditional surrender and were saved at the entreaty of the Remi. The Suessiones delivered up as hostages the chief men and two sons of king Galba: all the arms in the town were given up, and the surrender of the Suessiones was unconditional. It was Caesar's practice to strip his enemies of their arms and to take hostages as a security for their submission. He then advanced against the Bellovaci who had taken refuge with all their movables in the town of Bratuspantium, probably near the site of Breteuil, which is N.N.E. of Beauvais. When Caesar was about five miles from the place, all the older men came out to meet him, and stretching out their hands declared their readiness to submit and place themselves under his protection. The children and women also, when he had reached the town and was making his camp, appeared on the walls and by gestures after their fashion implored the pity of the Romans. Divitiacus, who was present, for he had returned to Caesar after the dispersion of the Belgian army and had sent away the forces of the Aedui, because, as we may assume, they were no longer wanted, spoke on behalf of the Bellovaci. He said that the Bellovaci had always acknowledged their dependence on the Aedui and had always been on friendly terms with them: that they had been urged on by their chiefs, who told them that the Aedui being reduced to subjection by the Romans suffered all kinds of bad treatment from them, in consequence of which statements the Bellovaci had fallen off from the Aedui and made war on the Roman people. The leaders in this matter, seeing what misfortune they had brought on their

---

* The "vineae" were covered galleries constructed of wicker work (vimina) generally, and sometimes of wood, for the purpose of covering the approach of the besiegers. (Rüstow, Heerwesen, p. 146.)

country, had run away to Britain: the Bellovaci entreated Caesar, and the Aedui joined in the prayer, to show them his usual clemency: if Caesar should do this, he would increase the influence of the Aedui among all the Belgae, whom the Aedui had been used to employ as auxiliaries in war. Out of regard to Divitiacus and the Aedui Caesar promised to take the Bellovaci under his protection, but as they were a powerful people, he required of them six hundred hostages. The hostages were given, all the arms in the town were collected, and Caesar then marched against the Ambiani, who immediately submitted and surrendered all that they had. The chief place of the Ambiani was Samarobriva (p. 47).

The territory of the Nervii bordered on the Ambiani. In answer to his inquiries Caesar was informed that the Nervii did not allow the traders (mercatores) to enter their country, nor wine and other articles of luxury to be imported, because they thought that such things enfeebled men's courage: the Nervii were of a savage temper and great bravery; they abused the rest of the Belgae for having surrendered to the Romans, and declared that they would neither send ambassadors to Caesar nor accept from him any terms of peace.

When Caesar had made three days' march in the territory of the Nervii, he learned from some prisoners that his camp was not more than ten Roman miles from the river Sabis (Sambre); that all the Nervii having been joined by their neighbours the Atrebates and Veromandui had placed themselves on the farther side of this stream and were there waiting for the arrival of the Romans; that they were also expecting the forces of the Aduatuci who were on their march; that the women of the Nervii and the men who by reason of age were past fighting had been put together in a place which the marshes prevented an army from reaching*. On obtaining this information Caesar sent forward scouts and centurions to choose a fit place for his camp. Many of the Belgae who had surrendered and many of the Galli were with Caesar on his march, some of whom, as it was afterwards known from prisoners, having observed the form in which the Roman army

* This place is supposed to be Mons by the author of the "Histoire," but the place is certainly not Mons. See B. G. II. 28.

marched during the three days, went over to the Nervii by night and told them that a large quantity of baggage was placed between the several legions, and that it was a matter of no difficulty, as soon as the first legion had reached the place for encampment and the rest were some distance off, to attack the first legion while the men were still under their burdens (sub sarcinis); for if this legion were defeated and the baggage were plundered, the rest would not have the courage to resist the Nervii. The Nervii were the more ready to follow this advice, because the nature of their country was favourable to such an enterprise. This people had never had any cavalry, and accordingly to prevent the cavalry of their neighbours from molesting them, they had filled their country with hedges constructed in the following manner. The trees, being planted in rows, were cut short when they were young, and the branches, which grew out thick in a lateral direction, becoming intertwined, and brambles and briars also growing in the intervals, these hedges were like a wall, and not only impenetrable, but it was not possible even to see through them. The march of the Roman army was greatly impeded by these obstacles, and this was a reason for the Nervii not neglecting the advice which they had received. We may conclude, though Caesar does not say it, that the Romans must have made a road for the troops and the baggage by cutting through the hedges[1].

The nature of the ground, which had been chosen for the Roman camp, was this. It was a hill which sloped down from the summit regularly to the Sambre. From the other bank of the river and right opposite another hill rose with a similar upward slope of about two hundred paces or one thousand feet, bare in the lowest part, but in the upper so thickly wooded that it was not easy to see into it[2]. The

[1] This passage about the hedges is mistranslated by Goeler (p. 69) and the author of the "Histoire" (p. 108) in one part. The author of the "Histoire" remarks that the fields near the Sambre are still surrounded by similar hedges. Goeler also has a note (p. 60, n. 8) on the present hedges of this country, which he describes not as the same as those which Caesar speaks of, but still they are hedges of a peculiar kind.

[2] It is not quite certain whether the words "passus circiter ducentos" mean what I have stated in the text. The Critics are not agreed on this matter.

enemy kept themselves concealed in these woods: on the open ground along the river a few bodies of cavalry were posted to watch. The depth of the river was about three feet.

We might suppose that this description would be sufficient to enable us to identify the place; and Goeler has determined the spot by a comparison of the localities with Cassini's map. The author of the "Histoire de César" agrees with Goeler. The site of the Roman camp is fixed at Neuf-Mesnil, on the left bank of the Sambre, above Maubeuge: the woods on the right bank, in which the enemy concealed themselves, were on the heights of Hautmont. The ground corresponds exactly to Caesar's description, and the identification is confirmed by a fact which Caesar mentions incidentally (c. 27), where he is describing the final defeat of the Nervii. If the site of the battle is rightly determined, and we assume that after the surrender of the Ambiani Caesar marched from Amiens or thereabouts, his course would be in an E.N.E. direction past Cambrai (Camaracum) and Bavai (Bagacum), which is about eight Roman miles west of the Sambre. On this route he would cross the Schelde at Cambrai, and between Cambrai and Bavai he would cross three other tributaries of the Schelde. It has been conjectured that the Schelde was the river on which Caesar defeated the Nervii, and a modern writer affirms that the ground between Bonavis and Vaucelles corresponds to the text of the Commentaries. But Caesar twice mentions the Sambre (Sabis), and if he did not mistake the name of the river, the battle was fought on the Sambre. In one passage of the Commentaries (vi. 33) Caesar says that the Schelde (Scaldis) flows into the Maas, where he ought to have said the Sabis; and so it might be conjectured that in ii. 18 when he wrote "Sabis," he should have written "Scaldis," as in vi. 33 when he wrote "Scaldis," he should have written "Sabis." The evidence of the text is however decisive in favour of the reading Sabis in the second book; and it is not probable that there is a position on the Schelde, which corresponds to Caesar's description so exactly as that on the Sambre does in all respects.

Caesar had sent the cavalry forward, and was following with all his force, but the order of his march was different

from that which the Belgae had reported to the Nervii. As
he was approaching the enemy, he had, according to his practice, six legions ready for action: behind these six legions he
had placed all the baggage; and the two legions, which were
last levied, closed the column and protected the baggage.
On reaching the Sambre Caesar's cavalry with the slingers
and archers crossed the river and attacked the enemy's cavalry,
who sometimes retreated into the woods, which concealed their
infantry, and then again advanced from the cover upon their
assailants, who did not venture to pursue them beyond the
open parts along the river. In the meantime the six legions
arrived at the site of the camp at Neuf-Mesnil, marked out
the limits and began to throw up the intrenchments. As
soon as the head of the baggage (c. 19) was seen by the
Belgae, who were concealed in the woods, which was the time
fixed for making the attack, they suddenly issued forth with
all their force in the order which had been formed under cover
of the forest. Falling on Caesar's cavalry they drove them
back in disorder, and descended to the river with such amazing
speed that almost at the same moment they appeared at the
border of the forest, in the river, and close upon the Roman
army. With equal speed they made their way up the slope
to the camp and to the men who were engaged in the works.

Caesar, who was on the spot, had every thing to do at once:
to hang out the flag (vexillum) which was the signal for arming, to summon the men to their ranks with the trumpet and
to recall from their work those soldiers who had gone some
distance for wood and turf, to form the order of battle, to
encourage the men, and to give the signal for the attack. The
shortness of the time and the rapid approach of the enemy up
the hill rendered a large part of these operations difficult; but
the skill and practice of the soldiers, who being taught by the
experience of former battles knew what they ought to do as
well as those who commanded them, and the fact that Caesar
had ordered the legati not to leave their several legions before
the camp was made, diminished the general's difficulties. For
as the enemy was coming on so quick and was so near, the
legati did not wait for his commands, but did what they knew
to be best.

Caesar after giving the necessary orders hurried to encourage the soldiers, and it chanced that he came first to the tenth legion. Using no more words than were sufficient to remind the men of their former courage, and to urge them bravely to resist the attack of the enemy, who were now within reach of the pila, he gave the signal. He then went from the left towards the right to cheer his men, and found that they were already fighting. So short was the time for preparation and so ready were the enemy to do battle, that the Roman soldiers had not time to fix the usual decorations[3] on their helmets, nor even to put on the helmets themselves and take the coverings off their shields. Whatever place any soldier first came to from his work, and whatever standards he first saw, there he took his station, that he might not lose time in looking for his comrades.

The army was thus arranged for battle conformably to the nature of the ground, the slope of the hill, and the exigencies of the occasion rather than according to military principles; for owing to the legions being disjoined they were severally in several parts resisting the enemy, and, as it has been already explained, the view was interrupted by the extreme thickness of the hedges. Under such circumstances it was neither possible to place reserves in convenient positions, nor to arrange what ought to be done on every part of the battle field, nor for one man to give all the necessary orders.

The soldiers of the ninth and tenth legions were on Caesar's left wing under Labienus and opposed to the Atrebates, who being exhausted by their rapid movement (c. 19), and many of them severely wounded by the discharge of the Roman pila, were quickly driven down the hill into the river, where a large part of them as they were attempting to cross in confusion fell beneath the swords of the Romans. The Roman soldiers crossed the Sambre after the enemy and followed them up the hill, where the Atrebates made a stand and renewed the contest, but they were at last put to flight, and Labienus took the Belgian camp. Two other legions, the eleventh and eighth, which were in Caesar's centre, had been attacked by the Veromandui, who formed the enemy's centre. The Vero-

[3] "Insignia:" ornaments of helmets, such as feathers, crests.

mandui also were driven down the hill, and the fight was continued on the banks of the river. The Roman order of battle generally formed a continuous or nearly continuous line in front of their camp, which an enemy could only reach by breaking the line or making a considerable circuit. But on this occasion the left wing of the Romans having crossed the Sambre and the centre being engaged with the enemy on the banks of the river, the left flank of the camp and the front were exposed; for the twelfth legion was on the right and the seventh was at no great distance from the twelfth. The position of the Nervii was on the enemy's left, opposite to the twelfth and seventh legions; and the banks of the river opposite to the enemy's left were, as Caesar describes them (c. 27) very high, a statement which is the strongest proof that the site of this great battle has been truly determined. The heights of Neuf-Mesnil, as they have already been described, descend to the river with a uniform slope; but at Boussières, a little farther up the stream, the heights which are connected with Neuf-Mesnil terminate on the river in escarpments from sixteen to about fifty feet high, which are not accessible at Boussières, but may be scaled lower down. The bank of the river on the right side opposite to Boussières is flat. Boduognatus the commander of the Nervii seeing the camp exposed led his men in a compact mass across the river and up the steep banks against the twelfth and seventh legions. Part of the Nervii attempted to surround these legions on the exposed flank, and part made their way to the height on which the camp was (c. 23).

Just at this time Caesar's cavalry and light infantry, which had been repulsed by the first attack of the enemy, and were making their escape into the camp, met the Nervii face to face, and turning their backs again sought safety in flight. The "calones" also or servants, who accompanied the six legions, having seen from the rear entrance of the camp and the summit of the hill the Roman soldiers victoriously crossing the river, had gone out to plunder, but when they looked back and saw that the enemy was in the camp they fled in confusion. At this moment also the baggage drivers, who were approaching, set up loud shouts of alarm, and in their fright began to run off in different directions. Caesar had with him some cavalry of the Treviri, who had the highest reputation among the Galli for courage, and had been sent as auxiliaries to the Roman army. But when these men saw the camp filled with the enemy, the legions hard pressed and nearly surrounded, the serving-men, horsemen, slingers and Numidians, scattered and running in every direction, they thought that all was lost, and hurrying homewards they reported that the Romans were defeated, and their baggage and camp taken.

After encouraging the tenth legion (c. 21) Caesar went to the right wing, which he found in great confusion. The men were hard pressed, and the cohorts of the twelfth legion so crowded together that the soldiers had not room to fight[4]: all the centurions of the fourth cohort with the standard bearer were killed and the standard was lost: of the remaining cohorts nearly all the centurions were either wounded or killed, and among them the Primipilus[5] P. Sextius Baculus, a most courageous man, was so severely wounded that he could no longer stand: the soldiers were growing weaker, and some in the rear ranks were retiring to avoid the missiles: the enemy in front were continually coming up the hill and falling on both flanks. Caesar seeing that matters were in great straits, and that there was no reserve to bring up, snatched a shield from one of the rear-rank men, for he had come without one, and rushed to the front. Addressing the centurions by name and cheering the men he ordered them to advance and to extend the front of the manipuli[6] that they might use their swords more easily. The arrival of the general gave the soldiers hope and renewed their courage, for even in this their extreme need every man was eager to do his

---

[4] "Signis in unum locum collatis" (c. 25).
[5] Primipilus, the first centurion of the first cohort, the highest in rank of the sixty centurions of the legion.
[6] "Manipulos laxare:" "this expression shows that the manipuli in the cohorts stood behind one another, and not, as Rüstow supposes, in the same line; otherwise Caesar would not have written 'manipulos,' but 'cohortes laxare.'" (Kœler (p. 77). There is nothing in this remark. I believe that Rüstow (p. 37) is right. Each manipulus formed one-third of the front of the cohort.

duty in the presence of Caesar, and so the attack of the enemy was checked a little (c. 25).

Observing that the seventh legion, which was near the twelfth, was also pressed by the enemy, Caesar commanded the tribunes to "bring the legions gradually together, and changing the position of the cohorts to lead them against the enemy." These words, which to us are scarcely intelligible, are explained to some extent, when Caesar adds, "that the result of this movement was that the men thus supported one another and having no fear of being surrounded on the rear by the enemy, they began to resist more boldly and to fight with more courage[1]." In the meantime the two legions, which brought up the rear and protected the baggage, having been informed of the fight that was going on quickened their pace and appeared on the top of the hill in sight of the enemy. Labienus also who was in the Belgian camp and from this more elevated[2] position saw the state of affairs on the other side of the river, sent the tenth legion to Caesar's aid. The men knowing in what danger their comrades were and the commander in chief also, hurried with all speed across the river to attack the Nervii. The arrival of the tenth legion gave such confidence to the twelfth and seventh legions that even those who were severely wounded and lying on the ground supported themselves on their shields and renewed the contest. Even the serving-men, though unarmed, when they saw that the enemy were struck with terror, rushed on the Nervii, and the cavalry eager to redeem their disgraceful flight placed themselves in front of the legionary soldiers in all parts of the field. But the enemy even in this desperate condition fought with intrepidity. When the first ranks fell, those behind stepped on the bodies and continued the contest. When these also were struck

---

[1] The two legions were placed back to back, as the passage is generally understood. But the flanks also must have been protected, and so the legions probably formed a square or parallelogram, as Rosch supposes that they did, and he shows how it could be done (Commentar ueber die Commentarien, &c. p. 205).

[2] The heights of Hautmont are 57 feet higher than the site of the Roman camp, 81 feet higher than Caesar's right wing, and 162 feet above the Sambre (Gorler, p. 78, note).

down, the survivors mounted on the piles of dead, discharged
their missiles against the Romans and threw back the pila
which had been directed against them.

This was the end of the bloody fight on the Sambre, in
which Roman discipline and military skill prevailed over
courage and superior numbers. The Nervii were almost annihilated on this dreadful day; they resisted to the last, for
nothing is said of a flight and pursuit[1]. On hearing of this
defeat the elders of the Nervii, who with the children and
women had taken refuge in the aestuaries and marshes (c.
16), sent commissioners to Caesar and made an unconditional
surrender. They said that by this battle their senators, as
Caesar expresses it, were reduced from six hundred to three,
and that out of sixty thousand[2] men there remained scarcely
five hundred able to bear arms[3]. To show his clemency towards this wretched people, Caesar gave them his protection,
left to them their territory and towns, and commanded their
neighbours to avoid molesting them. He says nothing of his
own losses; and the message of the Nervii is the only evidence
of the amount of their loss. But we find in other parts of the
Commentaries (v. 38, vi. 2, vii. 75) that the Nervii were not
so far reduced in numbers as it is stated in this second book.

The Aduatuci were on the road with all their forces to join
the Nervii, but when they heard of the battle, they immediately returned home. Leaving their towns and strong
places they carried all that they had into one town which was
strongly defended by its natural position. This place was
surrounded by high and steep rocks, except in one part where
there was a gentle ascent not more than two hundred feet
wide. The Aduatuci had fortified this part with a very

[1] Goeler (p. 70) thinks it probable that the Nervii may have retreated across
the Sambre to the wood of Quesnoy between the river and the Belgian camp,
and that the last struggle was made on this spot. He quotes Dimez (Lettre à
l'Académie Royale de Bruxelles) as evidence of arms, bones, cinerary urns, and
whole rows of graves having been found there. Caesar's narrative of the
battle ends abruptly, and does not absolutely exclude the hypothesis of Goeler;
but other battles may have been fought on this site long after Caesar's time.

[2] In c. 4 the contingent of the Nervii is estimated at fifty thousand.

[3] See Liv. Epit. 104. If the Epitomator has made no mistake, Livy compiled
this part of his narrative carelessly.

high double wall, on which they had placed heavy pieces of rock and beams pointed at the end. There was also a ditch before this double wall (c. 32). The Aduatuci were the descendants of some Cimbri and Teutoni, who were left here when the main body were going to invade the south of France and Italy (vol. ii. p. 46). As soon as the Romans appeared before the place, the enemy made frequent sallies, but they kept quiet when Caesar had shut them in with a rampart twelve feet high and fifteen Roman miles in circuit.

The author of the "Histoire de César" (p. 116) has assumed that this strong place of the Aduatuci was on the site of the citadel of Namur, in the angle at the junction of the Sambre and the Maas. He assumes that Caesar's "quindecim millium" (c. 30) means fifteen thousand feet, which cannot be admitted. The plateau of the citadel of Namur is also too small to contain so many persons as were crowded into the strong place of the Aduatuci; and the supposed line of contravallation, according to the author's plan, extended only from the Maas round the south side of the citadel to the Sambre, and so Caesar's lines would not surround the place.

Goeler (p. 83) affirms that the hill of Falhize, opposite to Huy on the Maas, corresponds exactly to the description of Caesar; and Goeler has examined the ground. Huy is lower down the river than Namur and about half-way between Namur and Liège. The hill of Falhize is about 600 steps in average width, 2000 in length and about 350 feet above the Maas. On the north-east side the surface of the hill is contracted to 94 steps, and at this part the ground slopes gently down with a fall of about 20 feet, and then gently rises again eastward towards the woods of Huy. The highest part of this ascent to the plateau of Falhize was the place which the Aduatuci fortified with a double wall and a ditch. "This ditch is now filled up, but above the material with which it has been filled some blocks of rock still rise, and others of about eight cubic feet lie scattered about. I have not seen any such rocks elsewhere on the hill." (Goeler, p. 86.)

Caesar's lines would be made on both sides of the river, and they would extend over the summits of the hills which lie round Falhize in a circular form. We cannot conjecture whether he found it necessary to block up the passage of the river at the two places where his lines of contravallation reached the stream; as Scipio did at the siege of Numantia (vol. i. p. 95). If the hill of Falhize was completely surrounded by the Roman lines, the circuit must have been many miles, and the number fifteen in Caesar's text may be no exaggeration. The line of circumvallation at Alesia (B. G. vii. 74) was fourteen miles in circuit. Caesar had seven legions with him, and a large body of engineers (fabri), as we infer with certainty from the work that was done here and on other occasions. By distributing the work among the different legions he would soon shut the people up. Five thousand of our regular navvies could in ten hours make a ditch 5000 yards long, 21 feet wide at the top and 12 deep, throwing the earth inwards and upwards as a parapet. If the Roman soldiers could only do half as much in the same time, the work would soon be accomplished. There are no springs on Falhize, and if the place was inhabited, the people must always have carried up their water from the Maas, which Caesar's lines would not prevent the besieged from doing now.

Covered galleries (vineae) were used for protecting the Romans while they were making a level embankment from the depression between the hill of Falhize and the wood of Huy to the double wall. On this embankment was raised a high tower for the construction of which the woods at Huy would furnish materials. When the besieged saw the tower building, they laughed at it and loudly rallied the Romans for setting up such an enormous machine at so great a distance: they asked how such little men expected to plant such a huge thing on the walls, for nearly all the Galli despised the Romans for the smallness of their stature compared with their own size. But when they saw the tower moving and approaching the walls, they were terrified by the strange appearance and sent men to Caesar, who said that the Romans must be aided by the gods or they could not have pushed forward so mighty an engine with such rapidity: they proposed to surrender themselves and all that they had, and they only begged that Caesar would not strip them of their arms: nearly all their neighbours were hostile to them, and if their arms were given up, they could not protect themselves; it would be better for them, if they were brought to this sad condition, to endure any thing from the Roman people rather than to be tortured to death by those among whom they had been used to rule.

Caesar replied, that more out of regard to his own practice than for their merits he would spare the people, if they surrendered before the ram had touched the wall; but he would not allow any terms of surrender unless the arms were first given up: he would then do what he had done in the case of the Nervii, and would give orders to the neighbouring peoples to abstain from molesting the subjects of the Roman people. The Aduatuci accepted Caesar's terms, and so large a quantity of arms was thrown into the ditch in front of the double wall that the pile reached almost to the top of the wall and of the embankment. As the Romans had begun to move their tower, it is certain that they had carried the embankment as far as they intended to do, and they may have filled up that part of the ditch which was between the embankment and the walls. The embankment[3] would not be wider than was necessary for the purpose of bearing the tower; and the ditch on each side of the embankment where it faced the wall, would remain as it was. Further, it would not be necessary for the embankment to be as high as the walls, for the purpose of the tower was evidently to avoid the necessity of raising the earth-works above the base of the walls. Caesar's description therefore may mean that the arms which were pitched down into the open part of the ditch on each side of the embankment filled it up; and, as Goeler suggests, the arms would naturally form a slope from the walls to the opposite side[4]. The besieged however, as it was afterwards discovered, concealed and retained about a third part of their arms. The gates were now opened, and the people remained quiet all that day (c. 32).

[3] The Roman agger was constructed of earth principally, but the sides were protected and supported by wood. Lucan, Phars. III. 396, quoted by Goeler, has a description of the construction.

[4] So Caesar might say correctly that the arms thrown from the wall "prope summam muri aggerisque altitudinem adaequarent," even if the embankment was much lower than the top of the walls (Goeler, Taf. 9. fig. 8).

As evening came on, Caesar ordered the gates to be closed and the soldiers to leave the town, in order that the people might not suffer any harm from them. The Aduatuci supposing that after the surrender the Romans would draw off the men from the forts or at least keep less strict guard over them, formed their design. With the arms which they had retained and shields hastily made of bark or wickerwork covered with skins, the besieged with all their force, during the third watch, made a sally from the place towards that part of the contravallation where the ascent to the Roman lines presented no difficulty[*]. Caesar had provided for such a surprise. Signal fires immediately blazed, and the Roman troops hurried from the nearest forts to the part which was attacked. The enemy fought as brave men ought to do, when fighting for their lives on unfavourable ground against men discharging their missiles from a rampart and towers. Four thousand perished in the attempt to break through the Roman lines, and the rest were driven back into the place. On the next day the gates of the town were forced open without any resistance, the soldiers entered, and Caesar made an auction in lots (sectio) of all the people in the place. The purchasers would be the dealers who followed the Roman army, and were both capitalists themselves and the agents of great capitalists at home, who invested their money in slaves. The number of those who were sold, as reported to Caesar by the purchasers, was fifty-three thousand.

At the time of the capture of this hill fort Caesar received news from P. Crassus whom he had sent with the seventh legion after the battle on the Sambre to the Veneti, Unelli, Osismi, Curiosolitae, Sesuvii, Aulerci and Redones, which are maritime states and border on the ocean. Crassus reported that all were reduced under the dominion of the Roman people. These states were in the parts between the lower course of the Loire and the Seine in the country named Bretagne and the peninsula Cotantin before the great French revolution. They correspond nearly to the modern departments of Morbihan, Finistère, Côtes du Nord, Ille et Vilaine, and Manche. A

[*] "Ascensus." This word shows that Caesar's lines were on high ground around the oppidum.

single legion was sufficient to compel the submission of these Armoric states; a fact which shows that there was no union among them and that they were terrified by the report of the proconsul's activity and daring. In fact Caesar affirms that this summer's campaign had reduced all Gallia to submission; and such was the fame of this military success among the barbarians that the nations east of the Rhine sent ambassadors to declare that they were ready to give hostages and to obey Caesar's orders. As he was hastening to Italia and to Illyricum, which was within his province, he ordered the ambassadors to come to him again at the beginning of the following summer.

Caesar placed seven of his legions in winter quarters along the Loire in the territories of the Andes, Turones and Carnutes, which states, as he remarks, "were near to those parts in which he had carried on war'" (ii. 35). The troops occupied a rich country, extending along the Loire from Angers to Orléans, where they would have abundant supplies. They were also near the states which had lately submitted to Crassus, and in this central position they stopped the communication between the people who were north and those who were south of the Loire. The friendly Senones and Aedui on the east bordered on the Carnutes; and the Sequani, who were east of the Saône were bound to the Romans. Thus the seven legions and the allies of Caesar occupied the whole country from Angers on the north side of the Loire to the Jura and the Vosges.

When Caesar's despatches were received in Rome, a thanksgiving (supplicatio) for fifteen days was decreed by the Senate, an honour never yet paid to any man (c. 35). Cicero informs us that he voted for this extraordinary honour. Perhaps he means that he proposed it, but it is not quite certain (De Prov. Cons. c. 11; Pro Balbo, c. 27). Cicero had returned from exile in B.C. 57, and at the beginning of September.

Before Caesar set out for Italy (B. G. iii. 1), he sent Servius Sulpicius Galba' with the twelfth legion and part of the

---

* The author of the "Histoire" proposes to write "where Crassus had carried on war;" because the winter quarters of the seven legions were not near those parts in which Caesar had carried on war. But see Schneider's critical note.

' Servius Galba was the grandson of Servius Galba who butchered the

cavalry into the territories of the Nantuates, Veragri and Seduni, three tribes which occupied the country from the territory of the Allobroges and the Leman lake and the Rhone to the summits of the Alps. The Nantuates were south of the lake in the country named Chablais, the Veragri in the lower part of the valley of the Rhone which enters the eastern end of the Leman lake, and the Seduni higher up the valley. The name of the Seduni is retained in the name of the town Sitten, which the French call Sion. Caesar's purpose was to open the roads over the Alps to the merchants who crossed the mountains at great risk and were compelled to pay heavy tolls to the natives. The road through the country of the Seduni was up the Valais, and is now continued over the Alps in the Simplon. There was also a road from Martigny by the pass of the Great St. Bernard, which road existed in the Roman time. Caesar allowed Galba, if he should think it necessary, to winter in these parts. After some successful battles and the capture of several forts, Galba received deputations from his enemies, who gave hostages and came to terms. He placed two cohorts among the Nantuates, and determined to pass the winter with the rest of the legion in a small town of the Veragri named Octodurus, which place lay in a valley with no great extent of level ground about it and surrounded by very lofty mountains. This town being divided into two parts by a stream, Galba gave the Galli one part of the town to pass the winter in, and assigned the other part to his cohorts, and fortified it with a rampart and ditch. Octodurus is Martinach, or Martigny, as the French name it, on the left side of the Rhone where it makes a great bend before it descends to the lake of Geneva. The river, which Caesar mentions, is the Drance which joins the Rhone near Martigny[a]. Several days had been passed in winter quarters and Galba had ordered corn to be carried thither, when he was informed by scouts that all the people during the night had quitted the other part of the town, and that the neighbouring

Lusitani (vol. I. p. 20), and the great grandfather of the Emperor Servius Galba (Suetonius, Galba, c. 3.)

[a] Martigny is on the right bank of the Drance. Octodurus is a Celtic name, the termination of which (dwr, water) occurs in other Gallic names, as for example in Divodurum, Two Waters, now Metz.

heights were occupied by a very large number of Seduni and
Veragri. The Galli had formed a design to surprise Galba,
thinking that a legion which was diminished by the absence
of two cohorts* and of many who were gone to look after the
supplies, was by no means formidable, and that if they
descended from the heights and discharged their missiles on
the Romans, the attack could not be resisted. They were
irritated also at having been compelled to give their children
as hostages; and they were persuaded that the Romans were
attempting to occupy the Alpine passes not only for the purpose of making the roads secure, but with the view of keeping
possession of the passes and adding those parts to the adjoining Provincia. The Roman occupation would have stopped the
Alpine people from exacting tolls from the traders.

Galba had neither completed his defences nor laid in all his
supplies, and he was taken by surprise. He immediately
called a council of war. The facts were these. Nearly all the
higher grounds were filled with armed men; there was no
possibility of relief coming, nor could supplies be brought up
in consequence of the roads being stopped, and all hope was
now nearly gone. Some members of the council proposed
that they should leave their baggage, sally out, and attempt
to escape by the same way by which they had come. The
majority however were of opinion that this determination
should be reserved for extremities, and that in the meantime
they should try their fortune and defend the camp. The
enemy scarcely allowed the Romans time for preparation.
They ran down at a signal from all directions and hurled
stones and javelins at the rampart. The Romans at first
made a vigorous resistance, and every missile from the rampart took effect. When any part of the camp being bared of
defenders was in danger, others hurried to the place to protect it; but the Romans were under this disadvantage that
the enemy when they were exhausted by long fighting retired
from the battle, and others with their strength unimpaired
took their places. The Romans owing to the smallness of

* This legion had been in the great battle on the Sambre, and we may suppose that the numbers were much diminished by death as well as by the absence
of the two cohorts.

their numbers could not do this: neither could those who were exhausted retire from the fight, nor could even the wounded leave their place and recruit themselves.

The contest had now continued more than six hours, and both the strength and the missiles of the Romans were failing: the enemy were pressing on harder, the resistance was growing feebler, and the Galli were tearing down the rampart and filling the ditch on all sides, when P. Sextius Baculus, who had distinguished himself in the battle with the Nervii, and the tribune C. Volusenus, an able and courageous man, hurried to Galba and told him that the only chance of safety was in sallying out. Galba summoned the centurions and through them quickly told the soldiers to stop fighting for a time, and only to catch the missiles that were sent, to recover a little from their exhaustion, and then when the signal was given to sally from the camp and trust to their courage. The soldiers obeyed the orders, and suddenly issuing from all the gates left the enemy no time to see what was intended or to rally their forces. The fortune of war was changed, and they who had come with the hope of taking the camp were surrounded and killed. Out of more than thirty thousand, the number of the barbarians, as it was ascertained, who assailed the camp, more than a third were destroyed; the rest were terrified and put to flight, and they were not allowed to halt even on the higher ground. After completely routing the enemy, who threw away their arms, the Romans returned to the camp. But Galba did not choose to run the same risk again, and he had not sufficient supplies. On the following day he burnt all the houses in the place, and set out for the Provincia: without meeting with any enemy he led the legion safely through the Nantuates into the country of the Allobroges, and wintered there (B. G. iii. 1—6).

The story in the Commentaries is in Caesar's style. The materials must have been furnished to the commander in chief by Galba.

CHAPTER IV.

P. CLODIUS, POMPEIUS AND CICERO.

B.C. 58.

We turn from Caesar's victorious career in Gallia to the ignoble events in Rome; from the plain, unadorned and veracious Commentaries of the Roman proconsul to blundering compilers and the dubious testimony of Cicero's letters and orations. Nothing can be more disgusting, more barren and less instructive than the history of this degraded commonwealth during Caesar's campaigns. While the great general with profound forethought was planning the subjugation of Gallia, and making all the necessary preparations to secure success, the wretched factions at home by their folly and wickedness were inviting the ruin which soon overwhelmed them.

Cicero had given up to his brother Quintus their father's house in Rome, and he bought after his consulship at great cost a house on the Palatine from a Crassus (Ad Fam. v. 6). After he fled from Rome, this house was plundered, and the movables were carried, as Cicero says on one occasion (Pro P. Sestio, c. 24) to the consuls; on another (In Pis. c. 11), he says they were carried to the house of the consul Piso's mother in law, and that the house was then set on fire by Clodius' rabble at the instigation of Piso. It was no new thing at Rome for a man's house to be demolished by the populace (vol. i. p. 288). The villa at Tusculum, once the property of L. Sulla, Cicero's favourite retreat on which he had spent much money, was also destroyed, and the furniture and ornaments, nay even the trees, were carried off to the neighbouring villa of the consul Gabinius. Cicero's wife Terentia was taken from Vesta's temple to the "tabula Valeria," on some affair of money no doubt, but we are not informed what it was. Cicero even says (Pro Sestio, c. 24) that his children were sought for the purpose of being murdered. If his enemies really had this design, they could easily have found the children.

The confused and spurious oration entitled De Domo is the authority for some facts. Clodius wished to have the ground on which Cicero's house stood, and as he was both buyer and seller, as it is said, but did not wish to appear as buyer, he employed a man named Scato to purchase for him (De Domo, c. 44). The purchase-money of course would go into the treasury. Clodius intended to build a fine mansion on the site, and as the space was not sufficient, he demolished the adjoining Porticus or colonnade of Catulus, which Q. Catulus after his victory over the Cimbri (B.C. 101) built on the site of the house of M. Fulvius Flaccus (vol. i. p. 288). In order to secure himself Clodius dedicated about the tenth part of the area of Cicero's house, and kept the rest for his own use. On the dedicated part he erected a temple to Liberty or to Licence as Cicero says (De Legg. ii. 17), and placed in it a statue. This statue, stolen by Appius the brother of Clodius, from the grave of a harlot of Tanagra and given by Appius to his brother Publius, was a representation of the woman, and was now converted into the image of Liberty. This incredible stuff is in the oration De Domo (c. 43).

Cicero (Pro Sestio, c. 25) after enumerating some of the laws enacted in the tribunate of Clodius, which laws have already been mentioned (vol. iii. c. 21), speaks (c. 26) of Clodius by a "tribunician law" depriving of his office the high priest of the Great Mother at Pessinus in Galatia and selling the place for a large sum of money to a fellow named Brogitarus, a son in law of Deiotarus, and even conferring on this man the title of king, though such a title, according to Roman usage, could only be conferred by the Senate. This may be taken as a sample of the means by which Clodius is said to have raised money for the purpose of paying his partisans. (Comp. De Harusp. Resp. c. 13.)

Tigranes, the son of the Armenian king, after the triumph

of Pompeius was kept at Rome in chains in the custody of
Flavius, who was now a praetor. To obtain his liberty
Tigranes offered Clodius a sum of money, but it could be no
more than a promise. The story is thus told by Asconius
(in Mil. c. 7). Flavius was supping with Clodius, who expressed a wish to see Tigranes, and the young prince was
brought to the house of Clodius, and seated at the table; but
Clodius would not give him up to Flavius, nor even to Pompeius who demanded him. Finally he put Tigranes on board
a vessel to make his escape, but the ship being driven to
Antium, Clodius sent his man Sex. Clodius to bring Tigranes
back to Rome. Flavius also hearing of the matter went to
seize his prisoner. The two parties met on the Appian Road
at the fourth milestone, and there was a fight in which many
were killed on both sides, but more on the side of Flavius,
and among them M. Papirius, a Roman eques and Publicanus,
and a friend of Pompeius. Flavius alone and without any
companion with difficulty fled to Rome. Tigranes, we must
suppose, made his escape, for nothing more is said of him.
Cicero appears to allude to this affair in a letter dated from
Thessalonica on the 29th of May (Ad Att. iii. 8, 3). Clodius
and Pompeius were now no longer friends, but the great man
had no means of resisting the turbulent tribune. The consul
Piso stood aloof: he would not declare against Clodius. The
other consul Gabinius was roused at last against his once
dear friend Clodius, and took the side of Pompeius (in Pis. c.
12). The people, says Cicero, were wonderfully indifferent.
They did not care whether Clodius or Gabinius perished in the
quarrel, and would have been well pleased if both had been
killed. Still Gabinius had one recommendation: he was on the
side of Pompeius. A consul and a tribune at the head of their
respective bands fought in the streets of Rome; missiles and
stones were flying about daily. In one conflict the fasces of
Gabinius were broken. Even the ceremonies of religion were
used by the opposite factions to strengthen their cause. The
tribune in solemn form and with the usual solemnities consecrated the property of Gabinius to the gods; and L. Ninnius
repaid the tribune by consecrating his property also in the same
way (De Domo, c. 47, 48). But it is one of the spurious

orations which is our authority for these facts. The quarrels in Rome gave Cicero's friends some hope. His son in law C. Piso, who was a quaestor, entreated his kinsman the consul Piso to exert himself for the recall of Cicero from exile, but Piso would do nothing. Cicero himself was not inactive, for in the letter to Atticus of the twenty-ninth of May he says that he had written to Pompeius, and he sent Atticus a copy of the letter (iii. 8. 4).

On the first of June on the motion of the tribune L. Ninnius a full senate came to a unanimous resolution in favour of Cicero being recalled, but the opposition of Aelius Ligur, one of the tribunes, nullified the vote. Cicero's brother Quintus now returned from his government of Asia. He was met on his approach to Rome by almost all the city with expressions of sorrow and sympathy. Quintus was in Rome early in June, as appears by a letter of the thirteenth of June from Thessalonica addressed to Quintus (Ad Qu. Fr. i. 3. 8), in which the exile accuses Hortensius of treachery, declares his opinion that Pompeius is a double dealer, recommends his family to his brother's care and asks him to send all the news of Rome. But Pompeius, though Cicero doubted his sincerity, was the man who could help him most; and it appears that the hostility of Clodius did move Pompeius to assist in Cicero's recall more than any love for Cicero himself. The tongue of the orator, when it was again let loose, was an ally too powerful to be neglected. Asconius in a note on the oration for Milo (c. 7) states that on the eleventh of August when Pompeius came into the senate, it was said that a dagger dropped from a slave of P. Clodius, that it was brought to the consul Gabinius, and it was said that P. Clodius had commanded the slave to kill Pompeius, who immediately returned home and shut himself up in his house. The story is badly told, and the alleged design of assassinating Pompeius in the senate house is hardly credible, if that is the meaning of Asconius; but he may mean that the design was to murder him on the way to the senate[1]. Asconius adds that Pompeius was blockaded (obsessus) or at least watched in his house by

[1] Comp. Plutarch, Pomp. c. 40. The writer of the oration De Harusp. c. 23 says, "Tum est illa in templo Castoris scelerata et paene deletrix hujus imperii dies deprehensa."

Damio a freedman of Clodius, as he found in the Acta (vol. iii. p. 410) of the eighteenth of August of this year, in which it was recorded that when Damio was appealing to the tribunes against the praetor Flavius, who, as we may conjecture, had disturbed Damio in his operations, L. Novius one of the colleagues of Clodius declared that he also had been wounded by this agent of Clodius, and prevented by armed men from taking part in public affairs.

Whatever may be the truth about this attempt on the life of Pompeius, he came no more into public during the tribunate of Clodius. He certainly acted with prudence and dignity in avoiding all contests with the tribune, for he was himself only a private person and the power of Clodius would soon terminate with his office. Culleo, supposed to be Q. Terentius Culleo, advised Pompeius to divorce Julia, to break with Caesar and join the senate. Pompeius would not do this, for besides his political connexion with Caesar, he was very fond of his young wife, and, as Plutarch reports, his love for Julia made him indisposed towards public life, and he passed his time chiefly with her in the country and in his gardens without troubling himself about what was going on in Rome. But he now saw that his old ally Cicero might be made useful, and he did what he could to bring him back. With the view of obtaining Caesar's consent, as we must infer, P. Sestius, tribune elect for the next year made a journey to Caesar (Pro Sestio, c. 33); but Cicero does not tell us the result of this visit, nor can we determine exactly the time. The conjecture that Clodius was moved by these supposed negotiations with Caesar to attempt the repeal of the laws enacted in Caesar's consulship is not sufficiently supported by the passages in the oration De Domo (c. 15), and in the oration De Harusp. (c. 23), even if we admit the genuineness of these orations. There was some correspondence between Pompeius and Caesar about this time, as we learn from a letter of Cicero (Ad Att. iii. 18), which may have been written in September.

The consuls elected for the next year were P. Cornelius Lentulus, a friend both of Pompeius and Cicero, and Q. Metellus Nepos, who was no longer hostile to him. Eight of the tribunes now undertook Cicero's cause, and on the twenty-ninth of October they promulgated (published) a bill for his recall, which was supported by the consul elect P. Cornelius Lentulus, but opposed by the consuls Piso and Gabinius, and by the tribune Ligur. Atticus wrote to Cicero on the twenty-ninth of October and told him all about this matter. Cicero's answer (Ad Attic. iii. 23) is dated the last day of November, and he was then at Dyrrachium to which place he had removed from Thessalonica (Ad Att. iii. 22). In his letter of the thirtieth of November Cicero says that the proposed law only restored his citizenship and his rank. He also speaks of the introduction into the bill of the usual clause of indemnity, in case this bill should contain any thing contrary to existing laws. There was a third matter on which he had something to say. Clodius in his law for the banishment of Cicero had attempted by a clause to prevent either the senate or the people from repealing the law. This clause was to the effect that no motion should be made, and nothing said about Cicero's restoration (Ad Att. iii. 15. 6). This was a foolish and common Roman fashion to attempt to limit the power of a legislative body. Cicero says, Atticus knows that such prohibitive clauses were never observed when the laws which contained them were repealed: indeed if they were observed, scarcely any law could be repealed, for all the laws endeavoured to protect themselves by such prohibitive clauses. Accordingly he says truly, that when a law is repealed, the clause which forbids the repeal is repealed also. But the eight tribunes inserted in their bill a clause which declared that their bill should have no effect if any thing in it should be against the prohibitive clauses, by which Clodius had attempted to protect his bill. It seems a very great absurdity for the tribunes to have proposed a bill which defeated its own purpose; but this is the meaning of the passage in Cicero[7]. He tells Atticus that he shall be content if he is simply recalled.

In a letter of the twenty-sixth[8] of November, addressed to Terentia and dated from Dyrrachium (Ad Fam. xiv. 1. 5), Cicero laments that his wife is intending to sell a piece of land (vicum). What will become of their boy, if there is nothing

---
[7] See the notes of P. Manutius on Cic. ad Att. III. 23.
[8] The same date as the letter to Atticus (III. 22).

left for him? If their friends remain true, she will not want
money. If Atticus gave Cicero a large sum of money when
he went into exile (Nepos, Atticus, c. 4), it is not likely that
Atticus would let the wife want any thing, when he continued
so faithful to the husband. We may conjecture that Terentia
had a higher spirit than her husband and did not wish to
trouble her friends. A letter to Atticus (iii. 27) seems to
mean that Cicero entreated him to assist his wife with money,
and Atticus was able to do so, for he was now become still
richer by the death of his very wealthy uncle Q. Caecilius, who
left him the whole or at least the greater part of his property.
From this time Atticus took the name of Q. Caecilius Pomponianus Atticus.

On the tenth of December Clodius and the old tribunes
went out of office and the new tribunes came in. On the same
day Cicero wrote a letter of complaint to Atticus (iii. 24) who
was continually occupied about his friend's restoration, and
negotiating with those who might put any difficulties in the
way. According to the Sempronian law the provinces for the
consuls elect of this year had been fixed before their election,
but it was not the custom to determine what the allowance and
outfit[4] of the consuls should be before they entered on their
office. Atticus and his friends had consented that the allowance of Lentulus and Metellus should be settled before the
new tribunes were in power. Cicero thinks that such a thing
was never done before. It was done on this occasion to please
Lentulus and Metellus; and Atticus and his friends by consenting to it expected to secure the aid of the new consuls for
Cicero's restoration. Cicero thought that the new tribunes
might be offended at this measure, which deprived them of
the power, which really belonged to them, of assenting to or
refusing the consuls' allowance; for though they did not intend to make any difficulty about the matter, they wished to
have the power of fixing the consuls' allowance in order to
secure Cicero's interests. Thus the result of the measure, as
Cicero supposed, might be that he would lose the new tribunes'
support, and the consuls would now be independent of them

[4] The expression is "provincias ornatas esse" which we cannot imitate. The Germans can translate "ornare" by "ausstatten."

and of the senate. He was often wrong in his political reckonings, and he was wrong in this.

The consuls Piso and Gabinius, "the two vultures," left Rome for their provinces, Piso for Macedonia, Gabinius for Syria. They went off with evil omens and the curses of the people (Pro Sestio, c. 33; In Pis. c. 14). Before the end of the year Atticus left Rome apparently on some business. He had done all that he could for his friend, and no more could be done until the beginning of the next year. Cicero concluded (Ad Attic. iii. 25) that if there had been any hope of his restoration, Atticus would not have left Rome at this time. The exile was impatient, and dissatisfied with his best friends. He urged Atticus to come and see him before the first of January[a].

I have deferred to the present the history of the most memorable event of the year B.C. 58 next to Cicero's exile.

Ptolemaeus Lathyrus king of Egypt left a legitimate daughter Berenice, also named Cleopatra, and two illegitimate sons named Ptolemaeus. After the death of Berenice and her husband Alexander (vol. ii. p. 381), one of these Ptolemaei named Auletes succeeded to the throne of Egypt. The other Ptolemaeus had the kingdom of Cyprus, that fertile island which could furnish all the materials for a ship from the keel to the ropes and canvas, and fit it out complete (Ammianus Marcell xiv. 8). This Ptolemaeus was rich, and defenceless; and the Romans coveted his wealth and his country. Velleius (ii. 45) says that he deserved to be deprived of his kingdom for his vices, a remark by which we may measure the sense and the honesty of this unscrupulous writer. Even such a compiler as Florus (iii. 9. 3) knew better, for he says that such was the report of the wealth of Ptolomaeus, that the people who subdued nations and were accustomed to give kingdoms confiscated in his lifetime the property of one who

---

[a] There is no date to the letter (Ad Att. III. 25). The words "a me" at the beginning are clearly spurious, and there may be some doubt about the meaning of the last sentence. I think however that I have given the true meaning.

I have endeavoured to show what was done as to Cicero's restoration up to the end of B.C. 58. Much more might be written, but this is enough to make the History intelligible, and as much as the matter is worth.

was their ally. Cicero (Pro Sestio, c. 26, 27) says that Ptolemaeus of Cyprus had not received the title of ally (socius) from the Roman Senate; but Cicero does not mean that this was a reason for plundering a prince, who was on friendly terms with the Roman people, nor does he charge him with any vices. On the contrary he speaks of this wicked transaction in terms of condemnation. The history of the annexation of Cyprus may be interesting to a people who have done the same thing. Whether the annals of British India contain so foul a crime, I leave those to determine who know more of Indian affairs than I do.

Clodius, it is said, bore a grudge against the king of Cyprus for not having sent him money enough when he was taken prisoner by the pirates (vol. iii. p. 103). This may be true, but the enmity of Clodius could have done the king no harm, if the Roman people had not coveted his possessions. Plutarch's narratives are never quite satisfactory. In the life of Cato he says that Clodius wished to send Cato out of Rome, in order to have the opportunity of executing his design against Cicero, and that as soon as he was in office he offered Cato the mission to Cyprus, that Cato refused, and Clodius told him that if he would not go willingly he should go against his will. The proposed mission to Cyprus was confirmed by the popular vote, and Cato was sent with the rank of praetor, to take possession of Cyprus, to strip the king of his money and bring it to Rome. "Cato was allowed neither ship nor soldier nor attendant except two clerks, one of whom was a thief and a thorough knave, and the other was a client of Clodius" (Plutarch, Cato, c. 34). Cato was also commissioned to restore certain Byzantine fugitives, for it was the design of Clodius to keep him from Rome as long as he could during his tribunate.

The chief agent in the robbery of the Cyprian king was Cicero's enemy Clodius. Cicero attempts to justify Cato for undertaking this odious mission which was imposed on him. The act, he says, was already committed when the bill for the annexation of Cyprus was passed; there was a special enactment for the appointment of Cato as commissioner (Pro Sestio, c. 29); and it was better that whatever good could come out

of this bad business should be secured by Cato rather than by
any other. This is a poor apology. Cato might have refused
to discharge this dirty commission. He set out from Rome
after Cicero had left the city (Pro Sestio, c. 28), and sent one
Canidius to inform the king of the enactment about his kingdom, and, according to Plutarch, Canidius prevailed on the
king to yield without a struggle, on the assurance that he
should not want money and that he should have the priesthood
of the goddess at Paphos.

In the meantime Cato was staying in Rhodes, where he saw
the Egyptian king Ptolemaeus, who being driven out of Egypt
by his people was on his voyage to Italy to seek the aid of the
Romans. As the king wished to see Cato, he sent him a
message expecting that Cato would wait on him. Cato answered
that if the king wished to see him, he must come, and when
he did come, Cato neither advanced to meet him nor rose, but
saluted him as an ordinary visitor. Cato advised the king not
to go to Rome, where the chief men were only looking after
money, but to return and to be reconciled to his people. The
king at first was disposed to follow Cato's advice, but his
friends turned him back to his original design, and he continued his voyage to Rome, where he found that Cato had told
him the truth.

The anecdote collector Valerius (ix. 4) reports as a proof
of the avarice of the Cyprian king that when he knew that he
was going to be plundered, he embarked all his treasures in
ships and put out to sea with the intention of scuttling his
vessels and perishing with his wealth. But he could not endure to sink his precious things in the sea, and he sailed back
with them. He ended his life by suicide, but whether before
the Romans arrived in Cyprus or after, we are not told[4].

Cato (Plutarch, Cato, c. 30) first went to Byzantium, but
as he did not quite trust Canidius, he sent his nephew M.
Brutus to Cyprus. At a later time Brutus had large sums out
at interest in Cyprus, from which we draw the almost certain

[4] Appian (B. C. ii. 23) says that he killed himself as soon as he heard of the
enactment of the law under which he was plundered. But Appian also says
that the king threw his treasures into the sea; and that Cato was not sent to
Cyprus until B.C. 52, which is a great error.

conclusion, that this virtuous Roman helped himself to some of
the king's money. After restoring the exiles to Byzantium
and settling the affairs of that city, Cato sailed to Cyprus.
The king's valuables were sold there, and we may therefore
infer that the people were rich enough to pay a good price for
them. Cato took great pains to make the sale as productive
as possible to the Roman state, and thus he offended the Romans
who accompanied him, and particularly Munatius Rufus, who
afterwards wrote a book about Cato. Munatius says that it
was not Cato's distrust, but his contemptuous behaviour which
vexed him, and was the cause of his dislike. In fact though
Munatius went to Cyprus in some capacity under Cato, he
would not obey his orders and left the island without his
permission. The only thing which Cato did not sell was a
statue of Zeno, the founder of the Stoic school, to which Cato
belonged. (Plin. H. N. 34. 8, 19 § 34.) The sum of money
which Cato raised in Cyprus was nearly seven thousand talents
of silver, which with the exception of a small part was brought
to Rome. The accounts of his administration were drawn up
in two books, but both of them were lost; one in a vessel
which sailed from Cenchreae, the eastern port of Corinth, and
was wrecked with the loss of all that it contained; the other
was burnt together with Cato's tent in the island Coreyra
where he called on his way home. Cato was met on his
arrival in Italy, as he was ascending the Tiber, by all the
magistrates, the priests, the Senate and a large part of the
people, but without landing or stopping his course he swept
along in a royal galley, and moored his ships in the dockyard.
The money was carried through the Forum to the great
admiration of the Romans, and the Senate rewarded the plun-
derer of Cyprus with thanks. Cato did not return to Rome,
according to Plutarch's chronology, until B.C. 56, in which year
his father-in-law L. Marcius Philippus was one of the consuls.
The island of Cyprus was annexed to the Roman provincial
government of Cilicia[7].

[7] The unfortunate king of Cyprus, who was on friendly terms with the
Romans, was plundered for no reason that we can discover, except that it was
affirmed in the bill which Clodius proposed that he had given aid to the pirates
(Schol. Bob. in Ciceronem Pro. P. Sestio, c. 26); but the real ground of Clodius'

This year was memorable for an example of Roman magnificence and profusion. M. Aemilius Scaurus, curule aedile, was the son of M. Aemilius, consul B.C. 115, and his wife Caecilia, who after her husband's death married the Dictator L. Sulla. Caecilia acquired large property in the time of her second husband, either by his grants of confiscated lands or by pretended purchase; and we may assume that her son received what she had unworthily obtained. Scaurus served under Cn. Pompeius in Syria and Judaea (vol. iii. pp. 175, 190), and Pompeius left him there with two legions. He was succeeded by L. Marcius Philippus (Appian, Syriaca, c. 51). Scaurus is charged with extorting three hundred talents from the Arab prince Aretas. On his return to Rome he was elected a curule aedile, and the year of his office was B.C. 58. The wealth which Scaurus inherited from his mother and his own acquisitions enabled him to exhibit most splendid shows, but even his immense wealth was insufficient for the expenditure, and he incurred a large debt by borrowing. He erected for his games a wooden theatre, which only stood one month. It accommodated eighty thousand spectators. The scena was 'triple,' as Plinius says (36. c. 15), of three hundred and sixty columns, three orders, as it seems, one above the other: the lowest columns were thirty-eight feet high. "The lowest part of the scena was of marble, the second of glass, and the highest of gilded planks." There were three thousand bronze statues between the columns. There were paintings from Sicyon, which this famous seat of art sold to pay the town debts; splendid hangings, once the property of the last Attalus of Pergamum, (vol. i. chap. xiv.), and other ornaments, some of which, for there was more than was wanted, were carried to the Tusculan villa of Scaurus and there destroyed by fire, when the slaves burnt their master's country-house. Scaurus also exhibited animals unknown to the Romans, five crocodiles and a hippopotamus in a Euripus or artificial lake. One hundred and fifty panthers appeared in the circus. But the most wonderful thing in the exhibition was the bones of the monster, to which

---

enmity may have been the king's small contribution to the ransom of Clodius when he was in the hands of the pirates (Appian, B. C. ii. 23; Strabo, p. 684. Vol. III. p. 103).

Andromeda was exposed. The bones were brought from Joppa in Judaea. The beast was forty feet in length (Plin. N. H. 0. c. 5). There is a coin of Scaurus and Hypsaeus which belongs to their curule aedileship. It bears on one side the name of Rex Aretas, who is kneeling near a camel and presenting an olive-branch. This is the man of Petra (vol. iii. p. 175) whom Scaurus plundered.

CHAPTER V.

CICERO'S RESTORATION.

B.C. 57.

On the 1st of January, B.C. 57, the consul P. Cornelius Lentulus proposed Cicero's restoration in the Senate without any opposition from his colleague Q. Caecilius Metellus, though Metellus was the man who had said that the execution of Catilina's associates was murder, and had prevented Cicero from making the usual speech at the end of his consulship (vol. iii. 350). All the praetors were in favour of Cicero, except Appius the brother of P. Clodius, and even he did not venture to make any opposition. All the tribunes also were on Cicero's side except Numerius Quintius and Atilius Serranus, who, as Cicero says, were bought by Clodius. L. Aurelius Cotta (consul B.C. 65) was first asked to give his opinion. Cotta declared that a man could not be deprived of his citizenship except by a law enacted by the Comitia Centuriata; that Cicero had merely retired for the good of the state; he ought not only to be recalled, but to be honoured by the Senate. Pompeius agreed with Cotta, but he said that for the sake of Cicero's quiet, he thought that a resolution of the Senate should be confirmed by a vote of the people. All were in favour of the proposal of Lentulus, and were going unanimously to vote for it, when the tribune Atilius rose, and asked time to consider, only one night. This was a polite form of putting a veto. Atilius was received with shouts and murmurs: he was also pressed by entreaties; and even his own father-in-law Cn. Oppius threw himself at the feet of his son-in-law. Atilius declared that he would not make any obstacle on the following day, and the Senate separated. A long night intervened, as Cicero expresses it, and the tribune's bribe was doubled, for which fact there is Cicero's assertion. There were only a few more days in January on which the Senate could meet; and on all these days the matter of Cicero's restoration was discussed. (Pro Sestio, c. 33, &c.)

Cicero's narrative is not quite clear. He says "that the resolution of the Senate was hindered by delay, trickery, and fraud, and that the 25th of January came at last, the day fixed for the decision of the assembly about his case" (Pro Sestio, c. 35). The tribune Q. Fabricius, who had undertaken to propose the bill (rogatio), occupied the place of meeting some time before daylight; but his opponents were there still earlier with armed men, and slaves and gladiators. Fabricius was attacked; some of his party were killed and many were wounded. When the tribune M. Cispius was entering the Forum, he was driven back. Cicero's brother Quintus, who was present, was expelled from the rostra which he had mounted to address the people on behalf of the exile, and, if we understand Cicero right, Quintus was wounded. With the aid of slaves and freedmen and under cover of the darkness, Quintus made his escape[1]. "You remember, jurymen," says Cicero, when in the following year he was speaking in defence of Sestius, "that on this occasion the Tiber was filled with dead bodies, the drains were choked, and the blood was wiped up in the Forum with sponges." Never was there such a slaughter, never such a pile of corpses, except perhaps on that day when Cinna and Cn. Octavius had their bloody fight in the Forum (vol. ii. p. 236). The tribunes Sestius and Milo, who were on Cicero's side, had not yet made their appearance on the field of battle.

On a subsequent occasion Sestius appeared in the temple of Castor and opposed some measure of the consul Metellus (obnuntiavit consuli). The tribune trusting to the sanctity of his office came unprotected; but the band of Clodius taking advantage of the opportunity attacked him with

[1] Plutarch (Cicero, c. 33) says that Quintus only escaped by lying among the bodies as if he were dead. Perhaps he used the passage of Cicero (Pro Sestio, c. 35), and misunderstood it.

swords, pieces of the wooden enclosure of the Forum, and clubs.
The tribune fell with more than twenty wounds under the
blows of his enemies and only escaped with his life because
they thought he was killed. In a letter to his brother (Ad
Q. Fr. ii. 3. 6) Cicero says that Sestius was saved by Bestia.
The assassins were so shocked at what they had done that they
thought of murdering a tribune on their own side, Numerius
Quintius, for the purpose, as we are told, of charging their
adversaries with the crime. Cicero, who attempts to make
this tribune ridiculous, reports that the cunning fellow seeing
what his own party were intending to do, for the rascals could
not hold their tongues, hastily put on a muleteer's cloak, a
dress in which he first made his appearance in the Roman
comitia and covered himself with a basket such as reapers use.
The tribune was not safe until it was known that Sestius was
still alive. Cicero expresses a wish that the rioters had not
found out their mistake so soon, for then they would have
murdered Quintius, who would have got what he deserved.

The gladiators, who had been employed in this recent brawl,
and belonged to the praetor Appius Clodius, were seized,
brought before the Senate, where they confessed, and then
were put in prison by Milo. But the tribune Atilius Serranus
set them free; and there was no further inquiry (Pro Sestio,
c. 39). It was now time for Sestius to look after his own
safety, and he collected a force which enabled him to resist
any attack (Pro Sestio, cc. 38, 39, 42). Clodius is charged
by Cicero (Pro Milone, c. 27) in several passages with burning
the temple of the Nymphs, in which the censors' records were
kept, but it is impossible to fix the time when this happened.
When L. Caecilius, one of the praetors, was celebrating the
games of Apollo (Ludi Apollinares) in the month of July, a
number of the lowest citizens having assembled at a time
when bread was dear made such a disturbance that all the
spectators in the theatre were driven away. This is from a
note of Asconius on the oration against Milo (c. 14): Cicero
himself says nothing of this disturbance at the games, but he
speaks of Clodius attacking the house of L. Caecilius, about
which fact Asconius observes that he had not found any other
evidence than Cicero's statement.

Milo twice attempted to bring Clodius to trial under the
Lex Plautia, as Cicero says (Pro Milone, c. 13, 15) on a charge
of disturbing the peace (de vi). One of these occasions was
in this year B.C. 57 [1], but a consul, a praetor, and a tribune
put forth new edicts of a new kind to this effect, "That the
accused do not make an appearance, that he be not summoned,
that no judicial inquiry be made, that no person be permitted
to speak of judices (jurymen) or trials." As this stands in
Cicero's text (Pro Sestio, c. 41) it is perfectly unintelligible,
and it is difficult to discover why he should have left it so, for
he must have known that a reader would either not see what
he meant or would attach some wrong meaning to it. The
following passage of Dion (39, c. 7) seems to explain the
matter: "Clodius was a candidate for the aedileship, in order
that, if he should be elected, he might escape trial for disturbing the peace, for Milo commenced a prosecution against him,
but did not bring it into court. For neither were the quaestors
yet elected, whose duty it was to determine the jurymen
(judices) by lot, and Nepos (the consul Metellus Nepos) forbade
the praetor to admit any prosecution before the jurymen were
appointed. And as it was the rule that the aediles should be
elected before the quaestors, this circumstance was the chief
cause of delay." In this instance the historian has been useful
in helping us to understand the contemporary writer. The
friends of Clodius wished to secure his election to the aedileship,
after which Clodius could only be tried during that year
(B.C. 57) for bribery at his election, if there should happen to
be bribery. As the law was powerless either for the punishment of Clodius or the protection of his enemies, Milo now
got his men together and was ready to repel force with force.

The Senate met in the temple of Virtus, which was built
by Cicero's countryman, C. Marius, and on the motion of the
consul Lentulus passed a resolution to thank Cn. Plancius for
protecting Cicero at Thessalonica, to recommend him to the
care of foreign nations, and to the protection of governors of
provinces, quaestors and legati, and to summon the people
from all parts of Italy to defend the interests of the exile.

[1] Plutarch (Cicero, 33) says that the tribune Milo was the first who ventured
to bring Clodius to trial.

When the people heard of this resolution, they were delighted and applauded the senators as they came from their sitting to the theatre[a]. When Lentulus entered, who presided on this day, the whole assembly rose and with outstretched hands thanked him, and with tears of joy showed their affection to Cicero. Clodius came too, but he was received with abuse and threatening gestures. There were verses in the play which the poet Attius seemed to have written for the occasion, and the great actor Aesopus gave them full force, particularly when he turned to the Senate, to the Equites, to all the people, and uttered the verse:

"Exulare sinitis, sinitis pelli, pulsum patimini."

In this play entitled "Brutus" it happened that the name of Tullius occurred, which name was of course applied to Cicero:

"Tullius qui libertatem civibus stabiliverat."

The name Tullius was no doubt Servius Tullius, the founder of Roman liberty, and there is no reason to suppose, as some have done, that Aesopus changed the name in the play and made it Tullius (Pro Sestio, c. 57, 58). But the popular feeling was best shown on an occasion, when the people came in greater crowds than they ever came to hear a speech or give their vote (Pro Sestio, c. 58). Scipio was exhibiting gladiators in honour of his adoptive father who had been dead some years, Q. Metellus Pius, when the tribune P. Sestius, Cicero's steadfast friend, appeared and was received with such shouts of applause that the disposition of the Roman people was never more clearly shown.

Pompeius had now taken up Cicero's case in earnest, and Cicero says that he has the evidence of Pompeius himself that Caesar was not opposed to his restoration (De Prov. Cons. c. 18). Pompeius visited some of the Italian towns to recommend Cicero's interests, he constantly co-operated with the consul Lentulus, and in his harangues to the people proclaimed himself the defender of the exile, and even entreated them in his behalf (In Pis. c. 32). The consul Lentulus summoned the Senate to the temple of Jupiter on the Capitol to consider

---

[a] "In templo Virtutis hoc esse decretum, quum tempore ludorum, qui Virtutis et Honoris dicebantur, populi reditum M. Tullii flagitaverint" (Schol. Bob. in Or. pro Sestio, c. 66).

the question which would be proposed to the popular assembly, the restoration of Cicero. The other consul Metellus made no resistance to the proposal[1]; and the conqueror of the three divisions of the globe read a written speech, in which he declared that the preservation of the state was due to Cicero only; and a very crowded Senate with one dissentient voice from P. Clodius confirmed by their vote the declaration of Cn. Pompeius. The number of votes in favour of Cicero, according to the oration Quum Senatui, &c. (c. 10), was four hundred and seventeen. The author of the oration De Domo (c. 9) says that the price of grain at this time was very high at Rome, but that on the day on which this resolution of the Senate was made prices fell contrary to expectation. If this was true, the dealers had kept their corn back and there was some stock on hand. There was once, if not now, a penalty against the dealers who kept their corn back (Livy, 38. c. 35). On the day after this vote and on the motion of Pompeius the Senate made a resolution that if any person hindered Cicero's return, he should be considered an enemy to the State, as it is said in the oration against Piso (c. 15); but in the speech for Sestius (c. 61), the exact terms of the resolution are given, as we may suppose, and they were to this effect: that no man should watch the heavens (ne quis de caelo servaret) or in any way impede the rogation which would be proposed to the popular assembly; if any man should do so, he would be an enemy to the State, and the matter should immediately be brought before the Senate; and further, if within the five days during which the vote of the people might be taken, it was not taken, Cicero might return to Rome and resume his former station. Quintus immediately wrote to his brother and sent him a copy of the resolution of the Senate[2]. Cicero informed Atticus that he would wait for the enactment of the laws (so it stands in the text), and if there should be opposi-

---

[1] Cicero pro Sestio (c. 62) says, "Ut etiam Q. Metellus consul . . de mea salute rettulerit," which might mean that he made the motion for the S. C. But I am not quite sure what Cicero means. Compare In Pis. c. 15, "de me quum omnes magistratus promulgassent," &c., and "Quum Senatui," c. 10.

[2] The letter to Atticus (III. 26) has been assigned to the year B.C. 58; but Drumann assigns it—correctly, as I think—to B.C. 57.

tion, he would rely on the resolution of the Senate and rather lose his life than remain an exile.

The people met to vote upon Cicero's restoration on the fourth of August. There were voters from all parts of Italy; the shops in Rome were closed; nay, to use the rhetorical language of the author of the oration De Domo (c. 33), even the Italian towns were closed. The voting was in the Campus Martius, and never had it been seen so crowded. Lentulus proposed the bill to the Comitia Centuriata. Cicero's friends distributed the ballots and looked carefully after the voters. If Clodius intended to make any opposition, he was kept in check by Milo and his band. Indeed to this bold tribune Cicero appears to have been principally indebted for his restoration; and that which was accomplished quietly in legal form had been made possible by Milo's armed force (Dion, 39, c. 8; Velleius, ii. 45). The popular vote confirmed the bill, and on the fourth of August Cicero ceased to be an exile. On the same day he left Dyrrachium and on the fifth he reached Brundisium where he found his daughter Tullia.

This fortunate day happened to be his daughter's birthday, the anniversary of the foundation of the colony of Brundisium, and of the temple of Salus or Safety at Rome, near which Atticus lived, three most happy coincidences. Cicero was entertained in the same hospitable house which had received him the year before when he was flying from Italy (vol. iii. p. 458). On the eighth while he was still at Brundisium, he was informed by a letter from his brother that the bill for his return had been enacted at the Comitia Centuriata. After a most honourable reception by the people of Brundisium he set out for Rome. All along the way by which he travelled the Italian towns made holiday to celebrate his coming; the roads were filled with deputations sent from all parts to meet him. As he approached the city every man, who was in any way known, came out to welcome his return; and from the Porta Capena, by which gate he entered the city, the steps of the temples were crowded by the lowest sort, who received him with loud applause. The same popular demonstrations accompanied him to the Capitol, on which and in the Forum there was a wonderful crowd. He has himself told the story of his triumphant return (Ad Att. iv. 1; Pro Sextio, c. 63; In Pis. c. 22). The day was the fourth of September, in the sixteenth month of his exile, as Plutarch and Appian reckon, but if he left Rome about the end of March, B.C. 58, it would be in the eighteenth month (vol. iii. p. 457). Plutarch has reported that even M. Crassus met Cicero and was reconciled in order to please his son Publius, who admired Cicero. Publius, however, was at this time with Caesar in Gallia (B. G. ii. 34).

On the fifth of September Cicero thanked the Senate for what they had done, and thanked them in a written speech which he read on the occasion (Ad Att. iv. 1, 5; Pro Plancio, c. 30). There is extant an oration entitled "Quum Senatui gratias egit," in which Cicero thanked the Senate in general: he thanked the consuls; he thanked Cn. Pompeius, P. Servilius, L. Gellius, L. Ninnius: he thanked Milo and Sestius with the other tribunes who had been friendly to him: he thanked the Praetors; he thanked Cn. Plancius, and his brother Quintus; and he spoke gratefully of the services of his deceased son-in-law Piso. He pardoned his timid friends; he would say nothing about those who had betrayed him. Though he was assailed by some magistrates, betrayed or deserted by others at the time when Clodius was attacking him, he might, if he had followed the advice of many most excellent men, have defended himself by arms, "for the courage which he possessed, and which the Senate were well acquainted with, did not fail him." However he did not choose to defend his own interests by force, and he went away. But "when he left Rome, the laws, the courts, the authority of the magistrates, and of the Senate, plenty, every thing that is holy among men and gods quitted Rome at the same time with himself" (c.14).

If Cicero really wrote this speech (Quum Senatui, &c.), we must form a very low estimate of his sense and of his taste at the time when he returned from exile. In the speeches which are undoubtedly genuine there is much that we may find fault with, but this address to the Senate has no merit, and it has so many defects that some good critics have denied that it is Cicero's work. There is extant also a speech entitled "Quum populo gratias egit," which is not mentioned in the letter to

Atticus. Dion Cassius, however (39. c. 9), says that Cicero gave his thanks in a speech both to the Senate and the people; and we have a speech of thanks to the people, and it is attributed to Cicero on as good external authority as any of his speeches. This speech to the people is very like that to the Senate: it is a kind of abridgment of it in the matter, and the words in many parts are the same. If any reader shall think the first speech bad, there is no doubt that he will think the second a great deal worse*. Drumann remarks that this speech of thanks to the people could not have been delivered on the sixth, the day after the Nones, for that was what the Romans called a black day (Macrob. Sat. i. 15), and it could not have been delivered with propriety on a later day. He assumes that it was delivered on the same day with the speech to the Senate, and that Cicero stepped out of the Senate-house to address the people in the Forum. This is not an unreasonable conjecture; but it will be quite unnecessary, if we assume that Cicero never delivered such a speech to the people, which assumption is a reasonable conclusion from his not mentioning it when he mentions the speech to the Senate. That which Dion read or saw may be that which we now have.

On the fourth and fifth of September there was again scarcity at Rome. The people came in crowds first to the theatre, then to the Senate-house at the instigation of Clodius, and cried out that Cicero was the cause of the scarcity. If the words "eo biduo" (Ad Attic. iv. 1. 6) have been rightly explained here, this popular disturbance was made both on the day of Cicero's return and on the day when he thanked the Senate; and on these two days the Senate also deliberated on

* There is an edition of four of the doubtful orations of Cicero by F. A. Wolf, Berlin, 1801. This edition contains the two orations which I have mentioned and the De Domo, and De Haruspicum Responsis. Wolf's preface contains the history of the controversy about these four orations and some remarks on them. Markland first called in question the genuineness of these orations. Opinions are still divided on the matter, and any man's assertions or even arguments on either side cannot decide the question. Those who would form a judgment of their own must take the trouble of reading these four orations. I venture to say that very few, who can form an opinion, will think that they are worth the trouble of reading.

the scarcity. If the scarcity was very urgent, there is no reason why the Senate should not have discussed the matter on the fourth of September before the hour when Cicero entered Rome, and on the fifth after he had thanked them for his restoration, which he could have done in half an hour. It was the general talk at Rome among the common sort and even among the friends of order (boni) that Pompeius should be appointed to look after the supply of corn, an office which he desired to have, and the people called on Cicero to move the question. He did so, and spoke with great earnestness, though all the men of consular rank were absent except Messala and Afranius; and absent, as Cicero says, because they did not think that they could safely express their opinion. A resolution of the Senate was made to the purport which Cicero recommended, that Pompeius should be asked to undertake the superintendence of the corn supply, and that a law to that effect should be proposed to the popular assembly. The resolution of the Senate was read to the people, and there was loud applause when Cicero's name was heard; and he then addressed the people with the permission of all the magistrates except one praetor and two tribunes who were not present. This is the first occasion on which Cicero tells us that he addressed the people after his return. P. Manutius supposes that this address may be the extant speech entitled, "Quum populo gratias egit," a supposition which could not be admitted, even if the speech were genuine, for in this extant speech, which contains nothing about conferring on Pompeius the superintendence of the corn supply, the writer says that the immortal gods showed their approbation of his restoration by the abundance of the fruits of the earth and the cheapness of provisions (Quum populo, c. 8). On the next day there was a full Senate, and all the consulars were there. The demands of Pompeius were granted. He asked for fifteen legati, and he named Cicero one of them first, saying that Cicero should be like another Pompeius. Cicero accepted the office on condition that the acceptance should not prevent him from being a candidate for the censorship, if the consuls of the next year should hold an election of censors, or from taking what the Romans called a votive legation, or leave of absence on a general pilgrimage to sacred places (Ad Att. iv. 2. 0, xv. 8). But he did not leave Italy, and he transferred the office to his brother Quintus before the end of the year as it seems (Ad Q. Fr. ii. 1. 3). The reconciliation between Pompeius and his humble and despised suppliant (vol. iii. p. 450) seemed now complete. The consuls drew up the bill which would be presented to the popular assembly: it gave to Pompeius all over the world supreme power in the matter of the supply of grain for five years, which was the same length of time that the bill of Vatinius had fixed for Caesar's proconsular government. The Tribune Messius proposed another bill, which as Cicero says, whatever he may mean, gave Pompeius "power over all money," probably over the treasury, a fleet, an army, and greater authority in the provinces than the governors of them. Cicero might well say that the bill proposed by the consuls was moderate compared with this extravagant bill of Messius, which the friends of Pompeius said that he preferred, though Pompeius said that he preferred the bill of the consuls. The men of consular rank expressed their dislike of Messius' bill. Cicero said nothing, because the court of the Pontifices had not yet given a decision about his house. This confession (Ad Att. iv. 1. 7) leads to the conclusion that in return for his services to Pompeius, Cicero expected his patron's assistance in the matter of his house; and if any man should further conclude that Cicero would have supported the bill of Messius if it had been necessary to secure Pompeius' favour, it must be admitted that it is a probable conclusion.

No doubt it was the consular bill which was passed, and it gave Pompeius employment again. When Dion says that Pompeius received proconsular authority in Italy and all other parts of the empire, he appears to be writing carelessly. Plutarch found some authority for telling us that Clodius complained that the scarcity of grain was brought about in order that Pompeius might be invested with power. If Clodius did say so, we do not gain much by his assertion, for the tribune's veracity, particularly on such a matter, cannot be rated high; and the assertion is not consistent with the fact of Pompeius sending his deputies to many places and himself sailing to Sicily, Sardinia, and Africa, to collect grain, with which he filled the market at Rome (Plut. Pomp. c. 50).

It was at this time according to Dion (39. c. 10), though his chronology cannot be trusted, that Cicero wrote a book with a title which imported that it was a defence of his political conduct. It contained a good deal of invective against Caesar, Crassus, and others, whom he did not dare to attack openly. He considered Caesar and Crassus, says the historian, as the men who had been the chief cause of his exile, and that they consented to his return because they could not prevent it. Cicero being afraid that the book might appear in his lifetime, sealed and gave it to his son with injunctions not to read or publish it until his death. It has been conjectured that Dion alludes to what Cicero calls his Anecdota or Anecdoton (Ad Att. ii. 6. xiv. 17), though in the second letter he speaks of the work as unfinished. This may be the work which Asconius also mentions (in Orat. in Toga Cand. p. 83, ed. Orelli), where he is speaking of C. Caesar and M. Crassus being the most active opponents of Cicero when he was a candidate for the consulship.

Cicero says in a letter to Atticus (iv. 2, 2), "I spoke before the Pontifices on the last day of September. The business was conducted by me with great care, and if ever I showed any power of eloquence, or indeed if I never did before, on this occasion certainly the feeling of the great wrong that I had suffered gave me a certain energy of speech. This oration therefore must not be kept from our young men, and I shall soon send you a copy, even if you do not want it." There is extant an oration entitled De Domo, and it is attributed to Cicero. There is the same difference of opinion about the genuineness of it that there is about the speech of thanks to the Senate and that to the people. The first twelve chapters of the speech on his house, which are about one-fifth of the whole, and directed against Clodius, who is addressed as if he were present, are, as the writer admits (c. 12), nothing to the purpose; but he says that he will make amends for this prolixity by the brevity of his speech on the matter which was before the Pontifices, a promise which the writer does not keep.

The writer of the oration De Haruspicum responsis (c. 6)

gives the names of thirteen of the Pontifices who were present when Cicero spoke about his house. The chief Pontifex Caesar was in Gallia and was busy about this time with selling the fifty-three thousand Aduatuci (p. 66) who had fallen into his hands; and another Pontifex was absent from some cause. There were also present the Rex Sacrorum, three Pontifices Minores, and the Flamen Martialis and the Flamen Quirinalis. The Flamen Dialis is not mentioned, and for a good reason: none had been elected since the death of L. Cornelius Merula, B.C. 87 (vol. ii. p. 249, and Tacit. Ann. iii. 58).

The question for this ecclesiastical court was the validity of the dedication by Clodius of the site of Cicero's house. Cicero does not say that any person addressed the court on the side of Clodius. The judgment was (Ad Att. iv. 2, 3.), that if he who affirmed that he had made the dedication had not been appointed by name for that purpose either by a vote of the populus or by a plebiscitum, and had not been appointed to do this act either by a vote of the populus or a plebiscitum, then it was the opinion of the court that the part of the ground which was the matter in dispute could be restored to Cicero without any religious impediment. This was all that the court could do, to declare whether the ground was legally consecrated or not. Perhaps Dion Cassius (39, c. 11) means no more when he says that Cicero persuaded the Pontifices to restore the ground to him as not being consecrated. Dion also says that Cicero's argument was that Clodius had not been legally adopted into a plebeian family (vol. iii. p. 413), consequently he was not legally elected a tribune, and all his acts in his tribuneship were invalid. But the judgment of the Pontifices, as Cicero reports, was independent of the question whether Clodius was legally a tribune, and was founded simply on the illegality of the consecration by whomsoever it was made.

Cicero was congratulated on the judgment by his friends, for it was considered that his ground was virtually restored to him. But Clodius, with the permission of his brother Appius, addressed the people, and said that the Pontifices had decided in his favour, that Cicero was going to take possession of the ground by force, and he urged them to follow himself and

Appius to defend their dear Liberty (p. 72). Some even of the lowest sort were amazed, others laughed at the fellow's impudence; but Cicero had determined not to appear on the ground until the consuls conformably to a resolution of the Senate had made a contract for the rebuilding of Catulus' portico, which had been demolished.

On the first of October there was a full Senate, and all the Pontifices who were Senators were present (Ad Attic. iv. 2. 4, &c.). Cn. Lentulus Marcellinus, one of the consuls elect, was first asked his opinion, and he replied by asking what the Pontifices had done. M. Lucullus, one of the Pontifices, replied that he and his colleagues had given judgment on the question of religion; in the Senate they would give their opinion on the law. Each of the senatorian Pontifices being called in his turn spoke at length in Cicero's favour. When it came to the turn of Clodius to speak, he attempted to waste the day in talking, and after continuing nearly three hours he was at last compelled to conclude by the disgust and clamour of the Senate. A resolution being drawn up in the terms proposed by Marcellinus with one dissentient voice, the tribune Serranus interposed, upon which both of the consuls submitted the tribune's interposition to the consideration of the Senate. The opinions of the Senators were expressed with the greatest solemnity, and were to this effect: that Cicero's house must be restored to him, that a contract should be made for the rebuilding of Catulus' portico, that the resolution of the Senate should be supported by all the magistrates, and that if any acts of violence followed, the Senate would consider they were due to him who had put his veto on their resolution. Serranus was alarmed and Cn. Oppius repeated his old trick (p. 84): he cast off his toga and threw himself at the feet of his son-in-law. Serranus asked one night for consideration: the Senate refused, for they remembered the first of January. The Senate intended that Serranus should either interpose his veto then, or give up his opposition. However, at Cicero's request, a night's delay was granted, and on the second of October the resolution was passed without any opposition from Serranus. The consuls then made a contract for the rebuilding of Catulus' portico, and the undertakers (redemptores) immediately pulled down that which Clodius had erected. With the assistance of assessors the consuls estimated the value of Cicero's house at two million sesterces, though according to his own account he had paid three millions and a half for it (Ad Fam. v. 6, 2); but the estimate of the consuls only applied to the building on the land, and did not comprise the value of the ground, which was of course included in Cicero's purchase. Cicero says nothing about this estimate of his house at Rome; but he says that the rest of the valuation was very shabby, five hundred thousand sesterces for his Tusculan villa, and two hundred and fifty thousand for his country-house at Formiae. People generally were dissatisfied with the valuation. Why then did he not get more? They said, as he says, that it was through his modesty, because he neither objected to what was offered nor asked for more. That however, he tells us, was not so, for his behaviour might even have helped him. The real reason, as he informs Atticus, was that those men, whom Atticus knows well, who had clipped his wings, did not wish them to grow again; but they are already growing, as he hopes. When he wrote this letter to Atticus, the building of his house was going on, and he was repairing the villa at Formiae. He had put up for sale his villa at Tusculum (Ad Att. iv. 2. 7). We collect from this letter that he was in pecuniary difficulties, which were probably owing in some measure to his exile. But he was always a man of great expense and often wanted money.

Cicero describes (Ad Att. iv. 3) at this time the wretched condition of Rome, a city without police, distracted by riots, in fact without any government at all, though it affected to govern the world. This military state had not even a military force in the capital to protect it against turbulent citizens. On the third of November the workmen were driven from Cicero's ground by an armed band, and the portico of Catulus which had already risen nearly as high as the roof was thrown down. The house of Cicero's brother Quintus was damaged by stones thrown from Cicero's ground and then set on fire by the order of Clodius, in the sight of the city, as Cicero expresses it, and to the great sorrow of all people. Clodius went about like a madman thinking of nothing but

how he should get rid of his enemies, and promising the slaves
their freedom. It is almost incredible that a man should have
been allowed to disturb the city by his riots, when the Senate
could have armed the consuls with such authority that in an
hour they might have got rid of the turbulent demagogue and
his band by a vigorous and salutary exercise of authority.
But Clodius, we must assume, had many friends in the Senate,
and Cicero though recalled from exile had not many. On
the eleventh of November, as Cicero was going down the
Sacra Via, Clodius followed him with his men shouting and
armed with stones, sticks and swords. Cicero retreated into
the vestibule of Tettius Damio. He was not alone: he too had
his men about him, for he says that those who were with him
easily prevented Clodius' men from entering the vestibule and
could have killed Clodius. On the next day Clodius attempted
to take possession of and burn Milo's house in the Germalus.
He came in the morning at the fifth hour with men furnished
with shields, swords and lighted torches. Clodius did not lead
the assault: he fixed himself in the house of P. Sulla as his
camp from which he would make his attack. But Q. Flaccus
came out of another house belonging to Milo at the head of a
resolute body of men, and killed all the most notorious of
Clodius' blackguards, and he would have killed Clodius too, if
he had not retired into the inner part of Sulla's house. This
Sulla appears to be the man whom Cicero once defended
(vol. iii. p. 367). The Senate met on the fourteenth, but
Clodius stayed at home[7]. The consul elect Marcellinus behaved admirably in Cicero's opinion: all the senators were in
a state of irritation. The consul Metellus wasted the time by
abusive talk, and he was assisted by Appius the brother of
Clodius, and by another whom Cicero does not name, but he
was an intimate friend of Atticus, who in a letter had spoken
so truly of his firmness and goodness, as Cicero ironically says.
Perhaps Hortensius was the man. Sestius was in a great
passion: and P. Clodius afterwards threatened the city if the
elections should not be held, for he was a candidate for the

[7] Some persons read the text of Cicero as saying that Sulla came to the Senate; but I do not.

aedileship. The motion of Marcellinus was to this effect, and he delivered it from a written paper: that the consideration of the question of Cicero's ground, of the incendiary fires, and of Cicero's danger should precede the holding of the comitia. Milo[a] put up a notice that he would observe the heavens on all the election days, which was the same as saying that he would stop the elections. The meeting of the Senate was followed by the turbulent popular harangues of Metellus, Appius and P. Clodius. The result was, says Cicero, that the elections would take place, if Milo did not prevent them.

On the twentieth of November at midnight Milo entered the Campus Martius with a large force, and though Clodius had with him a choice body of runaway slaves, he did not venture to appear. Milo stayed in the Campus till mid-day to the great delight of the citizens, and "with the greatest glory," as Cicero says. If Cicero did not put himself at the head of armed men, he had no objection to others doing it; and indeed, if all that he tells us of Clodius is true, the government was powerless, and it was time for every man to look after himself.

Metellus now challenged Milo to make his opposition (obnuntiatio) on the following day and in the Forum: there was no occasion to go to the Campus in the night; he would be in the Comitium, that is, in a certain part of the Forum at the first hour to meet his adversary. Accordingly on the twenty-first of November while it was still night Milo came to the Comitium; but Metellus, who wished by a trick to anticipate Milo, went at daybreak into the Campus in a stealthy way by a circuitous road. Milo overtook Metellus at a place called the groves, forbade all proceeding (obnuntiat), and Metellus retired amidst the abuse of the praetor Q. Valerius Flaccus. On the twenty-second was the Nundinae[b],

[a] "Proscripsit ... servatorum." The nominative to "proscripsit" is omitted in the MSS., and we cannot supply "Marcellinus." Orelli has supplied "Scutius;" but I think with Drumann that the word which has been omitted is "Milo." Mongault in his French translation has "Milo."

[b] Macrob. Sat. l. 16: "Julius Caesar sexto decimo auspiciorum libro negat nundinis contionem advocari posse, id est, cum populo agi, idcoque nundinis Romanorum haberi comitia non posse;" also "Rutilius scribit Romanos instit-

when there was no public meeting, nor on the twenty-third. The letter to Atticus (iv. 3), in which Cicero tells him all this news, was written on the twenty-fourth of November during the early morning of that day long before it was light. Milo was then already in the Campus for the purpose of stopping the elections. Marcellus one of the candidates for the aedileship, and a neighbour to Cicero, was snoring so loud that Cicero could hear him; which means that he was indifferent about the election. It was reported to Cicero that the vestibule of Clodius was deserted; there were only a few fellows in rags there, without even a lantern among them. The party of Clodius complained that Cicero schemed all this, but they knew nothing, he says, of the spirit and prudence of the hero Milo. Cicero tells Atticus that he does not think that the comitia will be held, and he thinks that Clodius will be brought to trial by Milo, if he should not be killed first. If he should come in Milo's way, Cicero foresees that he will be killed. Cicero tells his friend that his mind is vigorous, even more vigorous than in the days of his great prosperity. His private affairs were in a poor condition; but he was repaying his brother Quintus, though Quintus did not wish it, as far as he could without exhausting his means, and for this purpose he was availing himself of the assistance of his friends.

On the tenth of December Milo's tribunate ended. The new tribunes, L. Racilius, Cn. Plancius, and some others were friendly to Cicero. The tribune P. Rutilius Lupus summoned the Senate when the feast days were at hand in December, from which we conclude that the consuls of this year had already quitted Rome for their provinces, Lentulus for Cilicia and Metellus for nearer Spain. The time when the Senate met would be about the middle of December, after which day the Saturnalia and other days on which the Senate could not meet, occupied part of the time to the end of the

<hr/>

tulisse nundinas ut certo quidem diebus in agris rustici opus facerent, nono autem die intermisso rure ad mercatum legesque accipiendas Romam venirent." But we read of a contio on the day of the Nundinae (Ad Att. L i. 14. 1). A lex Hortensia made the Nundinae "fastos," "ut rustici qui nundinandi causa in urbem venicbant litos componerent: nefasto enim die praetori fari non licebat." This lex, however, would not justify a "contio."

month. About two hundred senators met. Lupus discussed the matter of the Campanian land, in fact Caesar's agrarian law, for this subject was not yet set at rest; but he did not ask the opinion of the senators, and no one spoke. The consul elect Marcellinus said that in the absence of Pompeius the Campanian question could not be properly discussed. Racilius then spoke of the trials for the late disturbances, and asked the opinion of Marcellinus, who said that the trials ought to proceed, that the praetor[1] urbanus should appoint the jurymen, and then the comitia should be held. The tribunes C. Cato and Cassius were in favour of the elections being held first: they were on the side of P. Clodius. Philippus, the other consul elect, agreed with Marcellinus. Racilius put the question to Cicero first of those who were not in office. Cicero spoke at length of the turbulence of Clodius, and charged him as if he was on his trial. The Senato was pleased, and Antistius Vetus spoke highly of Cicero's speech: he was of opinion that the trials should be held before the elections. Clodius, who was then invited to speak, tried to waste the day in talking, and was greatly incensed at Racilius. His noisy followers were heard from the outside, from the Graecostasis and the steps of the Senate-house, crying out against Q. Sextilius and the friends of Milo, as Cicero supposed. This disturbance caused some alarm: the Senato broke up to the great dissatisfaction of the whole body, and nothing more was done. Clodius was not brought to trial, nor was he elected aedile this year (Ad Q. Fr. ii. 1).

At the end of this letter to his brother which, as Cicero says, contains the proceedings of one day in the Senate, Quintus is urged to set sail before December was over. Quintus was now in Sardinia looking after the supply of corn, for he had taken the office of legatus under Pompeius in place of his brother Marcus; but Quintus did not return for some time.

In this year the consul Cornelius Lentulus Spinther wished to make his young son Spinther a member of the College of

---

[1] If we read, " et ipse judices praetor urbanus sortiretur," Cicero ad Qu. Fr. ii. 1, 2.

Augurs. There was a law (Dion, 39, c. 17) which declared that two persons of the same Gens should not hold the same priesthood at the same time, and Cornelius Faustus, son of the Dictator Sulla, was already a member of the College. The consul evaded the law by giving his son in adoption to one of the Manlii Torquati, and he was then elected.

This is all that our authorities report of the events at Rome to the end of B.C. 57, a history barren of all instruction, a story of miserable quarrels, unrelieved by the record of a single public measure of any utility, except one which was only useful according to Roman notions, the supplying of a hungry capital with food. In excuse for the Romans we may say, that if they had at this moment trusted as we do to the principles of demand and supply, the dealers would have regulated their supply by the demands of those who could pay for it, and not by the wants of those who could not; and thus those who wished to eat and had not the means of buying would have perished of hunger. The fault of the Roman system was that the occasional appearance of the State in the market as purchaser and then as vendor at a low price disturbed the reckonings of the dealers, who, if the State had kept quiet, would soon have found out what was the annual consumption of Rome and would have brought sufficient to the market. There was at this time in Rome a large number of people, many of whom had been attracted to the city by the public allowances, the bounty of the rich and the chances of an idle but precarious life; and these people, who have existed and do exist and will exist in all large cities, must receive help in some way, or they will die. The regular artisans of Rome were a numerous body and could earn their living as artisans do now, when trade is not disturbed by some great calamity or extravagant speculation of knaves; and the State might safely have left their demands to be supplied by the regular dealers. But it was this indefinite body of idlers, of men with no occupation, immigrants from all parts of Italy and now from all parts of the world, men ready to enlist themselves under any leader to disturb the peace of the city, which made the difficulty of the administration at Rome. It was necessary to supply these men with food in some way, when they could not get it. The city of Rome accomplished this purpose by distributing corn instead of levying a rate on the rich and the industrious, as we do. Our system leaves the trade in corn undisturbed, and as the total annual consumption of a large city is known within certain limits, and rises and falls in price are the certain index of the state of the market, the supply is furnished with perfect punctuality, and could only fail in modern times by some calamity beyond the reach of calculation, such as a scarcity in all corn-growing countries. Scarcity at Rome could evidently exist at the same time with abundance in foreign parts, which is proved by the fact that the superintendent of the corn supply could find corn when he went to look for it. We must not suppose that the Romans robbed the Sardinians, Sicilians, and the provincials of Africa of their grain, though they may have given a low price for it in times of great dearth[a] at Rome. But if the Romans could find corn abroad when they wanted it to avert famine, they would have had a better supply by letting the corn countries know that they might bring it to Rome when they liked, and that the State would take no part in this business. In antient times the slowness with which news was transmitted, and the difficulty of knowing the state of the Roman market would be a hindrance to the corn-dealers: but even in those days, Sicily, Sardinia, and the African coast were not too remote to receive weekly intelligence of the Roman market[b].

[a] We may form some idea of the poverty which was crowded in Rome when we know that in the largest parish of wealthy and commercial London, with a population of 220,000, the parish board relieves a weekly average of 9000 to 10,000 poor, and disburses annually from £80,000 to £90,000. (*Times*, Sept. 14, 1869.) In 1870, the population of the metropolis was estimated at 3,215,000, the pauper class at 141,000, and the expenditure on the relief of this class was £1,468,000. (*Times*, May 6, 1871.) To this we must add the enormous amount of money given as charity.

[b] The chapter, "Of the Police of Corn in France," in Arthur Young's *Travels in France*, is worth reading.

CHAPTER VI.

CAESAR AND THE VENETI.

B.C. 56.

Caesar supposing that Gallia was reduced to submission set out for Illyricum at the beginning of winter, for he wished to make himself acquainted with that country and the people. Illyricum was included in his commission; and there will be an opportunity of speaking of it afterwards (B. G. v. 1). But Caesar had other business to do besides visiting Illyricum, if he really went there. Cicero (in Vatin. c. 16) in B.C. 56 speaks of Caesar being at Aquileia and talking of the affairs of Rome with some Romans who visited him there. In the meantime a fresh war suddenly broke out in Gallia in this manner.

Young Crassus had wintered with the seventh legion in the country of the Andes, nearer to the Atlantic than the troops which wintered among the Turones and Carnutes. The Andes are the people whom Tacitus names the Andecavi, and the copyists of Ptolemy (ii. 8. 8) have named Ondicavae. They were west of the Turones, and their position is defined by the town Juliomagus or Civitas Andecavorum, now Angers on the Mayenne, one of the northern affluents of the Loire. As there was scarcity of corn among the Andes, Crassus sent several praefecti and tribunes to the neighbouring states to look for supplies, and among them T. Terrasidius to the country of the Sesuvii[1], M. Trebius Gallus to the Curiosolitae, and Q. Velanius with T. Silius to the Veneti. The position of the

---

[1] "Sesuvii." There is great variation in the MSS. in the writing of this name. See Schneider's note. Aldus printed "Unellos" instead of Sesuvios.

Sesuvii, if this is the true form of the word, is doubtful: it has been conjectured that the diocese of Séez which bordered on that of Le Mans and Evreux may represent their position. The position of the Curiosolitae is supposed to be indicated by Corseult, a village in Bretagne between Dinan and Lamballe. There are said to be Roman remains at Corseult. Thus the Curiosolitae would be north of the Veneti, and the Redones* (Rennes) would be their neighbours on the east (p. 47).

The Veneti were one of the Armoric states of the Celtae. Their neighbours on the south were the Namnetes or Nannetes (Nantes), on the east the Redones, and on the north the Curiosolitae, and the Osismi in the north-west part of Bretagne, in the department of Finistère. The chief town of the Veneti was Dariorigum, now Vannes on the bay of Morbihan in the French department of Morbihan, which may correspond nearly to the country of the Veneti. The Veneti were the most powerful of all the maritime peoples who occupied the peninsula of Bretagne. They had many vessels in which they sailed to the island Britannia, to Cornwall and the parts along the south coast of England, as we may assume. They surpassed all their neighbours in skill and experience in naval affairs; and as the Atlantic was stormy and offered no shelter to the navigator except in the few harbours along the coast which were in possession of the Veneti, they levied tolls on most of the traders who visited those seas. The Veneti set the example of resistance to the Romans by detaining Silius and Velanius in the expectation of thus recovering the hostages whom they had given to Crassus. As Caesar remarks (c. 8), it is the nature of the Galli to form hasty and sudden resolves. The Sesuvii and Curiosolitae made Terrasidius and Trebius prisoners, and quickly sending messengers to one another they agreed through their chiefs to do nothing except conformably to the decision of the confederation and to risk their fortunes together. They stirred up the other neighbouring states also to maintain the liberty which their fathers had transmitted and not to submit to Roman slavery. All the

* There is also the town of Redon, lower down on the Vilaine than Rennes. Redon retains the same Redones exactly, with the exception of the Latin termination, "es."

coast people were soon induced to enter into a combination, and they sent a joint message to Crassus, by which he was informed that if he would have his own men back, he must return the hostages.

Caesar was too far off, when he received from Crassus the news of this Armoric confederation, to do any thing more than send orders to build ships of war on the Loire, to get rowers from the Provincia, which bordered on the Mediterranean, and to collect sailors and steersmen. The orders were promptly obeyed, and Caesar, as he says, set out to join his army " as soon as the season allowed; " but the time when he left Italy will appear more clearly from the date of the congress at Luca in the early part of this year (Chapter vii.). The Veneti and the other states hearing of his arrival, and knowing well what a crime they had committed in making prisoners of men who had come to them under the sacred character of ambassadors, made preparations for war proportionate to the danger which threatened them and got their vessels ready. Caesar here (B. G. iii. 9) represents the praefecti and tribunes sent by Crassus as ambassadors; but it is plain that Crassus sent them to make requisitions on states which had submitted (B. G. ii. 34, iii. 7), and Caesar's real ground of complaint was that after submission these Armoric people had made prisoners of the men who were sent to execute their commander's orders. This is an instance of false colouring from which the Commentaries are not always free.

The Veneti trusted much in the natural difficulties of their country. On the land the roads were interrupted by aestuaries; the navigation was difficult to those who were unacquainted with the coast, the ports were few; and it was supposed that want of food would prevent the Roman armies from staying long: and even if all these things should turn out contrary to the expectation of the Veneti, still they were powerful on the sea, and the Romans had no ships nor were they familiar with the shallows, the ports and the islands in those parts where they were going to carry on war, and navigation, as the Veneti knew, was a very different thing in a closed sea such as the Mediterranean from what it was in the wide and open ocean. With these opinions they fortified the

towns, stored corn in them collected from the country, and
brought together as many ships as they could into Venetia,
the territory of the Veneti, for it was certain that Caesar
would first make his attack here. The Veneti and the other
combined states gained or attempted to gain as allies the
Osismi, Lexovii, Namnetes, Ambiliati, Morini, Diablintes and
Menapii. The position of the Lexovii is indicated by the
town of Lisieux between Caen and Evreux, in the department
of Calvados. The position of the Ambiliati is unknown. The
Morini were on the coast opposite to Britain, and the Menapii
were still farther north (p. 47): it is evident that the Armoric
states would have no help from such allies. The Diablintes,
who were somewhere on the Mayenne, and the Namnetes and
Osismi, who were neighbours of the Veneti, might give some
aid. The confederates even applied for help to Britannia,
which Caesar describes as lying right opposite "to those
parts," but he does not say whether the Britons sent any
ships.

The coast of the two French departments of Finistère and
Morbihan is cut deep by numerous bays, inlets and aestuaries,
and bordered with small islands from Brest as far south as the
aestuary of the Vilaine. But we shall see that Caesar's operations were limited to the coast of the department of Morbihan,
which extends from the aestuary of Quimperlé to the mouth
of the Vilaine and corresponds to Caesar's description, for it is
broken by numerous aestuaries (concisa aestuariis), which
would make a march along the shore of this country very
tedious.

The difficulties of a war against the Armoric states have
been described; but still Caesar was urged to undertake it by
the wrong done in making prisoners of the Roman envoys, by
the revolt after hostages had been given, by the combination
of so many states, and particularly by the fear that the other
nations of Gallia might do the same, if the Armoric states
were not punished. He knew well that nearly all the Galli
were eager for change, and easily and quickly stirred up to
war; and further, that all men naturally love liberty and hate
servitude. Accordingly before any more of the Gallic states
could combine, he determined to divide his forces and distribute

them over a large part of the Gallic territory. He sent T. Labienus with some cavalry to the country of the Treviri, who bordered on the Rhine. His instructions were to visit the Remi and the other Belgae and to keep them to their duty; and if the Germans, who were said to have been invited by the Belgae to help them, should attempt to force a passage over the river in boats, he must prevent them. P. Crassus with twelve legionary cohorts and a large body of cavalry marched into Aquitania, to prevent the people in those parts from sending any aid to the people of Celtica and to hinder the combination of so many nations. Q. Titurius Sabinus, a legatus, with three legions, was sent to the country of the Unelli, Curiosolitae and Lexovii with the view of keeping the people of those parts in check and preventing them from uniting their forces. The words of Caesar literally might mean that Sabinus entered the country of these three several states, but it appears (c. 17) that Sabinus entered the country of the Unelli, the Cotantin of the ante-revolutionary period, the present department of Manche, and so he would be between the Curiosolitae and the Lexovii[a]. D. Brutus, a young man, was set over the fleet and the Gallic ships, which Caesar had ordered to assemble from the country of the Pictones and Santones and the other parts which had been reduced to obedience. The Pictones, whose name is represented by Poitou, and the Santones (Saintonge) occupied the coast between the lower Loire and the great aestuary of the Garonne. Brutus was ordered to go against the Veneti as soon as he could, and Caesar set out for this country with his men. Sabinus and Crassus had between them four legions and two cohorts, which would leave three legions and eight cohorts with Caesar; for there is no reason to assume, as Goeler does, that Galba's legion remained among the Allobroges (p. 70). The author of the " Histoire de César " conjectures that one legion was put on board Caesar's fleet.

The towns of the Veneti were built at the extremities of tongues of land, as Caesar names them, and promontories, so that

---

[a] Dion (39, c. 40) says that D. Brutus came to Caesar with ships from the interior sea, the Mediterranean; but Caesar says nothing of these ships, and there are good reasons for not accepting Dion's narrative.

when the tide rose, which it did once in every twelve hours, these towns were separated from the main land and could not be reached on foot, nor was it safe to approach them in ships, for when the tide turned and ebbed, the vessels might be damaged in the shoal waters. The examination of a good map of this part of France will explain Caesar's text. The most remarkable of these promontories is the peninsula of Quiberon, a long narrow strip of land which runs out southwards from the main and is insulated at high water. Caesar attempted to take these maritime towns in the following manner. The sea was excluded from the parts flooded at high water by making mounds of earth and moles, which were raised as high as the walls of a town. But when the capture of the place was imminent, the Veneti would bring up a large number of ships, which they could easily do, and putting on board all their moveables would go to the nearest towns and there defend themselves with the like advantages of position. A single mound or mole might be sometimes sufficient for making the approach to these Venetian sea towns; but in some cases, as Goeler remarks (p. 95), it might be necessary to make two parallel moles, and to exclude the sea from the space between them. Thus the war was carried on during a large part of the summer to the advantage of the Veneti, for the Roman ships were detained by bad weather, and the difficulties of navigation were great in an immense open sea, where the tides were high and the ports few, indeed scarcely any. The enemy were not under such disadvantages, for their ships were built and equipped in a different way. The bottom was flatter than that of the Roman ships and so the enemy's vessels could settle more easily on the shoals when the tide ebbed. The head and stern of the Venetian ships were built very high to enable them to resist the large waves and the storms. The ships were entirely of oak and strong enough to withstand any sea. The cross beams of these vessels were a foot deep and secured by iron bolts as thick as a man's thumb. Instead of ropes they used iron chains as cables for the anchors[4]. The

---

[4] Strabo (195) has here made a great mistake if his text is right or he has been understood right; for he appears to say that the sails were held by chains

sails were skins with the hair on, and tanned hides made thin, either because the Veneti had no flax and were unacquainted with the use of it, or, as it is more probable, because ordinary sails were not strong enough to resist the ocean storms and the violent winds, nor suitable for navigating such heavy ships. In opposing these vessels the only advantage that the Romans had was in the speed of their ships and the use of oars. In every other respect the Veneti had the superiority. The Roman vessels could do no damage with the beak to ships of such solidity, nor owing to the height of the Venetian vessels could missiles be easily discharged into them, and for the same reason it was difficult to seize them with grappling-irons. Besides all this, when the wind blew hard and the Venetian ships sailed before it, they could resist the storm better than the Roman ships, and settle down safer in shoal water, and when they were left aground by the ebb tide, they had no reason to be afraid of rocks and reefs.

Several of the towns of the Veneti were stormed, but Caesar discovered that all his labour was thrown away, and that the flight of the enemy could not be stopped by taking these places, and he could do them no harm. He therefore determined, as he says, to wait for his fleet, which seems to mean the complete fleet, for his narrative implies that he had already made some use of ships. As soon as all Caesar's ships were assembled and were seen by the enemy, the Veneti came out of port and put to sea with about two hundred and twenty vessels equipped with all kinds of arms, and took their position right opposite to the Romans. At this season of the year, the prevailing winds on this coast are east or north-east in the morning, and a dead calm comes on about mid-day. Such a wind would enable the Roman fleet to leave the Loire early in the morning and sail towards the Bay of Quiberon, which is bounded on the west by the peninsula of Quiberon and on the east by that part of the coast which terminates in Pointe St. Jacques[1]. At the same

instead of ropes. He says that the ships of the Veneti were caulked with seatang.—See Oruskurd's note.

[1] The author of the "Histoire de César" (p. 126) and Goeler refer to a memoir by Captain the Comte de Grandpré in the Recueil de la Société des

time the Venetian fleet could get out of the mouth of the river Auray by the passage which connects the bay of Morbihan with the sea, and the battle would be fought in the Bay of Quiberon off the heights of St. Gildas, from which Caesar and his troops had a full view of the spectacle. Neither Brutus, who commanded Caesar's fleet, nor the tribunes and centurions who severally had charge of the ships were quite clear what plan of battle they should adopt.

Caesar's description of the battle is very short. Dion Cassius (30 c. 40—43) has a much longer description, which contains some things which are not in Caesar and omits others. We may conclude that he had read Caesar, but it is difficult to say whether he had any other authority, or added to Caesar's description something of his own invention. However, all his military descriptions are useless, and clearly the work of a man who had a very imperfect conception of what he was writing about.

The Romans in previous conflicts had discovered that they could not injure the enemy's ships by the beaks of their vessels (B. G. iii. 14). They had also raised wooden turrets on their decks, but still the high sterns of the Venetian ships towered above the Romans, who could not discharge their missiles with much effect from a lower position, and those of the Galli came down upon the Romans with the greater force. The Romans had however prepared one contrivance which was very useful. They had long poles, not unlike those which were used in attacking fortifications and pulling down breastworks; and at the end of the poles there were fastened pieces of iron curved like a pruning-hook and sharpened at the end[a].

Antiquaires de France, t. II. 1820, who has fixed the place of this naval battle. I have not seen this valuable essay, but I have no difficulty in accepting the author's conclusions. If the Roman fleet was at the mouth of the Loire early in the morning, which we may assume, there is no other place from which the Venetian fleet could have come out to meet them at this hour except the estuary of the Auray. If we suppose the naval fight to have taken place somewhere on the north side of the peninsula of Quiberon, innumerable difficulties will arise.

[a] This "falx" is described by Vegetius (v. 15). When Caesar says not unlike "murales falces," he means, as Schneider says, hooks like those which the Germans use in pulling down walls to stop the spread of a fire (Feuerhaken).

When these hooks had laid hold of the ropes, which fastened the yards to the masts, the Roman vessel was put in motion by the oars, the hooks gripped hard on the ropes which were cut or broken, the yards tumbled down, and as the Gallic ships depended entirely on their sails and tackle, they became useless. It seems that the cutting-hooks must have been fixed in some way to the Roman ships.

When the Gallic vessels were brought to this condition, the victory depended on courage alone, in which, says Caesar, the Romans were very superior to the enemy, and they were animated by the presence of the general and all his army, who could see every act of superior valour; for all the hills and higher grounds were occupied by the Roman soldiers, who looked down on the ships which were fighting close to the shore.

Those ships whose yards had fallen were surrounded by two or three Roman ships, and the men made every effort to board the enemy. Many vessels were taken in this way, and the enemy seeing that the battle was lost attempted to escape. The ships which were not disabled were turned before the wind, when all at once the sea became so smooth and calm that they could not stir, for they had no oars. This singular phenomenon of the wind suddenly dropping is one of those facts recorded by Caesar in his brief manner which fix on his history the stamp of truth (p. 111). The Romans had now no trouble in dealing with the enemy, for they followed and took the Venetian ships one by one. Very few escaped to land and were saved by the approach of night. The battle had continued from the fourth hour to sunset, or, if it was fought about the autumnal equinox, from ten in the morning.

This victory terminated the war with the Armoric states, in which all the young men, and all those of maturer age, who were distinguished for talent and rank, took part, and all their ships were brought together. Those who survived this great defeat, having no place of refuge nor any means of defending their towns, surrendered themselves and all their property. Caesar thought it necessary to make an example and to teach barbarians, as he says, to respect the rights of ambassadors,

Such hooks, I have been told, are or were used in French villages for the same purpose.

as he again untruly names the officers who were sent by
Crassus in quest of grain. Accordingly he put to death all
the Venetian Senate, as he terms the great council, and sold
the rest of the people by auction. He says "the rest" which
must mean all whom he could seize. He has not said, as he
does on another occasion (ii. 33), how many were sold, but we
may infer that he depopulated the country of the Veneti at
least; and it appears from a later book (vii. 75) that all the
Armoric states must have been greatly reduced by this unfortunate war. The only naval power in Gallia that could be
formidable to the Romans was totally destroyed, and neither
the Veneti nor their allies gave the proconsul any more
trouble. While Caesar was carrying on his campaign against
the Veneti, Q. Titurius Sabinus with his troops entered the
country of the Unelli. Viridovix was at the head of the
Unelli, and he had the supreme command over all the revolted
states from which he had got together an army and large
forces[1]. Within a few days after the arrival of Sabinus in the
country of the Unelli, the Aulerci Eburovices[2] and the
Lexovii massacred their respective Senates, because they would
not give their consent to the war, closed the town gates and
joined Viridovix. There were also assembled from all parts of
Gallia a great number of desperate men and robbers, whom
the hope of booty and love of fighting made averse from
agriculture and daily labour. Sabinus having selected a
suitable position kept within his camp, though Viridovix had
placed himself right opposite at the distance of two miles,
and by bringing out his troops daily gave the Roman an

[1] Caesar says, "exercitum magnasque copias coegerat." A man who wishes
to explain the Commentaries would not willingly omit any thing which Caesar has
said; but it is sometimes difficult to discover his meaning. Schneider affirms,
and probably he is right, that when Caesar writes "copias cogi" or "coactas" he
always means men, not things, such as corn or provisions. Probably then Viridovix
had what might be called an army, and a rabble also; which may explain why
he was so easily defeated. We read in other parts of the Commentaries of there
being many idle men in Gallia, who hated work and were ready for any thing
that promised plunder or profit. The number of such men would be increased by
the devastation and disorder which would prevail in a country where war had
been carried on for three years.

[2] The Aulerci Eburovices were south of the Seine. Their chief town was
Mediolanum, which is represented by Evreux, in the department of Eure.

opportunity of fighting. The consequence was that Sabinus was not only despised by the enemy, but somewhat blamed by his own men, and so strongly were the enemy convinced of his fear that they ventured to come even up to the rampart of the Roman camp. Sabinus adopted this defensive attitude because he did not think that a subordinate commander should hazard a battle against such a large force, especially in the absence of the general-in-chief, except on favourable ground or unless some good opportunity offered. The opinion of the enemy that Sabinus was afraid being firmly fixed, the Roman selected for his purpose a crafty fellow, a Gaul, one of the auxiliaries who were with him, and induced him by great gifts and promises of more to pass over to the Galli. The man went as a deserter, and conformably to his instructions he informed the enemy of the alarm of the Romans, of the straits in which Caesar was kept by the Veneti, and he affirmed that on the following night Sabinus intended to draw his men unseen from the camp and go to help Caesar. When the enemy received this report, there was a universal cry that such an opportunity ought not to be lost, and that the camp must be attacked. The Galli were moved to this resolution by several circumstances, the previous inactivity of Sabinus, the cause of which was confirmed by the deserter, the scarcity of food among themselves for which little provision had been made, the hope of the successful resistance of the Veneti, and finally by the readiness with which men believe what they wish. The Galli would not let Viridovix and the other commanders break up the general meeting till they consented to allow them to take their arms and attack the Romans. Their wish was granted, and exulting as in a certain victory the Galli collected cuttings of trees and brush-wood for the purpose of filling up the Roman ditch, and advanced against the camp.

The Roman camp was on a height to which there was a gradual ascent of about one mile. The Galli hurried up the hill at great speed, to allow the Romans no time to recover from their alarm and to make ready for the defence. But the enemy were out of breath when they reached the camp, and Sabinus encouraging his men gave the signal which they were eagerly expecting. While the Galli were still encumbered by the bundles which they were carrying, Sabinus suddenly ordered a sally to be made from two gates of the camp, probably the gates on the two sides, for the Romans would resist the enemy in front and thus keep them employed there, while they attacked them on the two flanks. The enemy did not stand the Roman onset for a moment, but immediately turned their backs and fled. The Romans, who were quite fresh, following the fugitives who were embarrassed by one another in their flight and by the bundles which they threw down[*], killed a great number of them, and the cavalry pursuing the remainder left only a few alive of those who had escaped from the rout. Thus it happened that at the same time Sabinus heard of the naval fight and Caesar of the victory of Sabinus, and all the states immediately surrendered to Sabinus; for as the disposition of the Galli is ready and prompt to begin a war, so their resolution is feeble, and they show little fortitude in enduring defeat. This remark of Caesar on the character of the Galli is the same as Livy's (x. 28) who says that in the onset they are more than men, but at the close of the fight less than women[1].

The author of the "Histoire de César" (p. 130) supposes that the site of the victory of Sabinus is a hill which is part of the high lands which separate the basin of the Sée from that of the Célune, where there are now remains of a camp named du Chastellier, seven kilomètres east of Avranches in the department of Manche. But this is only a conjecture.

On arriving in Aquitania (iii. 20) P. Crassus remembered that he was going to carry on a campaign in those parts where a few years before the legatus L. Valerius Praeconinus had been defeated and killed, and from which the proconsul L. Manilius had fled with the loss of his baggage (vol. ii. p. 454). It was necessary therefore to be very circumspect. Having secured his supplies and summoned a large number of good

[*] This is the meaning of "impedimentis," and I think Dion (39, c. 45) understood it so. This chapter of Dion is clearly taken only from Caesar's text, and a comparison of it with Caesar shows how he paraphrased and embellished his originals.

[1] See Machiavelli's chapter, Discorsi III. 36: "La cagione perchè i Francesi sono stati e sono ancora giudicati nelle zuffe da principio più che uomini e dipoi meno che femmine."

soldiers, whose names were on the muster-rolls of Tolosa, Carcaso (Carcassonne) and Narbo (Narbonne), three towns of the neighbouring Provincia, Crassus led his army into the country of the Sotiates, whose name appears to be preserved in Sos, a place near Eause in the department of Gers. The Sotiates were the neighbours of the Elusates, who will be mentioned hereafter. The Sotiates, who had got together a large force of infantry and cavalry in which arm they were very strong, attacked with their cavalry the Romans on their march. When the cavalry was repulsed and the Romans were pursuing, the enemy all at once showed their infantry which had been placed in a defile in ambuscade, and now falling on the Romans, who were in disorder, renewed the battle. The fight was long and furious; the enemy trusting to their former victories and believing that the safety of all Aquitania depended on their courage; the Romans eager to show what they could do without the general-in-chief and the rest of the legions under their young commander. At last the enemy exhausted by wounds turned their backs: a large number were killed, and Crassus continuing his march attacked the town of the Sotiates. But he met with a stout resistance, and it was necessary to make a regular siege, a fact which shows that Crassus had with him a body of fabri or engineers. The siege was made in the Roman fashion with covered galleries (vineae) to protect the men while they were raising the earthworks and pushing forward the towers. The enemy made sallies, and drove shafts under the vineae and earthworks, in which the Aquitani showed great skill, for they worked copper mines in many parts of the country; but when they saw that the activity of the besiegers rendered defence useless, they offered to submit. The surrender was accepted and they were commanded to give up their arms. While the Romans were occupied about this matter, Adcantuannus, who had the supreme command, attempted to sally out of the town at another part with his six hundred "devoted," whom the Aquitani named "soldurii." It was the fashion of these "soldurii" to attach themselves to a chieftain in whose service they enjoyed all the good things of life: if the chieftain came to a violent end, the followers either shared his fortune or committed suicide, and within the memory of man no instance had occurred of one of the "soldurii" refusing to die when the head of the band had been killed (vol. ii. 450). When the "soldurii" were attempting to break out of the town, a shout was raised at that part of the Roman lines, the men ran to their arms and there was a fierce contest. Adcantuannus was driven back into the town, but Crassus granted him the same terms of surrender as before*.

After taking the arms of the townsmen and hostages Crassus advanced against the Vocates and Tarusates. The position of the Tarusates is uncertain, but the Vocates may be the Vasatii of Ptolemy (ii. 7. 15), whose chief town was Cossio, or Cossium, now Bazas, in a dry sandy country in the department of the Gironde. Crassus appears to have entered Aquitania in the east part and had now advanced westward into the dreary plains south of Bordeaux on the road to Bayonne.

The people of this country being alarmed at the capture of the strong town of the Sotiates after a few days' siege sent commissioners in all directions for help, formed a league, exchanged hostages and raised men. They also sent to those states of Hispania Citerior which bordered on Aquitania to ask for troops and commanders. On the arrival of this aid, the Aquitani prepared for war with great confidence and with a large force. Those men were selected as commanders who had been with Sertorius in all his campaigns and were supposed to have great military skill. Some of them may have come from Lugdunum Convenarum in the Pyrenees (vol. ii. 460).

* There is a Gallic coin with a lion's head in profile on the obverse, and the words REX ADIETVANVS: on the reverse a lion walking, and SOTIOTA. Another coin has the same obverse, and on the reverse a wolf walking, with the legend SOTIOTA (Mr. Lindsay). The orthography of the name in Caesar is not certain. Schneider (Caesar, lll. 22 note) mentions a coin with the inscription REX AALETVANVS partly in Greek and partly in Roman characters with a lion's head; on the other side is SOTIOGA.

Nicolaus of Damascus (cited by Athenaeus, p. 249. Cas.), as the text stands, gives the name of Silodunl to these Solduril, and says that they died with their chief, even when he died a natural death. This was the best part of the institution; for when the chief died, the country would be rid of his followers. However, as a tyrant seems a necessity in some conditions of society, a new chief and a new band would appear. Caesar (vii. 40) speaks of a similar custom among the Galli.

These old soldiers followed the Roman fashion of selecting fit places for their camps which they fortified, and endeavoured to intercept the Roman supplies. The young general was in a difficult position, in a strange country and opposed to men who were not ignorant of the art of war. It was not safe to divide his small army; the enemy covered the country in all directions while they left force enough to defend their camp; they cut off the Roman supplies, and their numbers were daily increasing. Crassus could neither advance nor retreat: if he stood still, he would be starved. It was therefore necessary to fight. A council of war confirmed the general's opinion, and the next day was fixed for the battle. As soon as it was light Crassus drew up his army in two lines, put his auxiliary troops in the centre, and waited for the enemy's movements. Though the enemy relying on superior numbers and their military renown thought that they could safely engage with the Roman army, still they considered it safer to occupy the roads, to stop the supplies and to gain a victory without fighting; and if the Romans should be compelled by scarcity to retreat, their design was to attack them on the march when they would be encumbered and their spirit damped by the weight of their burdens. The Aquitani were using the prudent foresight which they had gained by experience and by observing Roman discipline; the commanders were of the same mind, and they kept quiet in their camp. But this hesitation on their side made the Romans think that they were afraid, and being encouraged by this belief they demanded with loud cries to be led against the enemy. Crassus took advantage of the temper of his men and led them to attack the enemy's camp. Some began to fill up the ditch, others with missiles attempted to drive the enemy from the rampart and their defences, while the auxiliary troops, in whose fighting powers Crassus had not much confidence, were employed in supplying stones and missiles and carrying turf and earth. The enemy on their side made a vigorous resistance, and missiles from the ramparts fell with effect on the besiegers. In the meantime some cavalry who had gone round the enemy's camp reported to Crassus that it was not fortified with the same care on the rear and might be easily entered.

Crassus urged the commanders of the cavalry to excite their men by great rewards and promises of more[3], and told them what to do. According to their instructions they took out of the Roman camp four cohorts, who being left there to defend it were quite fresh, and led them round by a circuitous road that they might not be seen by the enemy. While the Aquitani and the Romans were intent on the battle, the four cohorts soon arrived at the rear of the enemy's camp and breaking through the defences were inside before the Aquitani could see them or know what was going on. The shouts from the back part of the camp redoubled the strength of the assailants at the prospect of victory, and the Roman attack became more furious. The enemy surrounded on all sides in utter despair did their best to escape out of the camp and to save themselves by flight; but the cavalry followed them through the wide plains of Aquitania[4], and scarcely one-fourth of the fifty thousand Aquitani and Cantabri who were said to have come together, escaped from the pursuit. It was late at night before the cavalry returned to the Roman camp.

The report of the victory was followed by the submission of the greatest part of Aquitania, which sent hostages to Crassus. Among the nations which submitted were the Tarbelli, Bigerriones, Preciani, Vocates, Tarusates, Elusates, Garites, Ausci, Garumni, Sibuzates, and Cocosates. The Tarbelli were in the lower basin of the Adour. Their chief place was on the site of the hot springs of Dax. The Bigerriones appear in the name Bigorre. The chief place of the Elusates was Elusa, Eause; and the town of Auch on the river Gers preserves the name of the Ausci. The names Garites, if the name is genuine, and Garumni contain the same element Gar as the river Garumna and the Gers. It is stated by Walckenaer (Géog. i. 303) that the inhabitants of the southern part of Les Landes are still called Cousiots. Cocosa, Caussèquo, is twenty-four miles from Dax on the road from Dax to Bordeaux. A few people who were most remote, in the higher valleys of the Pyrenees, seeing that winter was

---

[3] See Caesar's text, and Schneider's note.
[4] The plains of the department of the Gironde or the department of Les Landes.

approaching when they could not be attacked, did not make their submission. The simple narrative of this successful expedition is in Caesar's style, and we may presume that he founded it on the report of his young friend[1], whose success justified the proconsul in sending him on this hazardous enterprise. Crassus of course made his report to the proconsul, who has written the narrative of the campaign in his short and rapid manner. As the winter was near and Crassus was in Rome early in the next year, it seems probable that he did not lead the troops back to Caesar, but was sent on a mission to Rome to look after the proconsul's interests.

About the same time, though the summer was nearly past, Caesar expecting a speedy victory led his army against the Morini and Menapii, the only people in Gallia who were still in arms and had never sent to ask for peace. His march would be from the Bay of Morbihan on the coast of Bretagne towards the country of the Abrincatui, the territory of Avranches, the supposed scene of the victory of Sabinus, where he may have been joined by the three victorious legions. He would then proceed through the country of the Lexovii (Lisieux) to the Seine, which he would perhaps cross above Rouen. His march would then be due north through the territory of the Bellovaci and Ambiani, which he had seen the year before, to the lower Somme. After crossing this river he would be in the territory of the Morini or coast men, who extended northward perhaps as far as Dunkerque. It is not probable that he reached the territory of the Menapii.

There is not a word in the Commentaries about this long march. It is Caesar's way to speak only of his military operations, and the reader must sometimes supply what he omits by putting together two facts, the place from which he set out and the place at which he arrived. The Morini adopted a system of resistance quite different from that of the other Galli, who, as the Morini well knew, had met Caesar in battle and had been defeated. The country was a continuous marsh and forest into which the Morini retreated with all their moveables. When Caesar had reached the forest,

[1] Dion's story (39, c. 46) is founded on Caesar and disfigured in his usual manner.

and begun to make his camp, no enemy was visible, but while the Romans were dispersed and occupied with their works, they were assailed by the Morini from all parts of the woods. The Romans snatched up their arms, drove the enemy back into the forest, and killed a large number; but carrying the pursuit too far into the intricate parts they lost a few men.

During the following days Caesar cut a road through the forest; and to prevent any attack being made on his men while they were unarmed and off their guard, he turned all the trees which were cut down with their branches towards the enemy, and thus made a rampart for the soldiers on the right and on the left. In a few days a great extent of road was cut; and the Romans were on the point of coming up with the cattle and the rear of the retreating train, while the Morini were plunging into the thicker part of the forests, when such stormy weather broke out that the Romans could not work and the heavy rains made it impossible for them to keep the field any longer, or as the general expresses it, they could not be kept longer "under skins" (sub pellibus). The Proconsul did what has been done in modern times: he wasted all the cultivated lands, burnt the villages and solitary huts, and led back his army over the Seine. He put his men in winter quarters among the Aulerci and Lexovii, in the fertile country on the south side of the lower Seine, and in the other states in which he had carried on his summer campaign[4].

[4] Dion, 39. c. 44, has epitomised Caesar's two chapters, and as usual he has introduced falsehood. The Morini and Menapii, he says, carried their most valuable things to the most wooded part of the mountains, which mountains Caesar attempted to reach by cutting a road through the forests. But Caesar might have gone as far as Cassel, south of Dunkerque, before he came to the only hill in this flat country.

CHAPTER VII.

P. CLODIUS.

B.C. 56.

ON the twenty-second of January Clodius was elected a curule aedile, and thus was protected against the threatened trial. The first thing that he did was to commence a prosecution against Milo for disturbing the peace (De vi), though, if we have been truly informed, Milo only collected his gladiators and rabble to resist the attacks of Clodius. Public business was suspended. On the second of February Milo appeared before the people in answer to the charge of Clodius, and Pompeius was present for the purpose of giving Milo his countenance and support. M. Marcellus spoke in Milo's favour at Cicero's request. However the business was put off to the sixth of February. Cicero in a letter to his brother (Ad Q. Fr. ii. 3), who was then in Sardinia, gives a lively picture of that day's proceedings, from which we learn as much about a Roman public meeting as if we had seen one. Pompeius spoke, or tried to speak, for as soon as he rose, Clodius' rabble began their clamour, and continued to shout and abuse him all the time that he spoke. However he did finish his speech in spite of the noise, and now and then he was heard in silence. Clodius then rose, but he was received with such shouts by the opposite party that he lost his presence of mind. For two hours during which Clodius spoke, he was overwhelmed with abuse and assailed with the filthiest verses directed against himself and his supposed intrigues with his sister Clodia. Furious and pale with rage he at last raised his voice above the shouts of his opponents and called out to his

own partisans, Who is killing the people with hunger? His
men answered, Pompeius. Who wishes to go to Alexandria?
The answer was, Pompeius. Whom did they wish to send?
Answer, Crassus[1]. Crassus was present, and not at all well-
disposed towards Milo. About the ninth hour, as if it
were a concerted thing, Clodius' men began to spit on ours,
says Cicero, and this was the commencement of a fray.
Then they attempted to shove their adversaries from the
ground, upon which "our men," says Cicero, fell upon them,
and Clodius' rabble took to flight. Clodius was ejected
from the rostra, and Cicero with his friends ran off to avoid
the danger.

The Senate was summoned, but Pompeius stayed at home,
and Cicero did not go, for if he went, he could not be silent,
and he wished to avoid giving offence by defending Pompeius,
who was blamed by Bibulus and others. The matter was put
off to the next day, and Clodius deferred the prosecution to
the Quirinalia, the seventeenth. On the eighth the Senate
met in Apollo's temple, in order that Pompeius might be
present, for this temple was not within the city. Pompeius
spoke with dignity, but nothing was concluded. On the ninth
in the temple of Apollo the Senate resolved that what had
been done on the sixth was done against the interest of the
State; which was quite true, for there had been a great riot,
but such an idle resolution was of no use. On this day the
tribune C. Cato made a fierce attack on Pompeius all through
his speech, and said a great deal in praise of Cicero; but as
Cicero says, against his wish. When he abused Pompeius for
his perfidious behaviour to Cicero, he was heard with pleasure
by Pompeius' enemies, who said nothing. Pompeius made a
vigorous reply in which he pointed to Crassus as the author
of the attacks on him, and said that he would protect himself
better than Africanus did against the treachery of C. Carbo
(vol. i. p. 229). Pompeius told Cicero that there was a
design on his own life, that C. Cato was supported by Crassus
and that Clodius received money from him, that both Cato and

[1] Plutarch, Pompeius, c. 48, has something to the same effect, but he incorrectly places this affair before Cicero's return. The allusion to Alexandria refers
to the restoration of the Egyptian king Ptolemaeus Auletes.

Clodius were encouraged by Crassus, Curio, and Bibulus and others of his enemies; that he must therefore prepare against any attack now that the popular assemblies were almost alienated from him, the nobility had become his enemies, the Senate showed him no favour, and the young men had no principle. This was a wretched condition to which the conqueror of the East had sunk, according to his own confession. But he was roused at last. He sent for men from the country. Clodius also increased his bands. Both sides were preparing for a fight on the Quirinalia; but "we are much stronger," says Cicero. A large body of men was expected by Pompeius from Picenum, where he had great estates, and from Gallia, probably Transpadana, where Pompeius' father had planted colonies. Cicero was not unwilling to see the quarrel settled by force; and it would have been decided by force, if Clodius had not kept quiet and dropped the prosecution.

Cicero had some employment at this time. On the tenth of February his friend P. Sestius was charged with bribery by Cn. Nerius, and on the same day by one M. Tullius Albinovanus with a breach of the peace. Sestius was sick and Cicero went to his house to offer his services, though some persons thought that he had good reasons for being somewhat angry with him. Sestius had been a steady friend to Cicero, but he had not satisfied him, particularly in the matter of the indemnity for his house (Ad Att. iii. 20. 3); and Cicero was not really grateful to Sestius, for he tells his brother that he now aided Sestius in order that Sestius and others might think that he was grateful. On the same day, the tenth, the Senate made one of their feeble attempts to stop the street brawls of Rome by a resolution, That the clubs and combinations of people should cease to assemble, and that a law should be proposed by which those who should still persist in meeting should be liable to the same penalties as those who disturbed the public peace. On the eleventh Cicero defended L. Calpurnius Bestia, who was a candidate for the praetorship in B.C. 57. Bestia was not elected, and he was now prosecuted for bribery. Cicero does not say in his letter to his brother that Bestia was acquitted, and we should conclude that he was convicted, as appears indeed from another passage of Cicero (Phil. xi. 5).

The trial of Sestius for a breach of the peace was in March, and he was acquitted on the fourteenth of the month by the votes of all the jurymen (Ad Q. Fr. ii. 4., "pridie Id.," if that is the true reading). Cicero says nothing of the trial for bribery, but his long speech for Sestius against the charge of breaking the peace (De vi) is extant. Sestius was defended by Q. Hortensius and M. Crassus, and also by Cicero who spoke after Hortensius (Pro Sestio, c. 2). This oration, which has often been quoted before, is one of the chief authorities for some of the events which have already been described, and it is as much about Cicero himself as Sestius. It begins with a short sketch of Sestius' early life (c. 1—5), and then tells the story of Clodius' adoption (B.C. 59) to qualify him for the tribunate (c. 6—15), the history of Cicero's expulsion from Rome B.C. 58 (c. 16—24), and of the condition of the commonwealth in that year (c. 25—31). The orator then comes to the case of Sestius, and describes the disturbances at Rome in B.C. 57, the year of Sestius' tribunate, when he and others were exerting themselves about Cicero's restoration, and Sestius was nearly murdered in Castor's temple (c. 37). It was not till then that Sestius kept armed men about him for his protection, as Milo also did. Sestius was guilty of no violence: he only armed himself against it: and this was the substance of Cicero's defence, which lay in a single fact. The orator then (c. 45) makes a political dissertation, which, as he supposes, would be useful to those who heard him, and was not foreign to the case: he explains the nature of the two parties in Rome, as he understood the matter, the Populares and the Optimates. He then makes an attack on L. Gellius Poplicola, a stepson of L. Marcius Philippus consul B.C. 91, and one of those who intended to give evidence against Sestius (c. 51, &c.); and he answers what the prosecutor had said about the way in which Cicero's restoration had been effected (c. 60).

It was the practice for the evidence to be given after the speeches for the defendant had been made; and P. Vatinius, the notorious tribune of B.C. 59, and one of Caesar's tools, gave evidence against Sestius. Quintilian observes (Inst. Or. v. 7) that speeches could be made generally for or against the credibility of the witnesses. Sometimes the speech was directed against witnesses severally, and this kind of attack combined with the defence, says Quintilian, we have read in many orations, and published separately, as Cicero's speech against Vatinius (in Vatinium testem). This speech was directly intended to destroy the credit of Vatinius as a witness; indirectly to gratify Cicero's malignant temper. In a letter to Lentulus (i. 9. 7) he says that when Pompeius had come into the city to speak in favour of Sestius on his trial, Vatinius in his evidence, in the presence of Pompeius, said that Cicero had become friendly towards Caesar in consequence of his good fortune and success. Vatinius said what was true, and Cicero paid him off by a violent attack on his character in the form of a set of questions on his life public and private, and principally the year of his tribunate. The best evidence of the truth of what Vatinius said is contained in this speech, for while Cicero attacks Vatinius for what he did in his tribunate, he excuses Caesar's acts in his consulship: "the truth shall at last break out and I will say without hesitation what I think: if C. Caesar was somewhat violent on a particular occasion, if the greatness of the struggle, his thirst for glory, his superior ability, his exalted rank urged him to certain things, which in such a man might be then endured and afterwards forgotten by reason of the great things he has since done, will you, villain, presume on the same licence, and shall we tolerate Vatinius, a robber and a sacrilegious wretch, when he asks for the same indulgence which is allowed to Caesar?" (c. 6.) In another passage (c. 10) Cicero asks Vatinius whether he had heard what Caesar said when he was lately at Aquileia, that Vatinius in his tribunate had done nothing without being paid for it. Cicero does not tell us who heard Caesar say this. In a letter to his brother (ii. 4. 1) he boasts that he made mincemeat of Vatinius, and the saucy audacious fellow went off in great confusion. After all this abuse Cicero defended Vatinius in B.C. 54.

The affair of Ptolemaeus Auletes king of Egypt occupied the Romans in B.C. 57 and the beginning of B.C. 56. Ptolemaeus was named Auletes, or the piper, because he practised the flute and had musical contests in his palace in which he engaged as a competitor. This unkingly demeanour made him despised, but he was disliked also for his vices. The kings of Egypt after the third Ptolemaeus, says Strabo (p. 796), were luxurious men and mismanaged the kingdom. Auletes (vol. iii. 415) had bought the recognition of his kingly title by the Romans at a large price, part of which he paid out of his ready money, and the rest he borrowed. The money of course would ultimately be paid by the wretched cultivators of the basin of the Nile, a country which at that time, as at present, was heavily taxed to support the extravagance of one man. Auletes borrowed in Rome where the great lenders of that day lived: the modern Auletes has the larger market of London and Paris in which he can gratify his loan-making propensities. The people of Auletes were vexed at being fleeced to pay the king's loans, and also, as Dion says, because he would not demand Cyprus of the Romans, and if they refused, reject their alliance. As his subjects became unruly and the king had no hired troops, he left Egypt for Rome, and, as we have seen, called at Rhodes on his voyage, and saw M. Cato there (p. 80). The people of Alexandria, not knowing where their king was or what had become of him, made his eldest daughter Berenice queen of Egypt.

Pompeius received the king into his house, and openly gave him his support. This may have been the foundation of the improbable charge of the historian Timagenes, that Auletes left Egypt without any necessity at the advice of Theophanes, the friend of Pompeius, in order that Pompeius might have the office of restoring the king. Plutarch, who reports this matter (Pomp. c. 49), remarks that the villainy of Theophanes does not make the fact so probable as the character of Pompeius makes it improbable. The king's arrival was the signal for the Roman jobbers to make their attack on him.

A man named C. Rabirius Postumus, a speculator on a grand scale, had furnished Ptolemaeus with a loan before the king fled from Egypt, and he made him other loans, when he came to Rome, out of his own money and that of his friends. The prospect of repayment was doubtful, but Rabirius was afraid that he might lose what he had lent, if he made no further advances. So he did what loan contractors do now when they lend to extravagant princes, who pay the interest on old loans out of the new loans; an operation which must end some time in loss, as it did in the case of the Egyptian royal piper. Cicero (Pro C. Rabirio, c. 3) rejects the imputation that the king borrowed in order to bribe the Roman Senate. The money, he says, was borrowed from or through Rabirius for expenses of the king's journey, and to supply his royal splendour and the cost of his train: the bonds for the repayment were executed in the Alban villa of Pompeius, who at that time had left Rome. It was no business of Rabirius, says Cicero, to inquire how the borrower would spend the money, especially as he was a king, a friend of the Roman people, and his restoration was committed by the Senate to a consul. He means P. Lentulus, one of the consuls of B.C. 57.

When the people of Alexandria heard that the king was at Rome, they sent a deputation of a hundred men with Dion, an Academician, at their head, to answer the king's charges and to make their own complaints. The king contrived to have many of these men murdered on the road, and others in Rome; and he kept the rest quiet by threats or bribes. These crimes were so notorious that the Senate expressed their indignation, and they summoned Dion to give evidence; but Auletes used his money so well that Dion was never brought before the Senate, and nothing was said about the assassinations so long as the king was in Rome. Dion himself was afterwards murdered.

Strabo (p. 796) says, without giving any authority for so loose and in part so improbable a statement, that Pompeius gave his support to Auletes, recommended him to the Senate, and effected his restoration and the death of the greater part of the deputies who came to give evidence against him. A man named P. Asicius was tried on the charge of having aided in the murder of Dion and been privy to it. Asicius was defended by Cicero and acquitted (Pro Caelio, c. 10).

A senatus-consultum had been made on the motion of P. Lentulus (B.C. 57), that the governor of Cilicia should have the office of restoring the Egyptian king, and Lentulus would be governor of Cilicia in B.C. 56 (Cic. ad Fam. i. 1. 3; 1. 7. 4). On the tenth of December, B.C. 57, C. Cato entered on his tribuneship. Auletes had already left Rome, as Fenestella states, and gone to Ephesus, leaving an agent Ammonius to look after his interests. About this time, or in the beginning of B.C. 56, as Dion says, the statue of Jupiter on the Alban mount was struck by lightning, and the Sibylline books were consulted, in which it was found written that, if the king of Egypt should apply for aid, the Romans must not refuse him their friendship, but they also must not help him with any force; if they did, they would have trouble and danger. Upon this the Senate, on the motion of C. Cato, annulled all that been settled about the king's restoration, and Cato compelled or prevailed on the Fifteen to read the Sibylline oracle to the people before the Senate had given their consent.

In January, B.C. 56, the Senate was busy with the Egyptian question. Cicero's letters (Ad Fam. i. 1—7) to P. Lentulus contain the information about the various motions made in the Senate, and the intrigues. Cicero spoke on the king's restoration, and probably more than once. There are extant some fragments of an Oration de rege Alexandrino, which may have been delivered early this year; but it is not possible to collect any thing from them[1]. The consul Cn. Lentulus Marcellinus maintained the validity of the religious objection to sending an army to Egypt, and a decree of the Senate was made to that effect. The only question then was whether the proconsul of Cilicia or Pompeius should accompany Auletes to Egypt; and at first it seemed probable that Lentulus would have the commission. Cicero on the nineteenth of January informs his brother, who was still in Sardinia, that he had discharged his duty to Lentulus and completely satisfied Pompeius: he does not see clearly what Pompeius wants, but every body sees what his friends want. The king's creditors are manifestly using money to oppose Lentulus, and it appears certain that he has lost the commission, and Cicero is very sorry for it, though Lentulus has done many things for which, if it were allowable to do so, Cicero could justly blame him—Cicero's letters to his brother perhaps always express his real thoughts. In his letters to Lentulus Cicero

[1] Schol. Bob. ad Orat. de rege Alexandrino, ed. Orelli, p. 348.

only speaks in the strongest terms of gratitude.—On the
fourteenth of January (Ad Fam. i. 2, 3) Cicero had dined with
Pompeius, and he thought that he had turned his friend's
thoughts from all considerations except the interests of Lentulus.
When he heard Pompeius talk, he acquitted him of
any desire to have the commission; but when he looked to
those who were most intimate with Pompeius, he saw what
was plain to all, that there had been unfair dealing in this
matter for some time on the part of certain persons, and that the
king and his advisers were no strangers to it. After the sixth
of February, when Pompeius, as we have seen (p. 123), was
so ill-received in the popular assembly, Cicero informed Lentulus
(Ad Fam. i. 5. b.) that Pompeius seemed to have given
up all thoughts of the Egyptian commission, and it was
Cicero's hope that when the king knew that he could not be
taken back to Egypt by Pompeius, and that if Lentulus did
not restore him, he would have no other opportunity, he
would then go to Lentulus. "And there is no doubt," he
says, "if Pompeius would only give a slight indication that
this would be agreeable to him, the king will do it. But you
know the man's slowness and taciturnity." Here we have
Pompeius' character as Cicero understood it. He could not
discover what the man's thoughts really were. Finally the
Senate adopted the motion of Servilius Isauricus, that the
king should not be restored (Ad Fam. i. 7. 4), though the tribunes,
or some of them, opposed the resolution of the Senate;
and Cicero at last advised Lentulus, if he thought that he could
occupy Alexandria and Egypt, to go to Alexandria with a fleet
and an army, leaving the king at Ptolemais or some place
near, and when Egypt was quiet and secured, Ptolemaeus could
return to his country. Thus Lentulus would restore the king
conformably to the original resolution of the Senate, and he
would be restored without the aid of an army, which the
pious men had declared to be the meaning of the Sibyl.
Cicero states that after frequent communication with Pompeius,
he wrote to Lentulus in conformity to the opinion and
advice of Pompeius. It seems then that Pompeius had given
up all hope of restoring the king in such way as he wished,
for it was impossible to do it with an armed force, and he had

no inclination to undertake the business without one, and with only a couple of lictors. He still held his commission for the supply of corn, which we may suppose he did not wish to give up for a commission which he would discharge without any show of authority. The religious objection was too strong for the politicians. Lentulus did nothing in the affair of Auletes, and the king, seeing his hopes for the present frustrated, took asylum in the great temple of Diana at Ephesus, a sanctuary which would protect him against his creditors (Strabo, p. 641).

On the fourth of April Cicero's daughter Tullia, then a widow, was betrothed to Furius Crassipes (Ad Q. Fr. ii. 5); and on the fifth a decree of the Senate allowed Pompeius 40,000,000 sesterces for the purchase of grain. Money was scarce at Rome and corn was still dear. On the same day (Ad Fam. i. 9. 8) Cicero proposed, and the Senate consented, that on the fifteenth of May the matter of the Campanian land should be discussed in a full meeting. Want of money was probably the reason why the agrarian law of B.C. 59 had not been fully executed. It is difficult to conjecture why Cicero made this bold attack on the stronghold of the three confederates, as he calls the Campanian law, for he could not hope to succeed in repealing it. In his long letter to P. Lentulus (Ad Fam. i. 9) he alleges his motion of the fifth of April as one of various proofs that he retained his old political opinions. Pompeius did not show that he was at all offended with Cicero for what he had done on the fifth of April, and Cicero went to see Pompeius on the eighth, for Pompeius was going to leave Rome for Sardinia and Cicero was going the next day into the country, whence he did not return till the fifteenth of May was over. Cicero asked Pompeius to allow his brother Quintus to return to Rome, and Pompeius promised that he should return immediately. He said that he was going to sail either from Labro (Livorno) or Pisae (Pisa) (Ad Q. Fr. ii. 6).

Before sailing Pompeius visited Caesar, who was then at Luca (Lucca) on the river Serchio, a place which was perhaps not within the limits of Caesar's province of Gallia Cisalpina, though we might conclude from his being there that it was, and Suetonius says so (Caesar, c. 24)[1]. Caesar complained to

[1] It is generally supposed that the river Macra (Magra) was the boundary of

Pompeius of Cicero's motion about the Campanian land. He had already seen Crassus at Ravenna, who had irritated him against Cicero (Ad Fam. i. 9. 9).

There was a great assemblage of Romans at Luca. Appius Claudius, the governor of Sardinia, came; and Q. Metellus Nepos, the governor of nearer Spain. There were collected around the proconsul of Gallia one hundred and twenty fasces, the insignia of office, and more than two hundred senators. The purpose of the congress, as our authorities inform us, was to secure the interests of the three confederates, and the rest came to look after their own. It was agreed among Caesar, Pompeius and Crassus that Pompeius and Crassus should be consuls the next year, and in the following year should have provinces and armies; that Caesar's government should be prolonged for another five years, and he should have an allowance of money to pay the army which he had increased without the permission of the Senate. Caesar had money already, if it is true that he bribed his visitors, but he wanted all that he could get for the Venetian war and the British invasion of the next year[1]. Thus the Roman constitution was destroyed, and it only remained to see which of the confederates would be master. Cicero saw the coming revolution, and saluted the rising sun.

Caesar went off to the Venetian war, Crassus returned to Rome, and Pompeius sailed to Sardinia, where he immediately addressed himself to Quintus Cicero, and told him that he must be answerable for his brother. Pompeius complained loudly of Marcus, recapitulated his own services towards him, and reminded Quintus of the conversations between them about Caesar's measures in his consulship, and what Quintus had promised that his brother should do: Quintus

---

Gallia Cisalpina in Caesar's time. Luca was a Ligurian town (Strabo, p. 217, 218, and Groskurd's notes), and Liguria was a part of Caesar's Cisalpine Province. (See the notes in Oudendorp's Lucan, i. 443, on the verse, Et nunc tonse Ligur.) In the time of Augustus Luca was included in Etruria.

[1] Dion does not mention the meeting at Luca. Appian (B. C. fl. 17) places it after the invasions of Britain, and Plutarch (Caesar, c. 21) if he ever troubled himself so far as to think when this meeting took place, supposed that it was in B.C. 55. The true time is fixed by Cicero's letters and other evidence.

knew that Pompeius had assisted Cicero in his restoration
with Caesar's consent, and he urged Quintus to recommend
Caesar's interests to his brother, and to ask him not to oppose
them, if he would not or could not defend them. Pompeius
also sent Vibullius to Rome to ask Cicero not to compromise
himself in the affair of the Campanian land before Pompeius
returned. All this made Cicero reflect, as he says in his long
letter to Lentulus (Ad Fam. i. 9, 10), and he held a kind of
dialogue with the commonwealth, and claimed permission
after suffering and doing so much for it, to think of being
grateful to those who had helped him, to do what his brother
had promised on his behalf, and after having always shown
himself a good citizen to be allowed to be a good man.
Cicero's apology to Lentulus is a clever piece of sophistry,
which can deceive no man of common sense, and could not
deceive Lentulus. But after reading all his reasons for surrendering to the demand of Pompeius, we wish that he had
stated his reasons for having made this motion about the
Campanian land. If he had reflected, what could he expect to
gain by such a motion? It could only be a fit of vanity and
a foolish dream of making himself the head of a party against
the confederates that could have prompted so childish a thought.
But after the congress of Luca and the message from Pompeius
he saw his danger. His political life was ended. His enemy
Clodius was cherished and flattered by the very men who had
the same opinions as himself, and who were pleased, as he
found out, to see him displeasing Pompeius and becoming the
object of Caesar's hostility. If he persisted in his course, the
confederates were his enemies, the rabble of Clodius might be
turned against him, and death or a second exile were his certain fate. He bowed to the necessity, and from this time till
Caesar fell under the daggers of his assassins, Cicero flattered
and crouched before the man whom he hated and feared.
There is not the slightest doubt about Cicero's opinions and
his fears, about his folly and his meanness at this critical time,
for we have it all in his own words. On the fifteenth of May
there was a full Senate, but Cicero was not there. He was at
Antium. Nothing was said in the Senate about the Campanian land question. But the Senate refused Gabinius, the

proconsul of Syria, a thanksgiving (supplicatio) for some alleged victory. Cicero was pleased, and the more pleased that this was done in his absence. The refusal, he says, is a proof that the Senate did not believe the despatches of Gabinius (De Prov. Cons. c. 6). A letter to Atticus (iv. 5) without a date speaks of something which Cicero had written and sent to a person, whom he does not name: it was a recantation (παλινῳδία) and he was rather ashamed of it. But he resolved to impose on himself the necessity of keeping to this new alliance, and to cut off all chance of returning to his false friends. The only explanation of the letter is that he had written to make his absolute surrender to Caesar. He says, " since those, who have no power, do not choose to love me, let me try to gain the affection of those who have power." During Cicero's residence in the country Tyrannio arranged his books, which seem to have been at Antium. Cicero found the remains, as he calls them, better than he expected. Sometime, perhaps early in the year, he asked Atticus to send two young clerks to help Tyrannio to repair the books and make "summaries" (indices) "which you Greeks, I think, call σύλλαβοι" (Ad Att. iv. 4. b.). In the letter (iv. 5) he announces that the work is done.

Cicero had already celebrated the glories of his consulship in Greek and in Latin. While he was still in the country, he informed Atticus (iv. 6) that he had urged his friend L. Lucceius by letter to write the history of his acts from the conspiracy of Catilina to his return from exile; and he tells Atticus to thank Lucceius for promising to do it. He also entreats Atticus to ask Lucceius to show him the letter, " which is very beautiful." It is indeed a long and beautiful letter. Lucceius kept it, and we have it (Ad Fam. v. 12). It is worth reading, if a man would know Cicero's character. He asks Lucceius to set off this history even in more honourable terms than his judgment will allow, to neglect so far the rules of history, and to shew him even more favour than is consistent with truth. If Lucceius will not do the work, perhaps Cicero may undertake it himself, but he rather wishes Lucceius to do it, and to do it soon, that men may know from him who Cicero is, while he is still alive, and that he may have the full enjoy-

ment of his little glory in his life-time. He will furnish
Lucceius with the materials (commentarii). In the next year
Cicero sent Lucceius through Atticus "my book," as he calls
it; but he does not say what it was (Ad Att. iv. 11); and in
the same year he sent "my book" to his brother Quintus
(Ad Q. Fr. ii. 8. 1). It does not appear that Lucceius kept
his promise. Cicero and he were corresponding in a friendly
way in B.C. 55.

After Pompeius' return to Rome, Clodius was reconciled
to him. Clodius wanted his help, as we shall soon see.
Some wonderful things happened in this year (B.C. 56), which
Dion records: on the Alban mount a small shrine of Juno,
which was placed on a table and turned to the east, turned
round to the north; a meteor appeared in the south and
rushed to the north; a wolf entered the city, and there was
an earthquake; some citizens were killed by lightning, and
a subterraneous noise was heard in the ager Latinus. The
Senate consulted the Haruspices, who answered that the games
had not been duly celebrated; that places dedicated to sacred
purposes were made common; that ambassadors had been
wickedly murdered; that honour and oaths had been neglected;
that ancient and secret sacrifices had been carelessly conducted
and polluted. The speech de Haruspicum Responsis, which is
printed in the collection of Cicero's orations, mentions only
the great noise (c. 9. 10) in the ager Latiniensis, as the place
is there named. Clodius read to the people the answer of the
Haruspices and contended that part of it applied to Cicero's
house, the ground of which had been consecrated, and then
restored to Cicero and built upon by him. Cicero replied in
the Senate to this attack and showed that the answer of the
Haruspices applied to Clodius. The games, he said, were the
Megalenses, which had been irregularly celebrated by Clodius,
who had allowed a number of slaves to enter the "cavea," or
body of the theatre, though it was usual for free men only to
be admitted. The answer about the sacred places, he said, did
not refer to his house, but to the house of one Seius, which
Clodius had taken possession of after murdering the owner,
for the house contained a shrine and altars, which were now
not treated as sacred. As to the murder of ambassadors

(c. 16), the answer referred to those sent by the people of Alexandria, and to Theodosius, an ambassador from Chios, whom Clodius had caused to be murdered, and to Plator, who went on a mission from Orestis in Macedonia to the proconsul L. Piso, and was murdered by him. The broken honour and oath were the act of the jury in acquitting Clodius, when he was tried for violating the mysteries of the Bona Dea. The pollution of the sacrifices was manifestly the pollution of the mysteries of the Bona Dea by Clodius. The orator explains the warnings from the gods to apply to Clodius and those like him; the misfortunes which threaten the state are owing to the wickedness of Clodius; and he exhorts the Senate to attend to the observance of religious duties. "But prayers will find a ready hearing with the gods who themselves point out to us the way to safety: our own angry passions and quarrels must be settled by ourselves" (c. 28)*.

If Cicero wrote this oration, in which he preached concord (c. 28), he did not practise what he taught. It was after this speech, according to Dion (39. c. 21), that he went with Milo and some tribunes to the Capitol and took down the bronze tablets set up by Clodius or in his tribunate, which contained the enactments that drove Cicero from Rome. But Clodius coming upon Cicero and his party, and aided by his brother C. Clodius then praetor, took the tablets from them and, as we must suppose, restored them to their place. Cicero, however, watching his opportunity when Clodius was out of

* This speech de Haruspicum Responsis is the fourth of the spurious speeches, as some suppose them to be, which Cicero delivered after his restoration. Asconius (Ad Cornel. p. 69) speaks of a speech of Cicero de Haruspicum Responsis, and he quotes a passage from the beginning of c. 12. Why then should not the speech which we have be the speech of Cicero? If a man would know the answer, he must read the speech. If he then believes it to be Cicero's, there is nothing more to say. If he does not believe it to be Cicero's, it will be hard to convince him that it is. Objections have been made to this speech and the three preceding spurious speeches on the ground of the Latinity; but this is a dangerous argument to use. There are certainly strange expressions in this speech and in the others, but some which have been attacked as false Latin are true Latin. It is the absurdity of this speech which is the real argument against it. Cicero did write with very bad taste sometimes; but if he wrote this speech, we could not have believed him capable of writing such miserable stuff, if he had not done it.

Rome, took down the tablets again, and carried them home. Cicero and Clodius now renewed their mutual abuse, each of them using the foolest language, in which Cicero would be a match for his opponent. Indeed the author of the oration de Haruspicum Responsis shows himself a worthy rival of the great orator, for on the occasion of this solemn deliberation upon the omens which disturbed Rome, he declared that no profligate indulged himself so freely among prostitutes as Clodius did with his sisters (c. 27). Cicero always maintained that Clodius was illegally adopted, was consequently illegally made tribune, and that all the acts of his tribunate were void. Clodius maintained that Cicero was legally banished and that the vote for his restoration was illegally obtained.

M. Cato, who had now returned from the mission to Cyprus, was no friend to Clodius, but he could not allow this attack on the legality of his tribunate without admitting that his own mission was illegal and all that he had done in Byzantium and Cyprus. Accordingly, in the Senate he maintained the legality of Clodius' tribunate against Cicero, which offended Cicero, and for some time they ceased to be on friendly terms (Plut. Cicero, 34; Cato, 40). Plutarch's story of Cicero's taking these bronze tablets is not quite the same as Dion's. Cicero himself says nothing of the affair, even in his letters to Atticus. Dion, by naming the praetorship of C. Claudius, fixes this event in B.C. 56, which may be true; but it is almost impossible to believe that it took place after the congress of Luca, for such an attack on the tribunate of Clodius was an attack on the majesty of Caesar and Pompeius, to whom after the middle of April Cicero made his unconditional surrender. This foolish and intemperate act was probably committed about the time when Cicero gave notice of his motion about the Campanian land, and during that temporary delusion, which led him to attempt to regain the favour of the party opposed to the confederates, with the hope of making himself a power in the State.

During this time Cicero's pen and tongue were actively employed. The tribune Racilius was an enemy of P. Clodius, and Cicero wrote something abusive of Clodius, as a scholiast informs us, with the title "Edictum Lucii Racilii tribuni plebi"[a]. M. Cispius, one of the tribunes of B.C. 57, who was with Q. Fabricius on the twenty-fifth of January (B.C. 57, p. 65) and driven from the Forum, was now prosecuted on some charge, and he was convicted in spite of Cicero's tears and sobs (Pro Plancio, c. 31). The speech for Cispius is not extant; but we have the speech for M. Caelius which was delivered in this year. Caelius, the son of a Roman eques, M. Caelius Rufus, was born B.C. 82. His father introduced him to M. Crassus and to Cicero, that he might improve himself by intimacy with these distinguished Romans. Cicero is our evidence for the oratorical talent of his young friend, who in his short life acquired much reputation as a speaker. Quintilian (Inst. x. 1. 115) says that Caelius had great ability as a prosecutor. We may also reckon him as one of our authorities for the Latin language, as there is extant in the collection of Cicero's letters (Lib. viii.) a book of seventeen letters to Cicero, which are well written. Caelius began his oratorical career, in B.C. 59, by prosecuting to conviction C. Antonius (vol. iii. p. 411). In B.C. 57 he prosecuted L. Sempronius Atratinus for bribery. Atratinus was defended by Cicero and acquitted. In B.C. 56, Atratinus the son prosecuted Caelius on various charges which came under the Roman term Vis. Caelius had intrigued with Clodia, one of the sisters of P. Clodius, and wife of Q. Metellus Celer, consul B.C. 60. Clodia and Caelius afterwards quarrelled, and Clodia took her revenge by exciting Atratinus, assisted by her brother P. Clodius and others, to prosecute Caelius, who was charged with borrowing valuables from her for the purpose of procuring the assassination of Dion the Alexandrine, and also with attempting to poison Clodia. Caelius spoke for himself, and Quintilian (Inst. xi. 1. 51) quotes a passage from his speech. M. Crassus and Cicero also spoke in his defence, but Cicero only replied to the charge about poisoning. He had something to do to remove certain prejudices against Caelius for the disorders of his early youth and his alleged intimacy with Catilina (vol. iii. p. 224). The evidence for the poisoning was perhaps

[a] Schol. Bob. in Orat. pro Plancio, p. 269. ed. Or.

nothing, or of no weight (c. 23). Caelius was acquitted, and Cicero had in this oration one more opportunity, which he did not neglect, of pouring forth his venom on P. Clodius and his profligate sister.

Sometime in this year (B.C. 56) the question of the consular provinces was brought before the Senate. The consular provinces, as they were named, were the two provinces which, pursuant to the Lex Sempronia of B.C. 123, were assigned by the Senate before the consular elections of each year to the consuls who should be elected in that year. The Senate could select any provinces that they pleased. At this time Gabinius had Syria, Piso had Macedonia, and both of them administered their provinces badly. Caesar had the two Galliae, of which Gallia Transalpina was given to him by the Senate and Cisalpina by the people, each province for five years. The matter for deliberation was which two of these four provinces should be given to the consuls elected in B.C. 56. One proposal was to give Caesar's two provinces to the new consuls, and so to supersede Caesar. Another proposal was to give one of Caesar's provinces and either Macedonia or Syria to the new consuls (De Prov. Cons. c. 7. 15). P. Servilius proposed to give Macedonia and Syria to the new consuls, and Cicero supported the motion of Servilius (c. 1) in his extant speech on the consular provinces. This speech may be compared with that which he made (vol. iii. p. 132) on the proposal to give to Cn. Pompeius the command in the Mithridatic war. In that speech he declared his allegiance to Pompeius. He now accepted Caesar as his master. We may certainly assume that the speech de Provinciis Consularibus was delivered after the conference at Luca.

Cicero hated Piso and Gabinius, as we know; and in proposing to supersede them, he made a fierce attack on their bad administration (De Prov. Cons. c. 2—7). But even if the administration of Piso and Gabinius had been excellent, it was Cicero's opinion (c. 8) that C. Caesar should not be superseded at present. The second part of the speech contains his apology for supporting Caesar, who, as one of Cicero's intimate friends in the Senate affirmed, actively assisted in driving him into exile. But Cicero said that he could not be the enemy of a man, the fame of whose great exploits daily filled his ears with the names of new nations and new places. Men, he says, may think what they please, but he cannot be unfriendly to any citizen who serves the State well (c. 9). He had no other reason for hating even P. Clodius except that he thought him to be a dangerous enemy to the State, which Clodius showed by violating the mysteries of the Bona Dea[1]. Cicero admits that he had formerly differed from C. Caesar's policy, and had been of the same opinion as the Senate; and he is still of the same opinion as the Senate. They had decreed an extraordinary thanksgiving in commemoration of Caesar's victories, and Cicero only followed what the Senate had done. As long as the Senate did not altogether approve of Caesar's public measures, they knew that he maintained no close intimacy with Caesar. As soon as Caesar's victories changed their minds, Cicero shared their opinion and maintained it by his words.

Cicero states (c. 11) that there had been lately a motion before the Senate about an allowance to Caesar for his army, that he supported it, that he answered those who opposed it, and assisted in drawing up the resolution of the Senate (scribendo adfuit). This allowance was probably made after the congress at Luca, and before Caesar left Italy for the Venetian war, or soon after. Caesar says nothing of this matter in his commentaries, nor of any thing else, with a few rare exceptions, which was passing in Rome. There was also a discussion in the Senate about ten legati for Caesar, to which some opposition was made, but Cicero supported the proposal about the ten legati.

In his speech (c. 12) Cicero asks why should Caesar wish to remain in Gallia, except to complete the work that he had begun: the country was in no way inviting. For the interest of the State Cicero would keep him there, even if Caesar did not wish to stay, for Gallia is the only nation that still resists the power of Rome. Here (c. 13) he begins to sing the praises of the great proconsul as he had once sung the praise

[1] Drumann, in a note, vol. v. p. 710, can no longer contain his indignation when he reads these words: "Why," he says, "was there not some senator ready, in the name and for the honour of truth, to silence this shameless liar and hypocrite?"

of Cn. Pompeius. Rome, he says, had hitherto only repelled the Galli, but it was Caesar's design to reduce them to subjection. "Nature not without some Divine power had made the Alps the bulwark of Italy, for if the road had been open to the savage multitudes of Gallia, Rome would never have been the seat of supreme power. But now the Alps may sink down to the level of the plains, for beyond those lofty mountains as far as the ocean there is nothing for Italy to fear." He expects that in one or two summers all Gallia will be for ever secured in chains, if Caesar shall be allowed to prosecute his victorious career. Cicero argues against taking from Caesar either Gallia Ulterior or Citerior (c. 15, 16). He then states (c. 17) that Caesar from early manhood had been intimate with himself, with his brother, and his cousin C. Visellius Varro. Though Cicero did not quite agree with Caesar in what he had done in his consulship, still he was bound to be grateful to him, because he wished for Cicero's co-operation; grateful also for offering him a place among the Campanian land commissioners, for wishing to associate him with Crassus and Pompeius in their close union with Caesar, and also for offering him the office of legatus. It was not through ingratitude that Cicero refused these offers, but from a certain kind of obstinacy, the wisdom of which he will not discuss. The acceptance of Caesar's offers might have protected Cicero against his enemies, but still he firmly resolved not to desert the Senate or the position which he occupied. Indeed, he felt that Caesar was as well disposed towards him as to his son-in-law Pompeius. He did indeed assist in the matter of Clodius' adoption into a plebeian (vol. iii. p. 413) family, but even this was no wrong to Cicero, as he says; and he gives this reason for affirming that even this act of hostility was no wrong: "for Caesar afterwards not only advised me to accept the office of legatus under him, but he even entreated me." Cicero refused this offer, not because he thought the place beneath his dignity, but because he did not think that so much villainy from the consuls of B.C. 58 threatened the State. His conclusion is that his own pride may be perhaps more condemned, when Caesar was so liberal towards him, than Caesar's wrong to one who was his friend. He makes an artful apology (c. 18) for Caesar's behaviour to him at the time of his exile. Caesar made amends by consenting to his restoration, or at least not opposing it, for Pompeius himself assured Cicero of Caesar's favourable disposition. If Cicero's sufferings cannot be undone, they may be forgotten; and if any person shall object to Cicero saying that in the interest of the State he neglects his own wrongs, he may at least be allowed to affirm that he is a grateful man, and that he is deeply affected, not merely by great favours, but even by a slight indication of goodwill. He concludes (c. 20) that if he were an enemy to Caesar, it would still be his duty at this time to have regard to the State, and to reserve his hostility to another time; and for the sake of the State he could forget all hostility, after the example of some illustrious men whom he has already enumerated (c. 9, 10). But there never was any enmity between him and Caesar, and therefore if he ever supposed that Caesar did him wrong, this opinion shall be blotted out by Caesar's services to him; and by his vote he will show what is due to Caesar's merits, he will support the unanimity of the Senate, he will maintain their consistency in conferring honour on Caesar, he will consult the interests of the State with respect to the Gallic war, and as an individual will show that he is not ungrateful.

Cicero says in a letter to Lentulus of this year (Ad Fam. i. 7. 10) in answer to his questions about the state of the commonwealth, "that the struggle between parties is violent, but the contest is unequal: for those who are superior in influence, arms and power, seem to him to have gained so much by the folly and inconsistency of their opponents that they have the advantage over them even in public opinion. Accordingly this party (Caesar's party) has obtained through the Senate with little opposition what they did not expect to obtain even from the popular assembly without some disturbance: for the Senate granted Caesar pay for his army and ten legati, and there was no difficulty in preventing his being superseded by virtue of the Sempronia Lex. He writes to Lentulus with the more brevity because the present condition of the commonwealth is not satisfactory to him."

There is a passage in another letter to Lentulus (Ad Fam.

i. 9. 20), written in B.C. 54 after Cicero had defended Vatinius, in which he speaks of a quarrel between Crassus and himself about Gabinius. Drumann (v. 715) has connected this passage with what Cicero said of Gabinius in his oration on the consular provinces, but the quarrel seems to me to have been on some other occasion.

There was no immediate result of the discussion on the consular provinces. Caesar was not disturbed, nor was Gabinius superseded. But Piso was superseded in Macedonia either now or later (In. Pis. c. 30).

In this year and after the oration on the consular provinces Cicero, at the request of Cn. Pompeius, defended L. Cornelius Balbus, and he spoke after Pompeius and M. Crassus. Balbus, a native of Gades, had been made a Roman citizen by Cn. Pompeius (vol. ii. 470) with the consent of his advisers (consilium), and the gift of the Roman citizenship was confirmed by a Lex Gellia B.C. 72 (Pro Balbo, c. 3. 8). A man of Gades who had abandoned his own citizenship (c. 14) prosecuted Balbus for acting as a Roman citizen, and the ground of the prosecution was, as Cicero says (c. 8), that no citizen of a state, which had a foedus or treaty with Rome, could become a Roman citizen, unless his state "fundus factus esset," in the language of the Roman law. The motive of the prosecution is not stated by Cicero. We may conjecture that the prosecutor was the tool of a party, who not being able to attack Pompeius, attacked the man who was devoted both to him and Caesar. If this is so, it was a proof of want of sense in the party opposed to Pompeius, for the prosecution gave him and Crassus the opportunity of defending Balbus, and Cicero the opportunity of blowing the trumpet once more in praise of Pompeius (c. 4) and declaring his adherence to the three confederates.

The whole question turned on the words "fundus factus," which according to Cicero the prosecutor did not understand. The words, he says, were no more applicable to foederate states than to all free states. If the Roman people made an enactment, and if the allies (socii) of Rome and the Latini adopted that enactment, and thus the law (lex), which was established at Rome, was fixed among that people as on a firm foundation (tamquam in fundo rescdlisset), then such people were bound by such adopted law. As an example Cicero refers to the Lex Julia of B.C. 90 (ii. 198), by which the Roman citizenship was offered to the Socii and Latini, and the effect of the law was that those communities, which did not accept it (qui fundi populi non facti essent), did not receive the Roman citizenship. Free states then or foederate states, that is, states connected with Rome by a treaty, might adopt any Roman enactment; but such an act only affected those states which accepted it, and not the Romans. Cicero asks the prosecutor (c. 10) if the citizens of Gades shall not be allowed to accept the Roman citizenship, when conquered nations might accept the citizenship if it was given? (c. 18.)—To this it might be replied that the two cases were unlike. Conquered nations must accept the Roman citizenship, if the conquerors imposed it, and they must accept the citizenship on such terms and with such limitations as the conquerors chose to fix. The foederate state of Gades might refuse to admit that one of their citizens could become a Roman citizen.—Cicero sees this, for he asks (c. 12), if a Roman citizen could become a citizen of Gades, why cannot a citizen of Gades become a Roman citizen?—The answer is, that he could of course become a Roman citizen, if Rome chose to accept him, whether the Gaditani consented or not.—Cicero states (c. 14) that there are or have been treaties with some peoples, by which it was declared that none of their citizens should be admitted to the Roman citizenship; and he argues that if in these excepted cases the Roman citizenship could not be conferred, it could as a necessary consequence be conferred in those cases which were not excepted: there was no exception of this kind in the treaty with Gades; and if there was such an exception, it was removed by the Lex Gellia. The prosecutor is supposed to reply, that a treaty does make an excepted case, if it is "sacrosanctum." Cicero rejoins that nothing can be "sacrosanctum," unless it has had the sanction given to it by the populus or the plebs. The treaty with Gades was made by the Senate, and approved by the judgment of the Roman people, but not formally by the votes of the people (c. 16); and even if it had been, there was nothing

in it to prevent a Gaditanian from being made a Roman
citizen. All this, says Cicero, might be urged, if the Gaditani were opposing Balbus and demanding back their citizen
(c. 17), but now there is a deputation from Gades for the purpose of maintaining the case which Cicero defends.

The case which Cicero was arguing before a jury (judices)
is purely a question of law. It is impossible to understand
from him what was the legal status of the prosecutor (ac-
cusator), as he is named, nor how the question was raised,
nor under what enactment this proceeding against Balbus
was conducted. The result was that Balbus still continued
to be a Roman citizen, and even became a consul (B.C. 40).

We learn from the oration for Balbus the Roman rules of law
about a man changing his citizenship (c. 11,12). Cicero affirms
that by Roman law no man can be deprived of his citizenship
against his will; and if he chooses to exchange his Roman
citizenship for the citizenship of another state, he can do so,
provided he is admitted a citizen of that other state. No
act of renunciation was necessary. If a Roman citizen was
admitted as a citizen of another state, he then ceased to be
a Roman citizen, for by Roman law a Roman could not be a
citizen of Rome and of another state at the same time. The
rule of Roman law (c. 12) as Cicero expresses it was that
citizens of all states may become citizens of Rome, and Roman
citizens may become citizens of other states, but they cannot
retain their Roman citizenship. He adds that in the Greek
states a man may be a citizen of several states. He had
seen several ignorant Romans at Athens acting as jurymen
and Areopagitae, not knowing that, if they became Athenian
citizens, they lost their Roman citizenship. But a Roman
could recover his citizenship by the process called Postliminium.

The Roman principle was right. A man cannot owe absolute obedience to two sovereign powers. So long as a citizen
of one state is in the territory of another friendly state he has
the protection of that state and he owes obedience to the law.
But if a man were a citizen of two countries he might be
obliged to obey contradictory commands, if it were possible.
The Romans opened their door to the world as the United

States do, but they consistently allowed their own citizens to become citizens of other states, and to depart in peace. The English law does not allow a subject, as we term him, to renounce his allegiance by becoming a citizen of another country, though the English law allows a foreigner under certain forms to become an English subject. The English law also claims a man's obedience as a subject simply because he has been born within the dominions of the British crown, even though at the time of his birth by the law of a foreign state he may owe allegiance to such state; and it claims the allegiance of a person born of a father who is a British subject wherever such person is born. The English principle can no longer be maintained and circumstances will compel us to admit that an Englishman can become a citizen of another state; but he must at the same time cease to be an English subject. Some difficult questions may arise from this mutation of citizenship, as Cicero names it, but the power of making the change is absolutely necessary in the present condition of the world[a].

Dion (39, c. 24—30) has several chapters about Pompeius and the consulship. The distribution of corn had given him some employment; and since many slaves had been manumitted in order to qualify them to receive an allowance, and probably to save their masters the expense of maintaining the

---

[a] Since this was written the Naturalization Act of 1870 has been passed, chap. 14. The first part of this Act provides for the Status of Aliens in the United Kingdom. By section 4, any person who by reason of his having been born within the dominions of her Majesty is a natural-born subject, but who also at the time of his birth became under the law of any foreign state a subject of such state and is still such subject, may make a declaration in a certain form and he shall then cease to be a British subject; and any person who is born out of her Majesty's dominions of a father being a British subject, may make a declaration in a certain form, and he shall then cease to be a British subject. The sixth section provides for expatriation, and declares that, any British subject who has at any time before, or may at any time after the passing of this Act, when in any foreign state and not under any disability, voluntarily become naturalized in such state, shall from and after the time of his so becoming naturalized in such foreign state be deemed to have ceased to be a British subject and be regarded as an alien. The eighth section provides that a natural-born British subject, who has become an alien in pursuance of this Act, may under certain conditions be re-admitted to the status of a British subject. He has what Cicero (c. 12) calls a power of recovering his citizenship by Postliminium.

old and infirm, Pompeius made a list of them, that the distribution might be managed with decency. However in canvassing for the consulship he found some difficulty. Dion represents Pompeius as jealous of Caesar's popularity, and even advising the consuls to supersede him, which is directly contrary to the evidence of Cicero. Dion speaks of senators being sent, after Roman fashion, to assist in the settlement of Gallia as if it were completely subdued. As the number of such commissioners was generally ten, Dion seems to have read something about the ten legati who were assigned to Caesar, and to have misunderstood the matter (c. 25). His narrative is entirely at variance with the other evidence which we possess. He continues thus. Pompeius seeing that he could not alone prevail against Caesar allied himself more closely with Crassus, and both of them sought the consulship as the only means by which they could be a match for the proconsul of Gallia. But they had not given due notice of their intention to be candidates, and as they knew that others besides the consuls would oppose their election, they intrigued to ;prevent the elections being made in that year (B.C. 50). For this purpose they employed among others the tribune C. Cato, for they expected that if no consuls should be ready to enter on their office on the first of January, an Interrex would be appointed, and they might then legally be candidates and be elected consuls.

These intrigues continuing, and being accompanied with some violence perhaps, for Dion is often very obscure, the Senate resolved to put on mourning as in a public calamity, in spite of the opposition of the tribune C. Cato. In the mean time P. Clodius sought a reconciliation with Pompeius in the expectation of gaining something by aiding his intrigues. "What Clodius wants," says Cicero to his brother (Ad Q. Fr. ii. 9, 2), " is some embassy or commission, either from the Senate or the people, a free legatio (vol. iii. p. 270), or one to Byzantium or to Brogitarus or both: it is an affair of money." Clodius appeared before the people in his ordinary dress and made a speech against the consul Marcellinus and others. This behaviour excited the indignation of the Senate, some of whom, as we may suppose, were prewent, and Clodius stopping short in his speech went right to the Senate-house, but he was met at the door by the senators who would not let him enter, and he was surrounded by the equites who would have torn him to pieces, if he had not called on the people for help. His cries brought a crowd with fire-brands who threatened to burn the house and the senators in it, if any harm befell Clodius. Thus Clodius escaped with his life.

At last on some occasion the consul Marcellinus asked Pompeius before the people whether he really wished to be elected consul. Pompeius replied that so far as honest men were concerned, he did not want the office, but because of those who were making disturbances in the State he desired it very much. Plutarch reports that the answer of Pompeius was that perhaps he might, perhaps he might not be a candidate. When Crassus was asked the same question, he answered that he would do whatever was for the interest of the State. Marcellinus and others seeing what were the two men's designs came no more to the Senate-house; and as a sufficient number of senators did not meet to determine about the elections, nothing could be done, and the year passed away.

This is the substance of what Dion has written about the failure of the elections of B.C. 56. He must have found it somewhere, but his narrative is exceedingly feeble and confused, and sometimes, perhaps partly owing to corruptions in the text, hardly intelligible.

CHAPTER VIII.

CAESAR AND THE GERMANS.

B.C. 55.

CAESAR begins his Fourth book thus: "In the following winter, which was the year when Cn. Pompeius and M. Crassus were consuls, the Usipetes, who were Germani, and also the Tenctheri with a large multitude crossed the Rhine not far from the sea into which the Rhine flows. The reason of this movement was that they had been harassed for many years by the Suevi and prevented from cultivating the ground (Chap. 2). These two nations after being expelled from their home and wandering for three years in many parts of Germany reached that country on the Rhine which was occupied by the Menapii, who had lands, houses, and villages on both sides of the river. Terrified by the approach of such large numbers the Menapii fled from the right side of the Rhine, and placing their forces in convenient positions on the left bank they prevented the enemy from crossing. The Germans had no boats to enable them to force a passage, and the vigilance of the Menapii rendered it impossible to cross the river without being seen. Accordingly the invaders made a feint of retiring to their own country, but after three days' march they turned round, and having accomplished with their cavalry the whole distance in one night they fell on the Menapii unexpectedly, for these people having been informed by scouts of the retreat of the Germans had returned to the villages on the east side of the Rhine. The Menapii were slaughtered and their boats seized before their countrymen, who were living on the other side of the river, knew any thing about it. The invaders crossed the river and occupying all the houses of the Menapii lived for the rest of the winter on what they found stored up" (B. G. cc. 1—4).

Caesar's Menapii extended along the left bank of the lower Rhine to the ocean, where they were the neighbours of the Morini, who occupied that part of the French coast at which the channel is narrowest, and extended eastward towards the lower course of the Schelde. We have no evidence which determines the boundary on the coast between the Morini and the Menapii. The Menapii also possessed the country on both sides of the lower Maas (Mosa). Along the Rhine and south of the Menapii were the Eburones, who bordered on the Treviri (B. G. vi. 5), a people whose territory lay on the left bank of the Rhine and on both sides of the Mosella (Mosel). Trier on the Mosel was the head-quarters of the Treviri. The country of the Eburones was also on both sides of the Maas, and they occupied the parts about Tongern and Spa. Opposite to them on the east side of the Rhine were the Sigambri (B. G. vi. 35). Between the Eburones and the Treviri were the Segni and Condrusi (B. G. vi. 32), dependents of the Treviri. The name of the Segni is probably retained in that of Sinei or Segnei, a small town in the territory of Namur, which is on the Maas and higher up the river than Liège. The position of the Condrusi and Paemani, has been already described (p. 47). The Caeroesi are mentioned by Caesar (B. G. ii. 4) with the Condrusi, Eburones and Paemani under the general name of Germani; but we have no evidence of the position of the Caeroesi.

There is no indication of the place where the Germans crossed the Rhine, except that it was "not far from the sea," an expression which has no definite meaning. As far as we can infer from the Commentaries Caesar never saw the lowest parts of the Rhine. It has been conjectured by Goeler (p. 109) that the Germans crossed near Emmerich, and it is only a conjecture; but there are good reasons for supposing that they did not cross the Rhine below this place.

When Caesar heard of this Germanic invasion, he knew that he could not trust the Galli, who were always ready for change. It was their custom to stop travellers and to inquire about what they had seen or heard; and in the towns the common sort would crowd about the merchants and force them to say where they came from and to tell all that they knew. Under the excitement of such hearsay news they would often form resolutions on matters of the greatest weight, though they soon had reason to repent of what they had done, for they were governed by loose reports, and most of those whom they questioned gave such answers as they knew that the inquirers expected.

To avoid the necessity of fighting both the Germans and the Galli at the same time Caesar joined the army earlier than usual, and he then discovered what he had suspected. Messages had been sent by some of the Gallic states to the German invaders, who were invited to advance from the Rhine by a promise that every thing that they might require should be prepared for their reception. Induced by these expectations the Germani were now extending their ravages and had reached the country of the Eburones and the Condrusi. Caesar called a meeting of the chiefs of Gallia (Celtica), but he thought it prudent to say nothing about what he had heard. On the contrary he tried to put the Galli in good humour and to confirm them in a friendly disposition. He then required from them a force of cavalry and prepared for war with the Germans.

After providing supplies for the army and selecting his cavalry Caesar advanced towards those parts in which he heard that the Germans were. His men had wintered between the Seine and the Loire (p. 122), and he led them from this part of Gallia to the Maas and crossed it. All this he omits, as usual, and only reports the events of the campaign. When he was within a few days' march of the Germans, he was met by a deputation, who addressed him to this effect: that the Germans were not attacking the Roman people, but if they were provoked, they would not avoid the contest, for it was the ancient custom of the Germans to resist those who attacked them: so much however they had to say; they had come into Gallia against their will, and had been ejected from home: if the Romans sought their goodwill, the Germans would be useful friends: let the Romans either assign lands to them or permit them to keep what they had won by their arms: they acknowledged their inferiority to the Suevi alone, for whom not even the immortal gods were a match; but there was no other nation on the earth who was their superior. Caesar sent an answer the conclusion of which was this: that he could have no friendship with the Germans so long as they stayed in Gallia: it was not consistent that men who could not protect their own lands should seize those of others: there were no vacant lands in Gallia to give especially to so large a multitude without doing some wrong; but if they chose, they might settle in the territories of the Ubii, whose deputies were then with him and had come to complain of the Suevi and to ask for help; and he would give orders to the Ubii to receive them.

The Germans replied that they would report this proposal to their countrymen and after deliberating on it would return on the third day. In the meantime they asked Caesar not to approach nearer to their encampment, but he refused to comply with their request. In fact he had discovered that a large part of the German cavalry had been sent off a few days before into the territory of the Ambivariti[1] on the west side of the Maas to plunder and collect corn, and he conjectured that the enemy was waiting for the return of their cavalry, and that this was the reason why they asked for time. The cavalry of the Tenctheri were famous even in the time of Tacitus (Germ. c. 32).

When Caesar was not more than twelve miles from the enemy, he was met by the deputies who had returned from the Germans and now entreated him not to proceed farther. Caesar refused to grant their request, upon which they asked him to send orders to his cavalry, who had advanced in front of the army, to abstain from hostilities, and to allow them the opportunity of sending a deputation to the Ubii. If the chiefs and great council of the Ubii would confirm the agreement by an oath, they would accept the terms which Caesar

[1] Goeler (p. 105) founds a conjecture on a resemblance of names that a small place, named Ambrives near Givet on the French and Belgian frontier, may represent the Ambivariti.

offered; and for this purpose they required three days. Caesar thought that this proposal was still made with the view of gaining time for the return of the German horsemen, but however he promised not to advance farther than four miles on that day to a place where he would find water, and he told the Germans to come there the next day as many as could come, and he would take their demands into consideration. In the mean time he sent orders to the commanders who had preceded him with all the cavalry not to attack the enemy, and, if they should be attacked, to hold out till he came up with the army. Caesar's cavalry were about five thousand, and the German cavalry not more than eight hundred, for the horsemen who had crossed the Maas were not yet returned. Caesar's cavalry were accordingly under no fear, because the deputies had just gone away after asking for a truce for this day; but all at once an attack was made on them, and they were thrown into confusion. When they rallied, the Germans after their fashion leapt down from their horses, and stabbing some of the Gallic horses under the belly and dismounting the riders put Caesar's cavalry to flight and drove them forward in disorder till they came in sight of the Roman army. Seventy-four horsemen fell on the Roman side, and among them Piso of Aquitania, a very brave man, whose grandfather had held royal authority in his own state and had received the title of friend from the Roman Senate. Piso had just rescued his brother, whose retreat was cut off by the enemy, but his own horse being wounded he was dismounted. Piso resisted bravely as long as he could, but he was surrounded and killed. His brother, who had made his way out of the confusion, seeing at a distance what had happened drove his horse at full speed against the Germans and perished also.

Caesar now resolved to receive no deputation nor any proposals from an enemy, who had attacked him after asking for peace; and to wait till the enemy's force was increased and till their cavalry returned would be madness. Having had experience of the fickle character of the Galli, he was fully aware of the effect produced on them by the success of the Germans, and he would not allow them any time for forming

hostile designs. This remark must apply to Caesar's Gallic
cavalry, for he had no other Gallic troops with him, and the
defeat of the cavalry could have no immediate effect on those
Galli who were at a distance. Accordingly Caesar informed
the legati and quaestor of his intention not to neglect the first
opportunity of fighting a battle. It happened most fortunately that on the next day in the morning a great number
of Germans with all the chiefs came to Caesar's camp and
with the same perfidious intentions, as Caesar affirms, though
it was said, as Caesar reports, but he does not tell us who
said it, that their purpose was to clear themselves of blame
about the attack of the previous day which had been made
contrary to agreement and contrary to the terms of their own
request; and their intention also was to obtain a truce if
they could by practising further deception. Caesar gladly
seized the opportunity of laying hold of these Germans. He
then led on his troops, but he ordered the cavalry, whom he
supposed to be cowed by their recent defeat, to follow in the
rear. Besides this, as we may collect from what he has said
of the fickle temper of the Galli, he could not trust his cavalry
until he had defeated the enemy.

The army marched in fighting order (triplici acie, p. 15),
and quickly passing over the eight miles (p. 154) reached the
enemy's camp before the Germans knew what was going on.
Struck with terror at the sudden appearance of the Romans
while their chiefs were absent[1], and having no time to deliberate or arm themselves, the Germans were thrown into confusion and hesitated whether they should meet the Romans,
defend the camp or seek safety in flight. Taking advantage
of this disorder and hot with vengeance for the perfidy of the
previous day, the Romans broke into the camp. Those who
could seize their arms made some resistance and fought among
the waggons and baggage; but the women and children, for
the men had crossed the Rhine with their families, fled in all
directions pursued by the cavalry whom Caesar sent after
them. The Germans turned round at the cries of the fugitives and when they saw their wives and children falling

---

[1] Dion (39, c. 48) adds that the Germans were resting at mid-day. This
chapter is a sample of the way in which a Greek made history.

beneath the swords of the Gallic horsemen, they threw down their arms and fled from the camp till they reached the confluence of the Mosel and the Rhine, where farther flight was impossible. Many were killed in the pursuit: the rest plunged into the mighty stream and were swallowed up. This was the second German army which the Roman proconsul drove into the Rhine. Without the loss of a single man and with very few wounded Caesar destroyed, according to his own reckoning, about one hundred thousand fighters, for he estimates the total number of Usipetes and Tenctheri at four hundred and thirty thousand. Some of the women and children may have escaped, for they were too many even for the valiant horsemen of Gallia to destroy, and the pursuit would be stopped by night and the weariness of the pursuers. The Germans, who had been made prisoners in the Roman camp, had Caesar's permission to go away, but knowing what they might expect from the Galli, whose lands they had wasted, they preferred staying with Caesar, who allowed them to be free. This treatment of his prisoners may be taken as evidence that Caesar did not believe that they were guilty of a breach of faith. Dion's assertion that the German deputies blamed their young men for this attack is not in Caesar. The Roman proconsul has told the story, and we may form our own opinion. He certainly has not concealed facts which appear to be against himself. The truth may be that he believed the Germans came this second time with treacherous intentions; and this is possible, for barbarous nations are perfidious to those who come against them as enemies, and are often more than their match in cunning. Caesar's behaviour was not approved at Rome on this or some similar occasion (Sueton. Caesar, c. 24). Tanusius, quoted by Plutarch (Caesar, c. 22), reports that while the Senate were voting a thanksgiving for the victory, M. Cato said that they ought to give up Caesar to the barbarians and so purge themselves of the violation of the truce.

The site of this dreadful catastrophe is placed in all the manuscripts of Caesar, so far as they are reported, at the confluence of the Mosa and the Rhenus[1]. In the tenth

[1] "Ad confluentem Mosae et Rheni." This is a Roman expression. Justin

chapter (B. G. iv.) Caesar has contrary to his fashion interrupted his narrative by a geographical description[1]. He says that the Mosa rises in the Vosges (Vosegus), and that after receiving a branch from the Rhenus, named Vahalis or Vacalus (Waal), it forms the island of the Batavi, and the point where it enters the Rhine is not more than eighty miles from the ocean. The text of this passage is not certain. As it stands, the Mosa after the junction of the Waal forms the island by flowing into the Rhine, and the junction of the Mosa and Rhine is eighty miles from the sea. As to the distance of eighty miles we cannot trust the manuscript numerals, and if Caesar wrote eighty, he might be misinformed. If Schneider's text is right, Caesar supposed that the Mosa had no outlet into the sea, but joined the Rhine below the island of the Batavi. Caesar then describes the course of the Rhine from the source in the Alps to the country of the Treviri, and so far he describes it as a rapid stream. He adds, "where the Rhine approaches the ocean, it flows down in several directions and makes numerous large islands, many of which are inhabited by savage people some of whom are supposed to live on fish and birds' eggs. Finally the Rhine enters the ocean by many mouths." Any person, who will read Caesar's narrative with proper attention, will see that the Germans were not driven into the water at the junction of the Mosa and Rhine which is here described. Before Caesar saw the Germans, they had left the Rhine and advanced south of Liège (c. 6), and when the Roman crossed the Mans and approached them, they could not move westward, nor would they move northwards into the country where they had wintered and fed on the stores of the Menapii (c. 4, 15); and as they finally fled to the Rhine, it is plain

---

(xxxii. 5) has "in confluenti Danubii et Savi." Caesar might also have written, "ad confluentes Mosam et Rhenum." As the modern name Coblenz is a corruption of the Latin "confluentes," it is probable that Coblenz represents Caesar's "confluentem." We may infer that Coblenz in the Swiss Canton of Aargau, at the confluence of the Aar and the Rhine, was also named Confluentes by the Romans.

[1] It has been suggested that this chapter is an interpolation, and it may be; but there is no evidence from the MSS. which supports this conjecture; and Dion (39. c. 49) appears to have found this chapter in his copy of Caesar.

that the junction of the Rhine and Moss, of which Caesar speaks, is the junction of the Rhine and Mosel, whatever Caesar wrote. It is possible that both the Maas and the Mosel had the same name. It is possible too that Caesar may have written Mosella. Caesar then was somewhere about Mayen in the Eifel when he reached the place where he expected to find water (c. 11), and after advancing eight miles he arrived at the German camp, from which the enemy were driven towards Coblenz[b].

Caesar now determined to cross the Rhine, and chiefly because he saw that the Germans were so easily induced to enter Gallia; for he thought that they would fear for their own safety when they knew that the Roman army was able and bold enough to cross the great river. He had other reasons also. The cavalry of the Usipetes and Tenctheri, who were on the west side of the Maas, came back after the defeat of their countrymen and crossed the Rhine into the territory of the Sigambri. Caesar sent to the Sigambri to demand the surrender of the fugitives, but the Sigambri refused to

---

[b] See the Notes in Duker's Florus (lii. 10). The author of the "Histoire de César" (II. 143) places the defeat of the Germans at the junction of the Rhine and Maas, as others have done; but this conclusion is inconsistent with Caesar's narrative. Goeler (p. 110) places the defeat at the confluence of the Rhine and Mosel, a conclusion to which we are led by a strict interpretation of Caesar, compared with the geography of the Rhine land. Caesar's narrative of this campaign is exceedingly brief, but I cannot see why there should be such difference of opinion about the site of the place where the Germans were defeated. Many years ago I came to the conclusion that Caesar has determined the site by speaking of the junction of the Rhine with another river, named the Mosa in his text, and that this Mosa is the Mosel. Those who have sailed up the Rhine will not easily believe that the German defeat took place at the present junction of the Rhine and Maas, or at any other ancient and assumed junction; and if a man has examined the Eifel and the country between Mayen and Coblenz he may easily convince himself that he will find in those parts a more probable site of the place which he is looking for. Goeler, who gives good reasons for his opinion, has unluckily added one that is bad. He says that Cluver points out that Dion Cassius (39, c. 47, 48) places the destruction of the Germans at the confluence of the Rhine and the Mosel. The evidence of Dion would be worth nothing, if we had it, but he does not say what is attributed to him. The author of the "Histoire" (note ii. p. 139) relies for his opinion on the researches of Major Cohausen of the Prussian army, which agree with the results of MM. Stoffel and Locqueywic, but he does not give the arguments of these gentlemen. His own arguments appear to me to be inconclusive.

give them up. The Ubii, the only people on the east side of the Rhine who had sent ambassadors to Caesar, and had made an alliance with him and given hostages, earnestly entreated him to protect them against the attacks of the Suevi: if he was too busy to do that, they would be content if he would only bring his army across the river; the fame of his power since the defeat of Ariovistus and the late battle had spread to the remotest German tribes, and the Ubii would be safe when it was known that they had the friendship of the Roman people: they were ready to supply boats for the transport of the army. Though Caesar was resolved to cross the Rhine, he did not think it quite safe to cross in boats, nor, as he expresses it, consistent with his own dignity and the dignity of the Roman people. The difficulty of making a bridge was very great owing to the width, the rapidity and the depth of the stream, but still he determined either to cross in this way or not at all. The manner in which he accomplished the work shows that he had a body of skilful engineers. The bridge, as he describes it, was constructed thus (c. 17).

A pair of timbers, one foot and a half in the square, pointed at a short distance from one end, and of a length proportioned to the depth of the river, were fastened together with an interval of two feet between them. The pair of timbers was floated into the stream on boats to the proper position, and then driven into the bed of the river with rammers, not perpendicularly like piles, but sloping in the direction of the current. Opposite to this pair and at the distance of forty feet lower down was fixed another pair of timbers joined in like manner, but sloping against the direction of the current. Upon and between these pairs of timbers and extending from one pair to the other was placed a cross beam two feet in width, for such was the distance between the timbers; and the upper extremities of each pair of timbers were secured on both sides by braces[4]. The result of this construction was that the timbers on each side were kept at the distance of two feet by the beam placed between them, and were also held together by the braces; and, as Caesar says, such was

---

[4] "Fibulae." These "fibulae" are misrepresented in Planche 15 of the "Histoire de César," but they are correctly represented by Goeler, Taf. viii.

the firmness of the work that the greater the force with which the water flowed down, the stronger was the work held together. The number of such pairs of timbers placed opposite to one another would depend on the width of the river, and the width of the intervals between the pairs in each row; but Caesar does not say what this width was, nor the width of the river. Beams were then placed lengthways in the direction of the bridge from each cross beam to the next, and over these beams planks were laid at right angles and also hurdles (crates), and thus a floor was made. In order to strengthen the pairs of timbers, piles[7] were driven perpendicularly into the river on the lower side and in front of these timbers on two lines meeting at an angle and forming, as Caesar expresses it, a ram's head. These upright piles were fastened together and also connected with each pair of timbers. Other piles similarly placed were driven into the river at a small distance above the upper pairs of timbers in order that if trunks of trees or boats were sent down the river by the barbarians, their force might be broken by the rams' heads and the bridge might be protected.

The materials for the bridge were collected and the bridge was built in ten days. It was a short time for making so great a work, but Caesar had a body of engineers (fabri) and the legionary soldiers could assist. Strada (De Bello Belgico, Decas Secunda, Lib. Sextus) following Caesar's example, as he says, describes the bridge which Alexander Farnese, Duke of Parma, made over the Schelde below Antwerp when he was besieging that town. It was a more difficult undertaking than Caesar's owing to the width and depth of the river and the tides, but it was only built part of the distance from each bank towards the middle of the river, which was left open and afterwards closed with vessels anchored side by side.

Leaving a strong force to guard each end of the bridge Caesar

[7] "Sublicae ... oblique": these piles were perpendicular and in two lines oblique to the direction of the current, but meeting in an angle and so forming an aries or ram (pro ariete subjectae). These "sublicae" on the lower side of the bridge are represented in the French plate by a timber driven into the river obliquely in such a way as to be nearly useless. Oudier also misunderstands this part of the construction.

led his army across and advanced northwards into the country of the Sigambri. Probably he placed a tête de pont at each end of the bridge. Several German peoples sent commissioners to sue for peace and friendship, and all of them received favourable answers, accompanied with an order to give hostages. The Sigambri, however, as soon as the Romans began to build the bridge, made preparations for flight, to which they were urged by the Usipetes and Tenchtheri who had taken refuge with them: they left the country with all their movables and plunged into the depths of the solitary forests. During the few days that Caesar stayed in the country of the Sigambri he burnt all the villages and buildings, and cut all the corn. The consequence must have been that in the next winter many Germans died of cold and hunger. From the territory of the Sigambri Caesar returned, as he says, into the country of the Ubii, from which statement we learn indirectly that his bridge brought him into the country of the Ubii, who were opposite to the Treviri. He heard from the Ubii, that the Suevi on hearing of the bridge being built met in council, sent orders to all the Suevic nation to quit their towns (oppida, as Caesar calls them), and to hide their children, wives and movables in the forests. All the men capable of bearing arms were directed to meet at a place about the centre of the Suevic territory, to wait there for the Romans and to stake all on one great battle. The resolution was wise, but the Roman was too wary to accept the challenge. He had accomplished, as he says, all the objects for which he had crossed the river, and after passing eighteen days on German soil he returned to Gallia and broke down the bridge[a].

[a] The author of the "Histoire de César" (ii. 143) places Caesar's bridge at Bonn, a supposition entirely inconsistent with the narrative. The arguments on both sides would fill some pages; and those who have made up their minds on the matter either way, would probably not be induced to change it. Those who have read Caesar with care and know the country will place the bridge, as Goeler does (p. 112), in the open Rhine valley about Neuwied. Goeler selects Urmitz between Neuwied and Engers as the place. The island at Urmitz would certainly facilitate the work.

CHAPTER IX.

THE FIRST INVASION OF BRITANNIA.

B.C. 55.

AFTER returning to the Gallic side of the Rhine, Caesar says that he resolved to invade Britain, though there only remained a small part of the summer, and the winters begin early in these northern regions. He had joined his army earlier than usual (B. G. iv. 6), and his operations against the Germans were soon concluded. He had indeed spent some time in calling together the Gallic chiefs, providing his supplies and leading his men from their winter quarters on the south side of the lower Seine (B. G. iii. 29), a distance of more than three hundred miles, to meet the Germans. But all this does not explain why so little of the summer remained after he had destroyed his bridge over the Rhine.

His reason for invading Britain was, as he says, because he was informed that aid had been sent from the island to "our enemies" in almost all the Gallic wars[1]; but he has said nothing about the fact in the earlier part of the Commentaries except that the Veneti sent to Britain for help in the preceeding year (B. G. iii. 9, p. 108). If the season should be too late for military operations in Britain, he still thought there would be time enough for him to become acquainted with the country, the harbours, and the landing-places, all which were nearly unknown to the Galli. Few persons visited the island except the traders, and they were only acquainted with the coast and those parts which were opposite to the Gallic

---

[1] The words of the text (iv. 20) seem ambiguous. He may mean that he was informed, that in the Gallic wars generally aid was sent to "our enemies;" but there is hardly any sense in this.

shores. Cæsar summoned indeed traders from all parts, but
he could get no information from them, from which we conclude that they would not say what they knew. The Veneti
who traded to Britain (B. G. iii. 0) certainly must have been
able to tell him something, but they were perhaps too far off
for his inquiries; he might not choose to trust them[2], and
they probably could tell him nothing about the shortest
passage. In order to obtain information he sent C. Volusenus
with a ship of war to explore the country, and he marched
with his forces from the Rhine[3] into the territory of the
Morini, because the passage from those parts to Britain was
the shortest. This remark shows that his march was directed
to that part of the French coast which lies between Boulogne
and Calais. His march from the Rhine to the Straits in a
due west course would be in direct distance near two hundred
and fifty miles; but we do not know what route he took.

Cæsar ordered vessels to assemble on the coast of the
Morini from all the adjacent parts, and also the fleet which
he had used in the Venetian war the year before. In the
mean time information of his designs being carried to Britain
by the traders, commissioners came to him from several of the
island states to offer hostages and their submission. They
were well received, exhorted to persevere in their intentions
and sent back accompanied by Commius whom Cæsar had
set up as a king of the Atrebates after the defeat of that nation
(B. G. ii. 23). Cæsar had tried the courage and prudence of
his new king, and believed him to be devoted to his interests.
Commius had also considerable influence in those parts of
Gallia where Cæsar then was[4]. He was instructed to visit
such British states as he could, to urge them to be faithful to
the Romans, and tell them that Cæsar would soon be among
them. Volusenus returned to Cæsar on the fifth day and

---

[2] Strabo (p. 194) may have had some authority for saying that the Veneti before they were attacked by Cæsar were ready to prevent Cæsar's passage to Britain because the trade was in their hands.

[3] "In Morinos proficiscitur;" "he entered the country of the Morini." This is the meaning of this expression in Cæsar.

[4] So I understand "in his regionibus" or "in iis regionibus," as it stands in some texts. The author of the "Histoire" (ii. 155) supposes that Cæsar means "among the Britons;" but I think that this is a mistake.

made his report. He had examined the country as far as a man could who had not ventured to quit his vessel and trust himself to the barbarians.

While Caesar was waiting for his ships, he was visited by deputies from a large part of the Morini. These men came to apologize for their past behaviour (p. 121): it was through ignorance of Roman usages that they had resisted Caesar, but they were now ready to obey his commands. The Roman general accepted their submission, but required a large number of hostages. He had now got together eighty transports which were sufficient to carry over two legions, the seventh and the tenth, and he had some ships of war which were distributed among the quaestor, the legati, and the commanders of the auxiliary troops[1]. On the return voyage when the troops were close packed, two of the transports carried about three hundred men (B. G. iv. 37), but no conclusion as to the force of the two legions can be drawn from this fact (p. 1, note). Caesar had also eighteen transports in a port eight miles distant from the port in which the eighty vessels were. These eighteen transports were assigned to the cavalry, but they were prevented by the wind from joining the fleet. In another passage (iv. 28) he names this port the upper or higher port, which means a port north of his port of embarcation. The rest of the army under the command of Q. Titurius Sabinus and L. Aurunculeius Cotta was ordered to march against the Menapii and those districts of the Morini which had not sent deputies to Caesar. P. Sulpicius Rufus was left with a sufficient force to occupy the port of embarcation, to which Caesar gives no name. In the expedition of the next year he sailed from a port named Itius[2], and the simplest explanation of the passage (B. G. v. 2) is that Itius was the port from which Caesar sailed this year. But this conclusion cannot be deduced from the Latin text with certainty. Strabo (p. 200) supposed that Caesar sailed from Itius in this expedition.

---

[1] We see from chapter 25 that he had archers and slingers, and they were in the war-ships.

[2] It is uncertain whether the name in Caesar is "Itium" or "Iccium" or "Icium." See Schneider's critical note, and Gibson, De Portu Iccio Dissertatio Nova.

The narrative of the two expeditions to Britain is told by
Caesar in his usual rapid style, and there is little difficulty in
understanding his text. But there is difference of opinion
about the French port from which he sailed and the part of
Britain at which he landed. We must read the narrative of
each voyage before we can understand the matter and come to
a conclusion. I shall therefore first report Caesar's narrative
of both expeditions as accurately as I can, and I shall state
the result of some modern inquiries on the places of embarcation and landing. Whatever difficulties there may be in
Caesar's narrative, as for instance in iv. 20 and other passages,
the same difficulties will appear in this narrative, for the
object here is to state only what Caesar says. Some of those
who have discussed this matter have mixed up Caesar's statements with the evidence of late compilers who cannot be
trusted.

The weather being favourable Caesar (B. G. iv. 23) set sail
"about the third watch," which probably means after the
second watch was past, and half the Roman night was spent
(p. 9, note), or about our midnight. The cavalry were ordered
to advance to the other port, which Caesar here names the
"further port," to embark there, and to follow him; but these
orders were not executed with perfect punctuality. About
the fourth hour of the following day, or the beginning of the
fourth hour after sunrise, Caesar reached Britain with the
first vessels, and saw armed forces of the enemy on all the
heights. If he sailed just after midnight on the 26th of
August according to our reckoning, as we shall afterwards
see, he reached the British coast between eight and nine in
the morning or about half-past eight, and as the sun would
rise about five, he would see the coast several hours before he
reached it and also see the point which he wished to make.
The nature of the place which he had reached was such, and
the sea was bounded by heights so steep¹, that a missile
could be thrown upon the shore from the elevated parts. The
point to which Caesar had brought his vessels appears to have

---

¹ " Its montibus angustis mare continebatur." "Angustus" is a participial
form and means "contracted." In this passage the sense is "steep,"
"abrupt."

been the port which then existed at Dover, on the site now occupied by part of the town[e]. Finding the place not at all suited for landing he anchored and waited till the ninth hour for the rest of the ships. If the ninth hour means the beginning of the ninth hour, he waited five Roman hours or nearly until half-past two in the afternoon. In the meantime he called together the legati and tribunes, and informed them of what he had learned from Volusenus and what his intention was; and he recommended a prompt execution of his orders when the signal was given. After dismissing the officers he gave the signal when the wind and tide (aestus) were both favourable; and the anchors being weighed, he continued his course (progressus[f]) about seven Roman miles and brought his ships to an open and flat shore.

Whether Caesar sailed from Boulogne, as some suppose, or from some place between Boulogne and Calais, his course to Dover was between north-west and north, and if he continued his course, it was still a northern course, and after a seven miles' sail he would reach the open and level beach between Walmer Castle and Deal, which is correctly described by two words. "Open" means that from the beach he could see into the country; the word "level" or "flat" cannot be misunderstood. This is the plain meaning of Caesar's narrative and the true interpretation of his text[g].

[e] "Histoire de César," Planche 17, and the author's note, vol. II. 157.

[f] This word (progressus) always means in Caesar a continued movement in the same direction in which a movement has been made. This meaning, as we might suppose, is the same in other Roman writers. "Regressus" means "having returned" by the same way by which a man has advanced. Caesar says that he continued his voyage in the direction in which he had made it before reaching the high cliffs; and he had the wind and tide with him.

[g] Dion Cassius (39, c. 51) says that Caesar did not land where he ought to have landed, or where it was best to land, for the Britons had occupied all the landing-places opposite to the mainland. "Accordingly Caesar sailed round a certain projecting promontory to the other side." But we cannot tell from this passage in which direction he moved, nor could Dion, for he only copied some authority, which was not Caesar. Perhaps he followed Cotta who served under Caesar (Athenaeus, vi. 273, ed. Cas.). But in this passage Athenaeus or Cotta is speaking of the second expedition, for Cotta did not accompany Caesar in the first expedition. Athenaeus quotes Cotta's work under the title of a "History of the Roman Polity."

When the Britons saw the ships leaving the anchorage, they sent forward their war chariots and following with the rest of the force attempted to prevent the landing of the Romans. The difficulty of landing was great. The size of the vessels did not allow them to anchor except in deep water: the soldiers were unacquainted with the coast, their hands were embarrassed, they were loaded with their armour, and they were compelled at the same time to leap out of the ships, to gain a footing in the water and to resist the enemy, who either remaining on the land or advancing a short distance into the water, with all their limbs free and a perfect knowledge of the ground, discharged their missiles without fear and urged forward their well-trained horses. The Romans alarmed by all these circumstances and new to this kind of fighting did not show their usual alacrity and readiness for battle. Caesar then ordered the ships of war, which presented to the enemy an unusual appearance and were more manageable, to move away a little from the transports, to be brought with their broadsides to the shore and placed on the exposed flank of the enemy, for the purpose of driving him off with slings, arrows, and missiles from the engines. The barbarians terrified by the sight of the ships, the noise of the oars and the discharge from the engines, were checked and drew back a little. The soldiers however still hesitated chiefly on account of the depth of the water, when the eagle-bearer of the tenth legion offering up a prayer to the gods for the successful issue of his resolve, cried aloud, "Leap into the water, fellow-soldiers, unless you intend to betray the eagle to the enemy: I at least shall have done my duty to my country and the general." With these words he threw himself into the water and carried the standard right against the Britons. The soldiers cheering one another followed the leader's example and all jumped from the ship into the sea. Those on the nearest vessels in the first line did the same and supported their comrades. The fight was maintained obstinately on both sides. But there was great confusion among the Romans, for they could neither keep their ranks nor get a firm footing nor follow their several standards, and every man as he left his ship joined any standard that was nearest. The enemy on the contrary being well acquainted with all the shoal waters, when they saw any of the soldiers singly quitting the vessels, drove their horses against them while they were unable to resist, and in great numbers surrounded any small body; and if the Romans in any place formed a compact mass, the enemy discharged their missiles on the unprotected flank. Caesar observing this difficulty ordered the boats of the ships of war and the light skiffs used for reconnoitring to be manned and sent them to support those who were most exposed to attack. As soon as the Romans had a footing on the dry land, they fell on the enemy with all their force and put them to flight; but the pursuit could not be continued, for the ships which carried the cavalry had been unable to keep their course and reach the island.

As soon as the enemy rallied from their flight, they sent to ask for peace, proffered hostages, and declared their readiness to obey Caesar's orders. The deputies who came were accompanied by Commius, whom the Britons had seized and put in chains as soon as he landed, though he was the bearer of Caesar's message to them and invested with something of the character of an ambassador. The Britons now sent Commius back, and in their entreaty for peace they threw on the multitude the blame for what had been done, and begged pardon for their want of thought. Though Caesar complained that the Britons after having sent deputies to Gallia to ask for peace had attacked him without any provocation, he accepted their excuse, but he demanded hostages. Part of the hostages were given immediately, and the Britons promised in a few days to give the rest who were sent for from some distant places. In the mean time the deputies told their people to return home, and chiefs from all quarters began to visit Caesar and to recommend themselves and their people to his protection. Peace was thus confirmed.

On the fourth day after Caesar's arrival in Britain, the eighteen ships in which the cavalry were embarked, sailed from the upper port, as Caesar now names it, with a light breeze (c. 28). As the vessels were approaching Britain and were visible from the camp, a violent storm suddenly arose and not a single ship was able to keep its course. Some of them were carried back to the place from which they sailed; and others with great risk were driven to the lower part of the island¹, which, as Caesar says, was nearer to the west: still they cast anchor, but as the vessels were filling with water, they were compelled in the darkness to put to sea, and make for the continent.

On the same night it happened to be full moon, on which day the tides in the ocean are the highest, but this, says Caesar, was unknown to our men. Yet some of these men had seen the tides on the coast of Bretagne the year before and Caesar speaks of them himself (B. G. iii. 12). It is strange if he had not observed or heard of the spring tides during the Venetian campaign. The high flood filled the ships of war which had been drawn up on the beach. The transports which were at anchor were dashed about by the storm, and the Romans were unable to manage or protect them. Many ships were wrecked, and the rest after losing ropes, anchors and the other tackle were not seaworthy. The natural consequence of this misfortune was great uneasiness in the army, for there were no other vessels for their reconveyance to the Gallic coast, and they were deficient in all the means for repairing the ships; and as every body knew that the army would winter in Gallia, there was no provision made for staying in Britain. This full moon fell on the night of the thirtieth and thirty-first of August after midnight, as Dr. Halley computed it, and he concluded that Caesar landed on the twenty-sixth. But the expression "on the fourth day" is ambiguous, for the Romans sometimes reckoned inclusively and sometimes not. Examples of both ways of reckoning are common². If the day of landing is one day and the day of full moon is another, only two days intervened, and Caesar landed on the twenty-seventh. Caesar could not be certain about the exact time of full moon, but he could be certain about the spring tide, which falls on the day after the new and the full moon. Caesar then may have landed on the twenty-eighth of August.

The British chiefs, who had come to Caesar after the battle,

¹ "To the lower part" means "towards the south."
² Savigny, System des heutigen Römischen Rechts, iv., Beylage, xi.

now held a conference. They saw that the Romans had neither cavalry nor ships nor supplies, and they concluded from the narrow limits of the camp that the number of the soldiers was small, for as Caesar had crossed over without any encumbrance (impedimenta), his camp occupied less ground. Accordingly the Britons resolved to begin the war again, to prevent the enemy from taking corn or any thing else, and to prolong hostilities to the winter, being confident that if they could defeat this army or prevent it from returning, no invader would ever enter Britain again. They now began a few at a time to leave the camp and secretly to summon their people from the country.

Before discovering the designs of the Britons, Caesar suspected what would happen after the damage to his vessels, and he was confirmed in his suspicion by the fact that no more hostages were given. Accordingly he prepared for the worst. He set about bringing corn from the country daily into his camp; and taking the vessels which had suffered most, he employed the timber and copper (aes) in repairing the rest, and ordered materials to be brought from the continent for this purpose. The soldiers worked with the greatest goodwill, and Caesar with the loss of twelve ships was enabled to put the remainder in seaworthy condition.

While this work was going on, one legion as usual was sent to cut the corn of the Britons[1], and the legion was the seventh on the day of which Caesar is now speaking. Up to this time nothing had happened to make the Romans suspect an attack, for some of the Britons stayed on their lands, and others still visited the camp. But on this day those who were on guard before the gates reported to Caesar that more dust than usual was seen in the quarter to which the legion had gone. Caesar suspecting the designs of the Britons ordered the cohorts which were on guard to march with him towards the seventh legion, and two other cohorts to take their place[2]. The

[1] It has been said that no wheat grows between Deal and Sandwich. But this is not true. At Worth there is some of the best corn-land in England.
[2] If a cohort was stationed at each of the four gates of the camp, the text is intelligible. Caesar took these four cohorts, and sent two other cohorts to take their place; and so each gate would now be guarded by half a cohort.

THE FIRST INVASION OF BRITANNIA.   171

remaining cohorts of the tenth legion were ordered to arm and
follow immediately. After advancing a little farther from
the camp Caesar saw that the seventh legion was hard pressed
by the enemy and with difficulty sustaining the attack with
their closed ranks, for the enemy were showering missiles on
them from all directions. As the corn had been cut in these
parts except in one place, the Britons suspecting that the Romans
would come hither had hid themselves in the woods during
the night, and while the men who had laid down their arms
were dispersed and engaged in cutting the corn, the Britons
suddenly fell on them, killed a few, threw the rest into
disorder before they could form their ranks, and surrounded
them with the war chariots.

Caesar here introduces a description of the way in which
the Britons used their war chariots and attacked cavalry, but
he brought no cavalry with him, and the description seems to
be out of place. This, he says, is their way of fighting [1].
They begin by driving the chariots through the enemy's ranks
(perequitant) while they discharge missiles; and by the alarm
caused by the horses and the noise of the wheels they
generally throw the enemy's lines into confusion, and when
they have made their way among the cavalry, they leap down
from the chariots and fight on foot. In the meantime the
drivers severally according to circumstances move away from
the battle and place the chariots in such a position that, if the
fighters should be overpowered by numbers, they can easily

---

[1] Goeler (p. 123) interprets this passage in a different way. He supposes the cavalry to be the British cavalry and gives to the whole chapter a meaning, which I do not accept. It does not appear from Caesar that the Britons had any cavalry. Yet some critics misunderstanding Caesar, as I suppose, think that they had, and in this opinion they agree with Dion (39, c. 51). Frontinus (Strat. II. 3. 18) speaks of Caesar checking the attack of the scythe-armed chariots of the Galli by fixing stakes in the ground; but Caesar never mentions war chariots of the Galli, nor does he say that the chariots of the Britons were armed with scythes. Livy (x. 28) writing of the battle in which P. Decius the son devoted himself for his country speaks of the Gallic "esseda" and "carri." But this is probably an invention of the historian to ornament a description, and he may have had no other authority for these Gallic "esseda" in Italy than Caesar's description of the British "esseda." As to the verb "perequitant" in Caesar compare Gellius (xviii. 5), who says "equitare . . . et homo equo stans et equus sub homine gradiens dicebatur;" and as to the Britons having no cavalry, see Schneider's Caesar, B. G. v. 15, critical note.

retire to their own people. In this way the Britons in battle have the rapid movement of cavalry and the steadiness of infantry, and by daily practice they become so expert that they are able[7] to manage their horses at full speed on steep slopes without falling, and quickly to check and turn them, to run along the pole of the carriage, stand on the horses' yoke and then rapidly retire to the chariot.

The Romans were put into confusion by this strange kind of fighting, and Caesar came most seasonably to their aid, for on his arrival the enemy stopped the attack, and the soldiers recovered from their fear. Caesar considering the occasion not favourable for a fight with the enemy kept his position, and after a short time led the legions back. While the Romans were employed in their camp the Britons who had hitherto remained on their lands went off to join their countrymen. The weather was so bad for several successive days that it kept the Romans in camp and the enemy from attacking. In the interval the Britons despatched messengers in all directions to inform the people how small the numbers of the Romans were, and what an opportunity there was for making booty and of ridding themselves of their enemies for ever, if they stormed the camp[8]. In consequence of this message a large number of infantry and war chariots came to make the attempt. Caesar saw that if the enemy were repulsed, they would still escape as they had done before; however as he had been joined by about thirty horsemen, whom Commius[9] had brought over, he arranged his legions in front of the camp. The battle began, and the Britons soon turned their backs. The Romans pursued as far as they could and killed a great number. They burnt all the buildings far and wide, and returned to the camp. On the same day commissioners

---

[7] "Sustinere." I have followed Oscler's explanation of this word (p. 123). "Ihre Pferde in vollem Lauf vor dem Stürzen zu bewahren."

[8] If the Britons thought two legions a small army, we may conclude that they could muster a much larger force.

[9] He has not mentioned these horsemen before. Perhaps both they and Commius had been seized on landing, and the horsemen were given up at the same time with Commius. The fact of Commius crossing over to Britain with thirty horsemen proves that the passage between Gallia and Britain was a usual thing.

came from the enemy to sue for peace. Caesar demanded of them twice the number of hostages which he had already required and ordered them to be brought to the continent[1], for, as the autumnal equinox was near and his ships were not strong, he intended to leave the island before the bad season began. Taking advantage of favourable weather he set sail a little after midnight, and reached the Gallic coast with all his vessels. Two of the transports however could not make the same harbours as the other vessels and were carried a little further south. As soon as the soldiers, about three hundred, had landed from these two vessels and were marching to the camp, the Morini in those parts, who had made their submission to Caesar (c. 22), expecting to carry off some booty surrounded the men at first in no very large numbers and ordered them to lay down their arms, if they would save their lives. The Romans forming what they called a circle (orbis) presented a front to the enemy on all sides and defended themselves. The shouts brought more of the Morini to the spot, to the number of near six thousand. On the news reaching Caesar he sent all the cavalry from the camp to aid the three hundred men, who had been fighting bravely above four hours and had killed many of the enemy. As soon as the cavalry appeared, the Morini threw away their arms and fled, but a large number of them were killed.

On the following day Caesar sent T. Labienus with the legions which had returned from Britain to attack the rebellious Morini. The summer had been very dry, and the Morini could not save themselves in the marshes as they had done the year before. Most of them fell into the hands of Labienus. Titurius and Cotta, who had led the legions into the land of the Menapii, returned from their expedition. They had wasted the country, cut the corn, and burnt the houses of this unfortunate people, who only escaped by hiding themselves in the thickest forests. Caesar placed all his men in winter quarters among the Belgae. Only two of the British states sent their hostages to him. When Caesar's despatches reached Rome, the Senate ordered a thanksgiving of twenty

---

[1] Caesar knew then that the Britons had ships.

days, which was five days more than the thanksgiving for the victories of B.C. 57. The matter for rejoicing was not much, if the despatches contained no more than the Commentaries; but Caesar had opened a new world to the Romans.

CHAPTER X.

THE SECOND CONSULSHIP OF POMPEIUS.

B.C. 55.

WHEN Caesar says (B. G. iv. 6) that he went to his army in the spring of the year B.C. 55 earlier than usual, we may conclude that he spent the winter in North Italy, but he does not say that he did. He would learn in Cisalpine Gallia how things were going on at Rome. L. Domitius, one of the candidates for the consulship, threatened, if he were elected, to deprive Caesar of his army and his provinces, and it was necessary for Caesar's interest that his two confederates Crassus and Pompeius should be elected. The history of Caesar's intrigues at this time is not found in any contemporary writer. It was part of the arrangement at the conference of Luca, as Plutarch says (Pomp. c. 51), that Caesar should help Pompeius and Crassus in their election by sending many of his men to vote, and Dion (39, c. 31) states that P. Crassus, Caesar's legatus in Aquitania (p. 121), did bring soldiers to Rome for the election; but it is very difficult to believe this. We know from Cicero (Ad Q. Fr. ii. 9) that P. Crassus was in Rome before the middle of February, and his father was then consul.

On the day of the election L. Domitius, the only candidate who opposed the two confederates, came to the Field of Mars before daylight accompanied by his brother-in-law M. Cato. Here they were attacked by armed men who killed the linkbearer of Domitius and wounded Cato and others. Cato urged Domitius to stay and struggle as long as they had life, but Domitius, who was not so obstinate as his brother-in-law, fled to his house, and Pompeius and Crassus were elected. This victory was not enough. It was necessary for the confederates to secure the other magistracies for their partisans, and particularly to exclude M. Cato, who was a candidate for the praetorship. On the eleventh of February a senatus-consultum about bribery was made on the motion[1] of Afranius, as Cicero states (Ad Q. Fr. ii. 9); but he does not say what was the purpose of this resolution of the senate. He adds however that some senators proposed that the praetors who were going to be elected should not enter on their office for sixty days, and the consuls refused to listen to this proposal. On this day, adds Cicero, the consuls plainly rejected Cato as a candidate: "they have," he says, "all the power in their hands, and they mean to let people know it." A passage in Plutarch (Cato Min. c. 42) explains this letter. The consuls, he says, suddenly and without the knowledge of many of the body summoned the Senate and got a vote that those who should be elected praetors should enter on the office immediately, in order that there might be no time to prosecute them on the charge of bribery; for a magistrate could not be prosecuted during his office. Bribery was now safe, and the consuls brought forward their own friends as candidates for the praetorship and themselves gave bribes and stood by while the voting was going on; but as the election seemed likely to be in favour of Cato, Pompeius stopped the voting by declaring that he had heard thunder. Afterwards P. Vatinius, Caesar's tool in his consulship, was elected instead of Cato, who though an unsuccessful candidate went home "attended by such a crowd as not even all the praetors together, who were elected, had to accompany them." Whether the second voting was accompanied by violence, as Plutarch says, or there was no violence, as Dion reports, is perfectly indifferent. A more scandalous transaction never occurred in the long history of Rome than this election.

At the election of the curule aediles the opposite factions came to blows and some were killed. Pompeius himself was

[1] Drumann (III. 279) observes that this letter contains in the editions the date III. Id. Mai, which ought to be Id. Febr. See Orelli's edition, and the Excursus De Ordine Epist. ad Q. Fratrem; also p. 175 as to P. Crassus.

in the fray, and his garments were drenched with blood. His slaves went home to get other clothes for their master, and according to the story carried with them the blood-stained garments, at the sight of which Julia fainted, and the alarm caused a miscarriage, for she was then with child. However the elections terminated according to the wish of the consuls, who also gained to their side all the new tribunes except two, C. Ateius Capito and P. Aquillius Gallus.

In the month of April Cicero, who was in the country at his Cuman villa, received a visit from Pompeius (Ad Att. iv. 9). This visit was perhaps after the provinces had been assigned to the consuls by a vote of the people, for the Senate had not determined the consular provinces before the elections, as they ought to have done. The consuls employed as their agent the tribune C. Trebonius, as Caesar in his consulship had used the tribune P. Vatinius. Trebonius proposed a bill to the popular assembly, that the consular provinces should be Syria and the two divisions of Spain, and that they should be held for five years. Favonius obtained permission to speak against the bill, but only one hour's talk was allowed him. M. Cato obtained two hours' licence, and as he went on talking after the time was spent, he was removed from the Rostra by force. Even this did not stop his mouth, and he was put out of the Forum; but he soon returned and again made his way to the Rostra, calling on the citizens to aid him. At last Trebonius ordered Cato to be taken to prison, whither he was followed by a crowd listening to him, for he talked all the way. Trebonius however was prudent enough to let the man go; and nothing further was done on this day. On the next day the tribune P. Aquillius Gallus intended to put his veto on the proceedings, and in order to secure a place in the Forum he went to the Senate-house, or some place where the Senate met, to pass the night and to be ready for the morrow. He did pass the night there, and also a large part of the following day against his will, for Trebonius fastened the doors. The tribune Ateius, and M. Cato and Favonius with their followers were prevented from entering the Forum by men who had occupied it the night before. However Favonius, Ninnius, Cato and Ateius contrived to slip into the assembly, and Cato and Ateius mounting up on men's shoulders attempted to break up the meeting by crying out "thunder;" Cato, if the story is true, only helping Ateius with his voice, for he had no authority to make such a declaration. This was the signal for a fight, in which four men were killed and many wounded. Aquillius in the midst of the tumult broke out of the Senate-house and received some hard blows, and a senator L. Villius Annalis was struck in the face by the consul Crassus. The bill of Trebonius of course was carried. As the people were leaving the ground, Ateius presented to them his colleague Aquillius covered with his own blood, a magistrate whose sacred office ought to have protected him from insult and violence.

Another bill proposed by Trebonius and passed by the assembly gave to Caesar the administration of his provinces for five years more. By the bill of Vatinius Caesar could hold his provinces to the end of B.C. 54, if we reckon the first five years from the beginning of B.C. 58; and the new bill would empower him to hold them from the beginning of B.C. 53 to the end of B.C. 49. Cato made no opposition to this bill, for all resistance was useless, but he warned Pompeius of the consequences that would follow both to himself and the state. Of the provinces assigned to the consuls Crassus took Syria, and Pompeius had the two Spains with four legions. The statement of Plutarch and Appian that Pompeius had also Africa does not agree with Dion, who mentions only Spain.

Dion (39, c. 37) speaks of the consuls proposing and carrying a bill which contained severer penalties against bribery; as if, says the historian, they had committed a smaller offence in obtaining their office by force than if they had obtained it by giving money. This passage appears to refer to a Lex Licinia de sodaliciis proposed by Crassus to check the practice of candidates employing agents to corrupt the voters. The consuls also introduced a bill for limiting the luxurious habits of the rich, though both of them were notorious for their sumptuous style of living. The orator Hortensius, who was a man of great expense, persuaded the consuls to give up their foolish design by praising them for the splendour which they showed at home and their liberality to others, and urging their own practice in confirmation of his advice. We may conjecture that the consuls, if they did propose a sumptuary bill, had some reasons which we are not acquainted with, and that they had no wish to convert the bill into a law.

A Lex Pompeia Judiciaria was also enacted this year, and before Cicero delivered his speech against Piso (In Pis. c. 30). The purpose of this law is explained by Asconius (In Pis. p. 16, ed. Orelli). The Lex Aurelia of B.C. 70 (vol. iii. p. 52) made the Judices eligible from senators, equites, and the tribuni aerarii. This Lex Pompeia made no alteration in the three eligible classes, but it enacted that the Judices should be chosen from the richest persons in the three classes, and the richest would be determined by the census.

L. Calpurnius Piso, the father-in-law of Caesar, who went to his province of Macedonia in B.C. 57, returned to Rome in B.C. 55. Cicero says that an attempt was made in B.C. 57 to recall both Piso and Gabinius. In the speech on the consular provinces made in B.C. 56, Cicero flattered Caesar and abused his father-in-law. Asconius says that Piso and Gabinius were recalled in consequence of the opinion expressed by Cicero in his oration on the consular provinces, but this appears to be not correct. Piso was superseded, and probably Cicero was most active in the matter, by Macedonia being declared a Praetorian Province and being assigned to Q. Ancharius in B.C. 55. When Piso returned to Rome he addressed the Senate in answer to the charges which Cicero had made against him, and Cicero replied in a speech which is extant, but the beginning is defective. It was delivered a few days before the opening of the theatre of Pompeius. This speech of Cicero is unequalled for coarse invective and foul abuse, and it is disgraceful to the orator. We may admit that Piso's administration was bad, for if Cicero's charges had no real foundation, such a speech would have ruined him. The only way that Cicero had of proving his assertions was by prosecuting Piso, but he either could not prove what he said or he was not bold enough to bring to trial Caesar's father-in-law. Cicero's oration was published and Piso wrote an answer to which Quintus wished his brother to reply; but Cicero says that nobody will read Piso's oration if he does not reply to it, and that all the schoolboys are learning his oration against Piso as a lesson (Ad Q. Fr. iii. 1. 4. 11).

In this year Pompeius dedicated the theatre which he had built (vol. iii. p. 370) in the Campus Martius, near the Porticus Octavia, which was built by Octavius after his triumph in B.C. 167. This was the first permanent theatre erected at Rome, and except the scena was built entirely of stone. Cicero's friend Atticus gave Pompeius his advice about the arrangement of the statues with which the theatre was decorated, if the passage in one of Cicero's letters to Atticus (iv. 9) is rightly understood. It was a beautiful building, and according to Pliny (36. c. 14. 27. 7) had seats for forty thousand spectators, but this was only one half of the number which the great temporary theatre of M. Aemilius Scaurus accommodated. Pompeius also built a Porticus or colonnade near the scena of his theatre, which sheltered people in the great heats and the bad weather, and was ornamented with paintings of Polygnotus, Pausias, Nicias, and other great Greek artists. This colonnade also contained a hall or Curia, which was sometimes used for the meetings of the Senate, and was decorated with a statue of Pompeius. He also built a temple of Venus Victrix (Plin. H. N. 8, c. 7), for Plinius speaks of the elephant fight "in the Circus" at the dedication of this temple in the second consulship of Pompeius. It appears from a passage of Tertullian (de Spectac. 10) that this temple was built close to the theatre, the seats in which served as an approach to the temple. Cicero's freedman Tiro in a letter* quoted by Gellius (x. 1) speaks of a temple of Victoria, the steps of which served the purpose of a theatre; and this appears to be the same temple which Plinius names the temple of Venus Victrix, but the formal dedication of this temple was not made until the third consulship of Pompeius B.C. 52, according to Tiro.

Plutarch speaks of the games of Pompeius being celebrated after Crassus left Rome for his province about the end of the year, but it seems probable that the time was earlier. Cicero,

* Pompeius wished to know whether the inscription should be "consul tertio" or "consul tertium." The most learned men whom he consulted did not agree, and Pompeius asked the opinion of Cicero, who recommended the inscription "consul tert."

who witnessed this grand exhibition without being pleased, says something about the games in a letter to his friend M. Marius, but there is no date in the letter (Ad Fam. vii. 1). There were musical entertainments, and gymnastic contests, and fights of gladiators, and horse races in the circus or hippodrome, and plays, and fights of wild beasts, which the Romans named Venationes. The amusements lasted many days. The old actor Aesopus appeared on the stage, though he was no longer able to please as he once did; and Cicero says that in a certain passage, which ought to have been uttered with energy, his voice failed. The scenic exhibitions were more adapted to please the vulgar by pompous show than men of taste by good acting. In the play of Clytemnestra there appeared an immense number of mules on the stage, and in the Trojan Horse three thousand bowls (craterarum, if this is the true reading in Cicero). There were foot soldiers with various kinds of armour, and horsemen. There were Oscan plays and Greek plays. Last of all came the Venationes, which lasted five days, and were magnificent, as Cicero says; but he observes, what pleasure can a person of refinement have in seeing either a feeble man mangled by a powerful beast, or a noble animal transfixed by a spear? The incredible number of five hundred lions is said to have been killed in these five days. On the last day there were elephant fights, which greatly excited the admiration of the common sort, but did not give pleasure. The compassion of the people was even moved, says Cicero, and they formed an opinion that there was some kind of community between this brute and the human race. Eighteen or twenty elephants fought against armed men, criminals, as Seneca reports, or Gaetuli, as Pliny (H. N. 8, c. 7) says. Perhaps the men were of both kinds. One of these elephants having his feet pierced by javelins crept on his knees to attack his assailants, seized the shields and threw them into the air. The shields as they descended whirling round gave the spectators wonderful delight, for it seemed as if the animal had pitched them upwards with great skill, though in fact it was a sign of furious rage. One elephant was killed by a single blow of a javelin which entered his head under the eye. The arena was surrounded by an en-

closure, which the elephants in their fright tried to break
through. Finding escape hopeless they seemed to appeal to
the compassion of the spectators and uttered doleful lamentations, which moved even Roman spectators so much that with
tears in their eyes they rose from their seats, and forgetful of
Pompeius and his munificence uttered curses on his head which
soon afterwards had their effect. This is the story of Plinius
which to some extent is confirmed by Cicero's letter, and we
cannot doubt that Plinius had authority for what he wrote.
The Romans got their elephants from Africa. Plinius believed
that the elephant was found in Mauritania, and Herodotus
said so before him. If this is not true (vol. ii. p. 373), these
animals must have been brought from the countries south of
Egypt or from the regions beyond the Sahara. Plinius speaks
also of four hundred and fifty panthers being brought from
Africa by Pompeius. A one-horned rhinoceros was also
exhibited.

Dion mentions a report, which does not seem to be a truth,
that it was not Pompeius who built this theatre, but his
favourite freedman Demetrius of Gadara (vol. iii. p. 190), who
had enriched himself by accompanying Pompeius in his campaigns, and gave his patron's name to this great edifice to
avoid the imputation of having got wealth enough to meet
such an expenditure. The popularity which Pompeius gained
from his great exhibition, was impaired when he and Crassus
began to raise troops for the service of the provinces which
had been assigned to them. The tribunes, Ateius Capito and
Aquillius Gallus, we must suppose (p. 177) attempted to hinder
the consuls from mustering their legions, but Pompeius did
not trouble himself about this opposition, and immediately
sent off his legati to Spain. He stayed at home himself to
look after the affairs of Italy, for he still held the office of
superintendent of the corn supplies, which had been conferred
on him for five years. In B.C. 56 Q. Caecilius Metellus Nepos
(consul B.C. 57) was the governor of nearer Spain, and he had
attended the conference in Luca, probably with the view of
looking after his own interests. There was disturbance in
Spain at this time, which was the reason, as Dion says (39, c.
54), for Spain being assigned to Pompeius. The Vaccaei who

took the lead in the rebellion were defeated by Metellus, but they attacked him when he was besieging Clunia, a city of the Arevaci, obtained some advantage over him and saved the town. In other places the insurgents were worsted, but they were too numerous to be reduced to submission, and Metellus was content not to be molested.

Gabinius went to his province Syria probably in December B.C. 58 (Pro Sestio, c. 33). After Pompeius left Syria, it was under the successive administration of M. Aemilius Scaurus, L. Marcius Philippus, and Cn. Lentulus Marcellinus. Gabinius was the first governor of Syria with the title of proconsul. Cicero says that after the arrival of Gabinius in Syria he lost his cavalry or some cavalry, for the orator's allegation is vague and therefore worth nothing, and afterwards "excellent or the best cohorts were cut to pieces" (De Provinc. consul, c. 4); for both which statements we have only the assertions of an enemy. The proconsul of Syria however gained some military advantage afterwards, for he sent despatches to Rome early in B.C. 56, which announced a victory (p. 135).

Alexander, the son of Aristobulus, who made his escape when Pompeius was taking him to Rome (vol. iii. p. 180), found on his return to Judaea a party ready to aid him against his uncle Hyrcanus, and he began to rebuild the walls of Jerusalem or was designing to rebuild them, when he was interrupted by the arrival of Gabinius. Alexander, who had got together an army of fifteen thousand foot and fifteen hundred horse, strengthened the forts Alexandrium, Hyrcanium and Machaerus. Gabinius sent forward M. Antonius with his cavalry, and Antonius was joined by some Jewish troops under Malichus and Pitholaus, and by Antipater the Idumaean. When Gabinius came up with his legions, Alexander retreated, but he was compelled to fight near Jerusalem, lost three thousand men in the battle, three thousand more who were taken prisoners, and he fled with the remainder of his army to Alexandrium where he was besieged by M. Antonius. In the meantime Gabinius going about Judaea gave orders to rebuild the cities which had been demolished, and restored the inhabitants to those which had been deserted. Samaria, Azotus or Ashdod, Scythopolis, Anthedon, Raphia, Dora, and other cities were rebuilt, which had long been desolate. Judaea is represented by the Jewish historian as being in a wretched condition, and Gabinius as a great benefactor to the nation. Alexander was at length compelled to yield and give up his fortresses, which Gabinius demolished. Hyrcanus was brought back to Jerusalem and entrusted with the care of the temple. Gabinius divided all the country into five parts, or Conventus, as the Romans would name them. The chief cities in each were Jerusalem, Gadara east of the Jordan, Amathus also east of the Jordan, Jericho, and Sephoris in Galilaea. Thus, as Josephus says, the Jews were freed from monarchic authority and were governed by an aristocracy.

An insurrection soon broke out under Aristobulus who had escaped from Rome with his younger son Antigonus. He found some partisans, but he was quickly overpowered by the forces of Gabinius, and made prisoner with Antigonus. Aristobulus was sent back to Rome and kept a prisoner there, but the Senate let his children go free, upon being informed by a despatch from Gabinius that he had promised so much to their mother, the wife of Aristobulus, in return for her services to the Romans in Judaea.

It does not appear at what time in B.C. 56 Gabinius defeated Alexander, settled the affairs of Judaea, and took Aristobulus prisoner. If these events happened before the fifteenth of May, and if Gabinius had claimed a "supplicatio" for these services, he deserved it as much as most Roman commanders. Cicero's speech on the consular provinces was delivered after the fifteenth of May, but we do not know how long after, nor whether Gabinius' settlement of Judaea was then known at Rome. But we do know on the evidence of Josephus, that Gabinius did good service in Judaea, and the Jewish historian had authority for his statements, while Cicero does not say what authority he had for the assertions on which he founded his coarse abuse of Gabinius.

Gabinius was preparing to attack the Arabs, who had given trouble to both his predecessors, when his attention was diverted in another direction (Dion, 39, c. 56). Phraates the Parthian king had been murdered by his own sons, one of whom Orodes seized the royal power and drove his brother

Mithridates from Media, of which country he was governor. Mithridates went to Gabinius whom he persuaded to assist him against his brother. Gabinius, as Josephus states, crossed the Euphrates, but the Jewish historian, whose narrative is often very imperfect, says that he changed his mind. Whatever was the cause of his return, he was soon busy about another matter. Pompeius wrote to him and urged him to restore Ptolemaeus to his throne. Indeed Dion's statement is that Gabinius gave up his Parthian expedition on receiving Pompeius' letter, which the king brought, or he arrived at the same time with the letter. The king promised to pay large sums of ready money to Gabinius and his army and still more when he was restored to the throne, on which his daughter Berenice was seated. She or the people of Alexandria had summoned from Syria a man named Seleucus, who pretended to be of the royal family of Syria, but there is no evidence that he was. The queen married the man and shared the royal power with him, but in a few days she was disgusted with her partner and ordered him to be strangled. She soon found a new husband. A man named Archelaus, the son of the Archelaus who fought against Sulla (vol. ii. p. 270), and now high priest of Comana, happened to be with Gabinius in Syria, and was intending to join him in the Parthian expedition. However he saw a better prospect in Egypt, and secretly leaving Gabinius he was introduced to the queen by some friends, married her and was proclaimed king. According to Strabo, he pretended to be the son of the last Mithridates of Pontus in order to recommend himself to the Egyptians. Dion, who likes any improbable story, if it damages a man's character, affirms that Gabinius seized Archelaus on suspicion of his designs on Egypt, and if he had kept him prisoner, he would have had no trouble about the restoration of Ptolemaeus. But then he was afraid that Ptolemaeus would give him less than he had promised, if the work was done without trouble; and he reckoned that the vigour and reputation of Archelaus would be a reason for Ptolemaeus giving him more. Accordingly he allowed Archelaus to escape to Egypt after having received from him a large sum of money. Plutarch (Anton. c. 3) says that Ptolemaeus promised Gabinius ten thousand talents for his restoration.

When Gabinius was ready for his Egyptian expedition he sent forward M. Antonius with the cavalry and followed after. Antipater the Idumaean provided the Roman army with all necessaries, and Hyrcanus, if he did not assist, at least consented to what was done. The Romans were furnished with money, arms, corn and auxiliaries, and the Jews in Pelusium on the eastern frontier of Egypt were prevailed on by Antipater to let the invaders enter. The most dangerous part of the march was through the sandy waterless desert along the inlet named the Ecregma and the Serbonian swamp. Antonius advanced through this desert, and by taking possession of Pelusium secured the road for Gabinius: when Ptolemaeus entered Pelusium, he would have massacred the Egyptians in the place if he had not been prevented by Antonius. Gabinius defeated the Egyptian troops in a battle after he had advanced from Pelusium, and again in a battle on the Nile and by land. Archelaus lost his life, but Antonius, who had been his friend, interred the body of the king with due honours. His reign lasted only six months. His son afterwards obtained the priesthood of Comana (Strabo, p. 558). All Egypt now surrendered, Ptolemaeus was restored, and he began his new reign by putting to death his daughter Berenice, and the richest Egyptians in order to get their property, for he was much in want of money. Gabinius left with Ptolemaeus for his protection five hundred Gauls and Germans who were in his army (Caesar, B. C. iii. 4. 103). Gabinius sent no despatches home to announce his success, because, as Dion says, he did not choose to report his own illegal conduct. However the invasion of Egypt was soon known at Rome. Cicero writes in a letter of the 22nd of April, B.C. 55, from his villa at Cumae that there was then a rumour at Puteoli that Ptolemaeus was in his kingdom; from which we infer, if the rumour was true, that Ptolemaeus was restored in the first two or three months of B.C. 55[1].

[1] Cicero's letter (Ad Attic. iv. 10) is not conclusive about the time. Clinton (395) relying on the less conclusive evidence of Dion (39, c. 65) fixes the

During the absence of Gabinius, Alexander, the son of Aristobulus, again stirred the Jews to revolt. He raised a large force, massacred all the Romans whom he found, and besieged on Mount Gerizim in Samaria those who had fled thither. Gabinius on his return from Egypt employed Antipater to negociate with the rebels, many of whom were induced by this prudent agent to desist from their mad enterprise; but Alexander, who was at the head of thirty thousand men, would not submit. A battle was fought at Mount Tabor near Nazareth in which Alexander was defeated with the loss of ten thousand men and the rest of his army was dispersed. Gabinius now came to Jerusalem, where he settled the affairs of Judaea with the advice of Antipater, and then undertook an expedition against the Nabathaei whom he defeated. Before the arrival of his successor Crassus, Gabinius refused to surrender the government to one of his legati who had arrived in Syria, and he kept it till Crassus came, as Dion says. It appears probable then that the expedition to restore Ptolemaeus was not at the close of B.C. 55.

Josephus affirms that Gabinius did great and glorious acts, and he refers to Nicolaus of Damascus and Strabo of Cappodicia as the authorities for the expeditions of Pompeius and Gabinius against the Jews. The Syrians complained of Gabinius among other things that they were molested by pirates during his absence; and the Publicani alleged that these robbers prevented them from collecting their dues and so they fell in arrear of their payments to the Roman Treasury. There is no doubt that Cicero received his information about Gabinius from the Publicani, who were knaves themselves and indignant that a greater knave should have authority over them.

Crassus was now preparing to leave Italy for Syria, and it was generally known that he intended to make war on the Parthians. Though the Parthians were not mentioned in the

restoration of Ptolemaeus at the close of B.C. 55. Dion (39, c. 53) after speaking of Caesar's return from Britain, which was in the autumn of B.C. 55, and then (c. 54) of the disturbance in Spain, says (c. 55) "about the same time Ptolemaeus was restored," which assertion and from such a writer does not allow any exact conclusion.

law of Trebonius, the terms of Crassus' commission were large
enough to allow him to do what he liked, and Caesar, it is
said, urged him to this war. Cicero and Crassus had long
been on no friendly terms, though early in this year Crassus'
son Publius, who loved Cicero, had brought about a show of
reconciliation between his friend and his father (Ad Q. Fr. ii.
9. 2). But as Crassus was going to leave Italy, it was his
interest to secure a man whose tongue was so dangerous, as
Cicero had shown particularly by a recent attack on Gabinius
whom Pompeius and Crassus defended and at the same time
taunted the orator with the name of exile [a]. Pompeius earnestly urged Cicero to be fully reconciled to Crassus, and Caesar,
who was informed of every thing that took place in Rome,
wrote to express his vexation about the late quarrel. Cicero
therefore, as he tells us in the long letter to Lentulus (Ad Fam.
i. 9. 20), thought it best to yield, and Crassus made the advance
by proposing to dine with Cicero, who received him in the
garden of his son-in-law Crassipes.

On the fifteenth of November Cicero was in his villa at
Tusculum, and informed Atticus (iv. 13) that Crassus had left
Rome. When it was known that the tribune Ateius intended
to make some opposition to the consul's departure, Crassus
entreated Pompeius to escort him out of the city, and the presence of Pompeius secured Crassus against any expression of
popular displeasure. Ateius however protested against the
departure of Crassus, and ordered him to be seized, but as the
other tribunes would not allow it, Ateius placed a brazier at
the gate into which he threw incense and poured libations, at
the same time uttering terrible curses against Crassus. Ateius
was afterwards punished by the Censor Appius Claudius for
this denunciation, but as Cicero says (De Divin. i. 16), Appius
did not act like a skilful augur, when he declared that the
denunciation was the cause of the subsequent misfortunes of
Crassus and his army. The general embarked at Brundisium
in bad weather and lost many of his ships. He appears to
have landed at Ephesus, for he marched through Galatia,
where he found Deiotarus, now a very old man, building a

---

[a] Dion, 39. c. 60. But see Cic. ad Q. Fr. iii. 2, 2.

city. Among the legati of Crassus were the quaestor C. Cassius Longinus, and Publius the son of Crassus and once a legatus of Caesar. The author of the Parthica, attributed to Appian, states that Publius came from Caesar in Gallia bringing a thousand choice horsemen, and joined his father in Syria during the winter quarters of B.C. 54 and 53. It is certain that Publius was in Rome early in B.C. 55 (p. 175), but it is still true that he did not leave Rome before the end of B.C. 54.

CHAPTER XI.

BRITANNIA.

B.C. 54.

In the fifth book of the Commentaries Caesar has introduced three short chapters on Britannia. Some of his information may have been obtained in the second invasion; and he got the rest from hearsay and Greek authorities.

"The interior of Britannia (Caesar, B. G. v. 12) is inhabited by men, who according to tradition were aboriginal in the island. The coast is occupied by people, who crossed over from Belgium[1] and after defeating the natives settled in the island and cultivated the land. Most of these settlers retain the names of the Belgian states from which they emigrated." This statement is partially confirmed by the fact that a people named Belgae occupied Hampshire and some adjacent parts, and a people named Atrebatii occupied Berkshire and adjacent parts (Ptolem. ii. 3; compare vol. iv. p. 46).

"The population of the island is very large and the houses are very numerous, and like those of the Galli. The quantity of cattle is great. The people use copper coin, or thin bars of iron of a certain weight which pass as money[2]. White lead

---

[1] "Ex Belgio transierant." Schneider in his critical note on this passage (v. 12) defends the reading "Belgio." If it is correct, Caesar uses the term Belgium as the Romans use Latium, Samnium, Picenum.

[2] The reading of Schneider (B. G. v. 12) is "Utuntur aut aere, aut nummo aureo, aut taleis ferreis ad certum pondus examinatis pro nummo." It is difficult to determine what the true text is (see Schneider's critical notes). There is also a reading "aureo" in place of "aereo;" but Cicero writing to Trebatius (Ad Fam. vi. 7) says, "I hear that there is neither gold nor silver in Britannia," which

(plumbum album) is found in the interior of the country."— This white lead is supposed to be tin. Plinius (34, c. 16) states that there are two kinds of "plumbum," black and white, and he identifies the white with the "cassiterus" of the Greeks. But Caesar was misinformed as to the part of Britannia in which tin was got.—" In the maritime parts iron is produced in small quantities, but copper is imported."—The iron of which he speaks may be that of Sussex, where the making of iron was continued up to the early part of the eighteenth century.—"The timber trees are the same as in Gallia except beech and fir."—But both the beech and fir are natives of Britain; and we must suppose that Caesar did not see them. —" The natives abstain from the hare, the fowl, and the goose for religious reasons; but they keep these animals in a domestic state for amusement. The climate is more moderate than that of Gallia in consequence of the cold being less."

"The form of the island is triangular, and one side is opposite to Gallia. One angle of this side, which is in the country named Cantium (Kent), to which part of the island nearly all the Gallic ships come, is turned towards the rising sun, and the lower angle is turned towards the midday. This side is about five hundred Roman miles long. The second side turns

he might have learned from the letters of his brother Quintus, who was with Caesar in the second expedition. Strabo and Tacitus speak of gold in Britain; and there are gold coins of Cunobellin, whose sons Cataratacus (Caractacus) and Togodumnus were defeated by A. Plautius in the reign of Claudius (Dion, 60. c. 20). Suetonius (Caligula, c. 44) speaks of Adminius also, a son of Cunobellinus, who was driven from the island by his father in the reign of Caligula, and submitted to the Romans. Claudius himself in his British expedition took Camulodunum (Colchester), the royal residence of Cunobellinus. The legends on the gold coins of Cunobellinus are CAMV (Camulodunum) and CVNO (Cunobellinus) in Roman characters. It is said that there are also copper coins of Cunobellinus (Dion, 60, c. 21, note of Reimarus, who quotes Camden). The coins of Cunobellinus must have been made before the visit of Claudius to Britain, but it is not easy to conjecture how they were made, for we cannot believe that the Britons were able to strike coins at that time, nor, if they could, would they have used Roman characters. If alphabetic characters were used in Britain before the Roman conquest, they were Greek characters (vol. III. p. 473). There are however Gallic coins of a date as early as Caesar's time or earlier with legends in Roman characters, and if the Galli could make coins, those of Cunobellinus may be the work of Gallic artists in Britain. The reading "taleis" is not certain. There is also a reading "sagulis."

towards Spain and the setting sun, in which direction is
Hibernia, half the size of Britannia, as it is supposed, and the
passage across from Hibernia to Britannia is about the same
as that from Gallia to Britannia. About midway in this
passage there is an island named Mona (probably Man). Many
smaller islands also are supposed to lie in front of this second
side of Britannia, and some have written about these islands
that for thirty successive days in winter there is darkness.
We," says Caesar, " could learn nothing about this fact by inquiry; but we did see by the aid of certain water-measures
(clepsydrae) that the nights are shorter than on the continent*.
The length of this side, according to the opinion of those
writers, is seven hundred miles. The third side is turned towards the north, in which direction there is no land opposite
to Britannia, but the angle of this side (he means the angle
formed by the third side and the second side) is turned towards
Germania, if it can be said to be turned towards any country.
This third side is supposed to be eight hundred miles in length,
and consequently the whole island is two thousand miles in
circuit."

The position of the side opposite to Gallia is described by
Caesar not very accurately: and the position of the second
side with respect to Spain is described as incorrectly by him
as it is by Tacitus (Agric. c. 10) more than a century afterwards. The origin of this mistake may be explained by the
fact that the south-west angle of Britannia runs far into the
Atlantic Ocean, and by the additional fact that the voyagers
from Cadiz, who visited the Cornish peninsula, found that
their course from the north-west angle of Spain was nearly
due north (vol. ii. 139).

The meridian of Greenwich cuts the eastern Pyrenees, and
with the exception of a comparatively small nook in the north-
east the huge compact mass of the Iberian peninsula is west

---

* Caesar made these observations in the summer season in Britannia and in a
more northern latitude than he had made similar observations in Gallia. The
water vessel used for measuring time had a small hole in the bottom through
which the water dropped. The vessel was named clepsydra, and it was used
in camp to mark the division of the night into four " vigiliae" of three hours
each. (Vegetius III. 8.)

of this meridian and pushed out into the Atlantic beyond the coast of France. The error as to the direction of the third side of the island shows that Cæsar had no knowledge of the position of the east side of Britannia north of the æstuary of the Thames; and this ignorance, as we shall see, is consistent with a remark which he makes about his second voyage across the channel. The dimensions of the sea coast of Britannia given in the commentaries must have been derived from a better authority than Pytheas (vol. i. p. 304).

Strabo (p. 63) states that Britannia is in length about equal to Celtica, and extends in a parallel direction not more than five thousand stadia, being defined by the opposite promontories.—This might seem to be a sufficient description of the British coast from the North Foreland to the Land's End, and of the opposite French coast from Cap Gris Nez to Cap Ushant; and the length, five thousand stadia, is the same as Cæsar's dimension, if we allow ten maritime stadia to a Roman mile. Strabo adds: " For the eastern promontories are opposite to the eastern, and the western to the western; and the eastern promontories are near to one another, near enough to be seen, namely Cantium and the outlets of the Rhine. But Pytheas declares that the length of the island is more than 20,000 stadia, and that Cantium is some days' sail from Celtice." It is plain that Pytheas, if Strabo reports him truly, when he speaks of the length of the island means the same side which Strabo describes as five thousand stadia in length[4]. Strabo has however made a mistake in placing the promontory of Kent opposite to the outlets of the Rhine instead of opposite to Gris Nez. The geographer declares Pytheas to be the greatest of liars, and if he said, as Strabo affirms, that Kent was several days' sail from Gallia, he certainly made a great mistake. For though Pytheas may have had a voyage of several days from some parts of the French coast within the Channel to the coast of Kent, he could not have seen the

---

[4] Groskurd in his translation of Strabo (l. 169, note) says that Pytheas visited the southern and eastern sides of Britann's, which he named the length, and estimated at 20,000 stadia. But the length to which Pytheas assigned 20,000 stadia, was the side which Strabo names the length. Pytheas (Strabo, 104) estimated the circuit of the island at more than 40,000 stadia.

Kentish coast without also seeing that the distance across the Straits was not one day's sail. According to another passage of Strabo (p. 104) Polybius said that Pytheas had deceived many persons, for he declared that he had visited all the accessible parts of Britain, and he made the whole circuit more than forty thousand stadia.

Caesar observes (c. 14) that of all the Britanni those who inhabit Cantium, a country lying altogether on the coast, are by far the most civilized, and their habits differ little from those of the Galli. Most of those who inhabit the interior of the island do not sow grain, but live on milk and flesh*, and clothe themselves in skins. All the Britanni dye themselves with woad, which gives them a blue colour and makes them look more terrible in battle. They wear the hair long and shave all the body except the head and upper lip. Ten or twelve men unite and have their wives in common, and this community exists particularly between brothers, and between fathers and sons. The children who are born are reckoned the children of the several men who first have the mother as a virgin.

This is all that Caesar tells us about the island, and it is a proof that he troubled himself little about what others had written on the matter, and did not care to communicate all that he saw. He does not speak of the religion of the islanders, though he afterwards observes (B. G. vi. 13) that the Druidicial system was supposed to be of British origin, and that people went from Gallia to Britannia to be more completely instructed in this religion.

The two other extant authorities on Britannia who come next after Caesar are Strabo (lib. iv.) and Diodorus (lib. v.), but they give little information. The passages already quoted from Strabo might lead to the conclusion that he had a tolerably accurate conception of the English Channel; but we learn from his remarks on Britannia that this was not so. "The island," he says (p. 199), "is triangular, and the longest side is parallel to Celtice, and in length the same, for each

* "La consommation du lait sous toutes les formes a pris chez les Anglais un développement énorme; leurs habitudes sont anciennes sous ce rapport; et il y a bien longtemps que César disait d'eux : 'Lacte et carne vivunt.'" L. de Lavergne, "Essai sur l'Économie rurale de l'Angleterre," etc. p. 85.

side is about four thousand and three or four hundred stadia;
for the Celtic side extends from the outlets of the Rhine to
the northern extremities of the Pyrenees which lie close to
Aquitania; and the side of Britannia extends from Cantium,
the most eastern point of Britain, opposite to the mouths of
the Rhine, as far as the western promontory of the island,
which is opposite to Aquitania and the Pyrenees. This (the
four thousand and three or four hundred stadia) is the shortest
distance from the Pyrenees to the Rhine. The longest distance
as already stated (p. 103), is five thousand stadia. But it is
probable," he says, "that there is some mutual inclination
from the parallel direction both in the river and the mountains,
in consequence of each making a bend at the parts where they
severally reach the ocean." Here we learn that Strabo supposed the direction of the Rhine and the Pyrenees to be
parallel, which is distinctly affirmed in another place (p. 128);
and what is more wonderful still, but consistent with what he
has said of the parallel course of the Rhine and the Pyrenees,
he supposed the Pyrenees (p. 137) to form the east side of
Spain, to run from south to north, and to be at right angles
to the Cévennes in France.

Strabo wrote in the time of Augustus, and if any of those
who accompanied Caesar to Britannia, wrote any thing about
the island, he could use it as well as what Caesar wrote. But
the little that he knew of the form of the island and the few
facts which he adds to Caesar's description, prove that he took
very little either from the Greek writers before him or from
the contemporaries of Caesar, and that very little was known
about Britannia at the commencement of our aera. He says
"that the largest part of the island is level and wooded, but
there are many hilly tracts. It produces gold, silver and iron,
which with skins, slaves and excellent hunting dogs were
exported." In Strabo's time some of the British princes had
secured the favour of Augustus Caesar by sending embassies
and they had dedicated offerings in the Capitol, and thus they
had made the island in a manner friendly to the Romans.
Accordingly they were not subjected to heavy duties on articles
exported to Gallia from Britannia, nor on articles exported
from Gallia to Britannia. The articles imported into Britannia

were ivory armlets, necklaces, amber (?), glass vessels and
such small wares. Strabo remarks that there is no occasion to
put a garrison in the island: if this were done, it would require
at least one legion and some cavalry in order to collect the
taxes, and the expense of the army would be equal to all the
money raised by taxation, for it would be necessary to lower
the customs' duties, if taxes were imposed; and if force were
used in the collection of taxes, there would be some danger.
If the Romans had followed Strabo's wise advice, they would
have saved themselves the trouble of taking and holding the
island, as they did under the Empire. The Britons were taller
than the Celts, and their hair not so yellow. Strabo saw
some young Britons in Rome, who were half a foot higher
than the tallest men there, but they were ill made in the legs
and not well built. "Though they have plenty of milk, the
Britons do not know how to make cheese, and they are ignorant
of garden cultivation and of agriculture. The climate is more
rainy than snowy, and even in the clear weather mists prevail
so long that all through the day the sun is visible for only
three or four hours about midday." This bad character of the
British climate was early established, and it is maintained
among the inhabitants of the continent in spite of the evidence
of facts. Strabo adds that it is just the same among the
Morini and Menapii of Gallia and their neighbours.

Ireland (Ierne), says Strabo, a large island*, is parallel to
the north side of Britannia. He can say nothing exact about
the island, except that the people are more savage than the
Britons, being cannibals and great devourers, and they think
it is honourable to eat their dead fathers; they also openly
cohabit with any women, even mothers and sisters. He adds
however that he has no credible evidence for these stories.

Diodorus, who wrote in the time of Augustus, has two
chapters on Britannia (v. 21, 22), but he reserved his particular
description to that part of his work which treated of Caesar's
invasions, which part is not preserved. He describes the island

---

* The words τραχύτερα, μᾶλλον δὲ πλάτος ἔχουσα are unintelligible. Groskurd
(p. 340) supposes them to be corrupt, and he adopts Koray's emendation
τραχύτερα μᾶλλον ἢ πλάτος ἔχουσα, which he translates "extending more in
length than breadth."

as triangular with sides of unequal length. It lies off the coast of Europe in an oblique direction. The nearest promontory to the continent is named Cantium, and is said to be about a hundred stadia from it; the other named Belerium (the Land's End) is said to be four days' sail from the continent. The remaining promontory or angle, it is said, extends into the sea, and is named Orca. The shortest side, that which lies parallel to Europe, is seven thousand five hundred stadia long; the second from the Straits (of Dover) to the promontory extending (into the sea) is fifteen thousand stadia, and the remaining side is twenty thousand stadia: consequently the whole circuit is forty-two thousand five hundred stadia. This with a few lines about the people and the tin trade (vol. ii. p. 140) is all that we learn from Diodorus.

The conclusion is that the extant authorities to the time of Augustus show that the Greeks and Romans knew very little about Britannia; that Pytheas, if he did navigate the Atlantic, as we can hardly doubt, either did not go so far north as some have supposed, or he was a very careless observer and reported many things from hearsay; that Caesar did not know much about Britannia and has told us even less than he could have done; but that the island had been visited by traders from the French coast, and probably from the Iberian peninsula, for centuries before the Christian aera.

Britannia was neglected by the Romans after Caesar's invasion until the time of the emperor Claudius, who visited the island A.D. 43. Pomponius Mela, who wrote after the expedition of Claudius (Mela, iii. 6), and Plinius (N. H. 4. c. 16) add nothing to our knowledge of Britannia. Plinius on the authority of Pytheas and Isidorus states the circuit of Britannia to be three thousand eight hundred and twenty-five Roman miles. Agrippa supposed the island to be eight hundred Roman miles long and three hundred wide. Great progress in the knowledge of the British islands was made in the latter part of the first century of our aera, for Ptolemaeus of Alexandria, who lived in the second century, was able to construct a tolerable map of Britannia and even of Ireland.

CHAPTER XII.

THE SECOND INVASION OF BRITANNIA.

B.C. 54.

CAESAR did not leave Gallia for Italy before the commencement of B.C. 54 (B. G. v. 1). He ordered his legati to build as many ships as they could during the winter and to repair the old ships. In order that they might receive their cargo more easily and be hauled on shore with less trouble, he directed the ships to be built a little lower than the vessels used in the Mediterranean; and there was the more reason for doing this because he had observed that the waves in the English Channel did not run so high as in the Mediterranean, which he supposed to be due to the frequent changes of ebb and flow. He also ordered the ships to be built a little broader than those used in other seas, that they might be better adapted for a cargo and the transport of beasts. All these new vessels were "actuariae," vessels in which both sails and oars could be used, for which purpose the low form particularly adapted them. Caesar ordered all that was necessary for fitting out the vessels to be brought from Spain, ropes, anchors, sails and such things[1].

After crossing the Alps and holding his courts in Gallia Cisalpina Caesar visited his adjoining province of Illyricum, having been informed that it was ravaged by a people, named Pirustae, who occupied part of Pannonia (Strabo, p. 314). When the Pirustae heard of Caesar's preparations, they sent messengers to express their readiness to make satisfaction. The answer was that they must bring a certain number of

---

[1] Plinius (19, c. 2) describes the Spanish "spartum," of which ropes were made.

hostages on a day named, or they would be attacked. The hostages were brought and Caesar appointed commissioners to assess the damage that had been done and to determine the penalty. He then held his courts in Illyricum, returned to Gallia Cisalpina, and thence to his army beyond the Alps.

Caesar was in Gallia Cisalpina at the end of May of the unreformed Calendar. Cicero received on the second[*] and the third of June letters from his brother Quintus, who had gone to join Caesar, dated from Placentia, and a place named Blandenona in the MSS. Caesar was then probably on his road to Gallia Transalpina, for the second letter came to Cicero together with a letter from Caesar, which expressed his satisfaction at Quintus' arrival. Cicero was delighted with Caesar's affection towards him, and he tells his brother that he needs not his advice to direct all his attention to the man: he had long neglected to cultivate his favour, in spite of Quintus' urgent entreaties, but he will now make amends for the past. Quintus had informed his brother that Caesar approved of his poem, and Cicero says "only give me Britannia to represent by my brush, you supplying the colours." Cicero had sent and recommended to Caesar the lawyer Trebatius, and Caesar thanked him very humorously and kindly: he said that among all those who were with him there was not a man who could draw up a "vadimonium" in due legal form. Cicero had also asked Caesar to give a tribuneship to one M. Curtius for the next year. The letter in which Cicero recommended Trebatius to Caesar is extant, together with Cicero's letters to Trebatius (Ad Fam. vii. 5—22), some of which were addressed to him while he was with Caesar in Gallia. Cicero often wrote to Caesar during the year B.C. 54 and Caesar wrote to Cicero, who also kept up a correspondence with L. Cornelius Balbus, Caesar's chief engineer, and with his brother Quintus. Cicero had now absolutely surrendered himself: he says that he prefers Caesar's love to all the honours which he was encouraged to expect from him.

There is no indication of the time when Caesar reached his

[*] The passage at the beginning of the letter (Ad Qu. Fr. II. 15) is probably corrupt. "Laude Nonis," which now stands in the texts, is an emendation of Nigronius. I connect "postridie" with "accept."

troops who were wintering in the country of the Belgae. It was a long journey to the Seine and the parts bordering on the English Channel, but it was his fashion to travel quick. On his arrival he visited all the winter quarters. Though there was a want of materials, his soldiers had worked hard, and he found about six hundred vessels of the kind described above, and twenty-eight ships of war finished, and ready to be launched in a few days. After thanking his men and those who had been set over them, he gave instructions, and ordered all the vessels to assemble at the Portus Itius or Itium, "from which port he had ascertained that the passage to Britannia was most convenient, a distance of about thirty miles from the continent."

We might infer, but it is not a certain conclusion, that none of the vessels had been constructed at this Portus, and that all had been built and repaired at other places. Strabo says that when Caesar was preparing for his British expedition, he established his building-yard on the Seine (p. 103). It has been supposed by some critics that these words of Caesar prove that he did not sail from Portus Itius on his first voyage (p. 164). Strabo states that he sailed from Itius; and he says this when he is speaking of the first invasion. An examination of Caesar's text shows, whatever ambiguity there may be in v. 2, that he sailed on both voyages from the same place (compare iv. 21. v. 2. 8).

After leaving a sufficient force to protect the Portus, Caesar set out with four legions unencumbered, and eight hundred horse to visit the Treviri, for these people did not send their representatives to the meetings of the Gallic states which Caesar used to assemble, nor did they obey his orders, and it was reported that they were stirring up the Germans on the east side of the Rhine. The Treviri, who extended as far as this river, were far the most powerful of the Gallic states in cavalry, and they were also strong in infantry. At this time two of their chiefs Indutiomarus and Cingetorix were contending for the supremacy. As soon as Caesar's approach was known, Cingetorix came to him, and declared that he and his party would be faithful to the Romans; and he informed Caesar of the movements among the Treviri. Indutiomarus on the contrary began to muster his forces, after sending all those, who by reason of their age were unable to bear arms, into the great forest Arduenna, which extended from the Rhine through the central parts of the Treviri to the borders of the Remi. However when some of the chiefs, who were friendly to Cingetorix and alarmed at the approach of the Roman army, went to Caesar to look after their own interests, Indutiomarus being afraid that he should be left alone, made his submission also. He offered some excuse for not coming to Caesar at first, but he was ready to come now and to place in Caesar's hands his own interests and those of the Treviri. Caesar knew what had induced the man to abandon his designs, but as every thing was ready for the British expedition, he ordered Indutiomarus to come to him with two hundred hostages. The hostages were brought and among them a son of Indutiomarus and all his kinsmen. Indutiomarus was comforted by Caesar and advised to be faithful. Caesar however summoned the chiefs of the Treviri and reconciled them severally to Cingetorix, for he well deserved this attention on the part of Caesar, who also thought it of great importance that the man who had shown such a friendly disposition should have the chief authority among his own people. Indutiomarus was much annoyed at his credit among the Treviri being thus impaired, and his hostility to the Romans was greatly increased.

Caesar and his legions returning from the country of the Treviri marched to Portus Itius, where he learned that sixty ships which had been built in the country of the Meldi[a], had been unable to keep their course, and being driven back by the weather had returned to the place from which they sailed. The rest were ready for the voyage and fully equipped. The Gallic cavalry to the number of four thousand, and the chiefs from all the Gallic states were assembled at the port.

[a] It is not certain if "Meldis" is the true reading (Schneider's critical note). There was a people named Meldi, who seem to have been on the Marne, but it is impossible that Caesar built ships on this river to be brought down the Marne and the Seine, as some suppose. As these ships did not reach the Itius on account of the wind, either they set out from some place from which the others did not, or they sailed later and found contrary winds. D'Anville guesses that the Meldi may have occupied the district of Meld-folt (properly Maldeghem) near Bruges. These Meldi were certainly a maritime people.

Caesar determined to leave behind a very small number of the Gallic chiefs, those who had proved their fidelity, and to take the rest with him as hostages, for he was afraid of some disturbance in Gallia during his absence. Among these chiefs was Dumnorix the Aeduan (p. 13), whom particularly Caesar resolved to take with him, for the man was of a restless temper, ambitious, courageous, and had a high reputation among his countrymen. Dumnorix had declared in the great council of the Aedui that Caesar intended to make him king, and though the Aedui were much vexed about this matter, they did not venture to remonstrate with Caesar. Dumnorix earnestly prayed to be allowed to stay in Gallia: he was not used to the sea and afraid of the voyage; he had also religious scruples of some kind about going. But neither his fears nor his scruples produced any effect on Caesar, and he then began to intrigue with the Gallic chieftains and to urge them to remain behind. To excite their alarm he said that as Caesar could not venture to put them to death in Gallia, he would do it when he had carried them to Britannia. He tried to induce the other Gauls also to combine and promise on their oath that they would all act as was best for the interests of Gallia. Dumnorix was exciting to mutiny and rebellion, as Caesar would view it, and being informed of all that the man was doing, he resolved to stop his dangerous designs. He had now been detained about five and twenty days at Itius by a wind, which he names Corus, blowing somewhere between W.N.W. and N.W., which wind, as Caesar says, blows in these parts a large part of the year. During this delay he tried to keep Dumnorix to his duty, and at the same time watched him well. At last the wind changed and Caesar ordered the troops to embark. While the army was thus engaged, Dumnorix with the Aeduan cavalry left the camp to go home without Caesar's knowledge. As soon as this was reported to Caesar, he stopped the embarcation and sent a large part of the cavalry in pursuit of the fugitives with orders to bring Dumnorix back, and to kill him if he did not yield or if he made resistance. Dumnorix being summoned did make resistance, defended himself and called on his countrymen to help him, exclaiming that he was a free man and belonged to a free state. The pursuers followed their orders, surrounded the man and killed him. All the Aeduan cavalry returned to the camp. Caesar has been careful in relating the circumstances of the death of Dumnorix, as if he wished to show that he was justified in what he did (p. 13).

Caesar's march to the site of Trier on the Mosel, for we will assume that he went no farther, was about two hundred and thirty miles direct distance, and the march back to the coast the same. He settled the affairs of the Treviri in a short time; but it is hardly possible that he did all this in less than five and thirty days. He was detained at Itius twenty-five days by the wind, and this time added to the assumed thirty-five days will make sixty days. If we suppose that he left North Italy at the end of May, we must allow him ten days at least for reaching his troops and visiting all the quarters. Consequently we must count seventy days from the time when Caesar left the neighbourhood of Placentia to the time when he sailed for the British coast. According to this reckoning, he would not sail for Britain before the ninth or tenth of August of the unreformed Calendar; but, as it will presently appear, he must have sailed somewhat earlier. On the twenty-seventh of July Cicero writing to Atticus (iv. 15, 10) says that he infers from the letters of Quintus that he may at that time be in Britannia. On the thirteenth of September Cicero received from his brother a letter dated from Britannia on the tenth of August (Ad Q. Fr. iii. 1, 4). There is another letter without date from M. Cicero to Quintus (ii. 10, 4) in which Marcus speaks of receiving a letter from Quintus from Britain; and it may have been the first letter that he received from Britain. The letter of the tenth of August, says Marcus, contains "nothing new except Erigona," a tragedy, written by Quintus and sent, as it seems, to his brother from Britain, but the tragedy never reached Marcus. In the other letter (ii. 16, 4) Cicero says that the Comitia were deferred to September, from which I infer that this letter was written in August, and Cicero had therefore even in August heard of the arrival of Caesar in Britain, which makes it probable that Caesar landed in July, for a letter from Britain would be about four weeks on the road to Rome.

The activity of Caesar during this year is wonderful. He travelled from the Channel into North Italy, and from North Italy into his province of Illyricum, the limits of which we have no means of determining, but it extended east of the Carnic or Julian Alps. From Illyricum he returned through North Italy to his troops on the Channel and thence made his hasty expedition to the Mosel and back to the Channel. He must have travelled above two thousand miles between the beginning of the year and the expedition to Britannia, and he crossed the Alps twice.

Caesar left Labienus on the continent with three legions and two thousand horse. Labienus was directed to protect the ports, to look after the supply of corn, to observe what was going on in Gallia and to act as circumstances might require. Caesar himself set sail with five legions[4] and two thousand horse at sunset with a gentle wind from s.w. by w. or thereabouts. About the middle of the night the wind dropped, and he did not keep his course, but was carried too far by the tide (aestus). The expression too far (longius) means that he was carried too far north and past the place where he had landed the year before. When day broke he saw Britannia on his left hand, and "left behind." He had drifted to a point some miles off the North Foreland, and as he would not see the British coast north of the aestuary of the Thames, he might suppose that he had left the island, which opinion would be consistent with his notion that one side of Britannia looked to the north (p. 192), for with this opinion he could properly say that he had left behind him not only his landing-place but the whole island. Taking advantage of the turn of the tide and using his oars he made for that part of the coast, "where in the previous summer he had found the landing to be best." If he was, where I have supposed him to be, some miles off the North Foreland, he would see his old landing-place. The soldiers in the heavy transports used the oars with such good will that they kept up with the ships of war. All the vessels reached the British coast about midday; but no enemy was seen. Caesar afterwards learned from

[4] It has been assumed that Caesar's legions contained 4200 men, but there is no evidence of the strength of his legions. See p. 1, note.

some prisoners that a large force of Britons had assembled in these parts, but being alarmed at the number of vessels, which all at once came into sight, they left the shore and retired to the higher land. There were more than eight hundred vessels of all sorts, including what Caesar names the "annotinae," perhaps provision-ships, and the "private ships," which were probably vessels belonging to the "mercatores" or traders, who accompanied the expedition [a].

The army was landed and a suitable spot was selected for the camp. From some of the natives whom he made prisoners Caesar learned the position of the enemy's forces, and he formed the design of surprising them. He left on the coast two cohorts of each legion and three hundred horse under the command of Q. Atrius to protect the ships, which were anchored on a soft and open coast. At the commencement of the third watch he set out to find the enemy, and probably took for guides some of his prisoners. As he set out about midnight, we must assume that he had moonlight and of course he had also the moon on the night on which he sailed from the Gallic coast. Having marched about twelve miles he saw the enemy, who had advanced with their war-chariots to a river, and from a higher position on the opposite side attempted to dispute the passage. Caesar's cavalry drove back the Britons, who retired into the forest to a spot which was naturally strong, and all the entrances were closed by numerous trees which had been felled. It was conjectured that the place had been fortified during some war among the natives. The Britons from various points threw missiles out of the wood and attempted to prevent the Romans from entering. However the soldiers of the seventh legion formed the "testudo" (p. 49) to protect themselves while they filled up the ditches, and then they took the place and drove the enemy out. Caesar would not allow his men to follow the fugitives, for he was not acquainted with the country, and as a good part of the day was spent he wished to have time to fortify his camp [b].

[a] Cotta, quoted by Athenaeus (vi. 273; see p. 166), speaks of a thousand ships; and he adds that Caesar took only three slaves or personal attendants with him.

[b] He means the place which he had selected for his camp (c. 9). He does not say that he had made this camp; he had only chosen the ground, and he

The river where Caesar found the enemy was the Stour, which flows past Canterbury. The author of the " Histoire de César" (ii. 186) assumes that the enemy opposed Caesar on the Little Stour, a branch of the Stour, and that the spot was the village of Kingston. If any person will visit Kingston, he will be amazed at the absurdity of the conjecture. In August there is no water in the shallow narrow channel of the Little Stour at Kingston, and both the banks are low. It is in fact at that season a small dry ditch. Mr. Jenkins' suggests Chilham on the Stour between Canterbury and Wye as the place where the Britons opposed Caesar and the site of their stronghold. Chilham is more than twelve English miles direct distance from any place from which Caesar probably began his march; but we ought not to assume that he calculated the distance very accurately, or that the numerals (xii) are free from all possibility of error.

On⁎ the morning of the following day Caesar sent infantry and cavalry in three divisions to pursue the enemy who had fled. When the men had advanced some distance and the rear was still within sight, some horsemen came to Caesar from Q. Atrius with the news that there had been a violent

---

left no men to make the camp. The ten cohorts and three hundred horsemen were appointed to guard the ships (c. 9). Schneider supposes that when Caesar says, " loco castris idoneo capto," he means that the camp was also made. If that was so, the legions must have been well tired, for they rowed the ships in the morning, made their camp in the afternoon, set out at midnight to find the enemy, fought a battle at early dawn, and took a strong place, and then made another camp to pass the night in, a camp somewhere near the place which they had taken, though they might safely have passed the night in and near the British fortress which they had won. Goeler (p. 135) also supposes that Caesar stopped the pursuit in order to have time to make his camp in the place where he then was, near Canterbury as he conjectures. If my explanation is right, Caesar's camp was not near the ships, but it is exceedingly difficult to follow his narrative in this part. It may be said that the men after returning from this expedition would be too fatigued to make the camp on the spot selected (c. 9); but they might do a little, the ten cohorts left to look after the ships might help while others took their place to watch the ships. The camp also might not have been quite finished on the day on which the soldiers returned from the expedition, and we may suppose that some of the army were working at it the next morning, for Caesar (c. 10) did not send all the army to pursue the enemy.

⁷ Mr. Jenkins is the Rector of Lyminge, where the springs of the Little Stour are.

⁎ These chapters (cc. 10, 11) are differently interpreted by different critics.

storm in the night, that nearly all the ships were damaged and cast up on the shore, as neither the anchors nor cables held firm, and the sailors and captains were unable to resist the fury of the wind; accordingly great mischief had been done by the ships falling foul of one another. Caesar immediately ordered the troops to be recalled, and went to visit the ships. He found things in the condition which had been reported, but with the loss of about forty vessels the rest could with a good deal of labour be repaired. Accordingly he took carpenters and smiths from the several legions and sent for others from the continent. He also sent orders to Labienus to build as many vessels as he could. Though it was a work of great labour, he determined to haul up all the ships and connect them with the camp by one line of defence. About ten days were spent over these matters, during which the work went on without interruption day and night. When the ships were hauled up and the camp was made perfectly secure, he left the same force as before to protect it, and advanced "to the place from which he had returned;" by which expression he means, as I understand the text, the British fort near the Stour. He found a still larger force of the natives assembled there under Cassivellaunus, to whom by common consent the conduct of the war was entrusted. Up to this time there had been continual hostilities between Cassivellaunus and the other British states, but the arrival of the Romans induced the Britons to give him the supreme command. His territory was separated from the maritime states by a river named Tamesis (Thames), which was about eighty miles from the sea. This estimate is evidently founded on the length of Caesar's subsequent march to the Thames. He knew nothing of the course of the river, but he would conclude that it entered the sea on that side of the island, which he supposed to be turned to the north (p. 192). If we assume that Caesar's camp was on the Stour about Richborough, where he would have a plentiful supply of water and would find corn in the fertile lands about Eastry and Worth, we may suppose that his ships were hauled up about Sandown Castle, and a single ditch and rampart from the sea to the Stour would protect his naval camp.

After speaking of Cassivellaunus Caesar interrupts his nar-native with the three chapters of the description of Britannia (p. 190); and then continues thus. The charioteers of the enemy, or, to use Caesar's own words, "the horsemen and charioteers (equites hostium essedariique)" had a fierce conflict with Caesar's cavalry on the march, but yet Caesar's cavalry had the advantage and drove them to the forests and the hills, after killing many of them. But the cavalry in following up the pursuit too eagerly lost a few of their own men. A short time afterwards, while the Romans were off their guard and engaged in making their camp, the Britons suddenly rushed from the forest and made a fierce attack on the pickets. Caesar sent to their relief two cohorts, which took a position at a very short interval from one another, but being frightened at this new kind of fighting they could not prevent the British chariots from boldly passing between them and returning uninjured. The enemy was finally repulsed by other cohorts being sent to attack them. On that day Q. Laberius Durus a tribune was killed.

This contest, which took place before the whole army and in front of the camp, showed that the legionary soldier being heavily armed could neither pursue the enemy nor safely quit his standard, and that the cavalry could not engage in battle without great risk, because the Britons often simulated flight, and when they had drawn the cavalry a little distance from the legions, would leap down from the chariots and fight on terms which were disadvantageous to their opponents. Thus the British mode of fighting was equally dangerous to the Romans whether they were retreating or pursuing. The Britons also never attacked in mass, but in small bodies at great intervals, and they had their men so placed that one body took the place of another, and those who were unhurt and fresh relieved those who were exhausted[*].

On the next day the enemy were on the hills far from the camp, and they only showed themselves in small bodies and harassed the cavalry less than the day before. About midday Caesar sent out three legions and all the cavalry under

[*] Caesar, in the third book of some writing addressed to Cicero, speaks of Britannia having many thousands of equites and essedarii. Philargyrius on Virgil, Georg. III. 204, referred to in the "Histoire de César," ii. p. 100.

C. Trebonius[1] (p. 177) to forage, but the enemy fell on the foragers with great fury and pursued them even to the standards and the troops who were under arms. The Romans by a vigorous attack repelled the Britons and continued the fight until the cavalry, encouraged by the legions which were following them, put the Britons to the rout and allowing them no opportunity of rallying, or making a stand or descending from their chariots, made a great slaughter of them. After this defeat the troops which had assembled from all quarters dispersed immediately, and the Britons never again opposed the Romans with united forces.

Caesar seeing that the enemy no longer intended to fight a regular battle led his men to the Thames and to the territory of Cassivellaunus. His narrative shows that after fortifying his camp (c. 11) he directed his march to the Thames. His course cannot be determined, but he may have passed from the valley of the Stour above Canterbury towards Ashford, and thence near the line of the South Eastern Railway as far as the neighbourhood of Reigate. His march would be on the south side of the chalk hills. At Dorking he might find his way by the valley of the Mole to the Thames about Hampton or Walton. The Thames, he says, is only fordable in one place, and that with difficulty; which means that he heard of only one ford at that part of the river to which he came. It may be assumed that he crossed the Thames at some point above the limit of tide-water. When he reached the river, he observed that a large force of the enemy was drawn up on the opposite bank, which was defended by sharp pointed stakes, and other similar stakes were covered by the water, as Caesar learned from prisoners and deserters[2]. The cavalry were

---

[1] Caius Trebonius, one of the tribunal of B.C. 55, who carried the bill which gave Caesar five more years in his government.

[2] He crossed, as it has been supposed, about Cowey stakes near the junction of the Wey and the Thames. Beda (Hist. I. 2) describes some stakes in the bed of the Thames, and he supposed that they were the stakes of which Caesar speaks, but Beda does not mention the name of the place. Camden identified the stakes with the Cowey stakes. The stakes which Caesar describes were placed on the river bank and others were under the water, but also along the bank, as the Latin seems to mean; but the Cowey stakes, it is said, "stood in two rows, as if going across the river," and according to a tradition reported by

ordered to go first and the legions to follow immediately after. They must have crossed of course either above or below the stakes. The soldiers forded the river with such speed and resolution, though the water came up to their heads, that the enemy unable to resist the impetuosity of the infantry and cavalry retired from the banks and took to flight [1].

Cassivellaunus now dismissed the greater part of his force, and retaining about four thousand "essedarii" watched the march of the Roman army keeping a little way out of their track. Sometimes he concealed his troops in places difficult of access and covered with the forest, and when he had discovered the route which the Romans would take, he drove all the cattle and people from the open parts into the woods [4]. If the cavalry spread abroad for the purpose of plunder and wasting the land, the British "essedarii" would issue from the forest by all the roads and paths with which they were acquainted and attack the cavalry, who were thus exposed to great danger and checked in their excursions. Caesar consequently did not allow the cavalry to deviate far from the line of march, and he could only waste the lands and burn the buildings of the Britons which lay near the road by which the legions advanced.

There is no indication of the direction in which Caesar was now moving except that he was in or near the country of the Trinobantes, one of the most powerful people in those parts. The Trinobantes occupied Essex: their chief town was Camalodunum or Camulodunum (p. 191), or, as it is in some texts of Ptolemaeus, Camoudolanum (Ptolem. ii. 3. 22), now Colchester.

[1] Thames fisherman were the remains of a bridge built by Julius Caesar. Mr. Lewin ("The Invasion of Britain by Julius Caesar," p. 107) suggests that the piles were the piles of an ancient bridge, and that if it existed in Caesar's time, Cassivellaunus would retreat over the bridge, "and then break it down and saw off the tops of the piles." This is like what Vercingetorix did in Gallia (B. G. vii. 34, 35). Mr. Lewin adds, "Who can say that Caesar did not himself construct the bridge?" Such a question requires no answer.

[3] Polyaenus, Strateg. viii. 23, 6, has a strange and incredible story of Caesar having an elephant with him.

[4] Gooler (p. 141) says, "We may conclude from this passage and the following narrative that the British chariots had very high wheels, which would enable them to pass more easily over the inequalities of the ground, that they were very narrow, and had only one horse or at most two horses, one in front of the other, that they might thus pass along the narrowest paths."

The Trinobantes had a king named Imanuentius, whom Cassivellaunus had put to death, upon which his son Mandubratius fled to Gallia and sought the protection of Caesar, with whom the young prince now was. The Trinobantes offered their submission, and asked Caesar to protect Mandubratius against Cassivellaunus, and send him to be their king. Caesar required of them forty hostages and corn for his army. The Trinobantes obeyed the order. Mandubratius was sent to them, and "they were saved from all damage from the soldiers," an expression which implies that some of the Roman soldiers at least entered the country of the Trinobantes.

The Cenimagni[1], Segontiaci, Ancalites, Bibroci and Cassi now made their submission by sending ambassadors. The Cenimagni, perhaps the Simeni of Ptolemaeus and Iceni of Tacitus, are supposed to have occupied Norfolk, Suffolk, and Cambridgeshire; the Segontiaci were in parts of Hampshire and Berks; the Ancalites in parts of Berks and Wilts; the Bibroci in parts of Berks, and the Cassi in Hertfordshire. But most of these positions are only conjectural. The name Bibroci has some resemblance to Berks. The hundred of Cassio or Cashio in Herts may preserve the name of Cassi, as Camden suggests. Caesar was informed by these ambassadors that he was not far from the town of Cassivellaunus, which was protected by woods and marshes, and that many men and much cattle were there. The Britons gave the name of town (oppidum) to a place which was protected by woods and a rampart of felled trees, and there they used to take refuge against the attack of an enemy (Strabo, p. 200). Caesar found that the place was strongly defended by natural position and art, yet he determined to attack it at two parts. The enemy did not long resist, but made their escape from the place. A great number of cattle was found in the town, and many of the Britons in their flight were overtaken and killed. There is no evidence for fixing the site of this British town. While these events were going on, Cassivellaunus sent a message to the four kings of Cantium to collect all their forces and attack the naval camp. The territory of Cantium, we

[1] Lipsius (Tacit. Ann. xii. 32) corrupted Caesar's text by writing "Iceni, Cangi," in place of Cenimagni.

may suppose, was divided into four parts, and each had a little king. The names of the kings were Cingetorix, Carvilius, Taximagulus and Segonax, the first of which is a pure Celtic name. When the Britons had reached the camp, the Romans sallied out, killed many of the enemy, captured a commander of rank named Lugotorix, and retired safely into their fortifications. Cassivellaunus hearing of this defeat, and moved both by the losses that he had sustained, and still more by the defection of the British states, sent ambassadors to Caesar to treat about submission. Commius, who was with Caesar, introduced to him the British deputation. Caesar intended to winter in Gallia, not, as Strabo says (p. 200), because there were already risings in that country and mutiny among the Roman soldiers, but because such disturbance among the Galli might always be expected. There was also not much remaining of the summer, and that little might soon be spent. Accordingly he required hostages and fixed the annual tribute which Britannia should pay to the Romans. Cassivellaunus received orders not to do any injury to Mandubratius or the Trinobantes.

Caesar led his army with the hostages to the coast, where he found the ships repaired. As he had a large number of prisoners, and some of the ships had been destroyed by the storm, he resolved to take his men back in two divisions. It happened that out of so large a number of ships and so many passages across the Channel both in this and the former year not a single vessel that conveyed soldiers was lost. But of those which carried over the first division and were sent back after landing the men, and of the sixty vessels which Labienus[*] had built after the damage by the storm, very few reached the British coast and the rest were driven back. Caesar waited some time, but fearing that the season might prevent his return, for the equinox was near, he stowed his men in the ships as well as he could, and the weather being quite calm he set sail at the beginning of the second watch, and reached the opposite coast at daybreak without any loss.

Cicero (Ad Att. iv. 16, 7, 13) had heard before the first of October from his brother and Caesar, that the end of the British

---

[*] Labienus had not much time for building these ships.

campaign was expected, but if these letters were written from
the interior of Britain we cannot guess how long they would be
in reaching Rome. Cicero (Ad Att. iv. 17, 3) also received on
the twenty-fourth of October a letter from Caesar and one
from his brother Quintus announcing the end of the war, and
that they were bringing back the army from Britain. The
letters were dated from the coast of Britain on the twenty-fifth
or twenty-sixth of September ("proximo a. d. vi. Kal. Oct."
perhaps "proximo" should be erased). The date of the return
of the second division is fixed by Caesar just before the equinox.

Cicero also received on the twenty-eighth of September a
letter from Caesar dated the first of September (Ad Q. Fr.
iii. 1. 7), in which Caesar tells him that he must not be surprised at not receiving a letter from his brother, for Quintus
was not with him when he reached the coast. Quintus might
have been bringing up the rear of the army. Cicero did not
answer this letter, and abstained even from congratulating
Caesar on the result of his expedition, for Caesar's daughter
Julia was dead and the father had no doubt heard of it.

In a letter to Quintus without date (Ad Q. Fr. iii. 3, 1)
Cicero says that it is more than fifty days since he had heard
from him or Caesar, or had any news, even a rumour from the
parts where they were. This letter was of course written
before Cicero received the letter of the twenty-fifth or
twenty-sixth of September, which he received on the twenty-
fourth of October, and if it was written just before the
twenty-fourth of October, he could say that it was more than
fifty days since he had heard from Britain, for he would refer
to the letter of the first of September. If we assume that
Caesar landed about the end of July of the unreformed
Calendar, which I have shown to be probable, there will be
fifty-five days between the last day of July and the close of
the campaign about the twenty-fifth of September, and
as we may allow a few days more before the embarcation of
the second division, Caesar was at least sixty days in Britain.
If then we assume that he sailed a few days before the
equinox, and if the equinox in this year was on the 26th of
September, we may reckon backwards and fix his landing in
Britain about the twenty-fifth of July.

The author of the "Histoire de César" (ii. 109) has fixed the landing on the twenty-first of July B.C. 54, the day before the full moon, and the return of the last division on the twenty-first of September of the true Calendar; which reckoning allows Caesar sixty-one days in Britain. The assumption that Caesar sailed on the eighteenth of July, when it was full moon (Lewin), has been made for the purpose of suiting an argument. It is impossible to say whether he sailed on the full moon or a few days earlier or later, as Mr. Lewin also admits. Mr. Appach (" Caesar's British Expeditions") makes it full moon on the twenty-first of July, and says that the second voyage took place on the night between the twenty-third and twenty-fourth of July B.C. 54, and that the first division left Britain on the tenth of September of the modern Calendar and the second on the fourteenth. From all the facts it seems a certain conclusion that Caesar landed in Britain in the second half of July. There are some remarks on the two British expeditions in the Appendix[1].

[1] There is an essay on the British expeditions of Caesar by M. de Saulcy in his volume entitled "Les Campagnes de Jules César," Paris, 1862. The author supposes that he has proved that Caesar embarked at Wissant in both expeditions, and that he landed at Deal. The essay is worth reading, but it contains some errors.

CHAPTER XIII.

THE WINTER OF B.C. 54.

AFTER he had hauled up the ships, Caesar held a council of the Gallic states at Samarobriva (Amiens). The summer had been dry in Gallia and the crops were less abundant than usual; and he found it necessary to place his troops in winter quarters in a different way from what he had done before, and to distribute them more widely. He gave one legion to Q. Fabius to lead into the country of the Morini; a second under Q. Cicero was led into the country of the Nervii. In a letter to Atticus (iv. 18) Cicero tells his friend that Caesar allowed Quintus the choice of winter quarters. Q. Roscius had a third legion in the country of the Essui, probably near the Aulerci, and certainly bordering on the Armoric States (B. G. v. 53). A fourth legion was placed under Labienus in the country of the Remi on the borders of the Treviri. Three legions were placed in Belgium under three commanders, one of whom was M. Crassus, a quaestor and the brother of Publius, who had left Caesar in order to go to Syria with his father. The other two were L. Munatius Plancus and C. Trebonius. One legion, which had been levied later than the rest in Gallia north of the Po, and half a legion or five cohorts were sent into the country of the Eburones, the greater part of which lay between the Mans and the Rhine, and was under the government of Ambiorix and Cativoleus. The legati Q. Titurius Sabinus and L. Aurunculeius Cotta commanded these troops. The winter quarters of all these legions, except that which Roscius was ordered to take to the country of the Essui, where all was quiet, were "comprised within one hundred Roman miles[1]," as Caesar says; by which I understand that no legion was more than a hundred miles from any other. Caesar determined to stay in Gallia till he had placed all the legions in their quarters and heard that the camps were made.

No certain conclusion can be derived from this limit of one hundred miles as to the position of the several winter stations, because Caesar could not know the distance accurately, and we can never trust the numerals in the manuscripts. We shall have the opportunity afterwards of determining the position of some of these winter quarters. When Caesar went to Britain, he had eight legions, and the legion last raised was not one of them, for he had eight legions at the beginning of B.C. 57 (B. G. ii. 2). He had therefore nine legions in Gallia after his return from Britain, but he has mentioned the winter quarters of only eight legions and five cohorts. Goeler (p. 144) suggests that Caesar distributed the other five cohorts among the legions to fill up the losses which their ranks had sustained. Caesar has been blamed by some critics for spreading his troops over so large a surface, but we may allow that he knew what he was doing better than his critics can tell us. The crops were short in this year, the conveyance of supplies to one or even two or three camps would have been very difficult, perhaps impossible, and so the only mode of feeding the soldiers may have been the distribution of the legions as Caesar describes it. Goeler remarks that Napoleon in his "Précis des Guerres de César" does not blame this distribution of the troops.

The first disturbance began in the country of the Carnutes, a name now represented by Chartres and also by Chartrain, one of the anterevolutionary small divisions of France north of the Loire. Among the Carnutes there was a man of very high rank, named Tasgetius[2]. His ancestors had been kings of the Carnutes; and in order to reward the man for his fidelity and great services in all the wars with the Galli Caesar had restored him to the kingly power which his ances-

[1] Goeler (p. 144) thinks that Caesar's expression is both clear and true. He explains the "hundred miles" thus: each winter camp was at the most a hundred Roman miles from the nearest camp. But I think that Schneider's explanation is right.

[2] There is a Gallic medal of a man named Tasgitios.

tors enjoyed. Tasgetius was now in the third year of his reign, when some of his enemies with the support of many of the Carnutes murdered him. Caesar being informed of his death and knowing that many persons were implicated in the murder was afraid that they might stir up the Carnutes to revolt, and he sent L. Plancus with a legion to winter in the country, to seize the assassins and to send them to him. In the mean time he heard that all the legions had reached their winter quarters and that the camps were fortified.

In about fifteen days after the arrival of the legions at their winter quarters, an insurrection broke out at the instigation of Ambiorix and Cativolcus. They had met Sabinus and Cotta at the boundaries of their kingdom and had brought corn to the winter quarters; but being moved by a message from Indutiomarus the Trevir they stirred up their people, and after surprising some of the Romans, who had been sent out to get wood, they came with a great force to attack the camp. The Romans seizing their arms manned the rampart and the Spanish cavalry were sent out to attack the enemy. The Spaniards had the advantage in the fight and the leaders seeing no hope of success withdrew. Then after their fashion the barbarians raised a loud clamour and called for some Roman to come out to a parley; they had something to say which concerned both sides, and they hoped that a conference would settle all disputes.

C. Arpineius, a Roman eques, a friend of Titurius Sabinus, was sent with one Q. Junius, a Spaniard, whom Caesar had on former occasions sent to Ambiorix, who addressed them thus.—He admitted that he was much indebted to Caesar for his kindness; that through him he had been released from paying tribute to his neighbours the Aduatuci, and that Caesar had restored to him his son and nephew whom the Aduatuci kept as hostages and treated as slaves. In attacking the Roman camp he had not followed either his own judgment or his inclination; he had been forced by the people who had as much power over him as he had over them. Further, the reason why his people had attacked the Romans was this: they could not resist the sudden combination of the Galli. This would plainly appear from the weakness of his

resources, for he was not so ignorant as to suppose that he
could defeat the Romans with such means as he had; but
there was a combination of all the Galli, and this was the day
fixed for an attack on all Caesar's winter quarters at once to
prevent any legion from aiding any other: it was not easy
for any Gaul to resist the importunity of the rest, when it
was believed that a design had been formed to recover the
liberty of all. After having done enough in respect of his
duty to his countrymen, he had now regard to what was due
from him for Caesar's favours, and he advised, he entreated
Titurius as his friend to look after his own safety and that of
his soldiers: a great force of the Germans had crossed the
Rhine, and would arrive in two days. The Roman commanders must determine, before the neighbouring people
should hear of the troops leaving the winter quarters, whether
they will lead their men to Cicero or to Labienus, one of
whom was about fifty miles distant and the other a little
more. He offered, and he confirmed his offer by an oath, to
give them a safe passage through his territories, and in doing
this he would be acting in the interest of his own people by
relieving them from the pressure of the Roman winter quarters, and he would be also making a proper return to Caesar for
his kindness.

Arpineius and Junius reported what they had heard. The
generals were much perplexed, and though this information
came from an enemy, they thought that it ought not to be
disregarded. They were chiefly moved by the circumstance
that it was scarcely credible that a people so weak as the
Eburones had ventured to attack the Romans without en-
couragement. The matter was referred to a military council
and hotly debated. L. Aurunculeius Cotta with many of the
tribunes and centurions of the highest rank were of opinion
that they should do nothing hastily, and that they ought
not to leave their winter quarters without Caesar's order:
they maintained that they could resist any number of Germans in their camp, and this was proved by the fact that
they had stood the first attack of the enemy and inflicted
many wounds on them: they were not in want of provisions:
in the mean time relief would come from the nearest winter

quarters and from Caesar. Finally, what could be more foolish or more disgraceful than to take an enemy's advice in a matter of such importance?

Titurius replied: it would be too late to take this advice when the forces of the enemy were increased by the arrival of the Germans, or some misfortune had befallen the men in the nearest winter quarters: the time for deliberation was short: he believed that Caesar had set out for Italy, for if this were not so, the Carnutes would not have killed Tasgetius, nor would the Eburones have been bold enough to attack the camp: he did not care whether the advice came from an enemy or not; he looked at the facts: the Rhine was near: the Germans were irritated at the death of Ariovistus and the victories of the Romans: all Gallia was burning for vengeance, having been reduced under Roman dominion after so many disgraceful defeats and the loss of their military reputation. In conclusion, who could suppose that Ambiorix had given such advice without some good reason? His opinion was safe either way: if they had no bad luck, they would reach the nearest legion without any risk: if all Gallia were combining with the Germans, their only hope was in moving quickly. What would be the result of the advice of Cotta and of those who agreed with him? It would be either immediate danger or at least a long blockade and the risk of starvation.

Cotta and the centurions of the first rank still persisted in their opinion, when Sabinus exclaimed, "Well then, have your own way, if you like," and he spoke loud enough for a large part of the soldiers to hear. "I am not the man," he added, "to fear death most; but the soldiers will judge, and if any calamity befall us, you must answer for it to those who, if you did not oppose it, might reach the nearest winter quarters the day after to-morrow and there with their comrades sustain the chances of war instead of perishing by famine or the sword far from their countrymen."

When the council broke up, the two commanders were earnestly entreated by their friends not to hazard the safety of the army by their obstinate disagreement: there was no difficulty either in staying or going, if they were only unanimous;

but if they could not agree, there was no hope. The dispute was prolonged to midnight, when at last Cotta yielded to importunity. Notice was given to the soldiers that they must set out at daybreak. The remainder of the night the men kept awake, occupied with considering what they should take with them and what utensils they should leave behind. They encouraged themselves in their resolution to leave the camp by reflecting that they could not stay without danger, and that the danger was increased by their lassitude and watches[3]. At daybreak they left the camp with the conviction that Ambiorix who had given this advice was their best friend. The army marched in a very long line and with a great quantity of baggage.

Caesar has not mentioned the site of the camp, but in the sixth book (c. 32) he names the place Aduatuca, which may be Tongern on the Jaar or Geer, a branch of the Maas[4]. The enemy, discovering by the noise and the wakefulness of the Romans that they were going to march out, placed two ambuscades about two miles from the camp in a convenient position in the woods where they could not be seen, and there they waited for the army. When the greater part of the Romans had descended into a long defile, the enemy suddenly showed themselves on both sides, pressed hard on the rear, prevented those in the front from emerging out of the defile, and attacked the Romans where they could least make resist-

---

[3] This passage is explained in various ways.

[4] Drumann (iii. 332) says that this Aduatuca must be distinguished from Aduatuca Tungrorum, or Tongern, which is west of the Maas and not far from Liège. He adds, "besides the distinct statement of Caesar about the position of this Aduatuca (vi. 32), there is also some weight in the remark that the Sigambri reached it from the Rhine without crossing the Maas (vi. 35)." The "distinct statement" is this: Caesar says that Aduatuca "fere est in mediis Eburonum finibus." That is all. The Sigambri crossed the Rhine of necessity to reach Aduatuca; and they must also have crossed the Maas, if Aduatuca was on the site of Tongern, and if they must cross it, there was no reason why Caesar should have told us the fact. Goeler (p. 148), who follows Drumann, also founds an argument on the supposed relative position of the several winter camps, and concludes that this Aduatuca must have been east of the Maas, and in the neighbourhood of Eupen or Limburg. In fact he comes to the conclusion that the castle of Limburg, which is built on a lofty rock, may be the site of the ancient Aduatuca. Those who have seen the place will not, I think, accept his suggestion.

ance. This defile is supposed with reasonable probability to be the valley of Lowaige[1], which is shut up by parallel hills and traversed in the direction of the length by the Geer. The defile is about four miles long. Then at last Titurius, who had not foreseen such an event, hurried in trepidation to put the cohorts in fighting order; but his movements were marked by timidity, and he lost his presence of mind, which is generally the case with those who are compelled to form some resolve in the midst of danger. On the contrary Cotta, as he had perceived that such a mishap might occur, and for that reason had not been in favour of leaving the camp, did every thing that was possible to save the army: he cheered and encouraged the men like a brave general and fought like a valiant soldier. As the length of the column made it very difficult for the commanders to see every part and to give the necessary orders, they passed along the word for the soldiers to abandon the baggage and form the "orbis[2]." But though such a movement on such an occasion could not be blamed, it had one disadvantage: it weakened the hopes of the Roman soldiers and encouraged the enemy to whom it seemed an evidence of fear and desperation. There was another unlucky consequence, an inevitable consequence of the order for this movement: many of the soldiers quitted their standards to pick out of the baggage what they valued most, and there was great shouting and lamentation.

The barbarians showed much prudence: their commanders passed the order along the whole line, that no man should leave his place: the booty, they said, was theirs and they would have all that the Romans left, and accordingly they must think only of getting the victory. Though Sabinus had failed in his duty, and fortune was against them, still the Romans trusted to their courage to save their lives, and whenever a cohort rushed forward, a great number of the enemy fell. Thereupon Ambiorix ordered his men to throw their missiles from a distance, not to approach the Romans, and whenever they were attacked, to retire, which the lightness of

[1] "Histoire de César," ii. p. 205.
[2] "Orbis." It was certainly not a full square, but a hollow square. Goeler p. 151.

their armour and daily practice easily enabled them to do, and to follow the Romans as they retreated to their standards.

This order was strictly obeyed. When any cohort advanced from the "orbis" and attacked, the enemy quickly retreated, and in the mean time the right flank of the cohort was exposed; and when the cohort began to retire, it was assailed on all sides. If the troops remained in the "orbis," there was no opportunity of displaying their courage, and the ranks being close packed received the numerous missiles of the enemy. Yet under all these disadvantages and though many of the men were wounded, the Romans still resisted; and though they had been fighting from daybreak to the eighth hour, they had maintained their character as brave soldiers. In this conflict T. Balventius, who the year before had been promoted to the first rank of centurions, a man of great courage and character, was pierced through both thighs with a javelin; and Q. Lucanius, who had the same rank, was killed while he was defending his son who had been surrounded by the enemy. Cotta, while he was encouraging the Romans, received a wound right in the face from a sling. Sabinus now in despair, seeing Ambiorix at a distance cheering his men, sent his own interpreter Q. Pompeius to entreat the king to spare him and his soldiers. The king replied that Sabinus might have a conference with him, if he chose: he hoped that he could prevail on his people to spare the soldiers: Sabinus himself should certainly suffer no harm and he gave his promise to that effect. Sabinus sent to ask Cotta to leave the fight and accompany him to a conference with Ambiorix: he expected to obtain from him terms of safety for all. Cotta declared that he would not go to an armed enemy.

Sabinus ordered the tribunes who were about him and the centurions of the first class to follow him. When Sabinus approached Ambiorix, he was commanded to throw down his arms, which he did, and he ordered those with him to do the same. Then began the conference about the terms; and while Ambiorix was purposely prolonging his talk, the enemy gradually surrounded Sabinus and killed him. The Eburones after their fashion proclaimed their victory by a howl, and falling on the Roman lines threw them into confusion. Cotta fell fighting and the greatest part of the soldiers with him. The rest retreated to the camp which they had left. L. Petrosidius, an eagle-bearer, being hard pressed by the enemy, threw the eagle over the rampart and died fighting bravely in front of the camp. The men within the camp with difficulty resisted the assault to nightfall, and then all to a man seeing that hope was gone killed one another. A few who escaped from the fight made their way through the tracks in the forests to the winter quarters of Labienus, and told him what had happened.

Caesar has very carefully recorded the treachery of Ambiorix, the error of Sabinus and the destruction of fifteen Roman cohorts, probably between four and five thousand men. He passes no direct judgment on Sabinus, but his narrative clearly shows that he considered him to be incompetent and the cause of the loss. Dion Cassius (40. c. 5, 6) has perhaps founded his story solely on Caesar's text, for the variations and the embellishments are no more than such a man would introduce through inaccuracy and love of rhetorical ornament. Caesar of course learned the facts from the few who escaped to Labienus, and he has taken great pains to make an intelligible story. He has not expressed in his Commentaries one word of indignation or sorrow; but still it may be true that after hearing of the massacre of his men he neither cut his hair nor shaved his beard until he had avenged them. (Sueton. Caesar, c. 67.)

Elated by this victory Ambiorix with his cavalry immediately visited the Aduatuci, who were his neighbours. The infantry was ordered to follow. These were the people whose town Caesar took in B.C. 57 (p. 60), and sold fifty-three thousand of them (ii. 29, 33), and we might conclude from Caesar's words that this number comprised all the population; but here we learn that some of them were left. After stirring up the Aduatuci Ambiorix hurried to the Nervii, a nation whose fighting men were nearly destroyed by Caesar, as he represents the fact (B. G. ii. 28), in the summer of B.C. 57; but here Ambiorix rouses the Nervii to revenge their wrongs, and persuades them to attack the winter quarters of Q. Cicero, which were within their territory. The explanation appears to be that in B.C. 57 Caesar wrote in his Commentaries that he had nearly destroyed the Nervii, and we may suppose that he believed it. In B.C. 54 he describes their rising, and he has not taken the pains to qualify or correct in his fifth book what he had said in the second. The plain conclusion is that he wrote his Commentaries at the time of the events, and that he did not correct them afterwards.

The Nervii immediately summoned the Ceutrones, Grudii, Levaci, Pleumoxii and Geiduni, who were their dependents, and with all the force that they could collect hurried to the quarters of Q. Cicero before he heard of the death of Sabinus. It happened that some of Cicero's men who had gone into the forest for firewood and timber were surprised by the enemy's horsemen, and this surprise was followed by a large force of Eburones, Nervii, and Aduatuci with their allies and dependents attacking the legion. The Roman soldiers seized their arms and mounted the rampart. The assault was with difficulty repelled on this day, for the enemy placed all their hope in the promptitude of their attack, and believed that if they got the victory now they would for the future be invincible.

Cicero immediately wrote letters to Caesar, and offered great rewards to the bearers if they should deliver them; but all the roads were stopped and the letter-carriers were intercepted. During the night one hundred and twenty towers were constructed out of the timber which the Romans had collected, and the defensive works were completed.—These towers were only scaffoldings tied together by cross pieces; and there may be an error in the number one hundred and twenty.—On the next day the enemy attacked the camp with a much larger force and filled up the ditch. The Romans repelled the attack in the same way as they had done the day before; and during the following days the attack and defence were continued in the same fashion. The Roman soldiers worked without intermission all night: neither the sick nor the wounded could take any rest, and the means for every day's defence were prepared the night before. A great stock of poles hardened at the end by fire and long pikes were got ready. The towers were furnished with floorings at different elevations for the men to stand on, and protected by battlements and breastworks made of branches intertwined. Though Cicero was in feeble health, he took no rest even during the night, until the importunity and entreaties of the men compelled him to spare himself.

The leaders and chiefs of the Nervii, who were accustomed to have access to Cicero and to talk with him, now proposed a conference, which was granted. They said just the same that Ambiorix had said to Sabinus, and they reported the death of Sabinus, pointing to the presence of Ambiorix as evidence of the truth of their statement. They further said that the Romans were mistaken if they expected any help from their friends, who were in the same difficulties; as for themselves, they only objected to Cicero and his men being quartered among them and to this becoming an established custom: they might leave their camp without any molestation and go in any direction they liked without fear. Cicero simply answered that it was not the usage of the Roman people to accept any terms from an armed enemy: if they would lay down their arms, they might employ his mediation and send ambassadors to Caesar, and he had hopes that Caesar with his usual regard to equity might grant their petition.

Failing in this attempt to deceive or intimidate the Romans, the Nervii surrounded the camp with a rampart nine or eleven feet high and a ditch fifteen feet wide, following the practice of the Romans, which they had observed in previous years, and the instructions of some prisoners; but as they had no suitable iron implements, they were obliged to cut the turf with their swords, and dig out the earth with their hands and carry it in their cloaks. From these facts a conclusion might be drawn about the numbers of the enemy, for in less than three hours they made a contravallation of "fifteen miles!'" in circuit; and on the following days they began to raise towers as high as the rampart and to prepare hooks* and tortoises

---

² "Fifteen miles." There is a reading "millium pedum xv in circuitu," fifteen thousand feet, but that is not the true reading. "Fifteen miles" is undoubtedly an error in the text. Some editions of Caesar have "ten miles," but even that is too much.

* "Hooks" or "long poles with hooks at the end," such as are described, iii. 14. (Oerler (p. 104) suggests that we should read "scalas" instead of "falces."

(testudines) or covered galleries, which they had learned to construct from the same captives.

On the seventh day of the siege there was a very high wind, when the assailants began to throw hot[1] balls of clay from slings and heated javelins against the soldiers' huts, which after Gallic fashion were covered with thatch. The huts soon took fire and the violence of the wind carried it to all parts of the camp. The enemy uttering loud shouts, as if they were sure of victory, began to push up the towers and covered galleries and to scale the rampart with ladders. But such was the courage of the Roman soldiers that, though they were scorched by the flames, assailed by showers of missiles, and all the baggage and property was in danger of being destroyed by fire, so far from deserting the rampart, scarcely a man looked behind him, and all fought with the utmost courage. This was the hardest day for the Romans, but the result was that a very large number of the enemy were killed and wounded, for they were crowded below the rampart and those who were farthest off prevented the nearest from making their escape. The flames were now a little abated, and in a certain part a tower had been pushed up by the enemy close to the rampart, when the centurions of the third cohort retired from the position which they occupied, and drawing off all their men invited the enemy by signs and shouts to enter the camp if they chose, but not a man ventured. The enemy was then dislodged by a shower of stones and the tower was set on fire.

As the attack daily became more difficult to resist, for many of the Roman soldiers were wounded, and those who could take part in the defence were reduced to a small number, Cicero was continually sending letters and messengers to Caesar, some of whom were caught and put to death with torture in the sight of the Romans. There happened to be in the camp a Nervian, named Vertico, a man of good condition,

[1] The author of the "Histoire" (p. 211) observes : "in the coal basin in the centre of which Charleroi is situated, the beds of coal reach the surface in several places. Even at present they knead clay with small coal." He adds that there have been found at Breteuil (Oise), as in the ruins of Carthage, many oval balls of baked earth." Goeler (p. 164) has ascertained that balls of clay heated to a white heat will retain their heat long enough to set straw on fire, when they are thrown.

who at the commencement of the blockade had gone over to Cicero and been faithful to him. Vertico induced a slave by the promise of freedom and great rewards to convey a letter to Caesar. The man carried out of the camp the letter secured in a javelin, probably hollowed, and as he was a Gaul he excited no suspicion among his countrymen. He reached Caesar safely, who was thus informed of Cicero's danger.

Caesar does not say where he was when he received the news. Dion Cassius (40, c. 9), as usual misunderstanding Caesar's text or perverting it, states that Caesar was on his road to Italy; but we may infer from the Commentaries that he was at Samarobriva (Amiens). Caesar received the letter about the eleventh hour of the day or about four in the afternoon, and immediately sent a messenger to M. Crassus, whose camp was in the country of the Bellovaci twenty-five miles distant. Crassus was ordered to set out at midnight with his legion and to hasten to Caesar. Crassus left his camp with the messenger. Another messenger was sent to Fabius, who was in the country of the Morini, with orders to lead his legion into the territory of the Atrebates (Artois) through which Caesar would march. Caesar also wrote to Labienus to tell him to advance to the territory of the Nervii with his legion, if he could do so consistently with the public interest. The rest of the army which was with Roscius and Plancus was too far distant for Caesar to wait for it; but he took about four hundred horsemen from the nearest winter quarters, whatever he means by these words.

At the third hour of the following morning, scouts announced the coming of Crassus, whom Caesar left in command at Samarobriva with a legion, for all the heavy material of the army was in that town, the hostages of the Gallic states, the books and accounts of the army, and all the corn which had been brought there for the winter supply. It does not appear from Caesar's narrative that he waited to see Crassus, for he set out as soon as he heard of his approach and marched on that day twenty miles. The narrative shows that Caesar was either at Samarobriva or close to it, and he left that place with one legion, that of Trebonius, and the four hundred horsemen, when he knew that Crassus was near enough to secure the stores at Samarobriva. Fabius with his legion joined Caesar on his march. Labienus, who had heard of the death of Sabinus, was threatened by all the forces of the Treviri, and he was afraid that if he left his winter quarters, his march might have the appearance of a flight and he might be unable to resist the attacks of the enemy who were elated at the recent disaster of the Romans. Accordingly he wrote to explain to Caesar how hazardous it would be to draw the legion from its quarters: he informed him of what had happened in the country of the Eburones, and that the whole force of the Treviri had fixed themselves within three miles of his camp.

Caesar approved of Labienus' resolution, though it deprived him of a legion, and he had only two legions to rely on. By forced marches he reached the country of the Nervii. There are no means of determining the position of Cicero's camp. If we accept the assumption that it was at Charleroi on the Sambre, Caesar's march from Amiens would take him through Cambrai and Bavai. Caesar learning from some prisoners in what danger Cicero was, induced a Gallic horseman by great rewards to carry a letter to him. The letter was written in Greek characters[1] that it might not be read by the enemy, if it was intercepted. If he should not be able to enter the camp, the man was told to fasten the letter to the cord (amentum)[2] of a javelin and hurl it within the

---

[1] So it is in Caesar's text, but the only characters, as far as we know, that any of the Galli were acquainted with, were Greek. We must conclude then that the letter was written in Greek also. Dion (40, c. 9) affirms that the letter was in Greek.

[2] The "amentum" was a loop of cord or leather fastened to the shaft of the javelin just behind the balance. When a man wished to throw a spear, he grasped the shaft in his hand, inserted his fingers in the loop and by means of the additional leverage was able to throw a heavy weapon a considerable distance. Ovid, Met. xii. 321.

"Inserit amento digitos—nec plura moratus
In juvenem torsit jaculum."

The Romans required an amentum for each spear. The New Caledonians require only one "ounep" or amentum. This "ounep" is a plaited cord or thong made of a mixture of cocoa-nut fibre and fish-skin: it is a foot or more long with a knob at one end and a loop at the other. Wood's "Natural History of Man," Part xxi. 205, 206. In this work there is a cut of a New Caledonian throwing his spear. He places only his forefinger in the loop and grasps the shaft of the spear with the other three fingers and the palm of the hand. In

lines. The letter stated that Cæsar would soon arrive with his legions, and urged Cicero and his men to maintain their courage. The Gaul fearing to attempt to enter the camp, threw the javelin, which by chance stuck in one of the wooden towers, and was not observed until the third day, when a soldier spied the letter and took it to Cicero, who read it to his men. The news spread joy through the camp; and now the smoke of distant conflagrations announced the approach of the avenging Proconsul.

The Gallic scouts brought the news of Cæsar's advance, upon which the enemy gave up the blockade and with all their force went to meet the Roman legions. The Gauls were estimated to be sixty thousand armed men. Cicero took advantage of the return of the messenger who had been sent to Cæsar, to send him again with a letter in which he advised the general to advance with caution, and informed him that the enemy had left the camp and were marching against him. The letter was delivered about midnight to Cæsar, who acquainted his men with the contents and encouraged them to prepare for battle. On the next day at early dawn Cæsar advanced about four miles, when he saw on the opposite side of a broad valley and a stream a great number of the enemy. It would have been hazardous to fight a battle with so large a force on unfavourable ground, and as he knew that Cicero was released from the blockade, he was well satisfied to check the rapidity of his march. Accordingly he made his camp on the most level spot that he could find, and though a camp for two legions, which hardly amounted to seven thousand men, would be of small dimensions, particularly as the army was without baggage, Cæsar made the space still smaller by contracting the width of the ways within the camp, which was done to

order to secure the ensep on the spear till it is released by the discharge, he "casts the end of the thong round the spear in a sailor's half-hitch, drawing it tight with his forefinger." Mr. Wood has made a mistake in explaining the word "torsit" in Ovid. He says, the spear was "flung with a whirling movement as a stone from a sling." But this is impossible, and the cut in his book contradicts his explanation, and also contradicts the two Latin lines which he quotes:—

"Amentum digitis tende prioribus
Et tot is jaculum dirigo viribus."

make the enemy believe that the number of the Romans was less than it really was. In the mean time scouts were sent in all directions to discover the best place for crossing the valley.

On that day there was some skirmishing between the cavalry close to the stream, but both armies maintained their position; the Galli waiting for fresh troops, which had not yet come up, and Caesar making a pretence of being afraid in the hope of drawing the enemy to ground favourable to himself and inducing them to fight on his side of the stream in front of the camp. If he failed in this design, he expected that when he was acquainted with the roads, he might cross the valley and the stream with less hazard. At daybreak the enemy's cavalry approached and engaged with Caesar's cavalry, who were ordered to give way and retire into the camp. At the same time Caesar ordered the rampart to be raised higher and the gates to be stopped up, and while the men were doing this, to hurry about the camp and exhibit all the signs of fear. The enemy were thus induced to cross the stream and draw up their force on unfavourable ground; and as the Roman soldiers were withdrawn from the rampart, the enemy came still nearer and threw missiles within. They also sent criers round the camp who proclaimed that any Gaul or Roman, if he chose to come over to their side before the third hour, might do so without any danger, but not after that time. They carried their contempt of the Romans so far that being deceived by the appearance of the gates being firmly closed, though in fact they were only stopped up by a single row of turf, they began to tear down the rampart with their hands and to fill up the ditch. The favourable moment was now come. Caesar ordered his men to sally out by all the gates and the cavalry with them. The enemy was so quickly put to flight that they made no resistance. A great number were killed and all the rest threw away their arms. The woods and marshes prevented the pursuit from being carried far; and indeed it would not have been possible to inflict any further loss on the enemy. On the same day Caesar with all his troops arrived safely at Cicero's camp. He saw with amazement the towers raised by the Gauls, and the "testudines" (covered galleries) and lines of the enemy. On

examining the legion he ascertained that not one man in ten
was without a wound, a sufficient proof of the danger to
which they had been exposed and of their courage. He commended Cicero and the soldiers as they well deserved, and
severally thanked the centurions and the tribunes who were
specially named to him by Cicero. He had learned from
some prisoners all the particulars of the death of Sabinus and
Cotta, and on the next day in a meeting of the soldiers he
told them all that had happened: he consoled and encouraged
the men: they ought to be the more content to bear the loss,
which had been sustained through the fault and rashness of
the legatus, because through the favour of the immortal gods
and by their own courage their comrades were avenged, and
neither the enemy's exultation nor their own sorrow lasted
long.

Caesar would receive from Q. Cicero the narrative of his
brave defence, and he has given it a conspicuous place in his
Commentaries (v. 38—52). He has even reported on the
authority of Cicero (v. 44) an anecdote of the rivalry and
courage of two centurions. Caesar had good reason to be
grateful to Cicero for saving the legion and the credit of the
Roman arms, but he also wished to please Marcus Cicero and
to keep him in his interest at Rome. The letters of Marcus
to Quintus (book iii.) show the intimacy between Caesar and
Marcus in B.C. 54, and their apparent friendship.

The news of Caesar's victory was carried to Labienus with
wonderful speed. Though he was about sixty miles from
Cicero's quarters, which Caesar reached after the ninth hour
of the day, a loud shout at the gates of the camp before midnight announced to Labienus Caesar's victory and the con-
gratulations of the Remi. The news being carried to the
Treviri, Indutiomarus, who had resolved to attack the camp
of Labienus on the following day, fled by night and led back
all his forces into the country of the Treviri. Caesar sent
back Fabius with his legion to his winter quarters. He himself with three legions determined to stay near Samarobriva
in three³ winter camps; and as there had been so much dis-

---

³ "There are still on the banks of the Somme near Amiens three camps not far from one another, which appear to belong this time." "Histoire de César," ii.

turbance in Gallia, he made up his mind to remain with the army. These three legions were the legion of Crassus, which had been left at Samarobriva, the legion of Trebonius, which returned from the expedition, and the legion of Cicero: Plancus, Labienus and Roscius remained in their respective positions. When the news was spread abroad of Sabinus' death, most of the Gallic states began to deliberate about war: they sent messengers and commissioners in all directions; they endeavoured to ascertain what resolutions the rest of the Galli were taking, and where the war was likely to break out, and they held meetings by night in lonely places. Scarcely any part of the winter passed without some anxiety to Caesar and some intelligence of the meetings and movements of the Galli. Among other reports he was informed by L. Roscius, who commanded the thirteenth legion, that a large force from those states which are named Armoric had met for the purpose of attacking him, and were not more than eight miles from his camp, when the news of Caesar's victory dispersed them as if they had been routed.

Caesar by summoning to his presence the chief men of every state, sometimes terrifying them by declaring that he knew what was going on, and sometimes exhorting them to their duty, kept a great part of Gallia in obedience. The Senones however, a powerful Gallic state, attempted by a public resolution to put to death Cavarinus, whom Caesar had set over them as king, whose brother Moritasgus was king of the Senones at the time of Caesar's arrival in Gallia, and his ancestors also had held the kingly power. Cavarinus being acquainted with the designs of the Senones saved himself by flight, and the people pursuing him to the borders expelled him from his kingdom and his native country. This is the third instance mentioned incidentally by Caesar of his having set up kings for the purpose of securing the fidelity of the Gallic states (B. G. iv. 21; v. 25, 54). The country was too large and Caesar's force too small to enable him to hold

128. In a note is added: "One is on the site of the citadel of Amiens, the second is near Tirancourt, the third is the Camp de l'Étoile;" and a reference is made to a dissertation on the Roman camps of the Somme by the Comte L. d'Allonville.

all Gallia in obedience, and he prudently made use of chiefs who belonged to great families in order to keep their people quiet and get from them what he wanted. The Senones sent commissioners to Caesar to explain their behaviour, but when he summoned all the Senate to his presence, they refused to come. This resistance encouraged the other Gallic states so much, that with the exception of the Aedui and the Remi there was hardly a single people whom Caesar did not suspect. Caesar had always treated the Aedui and Remi with the greatest consideration, the Aedui as old and faithful allies of Rome, and the Remi for their recent services in the Gallic war. Here Caesar, contrary to his practice, makes a remark in the first person. He says: " I am not inclined to think that there is any thing strange in this behaviour of the Galli, for they had many causes of complaint, and this particularly, that their nation which in martial merit used to be above all others had now so far fallen in general estimation as to submit to the dominion of the Roman people."

The Treviri and Indutiomarus never ceased during the winter to send commissioners across the Rhine, to stir up the states, offer them aid in money, and to assure them that the larger part of the Roman army had perished. However not a single German state could be persuaded to cross the Rhine: the Germans said that they had twice tried the experiment, in the war of Ariovistus and at the time when the Tenetheri passed over, and they had no inclination to try a third time. Though he was disappointed in the Germans, Indutiomarus continued to collect men and discipline them, to procure horses from the neighbouring states and to invite by great promises from all parts of Gallia exiles and condemned criminals. By these means he gained such consideration in Gallia that deputations came from all sides, and both communities and individuals sought his favour and friendship.

When Indutiomarus saw that people were coming to him even without being invited, that the Senones and Carnutes were moved to revolt by the consciousness of their disloyalty, and that the Nervii and Aduatuci were preparing to attack the Romans, and that he would not want volunteers if he advanced beyond the limits of his own country, he gave notice for the

people to assemble in arms[*]. This is the Gallic fashion of
beginning a war; all the men who have attained puberty
meet together according to the general usage: he who came
last was put to death with torture in the presence of all the
people. This council at the suggestion of Indutiomarus
declared Cingetorix, the head of the opposite party, to be an
enemy and his property to be forfeited to the state. When
this was done, Indutiomarus declared that he had been invited
by the Senones, the Carnutes and many other Gallic states,
that he would march in that direction through the territory of
the Remi and would ravage their lands, after first attacking
the camp of Labienus.

As the position of Labienus was naturally strong and well
fortified, he was not uneasy about the safety of his legion: his
only anxiety was not to lose any favourable opportunity. He
had been informed by Cingetorix and his kinsmen of what
Indutiomarus had said in the council, and he sent messengers
to the neighbouring states and summoned cavalry from all
parts to join him on a certain day. In the mean time Indutiomarus almost daily with all his cavalry was moving about
the Roman camp, with the view of making himself acquainted
with the position, and of entering into conversation with the
men of Labienus and frightening them. Most of the cavalry
during these visits to the camp threw missiles into it.
Labienus kept his men within their intrenchments, and confirmed in every way that he could the enemy's opinion that
he was afraid of them. As the contempt of Indutiomarus
for the Romans increased with his daily visits, Labienus one
night let into his camp all the cavalry whom he had summoned from the neighbouring states, and he kept all his men
so carefully within the intrenchments, that the arrival of
these horsemen could not in any way be known or reported to
the Treviri. Indutiomarus according to his daily practice
came up to the camp and spent a large part of the day there.

[*] Cæsar says "armatum concilium." The ordinary "concilia" of the
Galli were, as it seems (vi. 13), only attended by the nobles. On such occasions
as the present all the men were summoned: all were bound to fight; the whole
nation took up arms. The words "qui ex iis novissimus venit" must mean, "If
any man came late, and did not arrive in company with the rest."

His horsemen threw their missiles with insulting words, and challenged the Romans to fight. The Romans made no reply, and as evening came on, the enemy retired straggling and in disorder. Then all at once Labienus sent out his cavalry by two of the camp gates, with strict orders, after they had put the enemy to flight, which he knew that they would do, to pursue Indutiomarus only, and not to attack a single man until they had killed him. Labienus would not allow Indutiomarus any opportunity of escape, which he would have had, if the Roman troops followed the flying multitude. A large reward was promised to those who killed Indutiomarus; and the cohorts were sent after the cavalry to support them. Indutiomarus was caught as he was fording a river and killed. The position of Labienus' camp, as we may conclude from the Commentaries, was between the Mosel and the Maas; and the river where Indutiomarus* perished may have been a tributary of the Maas. The Ourthe has been conjectured to be the river; and the Semoy also. The head of Indutiomarus was carried to Labienus; and the cavalry as they returned to the camp overtook and killed all that they could. On hearing this news the assembled forces of the Eburones and Nervii dispersed, and Caesar now found Gallia somewhat more tranquil.

* Indutiomarus: there are extant brass coins with the legend "Indutiomarus." Lord Northwick's Catalogue, and Mr. Lindsay.

CHAPTER XIV.

THE TREVIRI AND THE EBURONES.

B.C. 53.

CAESAR began his sixth campaign with active preparations for war. He was one of those commanders who rise superior to difficulties; and like the Romans of the best times of the Commonwealth he was more formidable after defeat than before. He employed his legati M. Silanus, C. Antistius Reginus, and T. Sextius in raising fresh troops in North Italy. Cn. Pompeius, who with the title of Proconsul, was still near Rome looking after the interests of the State, as Caesar says, had enrolled troops in Gallia Cisalpina during his second consulship (B.C. 55), and Caesar requested Pompeius to order the men to muster and to come to him. It was necessary, as Caesar thought, for the Galli to learn that the resources of Italy were sufficient to repair quickly any losses sustained in war, and even to increase the forces employed against them. Pompeius granted Caesar's request out of regard both to the interest of the state and the friendship which still existed between them, notwithstanding the death of Julia, Caesar's daughter and the wife of Pompeius. Pompeius sent Caesar one legion, and his legati raised two more in Italy, all of which arrived in Gallia before the close of the winter[1]. Thus the loss of the legion and a half under Sabinus and Cotta was repaired, and

---

[1] Plutarch (Cato Min. 45) states that Pompeius lent Caesar six thousand legionary soldiers, and in two other (Pomp. 52; Caesar, 25) passages he says two legions. But compare B. G. viii. 54. Göler (p. 178) maintains that Plutarch's statement is right.

Caesar's army was increased by one legion and a half. Still he only reckons his whole force now to be ten legions (B. G. vi. 32, 33, 44; and p. 210).

After the death of Indutiomarus the authority was conferred by the Treviri on his kinsmen. As the son of Indutiomarus and all his kinsmen had been delivered as hostages to Caesar (B. G. v. 4, and p. 201), we must suppose that he had sent them home before the late rising. The new chiefs attempted to stir up the Germans and promised them money, but as they could not persuade those who were nearest, they addressed themselves to the Germans who were more remote. They found a few German states willing to listen to their proposals, and the alliance was confirmed by mutual oaths, and delivery of hostages by the Treviri as security for the money. The Treviri also formed a treaty with Ambiorix. Caesar was threatened on all sides: the Nervii, Aduatuci, and all the Germans west of the Rhine (B. G. ii. 4) were in arms; the Senones refused to obey his summons and were in league with the Carnutes and the neighbouring states; and the Germans were stirred up by frequent messages from the Treviri. Accordingly before the winter was past, Caesar with the four legions nearest to him unexpectedly entered the country of the Nervii and before they could either assemble their forces or escape, he seized a great quantity of cattle and made many prisoners. The booty was given to the soldiers, the lands of the Nervii were ravaged, the people were compelled to submit and give hostages. After this short winter campaign, which is described in a single sentence, Caesar led back his troops to their quarters. At the beginning of spring the states were summoned, according to custom, to meet, and all came except the Senones, Carnutes and Treviri, whose absence was considered by Caesar a sign of defection and the beginning of hostilities. In order to be nearer to the enemy, Caesar transferred the place of meeting from Samarobriva, as we conclude, for Caesar wintered there, to Lutetia, a town of the people named Parisii, and now the site of the capital of France. The Parisii were neighbours of the Senones, and within the memory of living persons had formed some kind of confederation with them, but the union may not have existed at this time, for the Parisii were not suspected of joining the Senones in their rebellion. Caesar declared before the assembly the state of affairs, and setting out on the same day for the country of the Senones he arrived there by forced marches, which he could make without difficulty through the level country along the banks of the upper Seine.

Acco, who was the leader of the revolt, hearing of Caesar's approach ordered the people to take refuge in the towns; but it was too late. The Roman troops were in possession of the country, and the Senones were compelled to sue for mercy. The Aedui, whose supremacy the Senones had acknowledged in former days, interceded for them with Caesar, who readily pardoned the Senones at the request of the Aedui and accepted their excuses: the season for the campaign was at hand and he had no time to spend in inquiries about the circumstances of the rebellion. The Senones were ordered to produce a hundred hostages, and they were delivered to the Aedui. The Carnutes also sent commissioners and hostages. They employed the Remi, whose dependents they were, to negotiate with Caesar, and they received the same answer as the Senones. Caesar, as we may infer (vi. 4) returned to Lutetia after the surrender of the Senones, and there received the submission of the Carnutes. He then closed the meeting of the states, and required from the several Gallic peoples their contingent of cavalry. The object of these annual meetings seems to have been to test the fidelity of the states which had submitted, and to fix their contingents for each year's campaign.

By his activity Caesar had stopped the hostile movements of the Nervii, Carnutes and Senones, and he could now direct all his attention to the Treviri and Ambiorix. He ordered Cavarinus (p. 232) to accompany him with the cavalry of the Senones, that no disturbance might arise among that people either through Cavarinus, if he were left behind, attempting to punish his enemies, or through their hostility to him. As to Ambiorix, Caesar was sure that he would not fight a battle, and accordingly he considered what he could or would do. Bordering on the Eburones, the people of Ambiorix, were the Menapii, who were protected by continuous swamps and forests, and they were the only people in Gallia who had never

sent deputies to Caesar about peace. He knew too that the
Menapii were in league with Ambiorix, and also that through
the Treviri Ambiorix had become friendly with the Germans;
and he determined to deprive the king of the Eburones of
these allies before attacking him, and so to prevent him, when
driven to desperation, either from hiding himself among the
Menapii or joining the Germans beyond the Rhine. With
this purpose he sent the heavy baggage of the whole army to
Labienus, who was now in the country of the Treviri, and ordered
two legions to join him. He set out himself with five legions
unincumbered to attack the Menapii, who did not assemble
their forces, but trusting to their natural defences fled into the
woods and marshes carrying all their property with them.

Caesar giving part of his forces to C. Fabius and the
quaestor M. Crassus, and making bridges to cross the rivers
of this watery region, fell upon the Menapii with his three
separate divisions. He burnt the scattered houses and villages, seized a great number of cattle and made many prisoners. The Menapii were thus compelled to sue for peace.
Caesar took hostages and told the Menapii that if they
received either Ambiorix or his ambassadors within their territories, he would massacre the hostages. He left Commius,
king of the Atrebates, with some cavalry to look after the
Menapii, and set out for the country of the Treviri.

While Caesar was thus employed, the Treviri collecting
a large force of infantry and cavalry prepared to attack
Labienus who had wintered in their country with one
legion, and they were not farther from him than a two days'
march, when they heard that he was joined by two legions
from Caesar. Accordingly making their encampment about
fifteen miles from Labienus they determined to wait for their
German allies. Labienus found out the enemy's design, and
with the expectation of their rashness giving him a favourable
opportunity for fighting, he left five cohorts to protect the
baggage, and with the remaining twenty-five and a large body
of cavalry advanced against the enemy and made a camp about
a mile from him. Between Labienus and the enemy there was
a river difficult to cross and with steep banks. Labienus
neither intended to cross this river himself nor did he think

that the enemy would cross. There is nothing in Caesar which enables us to identify this river, or justifies the assumption that it is either the Ourthe, or the Mosel, or the Alzette (Goeler, p. 184). The description agrees with the natural character of the Mosel, but it is hardly probable that Labienus had advanced so far into the territory of the Treviri. Caesar first describes the camp of Labienus as being in the territory of the Remi and on the borders of the Treviri (v. 24, 56), and afterwards as being in the country of the Treviri (vi. 5). Unless Labienus had moved from his first camp, and it is not said that he had, we must assume that he was still there when Caesar sent the baggage and two legions to him. All that we can say is that Labienus was somewhere between the Mans and the Mosel¹.

The Treviri were daily expecting help; and Labienus turned this expectation to his own advantage. He openly declared in a council of war that since the Germans were said to be approaching, he would not risk a battle and he would retreat at early dawn the following day. This information was quickly carried to the enemy by some of Labienus' Gallic cavalry. At night Labienus called together the tribunes and the centurions of the highest rank, explained his design, and in order to convince the enemy that he was afraid, he ordered the soldiers to quit their camp in a disorderly way contrary to Roman usage, and thus he produced the appearance of a hasty flight. The two camps were so near that the enemy's scouts brought the news of the Roman retreat before daybreak. Scarcely had the rear got out of the camp, when the Treviri began to urge one another not to lose the opportunity which they had so long wished for: it was not necessary to wait for the Germans when the Romans were in such alarm, and it was disgraceful to themselves who had so many men not to venture to attack a small force flying before them and encumbered with baggage. Accordingly without hesitation

¹ Goeler (p. 182) assumes that the winter camp of Labienus was at Arlon in Luxemburg, because he has seen the place, and he thinks that it was well adapted for a winter camp and that the position corresponds to Caesar's narrative of the fight. He conjectures that the stream with steep banks may be the Alzette (p. 184).

the Treviri crossed the river and prepared for battle on unfavourable ground. This was what Labienus had expected. Continuing his retreat leisurely, in order to draw all the enemy to his side of the river, he sent on the baggage a short distance a-head, placed it on a small knoll, and then addressed his little army. "Soldiers," he said, "you have the opportunity which you wanted: show the same courage under my orders which you have often shown under the commander-in-chief: imagine him to be here and looking on." Forthwith he ordered the men to face about and to form in line. A few companies of horse were sent off to protect the baggage, and the rest were placed on the flanks. The Romans with a cheer discharged their pila against the enemy, who seeing the supposed fugitives turning round to attack them did not stand even the first onset, but were routed and fled to the nearest parts of the forest. The cavalry of Labienus killed a great number, and also took many prisoners. In a few days the Treviri again acknowledged the Roman supremacy, for the Germans hearing of the defeat of their allies returned home accompanied by the kinsmen of Indutiomarus, who were the instigators of this defection. Cingetorix, who had always been faithful to the Romans, recovered the chief authority among the Treviri.

Cæsar now arrived after leaving the Menapii; and of course he was joined by Labienus, though he does not say so. He resolved to cross the Rhine a second time, because the Germans had sent aid to the Treviri, and to prevent Ambiorix from seeking refuge on the other side of the river. He ordered a bridge to be made a little higher up than the place where he made the first bridge, and as the mode of construction was known, and the soldiers worked with all their might, it was built in a few days*. He left on the Gallic side of the bridge a strong force to prevent any rising among the Treviri and took the rest of his troops across the river.

* Goeler (p. 186) thinks that the narrative of Cæsar shows that this bridge could only be constructed by taking advantage of a large island in the river, and this island must be Niederwerth between Coblenz and Urmitz. The author of the "Histoire," etc. (p. 230), places this second bridge near Bonn, which may be true, if Cæsar built his first bridge at Bonn. But see p. 161.

The Ubii, who had already given hostages and made their submission, sent deputies to inform Caesar that no help had gone from them to the Treviri and that they had been loyal: they asked for mercy and prayed that he would not punish the innocent for the hatred of the Germans towards the Romans: if he required more hostages, they were ready to give them. It seems that Caesar had suspected the Ubii of participating in the recent defection of the Treviri, but on investigating the matter and finding that the aid had been sent by the Suevi, he accepted the explanation of the Ubii and made inquiry about the road to the Suevi. A few days later he was informed by the Ubii that the Suevi were assembling their forces at one place and were sending notice to all the dependent states to furnish infantry and cavalry. Upon this Caesar prepared his supplies of grain, chose a convenient place for his camp, and ordered the Ubii to remove their cattle from the country and carry all their movables into the towns, with the view of preventing them from being seized by the Suevi, for Caesar thought that these stupid barbarians, if they were short of food, might be led to fight a battle on disadvantageous terms. He further ordered numerous scouts to be sent towards the Suevi to find out what they were doing. In a few days the scouts reported that all the Suevi after receiving certain intelligence of the arrival of the Roman army had retired with their forces to the remotest part of their territory, where there was a forest named Bacenis of boundless extent, which reached far into the interior, and like a natural wall separated the Cherusci from the Suevi, and protected them against one another: at the place where this forest commenced, at the west end, the Suevi had resolved to wait for the Romans.

This intelligence determined Caesar to advance no farther, for as few of the Germans cultivated the ground, he might not be able to supply his army with food. Accordingly he led his men back into Gallia. This is the reason that Caesar gives for not advancing against the Suevi, and it is a sufficient reason. Dion (40, c. 32), who is evidently following the Commentaries, says that Caesar retreated through fear of the Suevi, but in this instance as in many others he perverts

Caesar's text. In order to make the Germans believe that he might pay them another visit, Caesar only destroyed that part of the bridge, two hundred feet, which was near to the territory of the Ubii or the German side of the river, and built at the end of the bridge* a tower four stories high, which was defended by strong outworks and guarded by twelve cohorts left there under a young officer C. Volcatius Tullus. He does not inform us how long the cohorts stayed at the bridge. He succeeded however in terrifying the Germans, and we hear no more of their attempting to disturb him in Gallia.

The corn was beginning to ripen, and the time might be about the end of June or the beginning of July. Caesar had now no enemy except Ambiorix to deal with, and he marched through the Arduenna the largest forest in Gallia to chastise the king of the Eburones. The Arduenna extended from the banks of the Rhine and the country of the Treviri as far as the Nervii, a distance of more than five hundred miles, as it stands in Caesar's text, which is a great exaggeration, but even Strabo probably (p. 194) found these numerals in the commentaries, for he blames the historians who make the length of the Arduenna four thousand stadia, which is five hundred Roman miles. Ardennes is the name of one of the northern French departments which contains a part of the forest of Ardennes. Another part is in Luxemburg and Belgium. This old Celtic name exists in England in the Arden of Warwickshire, once an extensive forest.

Caesar sent forward L. Minucius Basilus with all the cavalry to surprise Ambiorix. He gave him orders to allow no camp fires, which might give the enemy notice of his approach, and said that he would follow immediately. Basilus caught many of the Eburones on their lands, and finding out from them where Ambiorix was said to be with a few horsemen, he hurried in that direction, and came upon the king unexpectedly. The house in which Ambiorix was staying was surrounded by forest, as most of the Gallic houses were, for it

---

* "Extremo ponte" is perhaps ambiguous. It might either mean at the end of the bridge on the Gallic side, or at the broken end of the bridge; and if the bridge was constructed across an island, the second must certainly be the right meaning.

was the habit of the Galli in the hot season to seek the vicinity of woods and streams. The king's companions and friends made a stand for a short time in this little nook against the cavalry of Basilus; and while they were fighting, one of his people mounted Ambiorix on a horse and the forest saved him from pursuit. But the king lost all military stores that he had with him together with his horses and waggons. It was doubtful whether Ambiorix had not collected his forces because he would not hazard a battle, or whether he was prevented by want of time and the sudden attack of Caesar's cavalry, which he supposed that the rest of the army was following close after. However he sent messengers through the country and advised the people to look after themselves. Some fled into the Arduenna, and others into the marshes. Those who were nearest to the ocean hid themselves in the parts which were insulated at high water. Many left their country and took refuge with all their movables among people who were entirely strangers. Cativoleus, the king of one half of the Eburones, who had joined Ambiorix in commencing hostilities against the Romans, was now an old man and too feeble either to fight or to fly. Cursing Ambiorix for advising the war he ended his life by eating the berries or taking poison extracted from the yew tree, which at that time was abundant both in Gallia and Germany.

While Caesar was on his march from the Rhine against the Eburones, he was met by deputies from the Segni and Condrusi (p. 161), who entreated him not to consider their people hostile, or to think that all the Germans west of the Rhine were of one mind: they declared they had never thought of war, and had sent no aid to Ambiorix. Caesar, after inquiring about the matter from some captives, sent orders to the Segni and Condrusi to bring to him all fugitive Eburones, and if they did, he would not touch their territory. Dividing his force into three parts, he took the baggage of all the legions to Aduatuca (Tongern), near the central part of the country of the Eburones, and the place where Sabinus and Cotta had wintered (p. 220). Caesar selected this spot for other reasons, and also because the works of the preceding year remained entire, and so the labour of the soldiers would be lightened.

He left in care of the baggage the fourteenth legion, one of the three which were last raised in Italy, with Q. Cicero in command and two hundred horsemen.

Caesar sent T. Labienus with three legions towards those parts on the ocean which bordered on the Menapii. C. Trebonius was sent with the same number of legions to ravage the parts adjacent to the Aduatuci. Caesar, with the remaining three legions, went towards the Scaldis (Schelde), which, ho says, flows into the Mosa (Maas), and towards the remotest part of the Arduenna, in which direction he was informed that Ambiorix had gone with a few horsemen. Caesar does not say, and perhaps he did not know, that the Schelde enters the North Sea. It has been suggested that this union of the Schelde with the Mosa was effected through the eastern branch of the Schelde, which may have been larger than it is now[1]. But, in fact, all the country between the mouth of the Schelde and the Maas may have been a swamp in Caesar's time.

When Caesar set out he said that he would return on the seventh day, on which day he knew that corn must be distributed among the legion which he was leaving at Aduatuca. He urged Labienus and Trebonius to return on the same day, if they could do so without neglecting the purpose for which they were sent, in order that, when they had discovered the designs of the enemy and all three had concerted their measures, they might commence hostilities again. Nine legions, more than thirty thousand men, and the cavalry, consisting of several thousands, were let loose in pursuit of these unfortunate Eburones, whom it was Caesar's settled purpose, as his narrative shows, to exterminate completely; and it seems that he did it, for we hear no more of them, and their place was occupied by the Tungri. (Plin. H. N. iv. 31).

The Eburones had no regular forces, nor town, nor place where they could defend themselves. The nation was scattered, and the fugitives hid themselves in retired valleys, forests, or marshes where the difficulty of approach offered a prospect of safety from the Romans. These places of refuge

---

[1] "Histoire de César." II. 233.

were well known to the people who lived in the neighbourhood, and it was necessary for the Romans to be very careful; for, though there was no danger to the mass of the army from the terror-stricken and dispersed natives, there was danger to the soldier, whom the love of booty might lead to wander too far; and it was also impossible for a large body of men to penetrate a forest where no one knew where the roads would lead, or it was not possible to discover them. If Caesar was resolved on finishing the business and extirpating "the brood of villains," as he calls them, it was necessary to send out numerous bodies of men, who would thus be separated from one another. If he kept his men together according to the Roman military practice, the people were sufficiently protected by the nature of their country, and they had daring enough to lie in wait and surprise the Roman stragglers. Against these difficulties Caesar took all possible precautions, and though the Romans were burning with desire for vengeance, he was content to spare the enemy rather than inflict any damage on them with loss to himself. But his fertile invention suggested a way of dealing with his enemies. He invited the peoples who bordered on the Eburones to come and plunder them, for in this way the Galli would run the risk of perishing in the forests instead of his own men, and the Eburones, being hemmed in by such numbers, might be completely extirpated, as they well deserved to be in Caesar's opinion. A large number of men quickly accepted the invitation.

The time was approaching when Caesar would return to Aduatuca, and there was nothing to fear from the Eburones. The news of the invitation to plunder had spread beyond the Rhine to the Sigambri, the people who had given shelter to the remnant of the Usipetes and Tencteri (p. 158). Two thousand horsemen of the Sigambri crossed the Rhine on boats and rafts thirty Roman miles below the place where the bridge was built and a garrison left. These Germans crossed somewhere about Bonn, if the site of the bridge has been rightly determined, and Bonn is due east of Aduatuca (Tongern). As soon as they touched the territory of the Eburones, many fugitives fell into their hands and they seized a great quantity of cattle. The prospect of booty led them on. Neither marshes nor forests stopped these men, who were bred up to war and pillage. The Sigambri inquired from the captives where Caesar was, and they were told that he was at some distance, and that all the army was with him. One of their prisoners suggested that, instead of seeking such miserable booty as they would find among the Eburones, they might in three hours reach Aduatuca, where the Romans had placed all their baggage and plunder. There was not force enough there, he said, to man the wall, and the Romans could not venture out of the fortifications. The Germans were tempted by the prospect. They concealed the booty which they had made, and, taking the informer as a guide, crossed the Maas about Maastricht and advanced on Aduatuca.

Following Caesar's orders Cicero had confined his men within the camp, and not allowed even one of the servants to go out. On the seventh day, however, he had no confidence that Caesar would keep his promise, for he had heard that the general had gone a long way off, and there was no report of his return. Moved by this consideration and by the clamour of his men, who said that if they were not allowed to leave the camp, it was almost the same as being besieged, and, knowing that nine legions and a very large body of cavalry had gone to meet the enemy, who were dispersed and almost destroyed, Cicero did not expect that any thing would happen to cause danger to his men within a range of three miles, and he sent five cohorts to cut the nearest corn, between which and the camp there was only a single hill. Many sick soldiers belonging to the several legions had been left in the camp; and those who had recovered since Caesar's departure, about three hundred, were sent out under one flag (vexillum). A great number of camp servants also, and of beasts of burden, which were kept within the camp, were allowed to go.

At this very time and when things were in this state the German horsemen arriving immediately attempted to break into the camp by the Decuman gate, nor were they seen before they were close upon the place, for the forest lay directly in front of the way by which they came. The traders whose tents were outside under the ramparts had no time to escape, and we may conclude that they were massacred. The Romans were thrown into confusion by this unexpected attack, and the cohort on guard with difficulty sustained the first onset. The enemy spread all round the camp, to see if they could find any other entrance into it. The Romans were hardly able to keep them out of the gates; the natural strength of the place and the fortifications protected other parts. All was confusion: every man was asking his neighbour the cause of the disturbance: nobody knew in what direction he should move or where they should assemble. Some declared that the camp was taken; others maintained that the army and the commander-in-chief had been destroyed and that the victorious barbarians had arrived. A great part of the men were struck with superstitious alarms suggested by the place where Cotta and Titurius had perished. Such being the universal terror, the barbarians were confirmed in the belief of what they had been told by their prisoners that there was no garrison in the place, and they persisted in the attempt to break into the camp and exhorted one another not to let such an opportunity slip from their hands. Among the sick who had been left in the camp was P. Sextius Baculus, who had served with Caesar as a centurion of the first rank and has been mentioned twice before (B. G. ii. 25, iii. 5). It was now the fifth day that Baculus had not taken food. Being alarmed for his own safety as well as that of the soldiers he went unarmed out of his tent. He then saw that the enemy was upon them and the danger was imminent: he got arms from those who were nearest and took his place at one of the gates. He was followed by the centurions of the cohort which was on guard, and all together they supported the enemy's assault. After receiving some severe wounds Baculus fainted and was with difficulty carried off by his comrades. In the meantime the soldiers recovered their courage so far as to venture to man the ramparts and make a show of defence. The foragers had just finished their work when they heard shouts in the distance, and the cavalry, who had accompanied them, hurried forward and discovered the danger. There was no entrenched place to which the terrified Romans could retreat. Being recently enrolled and without military experience they turned their eyes to the tribune and the centurions, and waited for their commands, but the sudden surprise had stupefied all. The Germans seeing the standards at a distance at first thought the legions had returned, and they abandoned the attack on the camp, but when they discovered how few the men were they fell upon them from all sides. The camp servants fled to the nearest eminence, from which being quickly dislodged they threw themselves among the ranks of the soldiers for protection, and thus terrified them still more. Some of the men advised that they should form what the Romans called a wedge and force a way through the enemy, as the camp was so near; others thought it would be best to occupy the heights, and for all to run the same risk. The veterans who had gone out under the flag would not consent to this second proposal, and encouraging one another and led by C. Trebonius, a Roman eques, who had been set over them, they broke through the enemy and reached the camp without the loss of a man. The camp servants and horsemen following immediately after were also saved by the impetuous onset and courage of the veterans. Those who had taken their place on the heights having no military experience neither persisted in the plan which they had formed of defending themselves on this spot, nor imitated the energy and rapid movement which had saved others, but they made an attempt to reach the camp and descended from their position to unfavourable ground. The centurions, some of whom had been raised for their merit from the lower rank of the other legions to the higher rank in this legion, not choosing to lose the military reputation which they had gained, fell fighting most courageously. The enemy being driven back by the valour of the centurions, part of the men contrary to all hope reached the camp in safety; the rest were surrounded and killed by the Germans, two cohorts out of five.

The Germans lost all hope of storming the camp when they saw that the Romans had manned the ramparts, and they retired across the Rhine with the booty which they had concealed in the woods. But so great was the alarm even after their departure that when C. Volusenus arrived that night with the cavalry, he could not make the men in the camp believe that Caesar with the army was at hand. Terror had so overpowered them that they had nearly lost their wits: they maintained that Caesar's forces were destroyed and the cavalry only had escaped by flight, for the Germans would never have ventured to attack the camp, if the army had been safe. The arrival of Caesar put an end to the alarm. The general well knew the chances of war, and only complained of the cohorts being removed from their posts and sent out instead of protecting the camp: he observed that there ought to have been no opportunity allowed for even the smallest risk: it was his opinion that fortune had shown her power in the sudden appearance of the enemy, and still more in turning them back after reaching the rampart and the gates; but the strangest of all was that the Germans, who had crossed the Rhine to plunder the country of Ambiorix, had done Ambiorix the greatest service by attacking the Roman camp.

Caesar's narrative of this mishap was of course founded on the information which he received either from Cicero or Cicero and others. He left at Aduatuca a legion which had seen no service under a commander who had proved his courage the year before; and his instructions were positive that the men must not leave the camp. Caesar like all great commanders was prudent, and only ran risk when it was necessary. Though there is not a word of direct censure either of Cicero or his men, the narrative is a severe condemnation of both. The men were cowards, except the three hundred and some of the officers, and the commander failed in judgment before the danger came, and lost his presence of mind when it did come; for Caesar tells us there was nobody to direct, nobody to give orders. Cicero saw his mistake when the Germans arrived, and he saw also that he could do nothing with his terrified recruits. If the men had been worth any thing, he might have made a sally from the camp when the Germans were cutting down the two cohorts. Probably out of regard to his brother Caesar refrained from blaming Quintus in direct terms, but by not even mentioning his name, while he represents the legion as without a head to direct them, he has left on record a report of this disaster which in the contemptuous language employed could hardly be surpassed[6]. The remarks about fortune, if they were intended to soothe Quintus a little, might also remind him that he ought not to have put himself in the power of such a goddess. Once before (vi. 30) Caesar has spoken of the power of Fortune. She was deified in Rome and men wrote and spoke as if she was a person. Caesar, whatever he may have thought, fell into the usual forms of expression when he wrote about Fortune and the immortal gods (i. 12, v. 52) as men often speak of Providence now, and mean nothing, or could not say exactly what they do mean. Cicero enumerates among the excellencies of Cn. Pompeius his good fortune, but he acknowledges that it was due to the gods. Machiavelli has a chapter (Discorsi, ii. 1) in which he examines the question whether the Romans acquired dominion more by their merit or through fortune.

Caesar now set out again to vex the enemy, as he expresses it. He summoned from the neighbouring states a great number of men and let them loose on the Eburones. All the villages and every building they came in sight of was fired. All the cattle were driven off. The corn was consumed by the men and beasts, or laid by the rains; and if any of the unfortunate people concealed themselves from the invaders, it was supposed that when the army was withdrawn they would perish by hunger. The king was hunted by numerous bodies of cavalry. The prisoners would sometimes tell them that they had just seen Ambiorix and that he was hardly out of sight, and thus the hunters having the hope of catching him, and undergoing incessant toil to gain Caesar's favour, made almost superhuman efforts, but still they failed of success, for Ambiorix saved himself by plunging into the forests or defiles, and after hiding himself by night made his way to other parts with an escort of four horsemen, the only persons to whom he ventured to entrust his life.

---

[6] Chrisius (l. 66, ed. Lindemann) quotes a passage from a letter of Caesar to M. Cicero, in which it is said : " He did not keep within the camp as a cautious and careful commander would have done." The words are, " Caesar epistularum ad Ciceronem, 'Neque,' inquit, 'pro tanto ac diligente se castris continuit.'" The passage appears to refer to this event in the Gallic war; and we conclude also that there was a collection of Caesar's letters to Cicero.

After this devastation Caesar led his army with the loss of the two cohorts, which were destroyed at Aduatuca, to Durocortorum (Reims), a town of the Remi, and, summoning a meeting of the Gallic states at that town, he made an inquiry into the conspiracy of the Senones and Carnutes. It is not said what was the result of this inquiry, except that a severe sentence was passed on Acco, who had been the chief mover in the rebellion. He was punished after the old Roman fashion (more majorum), which is described by Suetonius (Nero, 49). The man was stripped naked, his head was fixed in a kind of collar, and he was whipped to death. Some of those who were implicated in the conspiracy ran away, and sentence of banishment was pronounced upon them. Caesar placed two legions in winter quarters on the borders of the Treviri, two in the country of the Lingones, and the remaining six legions in the territory of the Senones at Agendicum (Sens on the Yonne, a branch of the Seine). After providing supplies for the army, he set out for north Italy to make his circuits in the province.

No great battle was fought in this campaign. The proconsul's purpose was to avenge the loss of his fifteen cohorts and to exterminate the treacherous Eburones. He set about the work with his usual ability and vigour. He stopped the rising of the Senones and Carnutes, held the Treviri in check, and cut off from Ambiorix all hope of finding a refuge among his neighbours, the Menapii, or help from the Germans over the Rhine. He made his preparations well before he turned his vengeance on his detested enemies. The unfortunate Eburones had corn-fields, houses, villages, and cattle. They were an industrious, thriving people. The vindictive Roman has disguised nothing. He let loose on the Eburones their savage neighbours: he killed and burnt, and wasted the land, and then left the survivors to die of hunger. Modern warfare is still the same, and the same excuse is made for the same retaliation. In 1852, in the Caffre war, we were informed by official report that "the crops of the Gaikas have been utterly destroyed." In the Indian mutiny (1857) the guilty rebels were punished with a severity which some of them well deserved, but innocent men perished too. So it is on the con-

tinent of North America. An Indian village is surprised
(1870), which, as it was supposed, had sent out men who
plundered and murdered. The retaliation was complete. The
villagers were massacred, men, women, and children, many of
them in the parents' arms. Thus a Roman general and a
modern soldier conduct warfare against their enemies exactly
in the same way. In 1870 and 1871 the German invaders of
France set fire to towns and burnt villages in retaliation, as it
was alleged, for Germans being killed not according to the
rules of war[1]. The Germans had also an excuse in the remembrance of what their country formerly suffered from the
armies of France.

[1] One of the best authenticated cases is the burning of Fontenoy, near
Toul, in January, 1871. The inhabitants were allowed to escape with the clothes
that they had on their backs, but the houses and all that they contained were
burnt. The people were deprived of home and food in a severe winter. (Letter
from Samuel James Capper, *Times*, April 6, 1871). The Christian Germans
treated these poor people as badly as the heathen Romans treated the Eburones,
and with less provocation.

CHAPTER XV.

M. CRASSUS.

B.C. 54, 53.

THERE is a letter from Cicero[1] (Ad Div. v. 8) to M. Crassus, then in his province, in which he speaks of the great zeal that he had shown in defending Crassus against the consuls and many men of consular rank. Probably some unfavourable reports had reached Rome about the behaviour of Crassus, and Cicero, as he says, gladly seized the opportunity of showing his friendly disposition to one who had been alienated from him for a time through the influence of wicked men. Both of the sons of Crassus, Marcus and Publius, were in Rome when this letter was written, and the date was B.C. 54. Publius, therefore, had not yet set out to join his father. Marcus, who was Caesar's quaestor in Gallia, and was with him till the latter part of B.C. 54 (D. G. v. 47), paid a visit to Rome before the end of the year and returned to join Caesar again early in B.C. 53 (B. G. vi. 6).

In B.C. 54 Crassus began his attack on the Parthians, though he had no instructions and no cause of quarrel with them, but he believed that the Parthian king, Orodes, Arsaces XIV. as he is supposed to be, was rich, and, being only newly settled in his kingdom, might he easily overpowered. Crassus crossed the Euphrates and plundered part of the Mesopotamia, or the northern part of the country between the Euphrates and Tigris, which contained Greek settlements

---

[1] Drumann incorrectly places this letter in the beginning of B.C. 54 (vi. 24, 25).

made in the time of Alexander's successors, but was now subject to the Parthians. As the Roman came unexpectedly, he met with no opposition till he reached Ichnae, a town on the Bilecha (Belik), a branch of the Euphrates. Here he defeated Sillaces, the satrap of the country, who had a few horsemen. Sillaces fled to the Parthian king and carried the news of the invasion. Crassus then took Nicephorium, also a Greek colony near the Euphrates. Apollonius, a Greek who had the command in a place named Zenodotium, invited some of the Romans into the place, and treacherously murdered them. Crassus retaliated by plundering Zenodotium and selling the people: but, instead of taking advantage of his success, he retired to spend the winter in Syria and to wait for his son Publius, who was coming from Caesar in Gaul with a thousand picked horsemen (Plutarch). This statement agrees with Cicero's letter as to the time when P. Crassus left Italy to join his father, though he did not come direct from Gallia, as Plutarch's words imply. Crassus had done enough to alarm and rouse the Parthian, and he gave him time to prepare for hostilities. He left garrisons in the cities which had surrendered, seven thousand infantry and a thousand cavalry, but he did nothing in the winter either to strengthen his force or to exercise his men for the next campaign.

Strabo (p. 514) says that Parthyaea, the country of the Parthians, was not large, and that the Parthians paid their contributions together with the Hyrcani both in the Persian times and under the dominion of the Macedonians. In the division of the Persian empire under the first Darius the Parthi are placed in the same nome with the Chorasmii, Sogdi, and Arii (Herod. iii. 93), and in the catalogue of Xerxes' army the Parthi and the Chorasmii are placed under one commander (Herod. vii. 66). The original country of the Parthians was wooded, mountainous, and not productive, but the extent was enlarged before Strabo's time. It is not easy to determine exactly where the original seat of the Parthians was. On the west it was bounded by Media, named Atropatene, and we may conclude that it bordered on Hyrcania, and was south of the Caspian, but separated from it by the mountains which are the southern boundary of this lake basin. Strabo places Apameia and Heracleia, two towns not far from Rhagae, within the Parthia of his day, and also Hecatompylos, a town with a pure Greek name. In the period which followed Alexander's death, and in the decay of the Greek kingdoms formed out of his empire, a Scythian as he is called, named Arsaces, seized Parthia, and became the founder of a dynasty named the Arsacidae. The time when this stranger began to lay the foundation of his power has been fixed about the middle of the third century before the Christian aera. Arsaces and his successors maintained a constant struggle against the neighbouring peoples, but at last the barbarian invaders maintained themselves securely and extended their power to the Euphrates and the countries along the Tigris as far south as the Greek town Seleuceia, which was founded on the Tigris by the Syrian king Seleucus Nicator.

Dion remarks (40, c. 15) that many* had written about the Parthians, and their country and institutions, but he limits himself to speaking of their mode of war. The Parthians use no shields, but they are mounted bowmen and pikemen, generally clad in mail, both horse and rider, which covers the whole body. The infantry are few and of the poorer sort, and they also are archers. They are all practised from infancy in using the bow and arrow, and the country being generally level is well suited for horses. They take great numbers of horses with them to war, and thus are enabled to have a change of horses, and to attack an enemy suddenly and suddenly to retreat to a distance. The atmosphere of their country is very dry and makes their archery most efficient, except in winter when they never go out to war. During the rest of the year the Parthians are most formidable enemies in their own country and in any country like it, for the sun is fiery hot and the Parthians can endure it. They are unable to make regular expeditions because they carry with them no supplies of grain and employ no persons to transport baggage.

Crassus was busy during the winter with getting money. He visited Bambyce, as the Syrians named the place, or Hierapolis, as the Greeks called it, and plundered the temple of

* Strabo (p. 515) among others, in his Histories (vi).

Atargatis, at which time his son Publius had joined him. He then went to Jerusalem, and took all the gold which Pompeius had left. The priest Eleazar gave him a mass of gold, which was in the temple, expecting by this offering to save the rest, for Crassus, as Josephus reports, swore that he would take nothing else, but he broke his oath and carried off all the treasure (Josephus, Antiq. xiv. 7, 1; B. J. i. 8. 8). He is also charged with requiring from the towns and princes contingents of men, and taking money instead of the men. This greediness seems almost incredible, but Plutarch, whose narrative is very minute, found, we must suppose, in some of his authorities evidence of the Roman general's avarice; and Josephus, who refers to Nicolaus of Damascus and Strabo's historical writings for the expeditions of Pompeius and Gabinius against the Jews, may have also found there the story of Crassus' plundering. Nicolaus and Strabo wrote near enough to the time of Crassus to be able to use whatever contemporary evidence there was. Josephus informs us that the great wealth of the temple of Jerusalem was created by the contributions of the Jews, who at that time were spread largely over the world. Cicero in his defence of Flaccus (c. 28) speaks of gold being yearly exported from Italy and the provinces to Jerusalem, and of Flaccus in his governorship publishing an edict to prevent the exportation of gold from the province of Asia. The gold in the temple was an offering of the Jews in foreign parts, and Josephus says, the Jews have no public money except that which belongs to God. But the exportation of the precious metal by the Jews was not limited to these donations. Gold came into Rome from the provinces, and the Jews and other eastern merchants took it off in the way of trade by supplying with foreign articles the demands of the wealthy and luxurious Romans.

While Crassus was making ready for his campaign he received from Orodes a message to this effect, that if the army was sent by the Romans, the Parthians would fight to the last; but if Crassus was acting without authority, the king would take pity on his age and let him withdraw his garrisons from Mesopotamia. To this insulting message Crassus replied that he would give an answer in Seleuceia; upon which one of the Parthian ambassadors showing the palm of his hand said, "The hair will grow here, Crassus, before you see Seleuceia."

It was the design of Orodes to march against Armenia to prevent the Armenian king from sending aid to Crassus; and his general Surenas was ordered to recover the places in Mesopotamia, which had fallen into the hands of the Romans. Tigranes, to whom Pompeius had restored the crown of Armenia (vol. iii. 154), was now dead, and his son Artavasdes or Artabazes, reigned in his stead. Before Crassus crossed the Euphrates, some of the places in Mesopotamia appear to have been recovered by Surenas, for Plutarch (Crassus, c. 18) states that some of the Roman soldiers who were in garrison there and had made their escape with difficulty, brought reports of the great numbers of the enemy and of their strange mode of fighting. This intelligence threw the men of Crassus into alarm, for they had expected that their greatest difficulty would be long marches and the pursuit of the enemy, but they now learned that they would have hard fighting. The chief officers also, and among them the quaestor Cassius, thought that the general ought to stop and submit the state of affairs to a council of war. The soothsayers too who accompanied the army declared that the signs were unfavourable; but Crassus paid no attention to them nor to the advice of his officers.

According to Plutarch, the Armenian king came to Crassus with six thousand horsemen. He promised ten thousand men clad in mail and thirty thousand infantry, who should be maintained at his cost, if Crassus would invade Parthia through Armenia, where the Roman army would find plenty of food and might advance safely through a hilly country, which was unfavourable to cavalry in which alone lay the strength of the Parthians. But Crassus persisted in marching through Mesopotamia where he had left many soldiers, and the Armenian king went away.

Crassus crossed the great river at Zeugma, which Seleucus Nicator founded on the west bank opposite to Apameia (Rumkala), which was also built by Seleucus. Zeugma is a little north of the parallel of thirty-seven. The army crossed the Euphrates by a bridge of boats and with unlucky omens

(Dion. 40. c. 18). One of the standard eagles obstinately refused to pass the river, and stuck in the ground, as if it were planted there, and when the men pulled it up, followed unwillingly. One of the colours (vexilla) also was blown from the bridge into the river; a story which appears in Julius Obsequens (c. 124) and in Plutarch in another form. As the men were crossing, a violent hurricane raised such a cloud of dust that they stumbled on one another and did not see the other side before they set their feet on it. In the midst of thunder, lightning and thick darkness the Roman general landed his men on the Mesopotamian side of the river; but the bridge broke down, as Dion states, before all of them had crossed. Crassus endeavoured to encourage the soldiers by telling them that the destruction of the bridge was no bad omen, for he swore that he had determined to return through Armenia; but he foolishly added, "None of us will return from this place." The words, if they were uttered, probably meant that the army would not return by the bridge; but the soldiers put a bad meaning on them and were still more dispirited. A companion of Plutarch and Dion appears to show that they followed the same authorities, but each has used them in his own peculiar way.

The hurricane described by Dion resembles that which in 1830 fell upon the two steamers of the Euphrates' expedition under Colonel Chesney. A little after one in the afternoon, in May, a storm from the west-north-west brought with it clouds of sand. The Euphrates steamer was safely secured, but the other vessel, the Tigris, perished and twenty men in her. Colonel Chesney escaped by swimming from the Tigris to the shore. He fortunately "took a direction which brought him to the land without having seen any thing whatever to guide him through the darkness worse than that of night." The hurricane lasted about eight minutes. Ammianus Marcellinus (xxiv. 1) describes a violent storm at Anatha (Annah) on the Euphrates during the eastern expedition of the Emperor Julian, when the wind rent in pieces many of the tents and stretched most of the soldiers on the ground.

The army of Crassus consisted of seven legions, near four thousand horsemen, and almost the same number of light-armed men. The number is magnified by Appian into one hundred thousand. The scouts, who had been sent out, reported that they had seen only the tracks of horsemen retreating, which gave the general and the army better hopes. Cassius, however, advised Crassus to give his troops rest in the garrisoned cities, till he should know what the enemy were doing; or as Crassus had resolved to march to Seleucia, he urged him to keep close to the Euphrates, which would protect his right flank, and the boats which carried the provisions would supply the army. While Crassus was deliberating, there came to the Roman camp an Arab chief of Osrhoene, named Augurus by Dion and Ariamnes by Plutarch. This man had received favours from Pompeius, and was supposed to be a friend to the Romans. He blamed Crassus for his tardiness in advancing against an enemy, who, as he said, had been long getting together his most valuable property and slaves with the intention of retreating to the Scythians or Hyrcanians. The king, said the Arab, was frightened, and had sent forward Surenas and Sillaces to receive the attack of the Romans, while he himself kept out of the way. Thus the cunning Arab persuaded Crassus to leave the river and to plunge into the waste and waterless plains of Mesopotamia, where neither tree nor plant appeared in the boundless wilderness of sand. Some of the Romans suspected treachery, and at this time messengers from the Armenian king reported that Orodes had fallen upon him and that he could send no aid to Crassus, but he advised Crassus to join the Armenians, or if he would not do this, to avoid encamping in places adapted to the movements of cavalry, and to keep close to the mountainous parts. Crassus returned no written answer to the king, but sent a message that he would at another time punish Artavasdes for his treachery. Cassius, as Plutarch reports, abused the Arab for leading the Romans into the wilderness, but he no longer advised Crassus, who was deceived by the barbarian to the last; and when Ariamnes rode off to join the enemy, Crassus still believed that he would serve the Romans. Both Dion and Plutarch show that they interpreted their authorities to mean that Crassus intended to march to Seleuceia, and if he did intend to attack the head-quarters of the

Parthian, Seleuceia was the proper object of his expedition. Dion states that the Arab prevailed on him to abandon the march to Seleuceia because it would occupy some time, and persuaded him to meet Surenas who was near and had only a small force, as the Arab affirmed. The march to Seleuceia might have been accomplished, if Crassus had kept close to the Euphrates and a fleet of boats had supplied the army. His road along the river would have taken him to the canals which joined the Euphrates and the Tigris, and by one of these canals, probably the Nahr Malcha, the boats might have passed to the Tigris and Seleuceia [3].

Surenas, whom the Parthian king had sent against Crassus, was in wealth, birth and rank next to his master, in courage and ability the first of the Parthians, and in stature and beauty without an equal. When he was on his own business, he travelled with a thousand camels to carry his baggage, two hundred carriages for his women, a thousand mailed horsemen, and a larger number of light cavalry. He had horsemen, dependents and slaves, not less than ten thousand. Surenas had restored Orodes to the Parthian throne, after he had been driven out of his kingdom, as Plutarch states, and he had also taken for him the great city Seleuceia on the Tigris. Surenas was not yet thirty years old, but he was prudent and cautious, and more than a match for Crassus, whose confidence and arrogance brought on his ruin.

While Crassus was continuing his march, some of his scouts reported that they had escaped with difficulty from the enemy, who had cut off the rest of their body, and were now advancing in great force. This unexpected news completely disconcerted the Roman general, who after placing his men in

---

[3] Dion's text is this (40, c. 20): "Crassus intended to march to Seleuceia, supposing that he could pass safely along the Euphrates and through it with his army and supplies, and after reaching Seleuceia, which he expected to gain over easily, as the population was Greek, he thought that he might reach Ctesiphon without difficulty." If there is no corruption in Dion's text, the words "and through it" are founded on some mistake made by him in using his authorities. If the great canal was then open, the boats of Crassus might have passed from the Euphrates to the Tigris by this canal, which Dion here calls the Euphrates. See Macmichael's Analasis, p. 302.

order of battle changed his plan and formed what the Romans called "agmen quadratum," an arrangement which allowed the army to advance and at the same time enabled it to resist attack. This moving square had twelve cohorts on each side, or forty-four cohorts in all, and a body of horse by the side of each cohort. But as Crassus had seven legions or seventy cohorts, the square, as Plutarch describes it, did not comprise all the legions. Cassius commanded one wing, Publius the other, and Crassus was in the centre. Marching in this way they came to a stream which Plutarch names Balissus, probably the Bilecha, (Belik), which enters the Euphrates near Thapsacus, where Xenophon crossed the river in the expedition with Cyrus. Some of the officers thought that they ought to stop here for the night, and learn what were the numbers and position of the enemy. Crassus would not listen to this advice, but pushed forward at a quick pace until the enemy were in sight, who did not seem formidable, for Surenas had placed the mass of his force behind the front ranks, and their bright armour was covered by cloaks and skins. When the Parthians were near the Romans, they began to beat their drums, which were furnished with bells and produced a sound compounded of the roaring of wild beasts and the crash of thunder, as Plutarch describes it. The Romans were startled at the noise, and the Parthians suddenly throwing off the coverings of their armour appeared with their helmets and breastplates flashing like flame, and their horses equipped in mail of brass and iron. The Parthians threw themselves round the Roman square, upon which Crassus ordered the light troops to spring forward, but a shower of arrows drove them back to seek shelter in the ranks of the legions, which were thrown into some disorder. The Parthians now dispersing discharged their arrows from all points on the compact ranks of the Romans, who if they stood still were wounded, and if they attempted to close with the enemy, they suffered just the same, for the Parthians still discharged their arrows while they were retreating.

The Romans endured for a time in the hope that the Parthians would exhaust their arrows or come to close quarters, but there were camels loaded with arrows to supply those who wanted more. The Parthians were now directing their attack on the wing commanded by Publius and surrounding it with their cavalry; from which we may infer that Crassus had changed the order of his battle, and no longer maintained the "agmen quadratum." Crassus seeing this danger sent orders to his son to force the enemy to engage, and Publius taking thirteen hundred horsemen, a thousand of whom were the Gauls whom he had brought from Caesar, with five hundred archers and eight cohorts, wheeled round against the Parthians, who immediately fled. The cavalry pursued and the infantry followed as quick as they could, but they had not gone far before the Parthians faced about and were joined by others. The enemy placed their mailed horsemen in front, and the rest of their cavalry riding round the Romans raised such a cloud of dust that they could see nothing, and being driven into a narrow compass were pierced by the Parthian arrows. Publius made a vigorous attack on the enemy with his cavalry, but the arms of his men were feeble against the Parthians. The Gauls indeed fought bravely, for they laid hold of the long spears of the Parthians and pushed the heavy mailed men from their horses, and many of the Gauls dismounting wounded the Parthian horses in the belly. The Gauls suffered dreadfully from the heat; and having lost most of their horses by driving them against the spears of the enemy they were compelled to retreat to the legionary soldiers, taking with them Publius who was badly wounded. The Romans made their way to a sandy hillock, where they placed the horses in the centre and close-locked their shields to resist the enemy; but the sloping ground which raised the men above one another only exposed them more to the Parthian arrows. Two Greeks of Carrhae, who were with Publius, advised him to escape to Ichnae on the Bilecha, which was not far off and had taken the part of the Romans, but Publius refused to desert his men and told the Greeks to save themselves. As his hand was pierced by an arrow, and he could not effectually use it, he ordered his shield-bearer to kill him. The Parthians transfixed most of the survivors with their spears, and made only a few prisoners. This was the end of the first act of the tragedy in which the brave young soldier perished, who had served Caesar so well in the battle with Ariovistus and in the Aquitanian campaign[1].

While Publius was pursuing the enemy, Crassus had a little rest from the attacks of the Parthians, and drawing his forces together on a sloping ground he waited for his son's return. Publius, when he found in what danger he was, had sent messengers to his father, but those who were first sent fell into the hands of the enemy, and the next messengers, who made their way to Crassus, reported that his son was lost, if aid was not speedily sent. The distracted father could not determine what he should do, but at last he put his troops in motion. In the mean time the Parthians advanced to attack him making loud shouts and beating their drums. They rode up to the Romans carrying the head of Publius on a spear, the sight of which instead of rousing the men to revenge his death, struck them with terror. For a moment the courage of Crassus rose above the danger and he went along the ranks encouraging the soldiers, but he could not raise their spirits, and when he ordered them to shout the battle-cry, the response was feeble and irregular, while the answer of the enemy was confident and loud. The Romans were again galled by the Parthian arrows, and the horsemen with their long spears drove the Romans together, and if any of them made a desperate attack on the enemy, they did little damage and were transfixed by the heavy spears of the Parthians. When darkness came on, the Parthians retired. The Romans passed a dreadful night in the plain where the dead and wounded, the living and the dying were lying together. Crassus wrapped himself in his cloak and lay concealed. Octavius one of the legati and Cassius attempted to rouse and comfort him, but finding that he had given himself up to despair they called together the centurions and tribunes and after deliberation it was determined not to stay on the ground. But when the army began to move and the wounded knew that their comrades were leaving

---

[1] Dion (40. c. 22, 23, 24) describes in three chapters the attack on Crassus after the death of his son. It is impossible to make use of his narrative, which is either an invention of the historian, or contains a few facts which he found in his authorities and perverted, embellished, and confused in a way which nobody but himself could do.

them, groans, shouts and confusion filled the camp, for the Romans after their fashion did not pass the night without throwing up some earthworks. As the men advanced, disorder and panic prevailed, and the march was slow. Three hundred horsemen with one Ignatius (Egnatius) at their head about midnight reached Carrhae, and calling out to the Roman watch on the walls told them to inform their commander Coponius that there had been a great battle between Crassus and the Parthians. Without saying more Ignatius and his men rode off and crossed the Euphrates at Zeugma. Coponius concluded from the words of the horsemen that they had nothing good to report, and as soon as he heard that Crassus was on his march, but we are not informed how he heard, he went to meet him and conducted him into the city.

If we knew the site of Carrhae, we should know within certain limits the place where Crassus was defeated; but there is no direct evidence. Carrhae is assumed to be the same as Haran, a small place two days' journey S.S.E. of Orfa, the ancient Edessa, as Niebuhr heard, but he did not visit Haran (Reisebeschreibung, ii. 410).

Though the Parthians knew that the Romans were escaping by night, they did not pursue, but at daybreak they came on those who were left in the camp to the number of four thousand and massacred them. They also overtook many stragglers, and four cohorts under the legate Vargunteius, which had separated from the rest of the army and lost their way. These men being surrounded by the enemy were destroyed except twenty, who were spared, as we are told, because the Parthians admired their bold attempt to force a passage with their swords, and they were allowed to retreat to Carrhae. Surenas did not know whether Crassus had made his escape or was shut up in Carrhae, and accordingly he sent one of his men, who knew the Roman language, as Plutarch says, but perhaps he ought to have said Greek, to approach the walls, to call out for Crassus or Cassius, and to say that Surenas wished to have a conference with them. The man did as he was ordered, and when Crassus and Cassius appeared on the wall, they were recognized by some Arabs who had been in the Roman camp. The Arabs said that Surenas offered to let the Romans go away safe, if they would leave Mesopotamia. Cassius, who is represented as the spokesman, asked for a time to be fixed and a place where Crassus and Surenas should meet; and the Arabs assenting to this proposal rode off. No conference followed, but Surenas appeared before Carrhae and bade the Romans, if they wished for a truce, to deliver up Crassus and Cassius in chains. Crassus with the Romans now prepared to make their escape by stealth. A man named Andromachus was entrusted with the secret and was appointed to guide the army, but he reported to the Parthians all that he knew. Crassus left the city by night during which time the Parthians never attack, but Andromachus contrived that they should not be far behind in the pursuit, for he led the Romans by circuitous and difficult roads. Some of the Romans suspecting Andromachus refused to follow him, and Cassius returned to Carrhae, whence he made his escape to Syria with five hundred horsemen. The retreat of the other Romans was towards the country north of Carrhae. Some of them, who had faithful guides made their way into a hilly tract, named Sinnaca, before daybreak, where they were safe. They were about five thousand men under the command of Octavius. At dawn Crassus was still in the low country with four cohorts and a few horsemen, and exposed to attack from the enemy, but he succeeded in making his way to a hill, and thence by a ridge, which connected this hill with Sinnaca, he joined Octavius.

Surenas fearing that the Romans might make their escape rode up the hill with his chief officers and invited Crassus to come to terms: the king was ready to make a truce with the Romans, if they would retire. Crassus after his experience of the Parthians would not listen to the proposal, but the soldiers urged him to accept the terms. In vain Crassus told them that if they held out for the rest of the day, they would be able to march by night through a mountainous country and secure their safety. The men became mutinous, and Crassus being alarmed advanced towards Surenas after protesting to the officers that he was acting under compulsion. Octavius and those about him descended the hill with Crassus. The rest of the story is very confused, but told shortly it is something like this. When Crassus and Surenas met, the

Roman general was on foot, but Surenas had a horse ready for Crassus, who was forcibly put upon it; for the purpose of the Parthian was apparently to carry him off. Octavius laid hold of the bridle of the horse, and other Romans attempted to stop the beast, and thus a fight began. Octavius killed the groom of one of the barbarians, and was then killed himself. Crassus fell in the struggle, but it is uncertain by what hand. The survivors fled back to the hill, and some of them surrendered on the demand of Surenas. The rest dispersed under cover of night: only a few escaped, and the remainder were hunted by the Arabs and put to death when they were caught. According to Plutarch, it was reported that twenty thousand men perished and ten thousand were taken alive. Other writers exaggerate the loss. It was in the early part of June that this great misfortune befell the Roman arms[4].

The head and hand of Crassus were sent to the king, who was then in Armenia. Molten gold, it was reported, was poured into the mouth of Crassus to indicate his greediness. Surenas sent a message to Seleuceia that he was bringing Crassus alive, and a mock triumph was prepared for the occasion. A Roman prisoner, who resembled Crassus, was put in a barbarian female dress, mounted on a horse, and instructed to answer as Crassus and Imperator to those who addressed him. There were trumpeters in front of the sham Crassus, and lictors rode on camels with purses suspended from the fasces, and by the side of the axes Roman heads freshly cut off. Courtesans of Seleuceia, singing girls followed in the procession, chanting obscene and ludicrous songs about the effeminacy and cowardice of Crassus.

Orodes the Parthian king had been reconciled to the Armenian king Artavasdes and had agreed to take the sister of Artavasdes as wife to his son Pacorus. There were banquets on the occasion and representations of Greek plays. Orodes had some acquaintance with the Greek language and literature, and Artavasdes wrote tragedies, speeches and histories, some of which, says Plutarch, are preserved. These eastern kings were sometimes the children of Greek women, who were

[4] Ovid, Fasti, vi. 465.

taken as wives or concubines by oriental despots. At one of
the entertainments presented to the Armenian and Parthian
kings, a tragedy actor named Jason recited that part of the
Bacchae of Euripides, which relates to Agave, and in the
midst of the applause Sillaces, who was standing at the door,
threw the head of Crassus before the company. The spectators clapped their hands with shouts of joy, and Jason laying
hold of the head and assuming the air of a Bacchante sung
with enthusiasm the verses of Euripides:

> "We bring from a mountain
> A young one new killed to the house,
> A fortunate prey."

In such a farce as this, says Plutarch, the expedition of Crassus
terminated.

According to Plinius (N. H. 6. c. 10) Orodes settled the
Roman prisoners in the city of Antiocheia Murgiana on the
river Margus, a site which is probably represented by Merv,
nearly due north of Herat, and on the river Murgh-aub. It
was supposed or said at Rome that these captives married
Asiatic women and served in the Parthian armies (Horace,
c. iii. 5).

CHAPTER XVI.

ROME.

B.C. 54, 53.

CICERO, who had gone to his Tusculan villa on the fifteenth of November, B.C. 55, informs Atticus that he intended to be in Rome on the nineteenth, and that he had finished his treatise on Oratory, at which he had long worked. It was now ready for copying and publication (Ad Att. iv. 13). We may assume that Atticus and his copiers (librarii) would do the work better than it was generally done, for Cicero complains that Latin books were copied and sold full of errors (Ad Q. Fr. iii. 6, 6). Strabo (p. 609), when he is speaking of Apellicon's library, which Sulla after the capture of Athens, carried to Rome, says that the books were much used by publishers, who employed bad copyists and the copies were not properly compared with the originals. This, he observes, was also the case with all the books which were copied for sale both at Rome and at Alexandria. We thus understand what is the origin of the numerous errors in ancient texts, which the industry of modern scholars has attempted to rectify. This Treatise De Oratore in three books is perhaps the best of Cicero's works. He had also finished a poem in three books on his own Times (De Temporibus meis), which in the next year he promised to send to his friend Lentulus, proconsul of Cilicia, if he could find a safe carrier. In B.C. 54 he was busy with his work De Re Publica, which was finally published in six books, and has been partially recovered within this century[1]. Cicero declares to his brother Quintus (Ad

---

[1] M. Tulli Ciceronis De Re Publica quae supersunt edente Angelo Maio.

Q. F. iii. 0, 4) that he withdrew altogether from public
affairs and devoted himself to literature; but he bitterly
laments that instead of enjoying the consideration in the
Senate to which his age entitled him, he was either harassed
with constant employment in the courts or only relieved by
his studies at home, visits to his villas, and the education of
his son and nephew: he was not at liberty to show either his
friendly feelings or his dislikes, and Caesar was the only man
who loved him as much as he desired, or, as some supposed,
the only man who had any inclination to love him at all. In
his letters to Quintus, who was with Caesar, he tells his
brother to be cautious about what he writes, for he is careful
himself not to say any thing in his letters about public affairs
for fear that they may be intercepted and give offence to any
one. But the transmission of letters does not appear to have
been very unsafe, for of all the letters sent by Quintus to
Marcus from Gallia the only one lost was that which contained the Erigona, one of Quintus' tragedies. Quintus
amused himself in his leisure with writing plays.

The chief business of the year 54 was the contest for the
consulship. There were four candidates, Domitius Calvinus,
C. Memmius, Messala and Scaurus, all eager to purchase the
prize. Milo and P. Clodius also were preparing for the
elections of 53, when Milo would be a candidate for the consulship and P. Clodius for the praetorship. There was talk
now and then of making Pompeius Dictator, for though Proconsul of Spain he was still staying near Rome. Cicero was
busy in the courts, and keeping up a regular correspondence
with Caesar, whose purpose was to secure Cicero in his interest, and Cicero was anxious to secure Caesar's protection.
L. Aemilius Paullus had laid the foundations of a new Basilica,
and Caesar in his absence wished to make the people think
of him by undertaking something for the embellishment of
Rome. Oppius, who was Caesar's agent at Rome, and Cicero
bought at Caesar's cost, for a new Forum, the ground which
extended from the old Forum as far as the Atrium Libertatis.
The site was covered with private houses, which were purchased, as Cicero says, for sixty millions of sesterces (Ad Att.
iv. 10, 14), but as Suetonius (Caesar, 26) states, the ground

cost above one hundred millions, and Pliny makes the cost still more. "We shall make a most glorious piece of work," says Cicero; "for we are going to build the Septa for the Tributa Comitia in the Campus Martius of marble, to cover them over and to surround the place with a lofty colonnade a thousand paces in length: at the same time the Villa Publica will be connected with this work." If the ground was paid for at this time, we may ask how Caesar raised the money. It is probable that he had made a great deal of money in Gallia, and particularly by the sale of prisoners (B. G. ii. 33; iii. 10). Cicero himself had a prospect of some profit from the Gallic war, for his brother (Ad Q. Fr. iii. 9. 4) promised him some slaves, and Cicero, as he says, was not well provided with them either at Rome or on his lands. Whether Cicero at this time received money from Caesar, either as a loan, as Drumann suggests (ii. 330), or as a gift, it is difficult to say. Cicero's own words, for we have no other evidence, are not decisive (Ad Fam. i. 9. 12; vii. 17. 7).

In February Cicero in the Senate opposed the petition of Antiochus king of Commagene (vol. iii. p. 170) for the possession of some small town on the Euphrates, and for permission to wear the "toga praetexta," which favour had been granted in Caesar's consulship. Cicero sneered and jeered about the poor king's petition and "exploded the whole affair," for what reason we know not. But as February was rogues' month[1], in which consuls and venal senators had the opportunity of taking money from provincial deputations and ambassadors of allied states, this kind of joking was a serious matter; and the consul Appius and Atticus also on his behalf begged Cicero to do no more in this kind, for Appius foresaw that if Cicero continued in this strain February would be an unprofitable month. "It is easy enough," says Cicero, "to explode all the other affairs;" but to avoid offending the consul, he went no farther (Ad Q. Fr. ii. 12. 2).

Cicero was in Rome on the ninth of July after a visit to Reate (Rieti), where he had gone to aid the Reatini in a

---

[1] Verr. II. 2. 31. and Ad Q Fr. II. 2. 1, where in Orelli's first edition we must read "legationes" for "legiones."

suit before one of the consuls and ten legati against the people of Interamna (Terni). The people of Reate complained of an artificial cut having been made or enlarged which carried off into the Nar above Interamna a great part of the waters of the lake formed by the river Velinus below Reate. Canvassing and bribery for the expected elections were now very active at Rome; and the proof is, says Cicero (Ad Att. iv. 15. 7), that on the fifteenth of July the rate of interest was doubled. "But you will not care for that," says Cicero, by which he means, as I understand the passage, that Atticus might derive some profit from the high rate of interest. The two consuls had made a bargain with two of the candidates Memmius and Domitius, by which they agreed to help them to the consulship, if Memmius and Domitius would aid the consuls of B.C. 54 in getting a proper outfit for their provinces. The candidates for the tribuneship showed more honesty, for they severally gave security to the praetor M. Cato for five hundred thousand sesterces on the condition that if Cato condemned any candidate of bribery, the deposit money should be distributed among the others (Plutarch, Cato, c. 44). The comitia for the election of the tribunes were held; and if no candidate should be convicted of bribery, Cato, as Cicero says, would have shown more power than all the jurymen who tried bribery cases. The consular elections were not held this year. Bribery had been long practised at Rome, and it appears that corruption had increased, for the majority, says Plutarch, were accustomed to receive money for their votes as if in the way of regular trade. In some English boroughs at the present day candidates offer bribes and voters accept without any shame: the voters care nothing for the candidate's character or his opinions; they have no political opinions themselves, and an election is for them only an opportunity of getting money.

In the month of July, and this was a very hot year, Cicero was busy in the courts. He defended C. Messius, and shortly afterwards, probably in August, Livius Drusus, who was accused of "praevaricatio" and acquitted. On the same day in the afternoon (Ad Q. Fr. ii. 16. 3) he defended P. Vatinius, Caesar's tool, whom he had well abused in an extant speech

(p. 127) in B.C. 56. Vatinius was now prosecuted by C. Licinius Calvus under the Lex Licinia de Sodalitiis, in fact, as we assume, for the bribery by which he obtained the praetorship in B.C. 55. Cicero defended Vatinius very unwillingly, but he could not help it. His apology for defending this liar, thief, robber and murderer, as he had once called him (In Vatin.) is contained in the long letter to Lentulus (Ad Fam. i. 9. 19)., Vatinius and Cicero were good friends afterwards, or they pretended that they were (Ad Div. v. 9. 10. 11)*. On the eighth of July M. Aemilius Scaurus, one of the candidates for the consulship, was charged before the praetor M. Cato with the offence of Repetundae under the Lex Julia. The prosecutor P. Triarius was the son of the Triarius, who had fought in Sardinia against M. Lepidus and under Lucullus against Mithridates (vol. iii. p. 89). Three other joint prosecutors (subscriptores) assisted Triarius. The charge against Scaurus was that during his propraetorship in Sardinia (B.C. 55) he had taken money illegally, and committed other crimes. The subscriptores were allowed thirty days for visiting Sardinia and Corsica in order to inquire into the evidence against Scaurus, but they did not avail themselves of this permission for fear that the Comitia might be held in their absence and Scaurus should gain his election by money. The trial was on the second of September. Scaurus relied on his father's great name, on the fame of his aedileship (p. 82), and, as Asconius says, on Cn. Pompeius, for the strange reason that when Pompeius put away his wife Mucia, who was suspected of adultery with C. Caesar, Scaurus married the woman and now had a son by her. Scaurus was defended by six advocates, among whom were P. Clodius, Cicero, and Q. Hortensius. Nine men of consular rank gave Scaurus a character (laudabant). Many of them were absent and sent their testimonials in writing. Pompeius being a proconsul was of course not within the walls, and though he did not give Scaurus any aid in his trial, he sent his written testimonial in favour of his former wife's new husband.

---

* Two letters from Vatinius to his dear Cicero (Ciceroni suo), B.C. 45, and a letter from Cicero to Vatinius Imperator.

Scaurus had also the testimonial of his half-brother Faustus Sulla, for Caecilia the mother of Scaurus married the dictator Sulla after her husband's death, and had by him Faustus and Fausta. Scaurus also spoke in his own defence, and moved the jury greatly by his tears, his squalid appearance, the remembrance of his aedileship, the favour of the people and his father's memory. His half-brother Faustus by his abject behaviour and his tears produced as great an effect on the audience as Scaurus. When the jury were voting, the scene in court was pathetic. The suppliants separated themselves into two parties who threw themselves before the knees of the jury. On the one side were Scaurus himself, M'. Glabrio his sister's son, C. Memmius a son of Scaurus' half-sister Fausta, and others. On the opposite side were Faustus Sulla, T. Annius Milo, whom Fausta had married a few months before after being sent away by her husband C. Memmius the father, and C. Cato, who had been just acquitted after trial, with some others. The jury consisted of twenty-two senators, twenty-three equites, and twenty-five tribuni aerarii. Four senators voted against Scaurus, two equites, and two tribuni aerarii, and he was of course acquitted. The Comitia were interrupted by the tribune Scaevola to the end of the month, but Scaurus after his acquittal gave bribes to the people at his own house, as Cicero says (Ad Att. iv. 16. 7), and though he gave freely, those candidates who had given before him, appeared to have gained the popular favour. All the four consular candidates were judicially charged with bribery; Domitius Calvinus, C. Memmius the father, M. Messala, and Scaurus who was again attacked by Triarius. Cicero defended Scaurus, who was convicted this time; but he was not tried until B.C. 52, if we can trust Appian (B. C. ii. 24). Cicero wrote out his speech for the defence of Scaurus on his first trial, but we have only fragments of it[4].

In this month of September Cicero had an opportunity of showing his gratitude to his friend Cn. Plancius who had kindly received him in Macedonia when he was driven from

[4] Asconius in Scaurianam, and the Argumentum (Orelli, p. 18). Other fragments have been more recently published by Mai and Peyron.

Rome (vol. iii. p. 459). The father of Plancius was still living and a distinguished member of the powerful body of Publicani, who farmed the provincial taxes. In B.C. 56 Plancius was a tribunus plebis; and in B.C. 55 he was a candidate for the curule aedileship with A. Plotius, Q. Pedius and M. Juventius Laterensis, the man who in B.C. 59 gave up his canvass for the tribuneship because he would not take the oath about Caesar's land bill (vol. iii. p. 422). For some reason the election of the curule aediles for B.C. 54 was not completed in B.C. 55, and the curule aediles for B.C. 54 were not elected until the summer of that year. Plancius and Plotius were elected and the unsuccessful candidate Laterensis prosecuted Plancius for bribery under the Lex Licinia de Sodalitiis. All that we know about the matter is contained in Cicero's oration in defence of Plancius[1].

In B.C. 56 the senate had made a Consultum, which was directed against the meeting of clubs and associations of a political character. The Consultum (Cic. ad Q. Fr. ii. 3. 5) declared that such meetings should not be held, and that a law should be passed by which the penalties De Vi should be applicable to those who disturbed the peace by such meetings. It has been assumed that the Lex Licinia de Sodalitiis was enacted in pursuance of this Senatusconsultum; but whether this was so or not, the Licinia was enacted in B.C. 55, and proposed by M. Licinius Crassus, one of the consuls of that year. Dion (39. c. 37) speaks of severer penalties against bribery being enacted in this year, and there is no other law than the Licinia to which his words can refer. This Lex Licinia de Sodalitiis was directed against clubs and associations which could be turned to the purposes of elections, and certain chapters (15, 18, 19) in the Oration pro Plancio help us to understand the business. The men who managed the canvassing would have a list of all the members (sodales) of a club, would agree with the club about the sum which should be paid and bring the members up to the poll, which would be a much easier way of

[1] There is a useful edition of this oration by Wunder, but, as I think, he has misunderstood the "sodalitia," and he has been followed by Drumann and others. The oration of Cicero is very difficult, but a man who knows no more of elections than Wunder does is not well qualified to explain it.

securing votes than dealing with the electors singly. There
is not the least reason for supposing that in this election
matter "sodales" had any other than the usual meaning. The
Lex Licinia was evidently an enactment directed against
those who made use of the existing clubs and associations for
election purposes. Wunder (Prolegomena, p. lxxiv) supposes
that certain men named "sodales," who were bribed by a candidate, compelled or brought together (cogebant) the multitude, to vote for the briber; and that to each "sodalis" a
candidate assigned a certain part of a tribe for him to look
after, and it was the business of those supposed "sodales" to
procure votes for the candidate in whatever way they could.
But this is a new meaning of the word "sodales," whereas
the law would take the word "sodales" in the usual, old
established acceptation; and if it did not, it would be necessary for the law to give a new meaning to the term and to
define it; and how, we may ask, could these election agents appointed by the several candidates form a "sodalitium," when the
only connexion between them was the fact of their working
for their employer, and "sodalitium" was a term already used
for clubs and associations, which were common in Rome?
Nor could the voting be managed in such a way as Wunder
supposes, for men could not be driven to the poll by force (vis),
and even if what we call undue influence and intimidation were
used, the voter had the ballot to protect him, and the ballot,
(Pro Plancio, c. 6) was effectual. "The people," Cicero says,
"like the ballot, for it enables a man to assume an open face
and to conceal his thoughts, and it gives him the liberty of
doing as he likes, but promising what he is asked." This is
the very reason why the ballot has been condemned by some
persons, who affirm that "it would enable a man to promise a
candidate his vote and give it to another: it would enable a
man to take money from one candidate and vote for another; and it would enable some lower scamp still to take a
bribe from both candidates and vote for neither." We
know that the ballot did not stop bribery at Rome; and
perhaps the secrecy of the ballot was not always secured; nor
will I say that secrecy could always be secured among us. It
is said that it is not secured in the United States, but it is

difficult to discover from what we read about secret voting there, whether the secrecy is not secured because in the nature of the thing it is impossible, or because the opposite factions do not choose to adopt all the means necessary to secure secrecy. If the ballot can do all that our modern objectors say that it can, a candidate would not be much disposed to give his money when he would know that he might get nothing for it*. If the voter did take money and did not do what he promised, he would be no greater rogue than he is now, when he sells a vote, not an opinion, for he frequently has none, and does not give the vote that he promises. In our very corrupt boroughs the briber is the great criminal. The voter who

* It has been said that "voting is a public duty, and should be discharged in the face of the people to whom the voter is responsible for the right exercise of it. The fact of responsibility is acknowledged when we punish those who vote corruptly." There are almost as many blunders here as there are words. There is no distinction of duties into public and private. There are legal duties, which are enforced by legal penalties or punishment, and there are duties, generally called moral, which are not enforced by legal penalties or punishment, but only by opinion or the disapprobation of society. Voting is not a legal duty. An elector may not vote if he chooses; and there is no legal penalty for not voting, nor does opinion condemn a man simply for not voting, and it would be most unreasonable if it did, for a man is the sole judge or ought to be whether he will vote for any candidate or for none at all. He may think all the candidates equally bad. The voter then is neither legally nor morally responsible for the exercise of his vote. He may legally vote for the greatest scoundrel in the world, if he is a candidate. There is no right or wrong voting, but there is a penalty for taking or giving a bribe for a vote. If we say that voting ought to be open, because the voter should act under the influence of opinion, we are in fact saying that he ought to vote under the influence of opinion, whether opinion is right or wrong; and who shall determine what opinion is right and what is wrong? But if a man has a vote, the meaning is that he should give the vote, as he pleases, and not be induced in any way to give it as other people please. Public voting therefore, if it does in any way affect the giving of a man's vote, contradicts the purpose for which the power of voting is given. The giving of a vote is an act of sovereign power, and there is no reason why any man should know how another votes. Before the day of voting comes, opinion, discussion, and the ordinary intercourse of society will have their effect on every man's mind; but the conclusion, the bare act of giving the vote, is and ought to be an irresponsible act, and therefore secret, if the voter is in danger of being affected in any way by giving it publicly. The act of voting is as much an act of sovereign power as the act of voting in either house of Parliament, but he who votes in the Commons' house, though not responsible for any vote, may lose his election at some future time, if his vote displeases that irresponsible member of the sovereign power, his constituents.

cares for neither side, and gets the best price that he can, is not a rogue because he votes for one man rather than another, for he may legally give his vote to any candidate, but he is a rogue because he takes money, and his roguery is not increased because he does not keep his promise to the man who has bribed him.

The constitution of the Jury under this Lex Licinia was peculiar (Pro Plancio, cc. 15, 16); but it is not easy to say what it was. It is generally supposed that Cicero means to say that the prosecutor named four tribes, of whom the accused could reject one, and the jury were chosen out of the remaining three; and chosen by the prosecutor, as Wunder affirms, without any power of challenge being allowed to the accused. But there is no evidence in Cicero's oration that the prosecutor named the jury: it is a supposition highly improbable, and contrary to Roman principle. Cicero says that the prosecutor named (edidit) the tribes, and he says no more. It is indeed very difficult in this oration to extract the facts out of Cicero's statements.

The peroration of Cicero's speech (c. 40) is a short sketch of his journey into exile and his kind reception by Plancius after he had crossed the sea from Brundisium. The closing words, the "miseratio" or pathetic appeal to the court was in the Roman style. He addresses the presiding judge C. Alfius: and entreats him thus: "Save for my sake by the vote of this jury a man by whose aid I have been restored to you and to them: your tears, Alfius, and yours, jurymen, not my own only, prevent me from saying more, but they give me hope in my great fear that you will show the same readiness in protecting Plancius that you showed in protecting me, for your tears now remind me of those which you shed often and abundantly in my behalf." So the scene closed in the midst of a general weeping, and Cicero expected an acquittal for his client. It appears (Pro Plancio, c. 3) that the penalty of the Lex Licinia was exile, but there is no evidence whether Plancius was acquitted or condemned. All we know of him is that he was living in Corcyra (Corfu) in B.C. 46 (Cic. ad Fam. iv. 14, 15).

In the early part of September during the excessive heat, the greatest that he ever remembered, Cicero retired to enjoy the cool retreat of Arpinum and the neighbourhood, from which place he wrote a long news-letter to his brother, but he did not finish it until after his return to Rome on the eighteenth of September (Ad Q. Fr. iii. 1). On the nineteenth Gabinius, who had returned from his province, arrived at Rome, but there was nobody waiting to greet him. On the twenty-seventh of September he slipped into the city by night, for he well knew what reception he might expect. On the tenth day afterwards he appeared in the Senate, and as he had declared that he intended to ask for a triumph, it was his duty to report his military success. Cicero does not say whether he made a report or not, but as he was preparing to leave the place, he was stopped by the consuls, and the farmers of the revenue (publicani), who were hostile to him, were introduced. Gabinius was assailed on all sides, and particularly by Cicero, who irritated him so much that the man with trembling voice branded his old enemy with the hateful name of exile[7]. This foul reproach roused all the senators from their seats and with loud clamour they pressed close round Gabinius. The Publicani followed their example, and Cicero was so much encouraged that he could hardly refrain, as he says, from being the prosecutor of Gabinius. But he did refrain, and the real reason for keeping aloof was fear of Pompeius, the friend and protector of Gabinius. He gives also other reasons: he could not trust any jury and was afraid of failing in the prosecution; he was also afraid of Gabinius[8] being convicted, if he did prosecute, and he had some hope that Gabinius might be convicted if he did not prosecute but only helped in the matter a little.

In fact Gabinius soon after entering the city received notice to appear before the praetor C. Alfius on the charge of Majestas or treason. His offence was the restoration of the Egyptian king without having a commission for that purpose. The prosecutor was L. Lentulus, who did his duty badly. Cicero

---

[7] Ad Q. Fratrem, III. 2. 2. It appears that Dion (39. c. 60.) made a mistake when he referred the use of this opprobrious name of exile to another occasion (p. 188).

[8] There is some difficulty in the words "ne illi me accusante aliquid accidat." P. Manutius interprets them differently.

appeared as a witness against Gabinius, but he could not have
said much, for the accused thanked him and did not cross-
examine him (Ad Q. Fr. iii. 4. 3). Cicero expected that
Gabinius would not be acquitted, but the great exertions and
entreaties of Pompeius, the weakness of the prosecutor, the
dishonesty of some of the jury, and vague fear of an impending
dictatorship saved Gabinius. The jury consisted of seventy
men, of whom thirty-two voted against him. (Ad Q. Fr.
iii. 4. 1.) The acquittal was followed a short time after by
dreadful rains and floods at Rome, which did great mischief,
and might be supposed to show the anger of the gods at the
escape of Gabinius. Dion (39. c. 61) has spoken of this great
flood as having happened before the trial of Gabinius, but a
letter of Cicero (Ad Q. Fr. iii. 7) corrects the mistake*.

There were two other charges against Gabinius, one for
Ambitus or bribery at some election, the other for Repetundae
or taking money from king Ptolemaeus. The tribune C.
Memmius was the prosecutor in the trial for Repetundae, and
Cicero defended the man whom he hated, despised and had
loaded with abuse. Before the trial for Majestas Cicero wrote
in a letter to his brother: " Pompeius earnestly urges me to
be reconciled to Gabinius, but hitherto he has not succeeded,
nor if I shall retain any portion of my liberty, will he succeed."
(Ad Q. Fr. iii. 1. 5.) In his speech for Rabirius Postumus
(c. 12) he says that he defended Gabinius on the charge of
Repetundae, because he had been reconciled to him, and he
denies that he defended him against his inclination and because he would not offend Pompeius. Dion (39. c. 63), whose
narrative is seldom trustworthy, says that the people were
called together outside the walls and addressed by Pompeius
on behalf of Gabinius, and that he read a letter from Caesar to
himself in favour of Gabinius, and entreated the jury. Dion has
here mixed up the fact of an address to the popular assembly
and the holding of a court, and Drumann (iii. 58) has followed
him in affirming that the trial took place outside the walls,
which is impossible to suppose. Cicero's statement (Pro

* Dion (39, c. 62) also falsely says that Cicero prosecuted Gabinius on this
charge.

Rabirio Postumo, c. 12) implies that Pompeius was not present at the trial, for his evidence was read, and it was to this effect that the King of Egypt had informed him by letter that no money was given to Gabinius except for military purposes. Gabinius was convicted by the jury, who may have found the evidence sufficient, but, as Dion after his fashion says, partly because the jury were afraid of popular indignation and partly because Gabinius did not pay them enough. The amount of the damages was, as usual in such cases, assessed against Gabinius, but neither security was given for the payment nor was the full amount recovered from the sale of his property. He went into exile and did not return until B.C. 49. No more is said about the charge of Ambitus. If the trial for Repetundae came on first, there would be no occasion for the other prosecution.

The trial of C. Rabirius Postumus followed, which was a kind of appendage (appendicula), as Cicero names it, to the case of Gabinius, and was held before the same judge and jury. Cicero defended Rabirius. C. Rabirius Postumus was the posthumous son of a father who had been a distinguished farmer of the taxes (Pro C. Rabirio Postumo, c. 2, &c.). The son also was a money-making man: he was much engaged in business, held many shares in the companies for farming the revenue, lent money to foreign states, employed it in the provinces, got men places, gave or perhaps sold them shares, and provided kings with loans. He corresponds to our directors of companies, jobbers, loan contractors, speculators and lenders of money to foreign states both in peace and in war, lenders to either side and to both sides, lenders to kings, and lenders even to him who now sits in the place of the Egyptian with whom Rabirius dealt. Rabirius lent money to Ptolemaeus before his expulsion from Egypt, and as such loans were used among other purposes for bribing senators at Rome, the first loan of Rabirius may have reached the pocket of Caesar in B.C. 59 (vol. iii. 415). Rabirius lent not only his own money, but his friends' also. When Ptolemaeus came to Rome in B.C. 57 he wanted more money, and Rabirius lent more (p. 128).

As Gabinius could not pay all that was declared due from

him, the prosecutors looked to Rabirius for the rest, and founded their demand on the clause of Caesar's law De Repetundis (vol. iii. p. 442), which enabled them to recover the ill-gotten money from the hands of any man to whom it could be traced. This was the case of Rabirius, who accompanied Gabinius to Egypt to look after his royal debtor. The king made him "controller" of the revenues of Egypt, with the power, we may assume, of paying himself and friends their loan with interest. In fact there was no other way of Rabirius getting the money except by collecting the taxes, which were mortgaged to the king's creditors. Rabirius (c. 11) was charged with collecting money for Gabinius to the amount of ten thousand talents, and also something for himself. Cicero means to deny that any of the money which Gabinius received came to the hands of Rabirius. The king gave money to Gabinius and did not pay his debt to Rabirius, who was at last imprisoned in Egypt, was in danger of losing his life, and finally escaped and carried off nothing. In fact, if Caesar had not shown wonderful liberality to Rabirius (c. 15), he would have become bankrupt and could not have shown his face in the Forum. The friendship of a single man supported Rabirius in his adversity, and Cicero glorifies the generosity of Caesar to an old friend whom he would not allow to perish. We see that Rabirius had been connected with Caesar, and he was not forsaken by him. Rabirius protected Cicero at the time of his leaving Rome for exile, assisted him with money, and was a friend to his wife and children during Cicero's absence; all which the orator gratefully records (c. 17). This speech was delivered during the cold weather of the winter, in which Cicero's brother was blockaded by the Nervii. It is not known whether Rabirius was condemned or acquitted.

At the beginning of November C. Pomptinus, who had reduced the Allobroges to submission (vol. iii. 390), enjoyed the triumph for which he had been waiting several years before the gates of Rome. The triumph had been refused by the Senate because it was alleged that Pomptinus had not received his commission (imperium) in due form. (Ad Att. iv. 10, 12.) Servius Galba, who had served under Pomptinus and afterwards under Caesar, was now praetor, and he called the people together before daylight, which was illegal, and thus secured to Pomptinus by an irregular vote the honour for which he had been waiting.

Julia the wife of Pompeius and Caesar's daughter died this year after giving birth to a child, which survived her only a few days. Pompeius intended to bury her in his Alban villa, but after the funeral oration was delivered, the people took the body to the Campus Martius, where it was burned and the remains were buried there, in spite of the opposition of the consul Domitius, who maintained that an interment could not take place in consecrated ground without some legal enactment. Plutarch (Caesar, 23) says that Caesar received the news of Julia's death immediately on returning from Britain to Gallia; but Seneca somewhere found the statement that he received the news in Britain. She died probably in September. Some time after, but it does not appear at what time, Caesar still wishing to maintain his connexion with Pompeius, proposed that he should marry Octavia, the granddaughter of Caesar's sister Julia and the sister of Octavius afterwards Caesar Augustus. Octavia was then the wife of C. Marcellus. Caesar also proposed that he himself should marry the daughter of Pompeius, who was promised to Faustus Sulla, though Caesar himself had a wife Calpurnia, the daughter of Piso. But the proposal had no result. (Sueton., Caesar, 27).

The new year (B.C. 53) began, but no consuls had been elected in the preceding year, and there was an Interregnum, as the Romans named it, during which time Interreges were appointed in succession until consuls were regularly elected. Each Interrex held office for five days (Appian, B. C. i. 98 and Ascon. in Mil. p. 43, Orelli). Cicero in a letter to Trebatius (Ad Div. vii. 11) makes a joke about the number of Interregna in this year. There is great difficulty in determining how these Interreges were appointed, and the discussion of this question belongs to a different place[1]. In this year when an Interrex attempted to hold the Consular Comitia, it was

---

[1] On the Interregnum and Interrex, see Becker, Handbuch, &c. ii. 1. 300.

sometimes found that the auspices were unfavourable; and the tribunes, or, as we may assume, a majority of them, also hindered the elections, and managed public affairs themselves. They even superintended the celebration of such games as it was the office of the praetors to superintend, from which remark of Dion we must infer that neither consuls nor praetors had been elected for this year. The tribunes further proposed the appointment of military tribunes instead of consuls, which had been done about three centuries before; and when this proposal was rejected, they recommended the appointment of Pompeius as dictator. A tribune, whom Plutarch names, incorrectly perhaps, Lucilius, is said to have first proposed the appointment of Pompeius to the dictatorship, but Cato attacked Lucilius for making the proposal, and many of Pompeius' friends declared that he did not seek the office nor wish it. Dion says that Pompeius was absent at this time, and when he returned, he refused the dictatorship, but there is no evidence except Dion's (40. c. 46) that it was offered to him. At last in the month of July the interregnum was ended by the election of Cn. Domitius Calvinus and M. Valerius Messala as consuls. The only recorded event of the year is the passing of a Senatusconsultum, which declared that neither a praetor nor a consul should hold a provincial government before the lapse of five years. In this year Milo was a candidate for the consulship of B.C. 52 with Plautius Hypsaeus and Q. Metellus Scipio as his opponents, and P. Clodius was a candidate for the praetorship. Rome was filled with brawls between hostile factions, blood was shed in the streets and the consul Calvinus was wounded. The result was that at the end of B.C. 53 neither praetors nor consuls had been elected for the next year.

Cicero strongly supported Milo in his canvass for the consulship. In a letter to C. Scribonius Curio, who was then returning from Asia (Ad Div. ii. 6), he says that he has directed all his efforts, and all his thoughts to Milo's consulship, on which in fact he rested all his own hopes. If Curio would support Milo, nothing else would be wanted, for Milo had already the favour of all honest people for his services to Cicero in his tribuneship, of the common sort for his munificence and liberality, and of the youth and those who had influence in elections, on account of his own exceeding popularity and activity in such matters. He earnestly entreats Curio to do his best for Milo, whose election would increase the credit of Cicero and indeed almost give him security. In speaking of "security" Cicero alludes to P. Clodius, who was a candidate for the praetorship, and who would not choose, if he could prevent it, to see his old enemy Milo in possession of the consulship. Pompeius who was now betrothed to Cornelia, the daughter of Q. Metellus Scipio and the young widow of P. Crassus, declared himself against Milo's election, and thus Pompeius and Clodius were again brought nearer. Clodius attacked Milo in the Senate: he charged him with being overwhelmed with debt, with rioting (vis), and bribing the electors. He attacked Cicero also as the friend and supporter of Milo, and the attack brought a reply from a man whose tongue was ever ready. Of this speech, which was afterwards published, a few fragments remain with the comments of a Scholiast on them, and an introduction which explains the occasion on which it was delivered and the meaning of the title (Interrogatio de aere alieno Milonis[1]). The speech of Cicero contained foul abuse of Clodius, as the fragments show, and as Clodius was a ready speaker with plenty of wit and impudence, we may assume that Cicero had heard a great deal that he would not like.

M. Antonius, the son of Creticus, the grandson of the great orator M. Antonius, who had accompanied Gabinius to Egypt, did not return to Rome, but went to Caesar in Gallia (Cic. Phil. ii. 19, 20). He came to Rome this year with letters from Caesar to Cicero, in which Caesar requested Cicero to allow Antonius to apologize for his past conduct, for in B.C. 58 Antonius was leagued with Cicero's enemy Clodius. Antonius came to be a candidate for a quaestorship and Cicero helped him. On this occasion, as Cicero says, Antonius attempted to kill his old friend Clodius in the Forum, being moved to the act not by Cicero, though Antonius declared, as Cicero wrote a long time after and perhaps not truly, that he

[1] Scholia Bobiensia, p. 341, ed. Orelli.

did not think that he could ever make sufficient amends for
his wrongs to Cicero, unless he killed Clodius. Antonius was
elected, and forthwith without waiting for the usual Senatusconsultum, and the determination of his province by lot or by
a vote of the people, he hurried back to Caesar in Gallia,
thinking that was the only place in the world where the impoverished, the debtor and the knave could find a refuge, and
where Antonius filled his pockets out of Caesar's grants and
his own plunder. Thus Cicero wrote about Caesar after his
death. Ten years before he was ready to do any thing that
Caesar asked him to do.

The news of the defeat of Crassus would reach Rome some
time before the end of B.C. 53. Publius the son was an augur,
and his death made a vacancy in the sacred college, which was
filled by the election of Cicero. In his long letter to Cato
from Cilicia written in B.C. 50, he says he did not seek a
priestly office (sacerdotium) before his exile, though he could
have obtained it without great difficulty, but after his exile he
was willing to be made an augur, though he had not cared for
the honour before. Drumann affirms that Cicero does not tell
the truth, and he is right in his assertion, for in B.C. 59 Cicero
wrote to Atticus that an augurship was the only thing by
which the three confederates could secure his services (vol. iii.
p. 415). It would be well for his credit if he had never told
a greater untruth than what he says to Cato. Cicero was
nominated, as he expresses it, by Cn. Pompeius and Q. Hortensius, and Hortensius declared on oath that Cicero was
worthy of the honour, upon which he was duly elected by the
college and consecrated (inauguratus) by Hortensius, whom
according to the rules of this ecclesiastical body he was bound
to respect as a father (Cicero, Phil. ii. 2, Brutus, c. 1). Cicero
was proud of his new office, for it gave him consideration in
the eyes of those whose superstitious notions he did not share.

CHAPTER XVII.

THE REVOLT OF GALLIA.

B.C. 52.

THERE were neither consuls nor praetors in Rome when the new year began, and Pompeius, who employed the tribune T. Munatius Plancus as his tool, prevented the appointment of an Interrex. On the twentieth of January Clodius and Milo with their followers accidentally met near Bovillae on the Appian road, and Clodius lost his life in the brawl which took place. The disturbance in Rome after the death of Clodius induced the Senate to make a resolution that the Interrex, for one had been appointed, and the tribunes and Pompeius, who was then at the gates of Rome with proconsular power, should look after the safety of the state (ne quid detrimenti res publica caperet), and raise troops in all parts of Italy, which was quickly done. Caesar informs us that he was in Italy, that is, in his province of Gallia Cisalpina when he heard of Clodius' death and the order for raising troops; and he raised troops himself in his province, but it does not appear whether he raised them on the authority of the resolution of the Senate by assuming that his province was comprehended in the term Italia, or that he did not trouble himself about any authority. A passage in one of Cicero's letters to Atticus (vii. i. 4) seems to mean that Cicero saw Caesar at Ravenna in this year, and was asked to use his interest in obtaining for Caesar permission to be a candidate for the consulship without being required to come to Rome.

The news of the disturbed state of Italy was quickly carried into Transalpine Gallia, and the Galli added to the report

what they wished to be true, that Caesar was detained by the
state of affairs at Rome and could not come to his army.
(B. G. vii. 1.) The opportunity seemed favourable for an
insurrection. The chief men met in retired places in the
forests to confer about their grievances, among which was the
execution of Acco, whose fate might be their own. They
deplored the condition of Gallia, and proposed great rewards
to those who should venture to begin the war. But above
all and before their designs were made public, it was necessary to prevent Caesar from returning to his army; and this
could be easily done, for the legions would not dare to leave
their winter camps in his absence nor could he join his legions
without the protection of troops; finally, it was better to die
in battle than not to recover their liberty. The Carnutes
offered to begin the rising, but as the Galli could not exchange
hostages for fear of betraying their design, the Carnutes
required an engagement from the rest not to desert them
after the war was begun. An oath to support one another
was taken over the military standards, which among these
people is the most solemn pledge of fidelity, the time for
the rising was fixed, and the meeting separated.

When the day came, the Carnutes headed by two desperate
men named Cotuatus and Conetodunus, hurried to Genabum[1]
(Orléans), where some Romans (negotiatores) had established
themselves in business, and among them one C. Fusius Cita,
a Roman Eques, who had been appointed by Caesar to look
after the supplies of corn. Orléans was a convenient place
for receiving the grain sent down the Loire and the Allier,
which flows through the fertile Limagne d'Auvergne, or
brought from the country to the north, the Pays de Beauce,
which now feeds Paris and the neighbourhood. The insurgents murdered the Romans and made plunder of their property. The news was quickly carried to all the Gallic states,
for it was the fashion of these people, when any great event
happened, to make it known through the country by shouts,
which were transmitted from one to another, as on this occa-

[1] The author of the "Hist. de César," II. 247, tries to prove that Genabum
was on the site of Gien, higher up the Loire than Orléans.

sion. The massacre at Genabum took place at sunrise, and before the end of the first evening watch, it was known in the country of the Arverni, a distance of one hundred and sixty Roman miles, as Caesar estimates it[1].

Vercingetorix a young Arvernian, and the son of Celtillus, who had been put to death by his fellow-citizens for aspiring to royal power, now called together his dependents and incited them to follow the example of the Carnutes. When his designs were known, his father's brother Gobanitio and the chief men of Gergovia, who were opposed to the rising, drove him out of the town. But he did not desist from his enterprise, and getting together a number of needy and desperate men he brought over others to his side, and at last with his forces greatly increased he drove his enemies out of Gergovia and was proclaimed king by his partisans. Vercingetorix sent his emissaries to all parts of Gallia to urge the people to be faithful to their undertaking. He quickly gained the Senones, Parisii, Pictones, Cadurci, Turoni, Aulerci, Lemovices, with the Andes and all the rest of the Oceanic states. The command-in-chief was conferred on him unanimously, and in virtue of his new power he demanded hostages of all these states, required each to send immediately a certain number of soldiers, and fixed the amount of armour which each state should make and the time when it should be ready. The cavalry was the principal object of his attention. His severity was equal to his activity; and he forced all waverers to obedience by cruel punishments. For great offences he burnt and tortured to death; for slighter, he would cut off a man's ears, or scoop out an eye and send him home to be an example to others.

By these means an army was soon brought together, and Vercingetorix sent Luctorius[2], a man belonging to the Cadurci and unequalled for audacity, to invade the country of the Ruteni which bordered on the Provincia. The Ruteni were between the Cévennes and the Cadurci, and occupied

---

[1] Caesar does not clearly explain how the news was transmitted so quickly. See Louis de Carné, "Un drame sous la Terreur," p. 43: the scene is Bretagne.

[2] Luctorius. There are coins which bear this name, and the name also appears on a Roman Inscription at Cahors.

the ante-revolutionary division of France named Rouergue, of which Rhodez was the capital. Vercingetorix himself marched into the territory of the Bituriges, who were north of the Arverni and separated from the Aedui by the Loire. The chief town of the Bituriges was Avaricum (Bourges), and a large part of their territory was within the basin of the Cher, one of the chief affluents of the Loire. The Bituriges sent messengers to the Aedui, whose dependents they were, to ask for help against the invaders, and the Aedui, following the advice of the legati, whom Caesar had left with the legions, sent cavalry and infantry to aid the Bituriges. These forces advanced to the Loire, and after having halted there a few days without venturing to cross the river, they came back and reported to the Roman legati that they had returned on account of the perfidy of the Bituriges, whose design it was, as they said they had discovered, to attack them on one side while the Arverni attacked them on the other, if they had crossed the Loire. Caesar says that he could not ascertain whether this excuse was founded in truth or the men were traitors; but as soon as they retired, the Bituriges joined the Arverni.

The news of the Gallic insurrection was brought to Caesar when he was in Gallia Cisalpina, and he did not leave Italy for the Transalpine province before he was informed that affairs at Rome were brought into a better condition by Cn. Pompeius, who was elected sole consul on the 25th of February. We cannot determine whether Caesar crossed the Alps before the twenty-fifth or after. On arriving in the Provincia he was in great straits about joining his men, for if he summoned the troops to come to him, they must fight on the march, and if he went to them, he must pass through some of the Gallic states whom he could not trust, though they had not yet risen in rebellion.

In the mean time Lucterius, who had been sent into the country of the Ruteni, brought over the people to the Arverni. "Having advanced to the Nitiobriges and Gabali," says Caesar, "he received hostages from both, and with the large force that he had got together he was preparing to enter the Provincia by the road which led to Narbo (Narbonne)." If

Lucterius came direct from his own country, he probably visited the Nitiobriges first, for they were the neighbours of the Cadurci on the west. The chief place of the Cadurci was Divona, now Cahors on the Lot, and the capital of the Nitiobriges was Aginnum (Agen) on the Garonne. The Gabali were in the Gévaudan, an old division of France in the mountainous region of the Cévennes, and the chief town of the Gévaudan is Mende, which lies in a deep valley on the Lot, and on the road from Nimes to Clermont in Auvergne. Caesar being informed of the designs of Lucterius hurried to Narbo, encouraged the people who were alarmed, and placed troops among the Provincial Ruteni, the Volcae Arecomici, whose chief town was Nemausus (Nimes), among the Tolosates, and around Narbo. The Provincial Ruteni were that part of the Ruteni who were south of the Tarn, which river Lucterius must cross if he marched upon Narbo. Caesar sent part of the Provincial forces and the troops which he had just brought from Italy to the country of the Helvii, who, as he says, are the neighbours of the Arverni. The Helvii were between the Rhone and the Cévennes, and their chief place was Alba (Alps or Aps) in the department of the Ardêche: their immediate neighbours west of the Cévennes were not the Arverni, but the Vellauni or Vellavi, who were however dependents of the Arverni.

Lucterius did not venture to cross the Tarn and enter the Provincia, where the Roman forces might fall on his flanks and rear; and Caesar now joined his troops in the territory of the Helvii. It was the coldest* time of the year, and the Cévennes were covered with snow to the depth of six feet, but by hard work the soldiers cut a road through the snow and reached the country of the Arverni. Caesar probably went up the higher part of the valley of the Ardêche, and having crossed the watershed between the sources of the Loire and Allier, he would descend into the valley of the Allier which leads to the central parts of the Auvergne. The Arverni were surprised at the appearance of Caesar's troops, for they thought that the Cévennes were a sufficient protection, and

* It was perhaps early in March, B.C. 52, of the unreformed calendar.

the mountains had never been crossed at this season of the
year even by single travellers. Caesar taking advantage of
this alarm ordered his cavalry to spread themselves over the
country and to strike terror into the people. Vercingetorix
was soon informed of this invasion, and at the earnest entreaty
of the Arverni, who were afraid of being plundered by the
enemy, he led his forces from the country of the Bituriges
into the territory of the Arverni, as Caesar expected that he
would do. After remaining two days with his troops Caesar
left them under the pretext of collecting more men. He
placed young Decimus Brutus over the forces in the Auvergne
with instructions to send his cavalry about the country, and
he promised not to be absent more than three days. But he
did not return, nor did he intend to return. Neither does he
tell us how Brutus effected his retreat, but we may assume
that he was informed about Caesar's purpose and that he retired
into the Provincia in a short time. Caesar now again crossed
the mountains at this inclement season, probably by the same
road, and travelling at a great rate he reached Vienna (Vienne)
on the east side of the Rhone, to which place he had sent forward many days before the cavalry which he had recently
raised. Continuing his journey day and night northwards
through the country of the Aedui he reached the Lingones
(p. 17), where two of the legions were wintering. By these
rapid movements he anticipated any hostile designs that the
Aedui might form against him, and sending his orders to the
other legions he got them all together at Agendicum (Sens)
before the Arverni could be informed of his arrival in these
parts. The feint of invading the country of the Arverni
which drew Vercingetorix southwards, gave Caesar the opportunity of joining his legions, which he accomplished by a winter
journey of four hundred miles. As soon as Vercingetorix
heard of this bold and successful enterprise he led his troops
back to the Bituriges and made preparations to attack the
town of the Boii, whom Caesar had planted in the territory
of the Aedui (p. 19) and placed in dependence on them. The
MSS. do not enable us to determine the true name of this
town.

It was still early in the year, and if Caesar kept his legions together in one place during the remainder of the winter, he had reason to fear that, if the dependents of the Aedui were compelled to submit to the insurgents, all Gallia would fall off from him, when it became manifest that he could not help his friends. If he left his winter quarters too early, there might be difficulty in bringing up supplies to his army. He resolved however to face all dangers rather than be disgraced and lose the good will of his adherents. Accordingly he urged the Aedui to send supplies after him, and he despatched messengers to inform the Boii that he was coming, and to exhort them to be faithful and resist the enemy courageously. Leaving two legions at Agendicum with the heavy baggage of all the army he marched with the other, eight legions in the direction of the Boii and on the second day arrived at a town of the Senones named Vellaunodunum, the site of which is not known. As he did not think it prudent to leave an enemy in the rear who might obstruct his supplies, he prepared to attack the place and in two days formed his lines of contrevallation. On the third day the townspeople submitted, and agreed to give up their arms and beasts of burden, and to deliver six hundred hostages. The legatus C. Trebonius was left at Vellaunodunum to look after the execution of the convention, and Caesar marched to Genabum which he reached in two days. The Carnutes did not begin to collect their men for the defence of Genabum until they heard of the attack on Vellaunodunum, for they expected that the siege would occupy Caesar some time. They were consequently taken by surprise and the town could make no defence. The Roman camp was planted in front of the town, but as it was late in the day, the attack was postponed to the morrow and all preparations were made. There was a bridge at Genabum which connected the town with the opposite bank of the Loire, and Caesar ordered two legions to be under arms all night to watch the townsmen if they should attempt to escape over the river. About midnight the people leaving the town silently began to cross the bridge, but the scouts informed Caesar, who had his legions ready, and his men set fire to the gates and entered the town. Very few of the enemy escaped, for the narrowness of the bridge and the approaches to it stopped the flight. "Caesar plundered and burnt the town, gave the booty to the soldiers, took his army over the Loire and arrived at the territory of the Bituriges;" all told in one short sentence, truly characteristic of the man's rapid movements and his brief contemptuous style.

When Vercingetorix heard of Caesar's approach, he gave up his attack on the Boii, and went to meet Caesar, who had determined to assault Noviodunum, a town of the Bituriges, which lay on his road. It is not agreed what modern town represents Noviodunum of the Bituriges, but it is a different place from the Noviodunum of the Aedui. The townsmen sent commissioners to Caesar to beg for mercy, and as he wished quickly to accomplish what he had undertaken, he ordered them to produce their arms, give up their horses, and deliver hostages. Part of the hostages were given up and some centurions and a few soldiers who had been let into the town were looking for arms and beasts, when the cavalry of Vercingetorix, which preceded the rest of the army, was discovered approaching. As soon as the townsmen saw this prospect of deliverance, they raised a shout, seized their arms, and attempted to close the gates and man the walls. The centurions who were in the town concluding from these signs that the people had changed their minds, took possession of the gates and drew off their men in safety. Caesar sent his cavalry out of the camp to meet the cavalry of Vercingetorix, and as they stood the attack of the enemy with difficulty, he supported them with four hundred German horsemen, whom, as he says, he had employed "from the beginning." This is one of the few instances in which Caesar's narrative is defective, for it is the first time that he mentions German cavalry being employed by him. The Galli could not stand the attack of the Germans and fled to the rest of their army after losing many men. The people of Noviodunum now fearing what might befall them seized those whom they charged with stirring up the common sort to resistance, handed them over to Caesar and made their surrender. Caesar continued his march towards Avaricum (Bourges), the largest and best fortified town of the Bituriges and in a very fertile country, being confident that if he got possession of this place, he would be master of all the territory.

After the loss of these three towns Vercingetorix held a council, in which he declared that the war must be conducted in a different way: they must prevent the Romans from getting forage and must cut off their supplies, which they could easily do by their superiority in cavalry and at that season of the year, for there was no fodder in the fields and the enemy must seek it in small detachments in the buildings where it was stored, and thus they might be destroyed daily by the Gallic cavalry. He also said that for the sake of the general interest they must sacrifice private property, and burn all the villages and scattered buildings in every direction in which the enemy might go for forage. They must also burn the towns which were not secured either by their walls or natural strength, that their own men might not fly to these towns to avoid the perils of war nor the Romans find supplies and booty in them. If these seemed hard conditions, it would be much worse for their children and wives to be made slaves and themselves to be killed, which is the fate of the vanquished. This proposal was unanimously accepted and in one day more than twenty towns of the Bituriges were set on fire, and the same was done in other states. These towns, or cities as Caesar names them, were the small places in the ante-revolutionary province of Berri which extended eastward to the Loire. The towns of upper Berri are small: those of lower Berri, which is a more fertile country, are larger. The flames of blazing towns and villages were seen in all directions, a piteous sight for the people, but they were comforted with the hope of almost certain victory and the confidence of recovering their losses. It was deliberated in the general council whether Avaricum also should be burnt or defended. The Bituriges entreated the confederates not to compel them to destroy a place which was the finest city of almost all Gallia and an ornament to their state; they said they could easily defend the place, for it was surrounded nearly on all sides by a river and marshes, and there was only one approach to it, and that very narrow. Vercingetorix at first would not listen to the remonstrances of the Bituriges, but at last he was moved by their entreaties and by pity for the common sort, who would have been turned out of their houses in the winter. A sufficient body of men was selected for the defence of Avaricum, and Vercingetorix following Caesar by short marches selected for encampment a spot protected by marshes and woods sixteen miles from Avaricum. There he was informed at every hour of the day by trusty scouts of what was going on at Avaricum, and he sent his orders back by them. He kept a strict watch on all the Romans who were sent to collect forage and corn, and as they were compelled to go great distances to get their supplies, the men of Vercingetorix fell on them when they were dispersed about the country and caused them some loss, though the Romans provided against such attacks as far as they could by going at uncertain times and in various directions.

Caesar had placed his camp at that part of the town of Avaricum, where a narrow tract of land between the river and the marshes allowed an army to approach. The upper town of Bourges[5] stands on a plateau bounded on the west by the Auron and on the north by the Evre or Yèvre which unite and fall into the Cher, one of the great branches of the Loire. The magnificent cathedral is in the highest part of the city which is connected with the narrow tract by which Caesar approached from the south-east and on which he placed his camp[6], between the Auron and the Yévrette. The appearance of the site has doubtless been much changed by the drainage of the low parts on the north and west of the town, and in some places the soil has been elevated by the accumulated rubbish of centuries. The nature of the ground made it impossible to surround the place with lines of contravallation, and Caesar prepared for the attack by constructing earthworks, bringing up his vineae or covered galleries and constructing two towers. The greatest height of the earthworks was eighty feet (c. 21), according to our text[7], and the

---

[5] Plan of Avaricum, Planches, No. 20, "Hist. de César."

[6] It is said on the Plan of Avaricum that part of the Roman camp has been discovered by excavation.

[7] The width, cccxxx feet, appears to contain an error; or as Rüstow (p. 143) suggests we should read "longum" for "latum."

top of the earthworks would not be higher than the top of the town wall, from which the author of the " Histoire de César" concludes that there was at this time a depression in the ground on the south-east side of the town at some small distance from the walls, and if this was so, it would be necessary to fill it up in that part where the earthworks were brought up to the wall.

Caesar was continually urging the Boii and Aedui to bring up supplies; but the Aedui showed little activity, the Boii, who were a poor people, soon exhausted their means; and the conflagration had destroyed the buildings in the country of the Bituriges. Caesar's army was for several days without corn, and only kept alive by eating the cattle which were driven from remote villages; yet no complaint escaped them unworthy of the great name of Rome and of their past victories. As Caesar visited the works, he addressed the several legions and told them that he would give up the siege, if they found the privations too great, but the men with one voice declared that they would consider it a disgrace to leave the undertaking incomplete, and they would rather endure any thing than not avenge their countrymen who had been treacherously murdered at Genabum. They made the same declarations to Caesar through the tribunes and centurions.

The towers had now been brought near to the walls, when Caesar learned from some prisoners that Vercingetorix being in want of forage had moved his camp nearer to Avaricum, and that he had gone with his cavalry and the light-armed troops which fought among them, to lay an ambuscade in a spot which he expected the Romans would visit the next day in quest of forage. On receiving this information Caesar set out at midnight and reached the enemy's encampment in the morning. The Galli being warned by their scouts of Caesar's approach removed their waggons and baggage into the thick forest, and drew up their forces on an open piece of ground. Caesar ordered his men to put their packs (sarcinae) together and prepare for battle. The hill on which the Galli stood had a gentle slope upwards, and was nearly surrounded by a marsh, which though only fifty feet wide made the approach difficult. The bridges were broken down, and the Galli confident in the strength of their position and ranged according to their several tribes watched all the fords and passages, ready to descend on the Romans if they should attempt to cross the marsh. A spectator viewing the proximity of the two armies would have supposed that the Galli were ready for a fair battle, but on perceiving the difference in the positions of the two armies he would have seen that the Galli had no intention to fight. The Romans were indignant that the enemy should dare to face them with such a small interval between the armies and called for the signal of battle. But Caesar told them that victory would cause the loss of many brave men, and as they were ready to encounter any danger for his glory, he should be most culpable, if he did not regard their lives more than his own reputation. Having thus pacified the men Caesar led them back to the camp and continued the siege.

When Vercingetorix returned to his army, he was charged with treachery for moving his camp nearer to the enemy, for going away with all his cavalry, for leaving his troops without a general, and thus giving an opportunity to the Romans of coming on them unexpectedly. All this could not have taken place without some design, and it was plain that Vercingetorix would rather receive the kingdom of Gallia from Caesar than accept it from his countrymen. Vercingetorix answered that he had moved his camp because they had no forage and moved it at their request, and he had been induced to approach nearer to the Romans by the facilities for defence which the new position offered; that the cavalry was useless in such a marshy place, and it was useful in the place to which he had led it; that he had purposely left them without a head that no one holding the command might be driven to fight a battle by the importunity of the soldiers, who as he knew were eager to fight because they could not endure the fatigues of war. If the Romans made their appearance accidentally, it was a lucky event; if some traitor invited them, they were under obligations to the man for giving them the opportunity of seeing from a safe position how few the enemy were and their want of courage in withdrawing because they were afraid to fight. He had no inclination to obtain through treachery and from Caesar the power which victory would give him, and of this victory he and all the Galli were well assured. Further, he would leave them to judge whether they were conferring authority on himself or were receiving every thing from him. "That you may know," he said, "that I am telling you the truth, hear what the Roman soldiers say;" and he produced some slaves whom he had caught foraging a few days before and kept in chains without food. These men having been taught what they must say declared that they were legionary soldiers, that hunger drove them out of the Roman camp to look for corn or cattle in the country, that the whole army was suffering from want of food and could not endure the siege labours, and that the commander had determined to withdraw the army in three days, if in the mean time he made no progress in the siege. This, said Vercingetorix, is what I have done for you, and you accuse me of treachery, who without allowing your blood to be shed have reduced a large victorious army to starvation, an army which has shamefully retired before you, and which through my foresight no Gallic state will receive within its limits. The army replied with general acclamations and a clatter of arms after their fashion: Vercingetorix was the greatest of generals; there could be no doubt of his loyalty and the war could not be conducted better. It was determined to send ten thousand men selected from the different divisions of the army to Avaricum, and not to entrust to the Bituriges alone the defence of the general interests; for if the Bituriges should succeed in saving the place, the victory would be due to them. The determination of the confederates was prompted by jealousy as much as by a desire to save Avaricum.

Modern criticism applied to ancient history would inquire what authority Caesar had for these two chapters (vii. c. 20, 21). It is not his way to say how he knew what he tells us, but we can generally see that he was an eye-witness of that which he describes, and as far as an examination of places can confirm his statements, we know that he had a sharp sight and that his descriptions are true. Where he was not an eye-witness, we can sometimes discover how he obtained his information, as in the case of the attack on the winter quarters of Galba (iii. 1), and the Aquitanian campaign of P. Crassus

(iii. 20). But it is impossible to conjecture how he knew what Vercingetorix said to his men on this occasion. His object was to show the character of Vercingetorix, the only opponent worthy of his talents that he met with in Gallia, and to exhibit the fickle temper of the Galli, which he often mentions. It may be supposed that, like other ancient writers, he has made the Gallic commander say what he might have said, and that a few facts either known or only probable are the foundation of a fiction; but if this is so, it is a way of writing which he does not often indulge in, for no narrative ancient or modern is more clear and simple, and more free from false ornament than the Commentaries of Caesar.

The perseverance of the besiegers was met with all kinds of contrivances by the Galli, as might be expected from so ingenious a people, who were always ready to imitate any thing that they saw. They turned aside the iron hooks[a] which were used for demolishing the walls, by laying hold of them with nooses and then by machinery drawing them inwards. They made mines under the "agger" or earth terrace and carried away the earth, which they did with the more skill, as there were large iron mines in the territory of the Bituriges, and they were acquainted with all kinds of subterranean galleries. Iron ore is still extracted in the department of Cher, of which Bourges is the capital, and it has been worked in the neighbourhood of Bourges, but this branch of industry is now discontinued, as I was told. The besieged also raised the town wall at the part which was attacked, and they did this by building wooden towers on it and protecting them with hides. Making frequent sallies by day and by night they applied fire to the woodwork in the "agger" and attacked the soldiers at their work. The Roman towers were daily rising by the addition of fresh material[b], and the besieged maintained their

---

[a] See Vegetius, iv. 14. The author of the "Histoire," ii. 250, translates "falces" by "béliers à tête aiguë;" which is a mistake.

[b] See Rustow's explanation of this difficult passage (p. 140). There was only one earth terrace made by the Romans, and it was protected by two towers, one on each side of the terrace and not on it. In the words "quotidianus agger expresserat," he assumes that "agger" is merely material, of course wood, for raising the towers higher. Rustow's plan, Fig. 22, explains his meaning.

towers at an equal elevation by fresh scaffolding. When the enemy had carried their mines far enough to break into the Roman galleries, they stopped up the passage with wood pointed at the end by burning, and with melted pitch and large stones, and thus prevented the enemy from reaching the walls[1].

This is the way in which Gallic town walls were constructed (c. 23). Straight beams of one continuous length were laid on the ground at the distance of two feet from one another; and of course at right angles to the direction of the wall. These beams were fastened together on the inside, and the intervals were filled up with earth except on the front or outside, where the intervals were faced with large stones. When the lower tier was well fastened together, another tier was placed upon it, and the same intervals were maintained, yet so that the beams did not touch those of the tier below, but the equal intervals were retained, and the several balks being separated by the several stones, the whole was held close together. Thus the work was continued until the wall attained the necessary height. This mode of construction with the alternation of timbers and stones in the several tiers was pleasing enough to the eye, and well adapted for the defence of towns, the stone protecting the wall against fire and the timber against the battering-ram, for as the woodwork consisted of a series of beams generally forty feet in length and fastened together on the inside, it was not possible to break through or to pull it in pieces[2].

By these obstacles the siege was prolonged, and though the Roman soldiers were working in the mud, exposed to the cold and to continual rain, they made in twenty-five days an embankment 330 feet wide and eighty in height[3]. When the embankment was approaching close to the walls and

---

[1] See Livy, 38, c. 7, and the operations at the siege of Sebastopol.

[2] The author of the "Histoire" (li. 260) translates "perpetuis trabibus pedes quadragenos plerumque introrsus revinctis," by "les pontres étaient reliées, du côté de la ville, par des traverses ayant habituellement quarante pieds de long;" which is not the meaning I believe. His Plan d'une couche (Planche 20) is constructed according to this interpretation.

[3] It is suggested by Göler that Caesar's text should be "330 feet long." See also Rüstow, p. 143, referred to above.

Caesar according to his custom was inspecting the operations and urging the men to their work, it was observed just before the beginning of the third watch that smoke was issuing from the embankment. In fact the enemy had fired the wood in it by a mine from below. At the same time a shout was raised from the town wall and the enemy sallied out by two gates on the two sides where the towers were placed, while the men on the walls threw torches and dry wood on the embankment with pitch and other combustibles. It was difficult for the besiegers to know how this sudden attack should be resisted, but as two legions were always keeping watch before the camp and other legions relieved one another in turns at the works, some of the men quickly met the besieged who had sallied out, others drew back the towers and cut the agger, while the rest hurried from the camp to extinguish the flames. At dawn of day the fight was still going on, and the enemy's hopes of victory were kept up, the more as they saw that the "plutei¹ turrium," or breast-works of the towers, were entirely burnt and that the Romans could not approach unprotected to defend their works. Fresh men also were continually pouring from the town to relieve those who were exhausted, for the enemy believed that the salvation of Gallia depended on the issue of this struggle. During this time there happened something which Caesar saw and considered worthy of being recorded. In front of one of the town gates there stood a Gaul, who received lumps of fat and pitch, which had been passed to him from hand to hand, and threw them in front of a Roman tower. This man was pierced in the right side by a javelin discharged from a scorpion, a kind of catapult, and fell dead. One of those who stood next to him stepped over the body, took his place, and was killed in the same way. He was succeeded by a third, and the third by a fourth, and so it went on until the fire in the "agger" was extinguished and the enemy was driven back at all points. The Galli had been unsuccessful in their attempts, and on the next day they determined to quit the town, in obedience to the exhortations

¹ "Plutei" is a general name for a screen or fence of skins or wood to protect the men. Rüstow, fig. 22, supposes that these plutei were placed on each side of the agger.

and commands of Vercingetorix. They hoped that they
might be able to do this in the night without great loss, for
the camp of Vercingetorix was not far from the town, and
a continuous marsh which intervened would delay the pursuit
of the Romans. Night came, and the men were preparing to
execute their design, when all at once the women ran out
into the streets and open places and throwing themselves at
the feet of their husbands most piteously entreated them
not to leave to the cruelty of the enemy wives and children
whose sex and age made them incapable of flight. But as
the men persisted in their resolution, for terror generally over-
powers pity, the women uttered loud shouts to signify to
the besiegers what was going on, and thus the men were
deterred from leaving the place for fear that the roads might
be occupied by the Roman cavalry.

The next day Caesar pushed forward a tower and continued
his works. A heavy rain coming on, he thought the opportunity favourable, and observing that the enemy were guard-
ing the walls with less care than usual, he ordered his men
also to relax a little in their labours and he let them know
what his design was. He concealed his legions within the
covered galleries ready for the assault, and urged them to
seize at last the prize of all their toils. Rewards were offered
to those who should first mount the walls, the signal was
given, the men rushed forward from every point and quickly
gained the walls. The enemy, surprised at this sudden assault
and driven from the walls and towers, formed in compact
bodies in the public place and the more open parts, with the
intention of resisting. But when they saw that the besiegers
did not descend into the town but spread along the walls,
they were afraid that their retreat would be cut off, and throwing down their arms they rushed straight towards the further
part of the town, now occupied by the fauxbourgs Taillegrain
and St. Privé[5]. Part of them while they were crowding the
narrow passages of the gates were destroyed by the Roman

---

[5] Plan of Avaricum, Planche 20, "Histoire de César." The massacre of Avaricum is told in as plain terms as the massacres by the Jews (Deut. lii. 6, 7.), "utterly destroying the men, women, and children of every city; but all the cattle and the spoil of the cities we took for a prey to ourselves."

soldiers, and part who had made their way out were cut down by the cavalry. Not a single Roman thought of making booty. Excited by the remembrance of the massacre at Genabum and the sufferings endured in the siege they spared neither the aged, nor the women, nor the children. Out of the whole number, which was about forty thousand, scarcely eight hundred, who escaped from the town as soon as they heard the cries of the assailants, reached Vercingetorix. It was late in the night when the fugitives entered the camp, where they were received in silence, for Vercingetorix was afraid that some disturbance might arise if they came in a body, and to prevent this result he had placed his friends and the chief men of the several states along the road to separate the men and lead them to the several parts of the camp which their countrymen occupied. The forty thousand persons in Avaricum appear to have been the whole population, which was probably raised to this amount by those who took refuge there after the towns of the Bituriges were burnt and by the troops which Vercingetorix placed in the town.

On the day after the capture of Avaricum Vercingetorix addressed his men: the Romans, he said, had not defeated them in battle, and had only shown their superiority in besieging towns, of which art the Galli knew nothing; success could not always be expected in war, and they knew that it was against his judgment that the town had been defended: he would soon make amends for this loss by bringing over the states which were not yet in the confederation, and would thus form a combination that the whole world would not be able to resist [5]: in the mean time it was reasonable that they should consent for the common interest to fortify their camps in Roman fashion and thus secure themselves against sudden attacks. This speech satisfied the men. They were pleased to see that the general had not lost his courage or slunk

---

[5] The author of the "Histoire de César" (ii. 451) makes this remark:— "Comme un chef ne manque jamais de se révéler lorsqu'éclate un grand mouvement national, Vercingetorix apparaît, se met à la tête d'une guerre d'indépendance et pose la première fois proclame cette vérité, empreinte de grandeur et de patriotisme: Si la Gaule sait être unie, et devenir une nation, elle peut défier l'univers." But the union is the difficulty.

away; and their opinion of his judgment was increased by his advice about the defence of Avaricum. Caesar observes that misfortune weakens the authority of most commanders, but that the influence of Vercingetorix increased daily after the capture of the town; which in fact strengthened his hands, for the Galli from this time began to make fortified camps, and though not used to hard work, were now ready to endure any labour.

Vercingetorix employed confidential agents to gain by bribes and promises the chief men of the states whose help he still wished to secure (c. 31). He armed and clothed those who had escaped from Avaricum; and to repair his losses he required from the confederate states a certain number of men to be sent to him at a fixed day, and all the bowmen, who were very numerous in Gallia, to be got together and brought to his camp. By these means he soon made up the loss at Avaricum. In the mean time Teutomatus, the son of Ollovico, king of the Nitiobriges, whose father had received from the Roman senate the title of "friend," came to Vercingetorix with a large body of his own horsemen and others whom he had hired in Aquitania.

Caesar found in Avaricum a great store of corn and other supplies, and he stayed there several days to give his soldiers rest after their labours and privations. He does not inform us what was done during his stay with the thousands of dead bodies which lay in the streets and in the houses. As he describes the massacre in the fewest words possible, so he says nothing of the disposal of the dead, and we might omit all conjectures on the matter, if he had not passed some days (complures), he does not say how many, in the midst of this dreadful carnage. The winter season was now nearly over, and he was preparing to begin the regular campaign either by drawing the enemy out of the marshes and forests, or if he could not do that, by shutting them in, when he received a visit from the chiefs of the Aedui. They informed him that their affairs were in a very critical condition: it was their practice to choose a chief magistrate who held the authority for one year (B. G. i. 16), but now they had two, and each claimed to have been legally elected. One of them was Con-

victolitanis, a young man of high rank; the other, named
Cotus, of a very antient family, possessed great influence and
had a large body of kinsmen. Valetiacus, the brother of Cotus,
had been chief magistrate the preceding year. All the state
was in arms, the senate and people were divided into opposite
factions, and if the quarrel continued the two parties would
soon come to blows. Caesar saw that if the Aedui, who had
been the close allies of Rome and always favoured by him,
should take up arms against one another, the weaker side
would call in Vercingetorix. Accordingly, though it interrupted
his plans, he resolved to prevent matters from coming to such
extremities, and to show his respect for their usages, which did not
allow their chief magistrates to leave the country, he summoned
the senate and the two claimants to meet him at Decetia
(Decise) an island and town on the Loire in the territory of
the Aedui. Nearly all the people assembled on this occasion.
By privately inquiring Caesar learned that the election of
Cotus was irregular both as to time and place, and the result
had been declared by his own brother, though it was not legal
for two persons of the same family to be elected so long as
both were living, nor even for two such persons to be members of the senate. The decision was that Cotus must resign
the office, and Convictolitanis must have it, who had been
elected by the priests in regular form. After delivering this
judgment Caesar urged the Aedui to forget their quarrels, to
direct all their energies to the war, and to look forward to the
rewards they would receive from him after the conquest of
Gallia. He required them to send him quickly all their
cavalry and ten thousand men, whom he intended to distribute in various places to secure his supplies. He divided his
forces into two parts. Labienus was ordered to take two
legions and part of the cavalry, and adding to this force the
two legions left at Sens (vii. 10) to march against the Senones
and Parisii on the Seine, who were in arms against the
Romans. With the six remaining legions and the rest of the
cavalry Caesar determined to enter the country of the Arverni,
the Auvergne in central France, the head-quarters of Vercingetorix.

CHAPTER XVIII.

GERGOVIA.

B.C. 52.

IF Caesar marched from Bourges by the shortest line to Decise, he crossed the Eluver (Allier) above the junction with the Loire; but if he passed by Noviodunum of the Aedui (Nevers), as it has been suggested ("Histoire de César," ii. 205), he crossed the Loire. On leaving Decise for Gergovia he came to the Allier and led his army south along the east side of the river, for Vercingetorix had broken down all the bridges and was marching in the same direction as Caesar on the west side of the Allier. Probably Caesar intended to cross the Allier at or near Moulins, and we may suppose that there were also bridges higher up the stream at Varennes and Vichy. The two armies moved in sight of one another, and made their camps nearly opposite. The Gallic scouts kept a sharp look-out to prevent the Romans from making a bridge, and Caesar was in danger of being unable to cross the Allier during a great part of the summer, for this river, as he says, is not generally fordable before the autumn. In July the Allier is nearly dry at Moulins and Varennes; but usually it is not fordable before the end of June, and in wet seasons not till a later time. To prevent this delay Caesar made a camp in the forest opposite one of the bridges which had been destroyed, and the following day lay concealed with two legions. He sent forward the other four legions with the baggage in the usual order, but having taken, as he says, every fourth

cohort[1] from the six legions to make up the two legions, he
ordered the remaining force to march in six divisions to deceive the enemy. The four legions were instructed to move
forward as far as they could in order to draw on Vercingetorix, and as soon as Caesar conjectured from the time of
day that they were in camp, he began to rebuild the bridge
on the old piles, the lower part of which remained entire.
This was soon done, the two legions crossed, made a camp,
and the four legions were recalled. As soon as Vercingetorix
heard that the Romans had passed the Allier, he hurried
on towards Gergovia that he might not be compelled to fight
against his will.

Caesar reached Gergovia in good time on the fifth day's
march from the place where he crossed the Allier. His road
was up the fertile valley of that river into the rich country
named the Limagne of Auvergne, one of the most fertile districts in Europe, where he would find supplies[2]. He had a
cavalry skirmish with the enemy immediately on his arrival,
and time enough in the rest of the day to see that the town
which was on the top of a mountain and difficult of access
could not be taken by assault, and he could not blockade it
until he had provided supplies (c. 36).

The Gergovian mountains are part of the high plateau on
which stand the volcanic peaks of the Lower Auvergne (vol.
iii. p. 405). Gergovia, which retains the name, is nearly four
miles south of Clermont-Ferrand, and is conspicuous as you
approach it either from the north or the south. It is a mass
of limestone capped by a stream of lava, about 2400 feet above
the sea and about 1250 feet above the plain. The summit is
nearly horizontal and in the form of a parallelogram about

---

[1] If Caesar took every fourth cohort out of the whole number of sixty,
"captis quartis quibusque cohortibus" may be explained consistently with the
Roman usage of the words by supposing that he took the first, fourth, seventh,
and so on, and in this way he would have twenty cohorts (Feldhausch, quoted by
Drumann, Geschichte Roms, iii. 316). Dion (40, c. 35) says that Caesar crossed
the Allier on rafts, which contradicts the Latin text; but he has rightly understood Caesar's manoeuvre about the legions.

[2] The light soil was, perhaps is, worked by the small proprietors with a plough
drawn by two cows, or the peasant's wife, it is said, took the place of one of the
cows. Cows are still sometimes employed as beasts of draught about Vichy.

4920 feet long from east to west, and 1968 feet wide from
north to south[*]. The northern and eastern slopes are precipitous. The southern side is steep on the upper part, but
descends to the plain by a series of terraces. On the west
side Gergovia is connected by a narrow neck about 400 feet
wide, named Les Goules, with the heights of Risolles which
are about 130 feet lower than Gergovia. Risolles is a mass
of high land of irregular form to which belongs the height of
Jussat or Jussac, which resembles a truncated cone. West of
the Risolles and separated from it by a valley is the Puy
Giroux, from the summit of which is taken the view in
Scrope's "Central France" of the hill of Jussat, and beyond
it the higher plateau of Gergovia. Right opposite to the
southern slope of Gergovia, and near the foot of the mountain
is the steep-sided elevation named La Roche Blanche, below
and south of which a small stream named the Auzon runs
into the Allier. To the north-west and near the base of the
plateau of Gergovia is another small stream, the Artières,
which also joins the Allier: the Artières receives the Clé-
mensat a rivulet which rises west of the plateau of Gergovia
and flows past Romagnat. As Caesar approached Gergovia
from the north-east, he would see the north face of the mountain, and as he marched past Gergovia to a position south-
east of the mountain, he would see the eastern and southern
sides. His conclusion that this hill-town could not be taken
by assault is completely justified by a view of the place.

Vercingetorix had placed himself on the southern slope of
Gergovia near the town, and around him at small intervals
and in separate detachments lay the confederate forces, which
occupied all the heights and presented a formidable appearance. The chiefs who formed the council of war came to him
every morning at daybreak either to make their report or
to receive orders; and Vercingetorix tried the courage of
his men almost daily in skirmishes of cavalry mingled with
archers. "Opposite to the town and at the foot of the moun-

---

[*] See "Histoire de César," Planche, 21; and "Gergovia," etc., von M. A.
Fischer, Leipzig, 1855. These two authorities agree in the length of the plateau;
but in the "Histoire" the width is said to be above 500 mètres.

tain was a hill exceedingly strong in natural position and scarped on all sides," as Caesar says. This hill appears to be the Roche Blanche, though it is described in the "Histoire de César" as scarped only on three sides[4]. If Caesar could get possession of this hill, which was occupied by the enemy, he expected to shut them out from their chief supply of water and forage. The place was not defended by a strong force, and Caesar leaving his camp in the silence of the night got possession of the hill before any help could be sent to the garrison from the town. He placed two legions on the Roche Blanche, and connected this camp with his large camp by two ditches each twelve feet wide, along which even a single man could go in safety without fear of a sudden attack from the enemy.

If the position of the Roche Blanche is determined, it will help us to find the position of Caesar's great camp. Fischer places the large camp south of the Auzon at Le Crest; and if this were so, the communication between the two camps was interrupted by the Auzon. But it is stated in the "Histoire de César" that the commandant Baron Stoffel in 1862 discovered the sites of both camps, the smaller on the Roche Blanche, and the larger on the north side of the Auzon, and north of the village of Orcet, which is about due east of the Roche Blanche[5]. As the traces of the larger camp have been really discovered, there is no longer any room for conjecture.

In the mean time Convictolitanis, the chief magistrate of the Aedui being bribed by the Arverni to desert Caesar, entered into negotiations with some young men, and among them

[4] In a note (p. 270), it is said that the Roche Blanche on the south side is nearly perpendicular like a wall, but that it has lost on the other sides the abrupt form by the falling of the earth.

[5] "The communication between the great and the little camp was a parapet formed by the earth dug from two contiguous ditches each four feet deep and six wide, and consequently the width of the two together was only twelve feet. If we are surprised at the Romans having made two small ditches six feet wide and four deep, instead of one eight feet wide and six deep, which would have produced the same amount of earth, the explanation is that two small ditches were made much sooner than one large ditch."—"Histoire de César," note ii. p. 271. But Caesar's ditches were each twelve feet wide (duodenum pedum). Planch. 23 contains the "Profile de double fossé," and a view of the plateau of Gergovia taken from the tower of the Roche Blanche.

Litavicus and his brothers, who belonged to a great family. He gave them part of what he had received, and reminded them that the Aedui alone stood in the way of the liberation of Gallia, that the other states were only prevented from rising by respect for them: he admitted that he was under some obligations to Caesar, but his duty to his country was superior. The young men were soon persuaded by the arguments and the money of the magistrate, and the confederates began to consider how they should accomplish their design, for they did not expect that the Aedui would be ready to engage in war. It was finally resolved that Litavicus should take the command of the ten thousand men who were going to Gergovia and that the brothers of Litavicus should hurry on before him to Caesar. The rest of their plan will appear from what followed. When Litavicus was within thirty miles of Gergovia, he called the men together and with tears in his eyes said, " Fellow-soldiers, whither are we going? All our cavalry, all our nobility have perished, and Eporedorix and Virdumarus chief men in our state, have been charged with treachery and put to death by the Romans without trial. You may learn this," he said, " from those who have escaped, for as my brothers and kinsmen have perished, grief prevents me from describing what has been done." He then brought forward some men whom he had instructed for the purpose, and they confirmed all that Litavicus had said. The Aedui unanimously entreated Litavicus to tell them what they must do to save themselves. "It needs no telling," he replied: " we must go to Gergovia and join the Arverni: after committing this crime the Romans will come to kill us; let us therefore avenge the death of our brethren and put to death these robbers." At the same time he pointed to some Romans, who relying on the protection of this escort were taking a great quantity of corn and supplies to Gergovia. The stores were plundered, the Romans put to death with tortures, and messengers were sent all through the country of the Aedui to stir them up by the same lies, and urge them to like acts of vengeance.

Both Eporedorix and Virdumarus were in Caesar's camp in his cavalry, and both of them had been particularly invited to join him. Eporedorix was of a great family, and Virdumarus, who was of low condition, had been introduced by Divitiacus to Caesar, and raised by him to high rank. Eporedorix having in some way heard of the design of Litavicus came about midnight to inform Caesar and to urge him to prevent the defection of the Aedui from the Roman alliance through the folly of a few young men, for the defection of the whole state would certainly follow, if so many thousands joined the Arverni. Caesar was much disturbed at the news, for he had always specially favoured the Aedui; but without a moment's delay he took four legions without baggage and all his cavalry*. There was no time to contract the limits of the camp, for every thing depended on the rapidity of Caesar's movements. He left C. Fabius with two legions to defend the camp; and ordered the brothers of Litavicus to be seized, but they had just escaped. The soldiers responded with hearty good will to the general's ardour, and after a march of twenty-five miles they came in sight of the Aedui. Caesar sent forward his cavalry to stop their march, but with instructions to kill no man. He ordered Eporedorix and Virdumarus, who were supposed to be dead, to show themselves among the cavalry to their countrymen, and as they were well known, the knavery of Litavicus was immediately detected, and the Aedui threw down their arms in sign of submission and begged for mercy. Litavicus made his escape to Gergovia with his dependents, whose custom it was never to desert their master (B. G. iii. 22; and p. 118, note). Caesar sent a message to inform the Aedui that he had spared those whom the law of war would have allowed him to kill, and after giving his men three hours rest during the night he set out on his return to Gergovia, taking the Aedui with him (vii. 50). When Caesar was about half way, he was met by some horsemen from

* Caesar took four legions out of his camp, the larger camp, and left two legions to defend it. These two legions were therefore transferred from the small camp (vii. 36) to the large camp, and the small camp was left undefended and might have been seized by the Galli, but it probably contained nothing that they would value, and they would not have been able to defend it when Caesar returned. The attack of the Galli was made on the large camp. The small camp was in Caesar's possession after his return to Gergovia, as appears from vii. 51.

Fabius who informed him that the camp had been attacked with great violence. The enemy were so numerous that they could relieve their own men when they were wearied, while the Romans were exhausted by continual exertion and the necessity of being always on the ramparts in consequence of the extent of the camp. The horsemen further reported that many of the Romans were wounded by arrows and other missiles, but that the engines had been very useful in repelling the attack; that when the enemy retired, Fabius began to stop up the gates of the camp except two, and to put blinds (plutei) on the ramparts in expectation of an assault on the following day. This intelligence roused the soldiers to exert themselves and they reached the camp before sunrise. Caesar had received the news from Eporedorix about midnight, and he set out without any delay, but it would require a little time to put his four legions in marching order. He met the Aedui twenty-five miles from his camp, which would be a march of eight or ten hours, settled his business with them, allowed his soldiers the first three hours after sunset for rest, and reached his camp the following morning before sunrise. Thus his men marched fifty Roman miles in less than thirty hours; but the whole of the second march was during the night, and the greater part of the first march.

As soon as the messengers from Litavicus reached the Aedui, these people without taking any time to inquire into the matter fell upon the Romans who were in their country, robbing, massacring them and seizing them as slaves. Convictolitanis urged on the common sort in the hope that they would carry their excesses so far that they could not recede. M. Aristius a tribune, who was on the road to join his legion, was induced to come out of Cabillonum (Chalon-sur-Saône) by the promise of a safeguard, and the Roman merchants (negotiatores) who were settled there were also compelled to leave the town. As soon as the Romans were on the road, they were plundered of all that they had. However they resisted the attack of the Aedui for a whole day and night, and after many had fallen on both sides, and the assailants were calling on their countrymen for more help, the news came that all the soldiers of the Aedui were in Caesar's power. Then with their usual fickleness of character the Aedui hurried to Aristius and protested that the state was in no way chargeable with this violence: they made search after the stolen goods, they seized on the public account the property of Litavicus and his brothers, and sent commissioners to Caesar to clear themselves of all blame. Their object was to get back their soldiers; but as a great number were involved in the guilt of the murders, had plunder in their possession, and feared Caesar's vengeance, they were at the same time secretly planning to take up arms against him and soliciting the neighbouring states to join them. Caesar knew all this, but he received the commissioners in the kindest manner, and declared that he did not condemn the state for the folly of the common sort, and that his friendly feelings towards the Aedui were undiminished. But in fact he was anticipating a general rising of the Galli and the possibility of being hemmed in by his enemies, and his thoughts were occupied about the best way of retiring from Gergovia and uniting all his forces, without giving to his retreat the appearance of a flight. Caesar was indeed in great danger, for the defection of the Aedui, who had been faithful to him from the beginning, would deprive him of his most useful allies.

While these thoughts were in his mind, it happened that on going to the small camp to examine the works Caesar observed that a hill, which was occupied by the enemy and on former days had been nearly covered with men, was now quite bare. He inquired of the deserters who came to him daily in large numbers, what was the reason, and all of them confirmed what Caesar had already learned from his scouts. The mass of Risolles, to which this hill belonged, was connected with the mountain of Gergovia by the ridge Les Goules, nearly level, but covered with trees and narrow at the part which gave access to the west end of the town[1]. The enemy were afraid that the Romans might seize this height, as they had seized the Roche Blanche, and then the Galli would be nearly

---

[1] "The foundations of the masonry and the approaches to this gate were laid bare in July, 1861. The broad road which led from the gate to the Col des Goules is distinctly seen."—"Hist. de César," ii. 273, note, in which the author has marked on his plan (Planche, 21) the part of Risolles where he supposes the Gauls to have been working.

shut out from foraging. It was for the purpose of fortifying this weak point that Vercingetorix had summoned all the allies. Just after midnight (c. 45) Caesar sent several companies of horse in the direction of Risolles with orders to beat about the low grounds and to make a noise. At daybreak he ordered a great number of horses and mules to be brought out of the camps, and the muleteers with helmets on their heads to mount the beasts and ride round the heights of Risolles, where the village of Opme stands. A few horsemen were sent with the muleteers, and all of them had instructions to go in the same direction by a long circuit. All this was seen from Gergovia, the high position of which commanded a view of the larger camp, but the people at so great distance could not see clearly what was going on. Caesar also sent one legion in the direction of Risolles, but ordered the men after advancing a short distance to hide themselves in the forest on the low grounds. The suspicions of the Galli were thus confirmed and they directed all their forces to the place which they were fortifying.

Caesar seeing that the Gallic camps were deserted brought his men in small detachments from the large to the small camp by the double ditch, under shelter of the earthworks, with plumes and helmets covered and standards concealed, that they might not be seen from the town. The legati, who commanded the several legions, four in number, were informed of the general's design. They were particularly instructed to keep the men in check, to prevent them advancing too far in their eagerness to fight or with the hope of booty: he pointed out the difficulties of the ground, which could only be overcome by a rapid ascent, and told them that the object was to make a surprise and not to fight a battle. He then gave the signal, and at the same time sent the Aedui from the large camp to ascend the mountain of Gergovia on the east side.

The distance from the town wall on the south side to the plain was in a straight line twelve hundred paces or six thousand Roman feet[a]; but the whole distance was made somewhat

[a] "It is in fact 1780 mètres from the foot of the mountain where Caesar would collect his troops between the Roche Blanche and the Puy of Marmant to the gate O on the south side of the town (Planche, 21). This line passes by the

longer by the necessity of deviating from the straight line to
make the ascent easier. About half way up the hill and extending from east to west the Galli had built a wall of large
stones six feet high to check an attack from the enemy. All
the part of the hill below the wall was unoccupied, but the part
above as far as the town wall was filled with the Gallic camps
closely crowded. When the signal was given, the Roman
soldiers quickly reached the wall, crossed it and got possession
of three camps. This was done so promptly that Teutomatus,
king of the Nitiobriges, was surprised in his tent where he had
gone to rest at midday, and hardly escaped with the upper
part of his body exposed and his horse wounded.

Caesar having accomplished his purpose, as he says, ordered
the signal to be given for the soldiers to return, and the tenth
legion halted with which Caesar was. It has been supposed
that he was on a small eminence west of the village of Merdogne
("Hist. de César," ii. 278). But the soldiers of the three other
legions being separated from the tenth legion by the valley
which lies between Caesar's position and Gergovia did not hear
the trumpet, for, as Caesar says, the depression or valley is
considerable; and though the tribuni and legati tried to check
their impetuosity, the men elated by the hope of victory and
by past success rushed forward in the pursuit till they came
close to the walls and gates of the town. Then a loud cry was
heard from all parts of Gergovia, and those who were farthest
from the part assailed by the Romans, terrified by the sudden
alarm and supposing that the enemy were within the walls,
rushed out of the town. The women threw down from the
wall articles of dress and silver, and exposing themselves as far
as the breast, with outstretched hands entreated the Romans
to spare them. Some of the women were let down the wall by
the aid of others and surrendered to the soldiers. There was
one L. Fabius a centurion of the eighth legion, who remembering the rich booty of Avaricum had declared that no man
should mount the wall of Gergovia before him. With the aid
of three soldiers of his maniple he climbed up the wall, and

ravine in which is the village of Merdogne: on the right and left the ground
is too irregular to be scaled by troops."—"Hist. de César, ii. 277, note."

then helped the soldiers to mount one after the other. The Galli who were employed on the works west of the plateau of Gergovia heard the distant shouts, which were followed by repeated messages announcing the capture of the town. The Gallic cavalry came first, and the infantry quickly followed. Every man as he arrived took his place under the wall and joined the combatants, whose numbers were thus increased. The women, who a little before were holding out their hands in supplication to the Romans, now encouraged their countrymen by displaying after Gallic fashion their hair loose and showing their children. Both the ground and the numbers made it an unequal contest for the Romans, who were also exhausted by running and the length of the fight, and they could not resist men who came fresh to the struggle. Caesar observing that his soldiers were fighting under unfavourable circumstances and the enemy's numbers increasing, sent orders to the legatus T. Sextius, whom he had left in the smaller camp, to bring out the cohorts immediately and place them at the foot of the hill on the right of the Galli, for the purpose of checking the pursuit of the enemy if the Romans should be driven from their ground. Caesar himself advancing* a short distance with his legion from the place where he had halted, waited for the result of the battle. While the contest was going on with great fury, the Aedui, whom Caesar had ordered to make a diversion by ascending the east end of the mountain of Gergovia, came in sight all at once. Their armour which resembled that of the Galli caused the Romans great alarm, and though it was observed that their right arms were bare, which was the established sign of friendly troops, yet the soldiers supposed that this was only done to deceive them[†]. Just at this time L. Fabius and those who had ascended the wall with him were surrounded, slaughtered and pitched down. M. Petreius, a centurion of the same legion as Fabius, attempted

---

* " Progressus:" the author of the " Hist. de César " (ii. 278, note) accepts Goeler's proposal to read " regressus," a word which Caesar never uses. He also gives a reason for accepting " regressus," which is a good reason for rejecting it.

† Fischer (" Gergovia," p. 19) describes a Gallic silver coin of Epadnactos, the reverse of which has an armed man with the head and one shoulder bare. He thinks that the coin may explain this passage in Caesar.

to break one of the gates, but overpowered by numbers and severely wounded he told his men to make their retreat while they could. He fell fighting bravely and thus saved his soldiers. The Romans pressed on all sides were driven down the mountain with the loss of forty-six centurions, but the tenth legion, which had taken a position on tolerably level ground, checked the enemy in their eager pursuit; and the tenth was supported by the cohorts of the thirteenth legion under T. Sextius which had occupied some higher ground. As soon as the legions reached the plain, they turned round and faced the enemy. Vercingetorix led his troops back from the foot of the mountain to their entrenchments. On this day Caesar lost near seven hundred soldiers. On the next day Caesar rebuked his men for their rashness and impetuosity[1]: he blamed them for determining how far they should advance or what they should do, for not halting at the signal, and not allowing themselves to be kept in check by the tribuni and the legati; he pointed out the difficulties in the nature of the ground, and reminded them of what he had done near Avaricum, when he surprised the enemy who were without a leader and without cavalry and renounced a certain victory to prevent his men sustaining even a small loss owing to the disadvantage of position (vii. c. 19; p. 208): he admired their courage in not being stopped either by the defences of the camps, the height of the mountain or the walls of the town, but he also blamed their want of discipline and their presumption in thinking that they were better judges than their general of the means to victory and of the issue of events: finally he told them that he required from them obedience and discipline as much as courage, and that they must attribute their disaster to the unfavourable character of the ground, and not to the bravery of the enemy. Though Caesar still intended to leave Gergovia, he drew out his legions after this address, and placed them in battle-order in a good position. Vercingetorix[2] came down to the level ground, but there was only a skirmish of cavalry, after which Caesar, who had the advantage, led his troops back

---

[1] "Cupiditatem," not "soif du pillage," as some French translators have it.
[2] I take the MSS. reading "nihilo minus in aequum locum descenderet."

to the camp. On the next day he offered the Galli battle a
second time, and thinking he had now done enough to abate
their arrogance and to encourage his own men, he broke up
his camp and moved towards the country of the Aedui without
being followed by the enemy. On the third day he reached
the Allier, repaired a bridge and took his men over the river,
at some place probably higher up than that where he crossed
before (p 308).

In this narrative, the author of the "Histoire de César" (ii.
281) remarks, "Caesar skilfully disguises a check. Evidently
he expected to take Gergovia by a coup-de-main before the
Galli attracted by a feigned attack on the west side of the
town should be able to return to defend it. Deceived in his
expectation he gave the signal for a retreat, but too late for it
to be made in good order. Caesar does not appear to be
sincere when he says that he had attained his object as soon
as his soldiers reached the foot of the wall. It ought not to
have been so, for what could be the advantage of taking the
camps which were almost without troops, if this capture should
not be followed by the surrender of the town itself?" All
that we know of this affair is contained in the Commentaries,
and Caesar's own statement is the answer to this censure.
Caesar by various devices (c. 45) confirmed the enemy in the
opinion that he might attempt to approach the town on the
west, and they saw from Gergovia that he had sent a legion in
the direction of Risolles and that the legion had disappeared in
the forest. It was for the purpose of preventing Caesar from
getting a footing on Risolles, and thus approaching Gergovia,
that the Galli had gone some distance west of the town to
fortify the place where Risolles might be ascended. Caesar
having got his men together told his legati what his design
was, and he enjoined them to keep the soldiers in check and
not to allow them to advance too far either through ardour
for fighting or love of plunder. He therefore, as he says
himself, gave orders that they must not advance beyond a
certain point. When they had crossed the wall and seized
three camps, and this is what the Roman says that his purpose
was, and not, as the critic represents it, the arrival of his men
at the foot of the town wall, Caesar gave the signal to return,

and the tenth legion which he had addressed, halted. Why should we not believe Caesar when he says that after accomplishing his design he gave the signal for the men to return who had driven away the enemy from the three camps? If his design was only to surprise the camps, in which he succeeded, he knew better than his critic whether he gained any advantage by doing so. He may have thought that this was enough for that day, and if he kept his position, he would see whether he could make any use of it. But it seems probable and it is consistent with all that he has said, that he had a further design, which was to plant his troops on the high ground immediately west of Gergovia, and the first thing necessary was to disperse the enemy who were below the walls on the south side of the city, and who were left there, as we may assume, to protect that part of the approach. When Caesar had got possession of the site of the Gallic camps, he was very near to the ridge at the west end of Gergovia, and there was, as far as we can judge, a possibility that he might have seized this place, and kept it against any attack of the Galli. That he did not intend to assault Gergovia on the south side, will be plain to any man who has seen the place, and it is expressed in his text as clearly as if he had said so, for he gave the signal to return as soon as his men had got possession of the three camps, and though they did not hear the trumpet, the tribunes and the legati attempted to check their impetuous rush up the steeps beneath the wall, "consistently with Caesar's orders" (c. 47). Nor when the men had broken loose and mounted to the south wall did he go to support them with the tenth legion, which is another proof that this assault was not his design, and evidence too that he thought it prudent to keep the tenth legion in reserve against a contingency which he might certainly expect. Accordingly he let his men fight until overpowered by the Galli, who hurried from their works on Risolles, and struck with terror at the sudden appearance of the Aedui, whom they took for enemies, they were driven back towards the tenth legion, which had remained where Caesar ordered it to stay. If Caesar's men had kept together after taking the three camps, he might perhaps have made his way to the west side of Gergovia before the enemy could return from the works at which they were labouring; and we may certainly conclude that when the townsmen saw the Aedui approaching on the south-east and Caesar at the opposite end of the plateau they would have deserted the town, as many of them did on the approach of the Romans to the south wall. If the legions had kept together and ascended the hill to Les Goules, they would not have seen the Aedui, who would have done all that Caesar expected from them by frightening the people in Gergovia. Even if Vercingetorix and Caesar had met at the west end of the plateau, the Gaul would not have easily dislodged the Roman in a close fight, when there was a possibility that the legion which was hid in the woods might ascend Risolles and fall on the rear of the Galli. It was hazardous for Caesar to attempt to seize the position at Les Goules, if that was his design; but every thing was well planned for such a purpose, an accident only caused it to fail, and if he had succeeded, Gergovia was won. The criticism of the author of the "Histoire"[*] is certainly founded on a misstatement of Caesar's meaning; it turns a plain, consistent narrative into an absurdity, and makes the Roman proconsul a blunderer in war and a disingenuous historian. Caesar lays the blame of his failure on the soldiers and his narrative fully justifies him.

After crossing the Allier (c. 54) Caesar was informed by Viridumarus and Eporedorix that Litavicus had gone with all the cavalry to stir the Aedui to revolt, and they urged that it was Caesar's interest to allow them to anticipate him in order to confirm the Aedui in their fidelity to the Romans. Caesar had already many proofs of the treachery of the Aedui, and he believed that if these men left him, they would hasten the revolt, but yet he did not think it prudent to retain them and

---

[*] The writer's exposition of Caesar is generally correct, and there is therefore the more reason for refuting his mistakes in this matter. Drumann ("Geschichte Roms," III. 349) has a similar comment on Caesar's attempt on Gergovia, in which he perverts the text and shows his conceit and want of judgment.

I have done the best that I can to explain the assault on Gergovia with the aid of Fischer and the author of the "Histoire;" but it is probable that what I have written may require some correction. I am not completely satisfied with the explanation of Caesar's operations about this place. Some of my countrymen who travel abroad may perhaps be induced to spend a few days on this memorable site, and examine it with Caesar in their hands.

incur the suspicion of using violence or being afraid. When
Virdumarus and Eporedorix parted from him, he briefly reminded them of his services to the Aedui, and of the low condition from which he had raised the nation to the present state
of honour and authority. With these words he dismissed the
two men, who went off to Noviodunum (Nevers), a town of the
Aedui advantageously situated, as Caesar says. Nevers is on
the slope of a hill on the right bank of the Loire, and Caesar
had made it his dépôt for all his Gallic hostages, his corn, his
military chest, most of the baggage belonging to himself and
the army, and for a great number of horses which had been
purchased in Italy and Spain. It has been suggested that he
established this dépôt on his way from Avaricum to Decetia
(Decise), and it may have been so, if he passed by this road
(p. 307). As he had long known that he could not trust the
Aedui, it seems strange that he had left the place unprotected,
when he advanced to Gergovia and sent Labienus to Agendicum (Sens), but as he does not explain his reasons, we must be
content with what he tells us. He was in great straits all
through the campaign of this year, and he did the best that
he could. If he had no troops to spare for the protection of
Noviodunum, he was compelled to trust to the Aedui, who had
not yet declared against him. When Virdumarus and Eporedorix arrived at Noviodunum, they learnt the state of affairs;
that Litavicus had been received at Bibracte (p. 14) the chief
town of the Aedui, that Convictolitanis and a large part of the
senate had joined him there, and that commissioners had been
sent by the state to Vercingetorix to negotiate for peace and
alliance. The opportunity was too good to be lost. Accordingly
the Aedui massacred those who had been left in charge of
Noviodunum, and the Italians who were settled there in business or happened to be passing through the town: they divided
among themselves the money and the horses, sent the hostages
to Bibracte, and as they could not hold the town they burnt it
to prevent the place being of any use to the Romans. They
carried off in boats all the corn that they could hastily remove,
and threw the rest into the river or burnt it. They began to
collect troops from the neighbouring parts, to post bodies of
armed men along the Loire, and to display their cavalry in all

directions for the purpose of alarming the Romans, and in the expectation of preventing them from getting supplies or crossing the Loire to reach the Provincia[e]. They were encouraged in this expectation by the fact that the Loire was now so swollen by the melted snows that it seemed impossible to ford it in any part. If these floods in the Loire were really caused by the melting of the snow on the Cévennes, the time of the year could not be farther advanced than the end of April or the beginning of May. Caesar being informed of all that had happened among the Aedui, saw that he ought to move quick, if he must run the risk of making a bridge over the Loire, in order that he might fight before larger forces were assembled on the river. Even in his present difficulties he saw no reason for changing his purpose and retreating into the Provincia, which would be a disgrace to the army and a difficult march also across the Cévennes. But his chief reason for attempting to cross the Loire was his fear for Labienus and his legions. Accordingly by forced marches day and night he reached the river before he was expected, and the cavalry found a ford[f] which under the circumstances was considered to be practicable, though it was so deep that the soldiers could only keep their shoulders and arms above water and so support their weapons. The cavalry[f] was placed across the stream above the ford to break the force of the current, and the army passed the river in

---

[e] In B. G. vii. 55 the words "aut adductos inopia ex provincia excludere possent" are obscure and perhaps corrupt. I have given what I suppose to be the meaning of the passage. Davis altered it thus: "et adductos inopia in provinciam repellere possent." Some German editors follow him, except that they write "expellere" for "repellere." The shortest way into the Provincia for Caesar would be by crossing the Loire. If he attempted to reach the Provincia without crossing the Loire, Vercingetorix would be in his way and the Cévennes also. The fact is that the enemy did not wish to drive him into the Provincia, from which he would soon have returned. They wished to starve him between the Allier and the Loire. The emendators have not understood the matter. Dion (40, c. 38) states that Caesar not being able to cross the Loire, turned to the Lingones, and had no success even there. Dion did not know the position of the Lingones.

[f] The author of the "Histoire" affirms that there has always been a ford at Dourdan-Laney.

[f] See Vegetius, lil. 7, who speaks of two lines of horsemen being placed across a river, and of the infantry passing between them. There is an English translation of Vegetius by Lieut. John Clarke.

safety before the enemy could recover from their surprise at the sudden appearance of the Romans. Caesar found corn and abundance of cattle, and having well supplied his men he directed his march towards the territory of the Senones. No doubt the Aedui paid dear for their treachery, and were well pillaged by the hungry soldiers. I do not suppose that Caesar found the corn standing ripe in the fields, though his words might bear that interpretation (in agris), for the remark about the Loire being swollen by the melted snows proves that it was not yet harvest-time. Indeed the winter was not quite past when Avaricum was taken (vii. 32). He therefore found the corn stored in the buildings, and how much mischief his men did besides carrying off the stocks and cattle of the Aedui, he has not cared to tell us.

By his courage and sagacity Caesar rescued his army from a dangerous position, effected his junction with Labienus, and was now ready with all his forces to resist the combination of the Galli which he had foreseen, and to crush the last effort to recover their liberty under a commander whose ability and resolution Caesar estimated justly.

Modern writers often pass judgment on the military events of antiquity, though they know only the facts which are reported, which may be very few, and are ignorant of many facts which are not reported. If Caesar's conduct during the difficult campaign of 52 requires any apology, it will be found in a careful study of his book, which will last longer than the books of those who either praise or blame him. The rising in the winter of 54 proved that Gallia was not reduced to submission; and the campaign of 53 was a war of extermination against the people in the north part of Gallia, whose treachery and intrigues with the Germans east of the Rhine threatened to give the Romans no rest. Caesar had the subjugation of Gallia on his hands and also the state of affairs in Rome to look after; and his visit to Italy in the winter of 53 and 52 gave the Galli an opportunity of attempting to throw off the yoke. At the beginning of the year 52 the state of affairs in Gallia and Caesar's separation from his troops formed a difficulty which a less able commander would not have overcome; and we have seen how boldly and successfully he brought his troops together. We may assume that he had sufficient reasons for sending Labienus with four legions against Lutetia, while he himself marched to Gergovia, and that he could foresee that the defeat either of Labienus or himself would endanger the safety of both. All Gallia was roused against him, and the Aedui his best friends were, as he well knew, very uncertain allies; and yet he thought it necessary to divide his force, for Gallia was too large for a single army to keep it in obedience. Before Gergovia he had a check, and his retreat from that hill-town exposed him to the greatest danger; but it was absolutely necessary to join Labienus and again unite his forces, for it was now plain that all the Galli would be brought against Caesar by Vercingetorix and that the issue of the campaign would depend on one great battle. During this year Caesar ran many hazards, and he could not avoid it. With his small army opposed to many nations he could only save himself by audacity; but his audacity was the cool calculation of a man who had a just confidence in himself, and his soldiers had equal confidence in the ability and vigilance of their commander.

CHAPTER XIX.

ALESIA.

B.C. 52.

WHILE Caesar was in the centre of Gallia, Labienus advanced from Agendicum (Sens) against Lutetia (Paris) with four legions: some troops, which had lately come from Italy, were left to protect the baggage (B. G. vii. 57). His march was along the left bank of the Yonne, and after the junction of the Yonne with the Seine along the left bank of the Seine past Fontainebleau. On Labienus' arrival being known, a great force was collected from the neighbouring states, and placed under the command of Camulogenus of the nation of the Aulerci, a man of very advanced age, who received this mark of distinction on account of his military skill. Camulogenus observing that there was a continuous marsh, which was connected with the Seine and made all the part on the south side of the river difficult to pass, took his position there and determined to prevent the Romans from crossing. Labienus attempted to make a road across the marsh by bringing up covered galleries to protect his men while they threw down brushwood and earth to form a way. Finding that it would be very difficult to do this in face of the enemy he retreated silently in the third watch of the night by the road by which he had advanced, and came to Melodunum (Melun), a town on an island in the Seine, like Lutetia. Here he seized about fifty boats, fastened them together, put his men on them, and got possession of the place without any resistance from the townsmen, a great part of whom had been summoned to the war, and the rest were

terrified by this unexpected attack. Labienus repaired the
bridge which connected the island with the right bank of the
river, for the enemy had destroyed it a few days before, led
his troops over it and marched along the right bank of the
Seine towards Paris. He took the boats with him and used
them, as we suppose, for crossing the Marne, but the Marne
is not mentioned. The news being carried to the Gallic army
by those who had fled from Melodunum, Camulogenus ordered
Lutetia to be burnt and the bridges which connected it with
the opposite banks to be destroyed. The Galli left the marsh
where they had opposed the passage of Labienus, and took
a position on the Seine opposite to Lutetia and opposite to
the camp of Labienus.

The author of the "Histoire de César" (ii. 280) contends
that the marsh, where Labienus was stopped on the south
side of the Seine, was not a marsh formed by the Bièvre,
which enters the Seine on the left bank opposite to Paris, but
a marsh formed by the Essonne, which joins the left side of
the Seine below Melun and nearer to Melun than to Paris.
He argues that it is very improbable that, if Labienus had
reached the Bièvre, he would have marched back all the way
to Melun in order to put himself on the right bank of the
Seine. If the marsh was that formed by the Essonne, he
contends that the retreat of Labienus becomes intelligible, his
object being to gain the north side of the Seine and march
upon Lutetia, where he arrived before Camulogenus. This is
all true except the fact of Labienus arriving at Lutetia before
the Galli who had stopped his march, for Caesar does not say
who reached Lutetia first; nor can we infer with certainty.
The author also affirms that the Bièvre flows in a calcareous
bed, and could never have formed a marsh capable of stopping
an army; and on the contrary, the ground along the Essonne
presents even now a very serious obstacle. It is intersected
by innumerable turf-pits, and it was behind the Essonne that
the Emperor Napoleon I. in 1814 placed the army while the
enemy was occupying Paris.

The narrative of Caesar rather leads to the conclusion that the
marsh was nearly opposite Paris. The words "cujus adventu"
(c. 57) are ambiguous, for they may either mean an actual

arrival at a place named (B. G. vi. 41, v. 54, i. 22) or a near approach. The length of the retreat from the Bièvre to Melun is in favour of the Frenchman's supposition; but there is nothing in Caesar's text which shows that the Galli advanced east of Paris to meet Labienus. Caesar's narrative is founded on Labienus' report, which is defective for the purpose of identifying the site of the marsh, but not defective as a military narrative, nor is it obscure, though it has been misunderstood.

At the time when Labienus was on the north bank of the Seine opposite to Paris, the news spread abroad that Caesar had retired from Gergovia and that Gallia was rising. It was the common talk that Caesar being stopped by the Loire and compelled by want of supplies had marched towards the Provincia. The Bellovaci were already inclined to rise, and when they heard of the revolt of the Aedui they began to collect troops and openly to prepare for war. Under these circumstances Labienus saw that he must change his plans, and that he could attempt no more than to carry his army back to Agendicum. On the north side of the Seine he was threatened by the Bellovaci, who had the highest reputation for courage of all the Galli (p. 40); on the other side by Camulogenus, who was on the south bank of the Seine with a well disciplined army; and his own men were separated from their head-quarters and baggage at Sens by a large river, for Labienus must cross the Seine somewhere on his retreat. In these unexpected difficulties the Roman general relied for safety on his courage and skill. At nightfall he called a council of war and urged his officers to execute his plan with the utmost exactness. He assigned each of the boats which he had brought from Melun to a Roman eques, and at the end of the first watch he ordered them to go down the river four miles in silence and to wait for him[1]. Five cohorts, on whom he could least rely, were left to guard the camp, and the remaining five cohorts of this legion were ordered to march at midnight up the stream with all the baggage and to make a great noise. He also got together some small boats, which

---

[1] Four miles, says the author of the "Histoire," would bring them to the heights of the village named Point-du-Jour.

were sent in the same direction to make a great splashing with
the oars. A little after midnight Labienus with three legions
marched down the river to the place where he had ordered the
boats to wait for him. When he had arrived there, the scouts
of the enemy who were placed along the banks of the river and
were not looking out in consequence of a sudden storm, were
surprised by the Romans, and the army and cavalry were quickly
carried across the river. Just before daybreak the enemy
learned that contrary to custom there was a great noise in the
Roman camp, that a large body of men was marching up the
stream, that the noise of oars was heard in the same direction,
and that a little lower down troops were crossing the river in
boats. They supposed that the legions were crossing in three
places, and that the Romans being terrified by the defection
of the Aedui were attempting to escape. Accordingly the Galli
divided their own forces into three parts, and leaving one part
to keep watch opposite the Roman camp, and sending a small
force up the river as far as the boats should go[1], they went
with the rest of the troops to meet Labienus. At dawn of
day all the Romans had crossed the Seine, and the enemy's
army was in sight. Labienus encouraged his men by bidding
them remember their past victories, and to imagine that
Caesar was present, under whom they had so often defeated
the enemy. He then gave the signal. On the first onset,
the seventh legion, which was on the right wing, routed the
enemy: on the left wing, which was occupied by the twelfth
legion, though the first ranks of the Galli had been transfixed
by the Roman pila, the rest made a vigorous resistance and
showed no disposition to fly. Camulogenus the commander
was there encouraging his men. The victory was still doubtful, when the tribunes of the seventh legion being informed of
the state of affairs on the left, came on the rear of the enemy
with their men. Not even then did a single Gaul give way,
but they were all surrounded and killed, and Camulogenus
among them. Those who had been left opposite to the camp
of Labienus, hearing the sound of battle, came to help their
countrymen, and occupied a hill; but they could not resist the

[1] "Parva manu Metiosedum versus missa." There is probably an error in "Metiosedum." See D'Anville, "Notice de la Gaule," art. Melodunum

impetuous attack of the Romans, and mingling with the fugitives, whom neither the forests nor the hills protected, they were cut off by the cavalry. Labienus returned to Agendicum, and then joined Caesar with all his force, but it is not said where Labienus joined Caesar[3].

The defection of the Aedui (c. 63) was the signal for a general rising of the Galli; and the Aedui, as Caesar's narrative seems to mean, sent commissioners in all directions and employed their influence and their money in stirring up the Galli. Their abandonment of the Romans exposed them to danger, but they hoped that the opportunity would be favourable for recovering their former authority and placing themselves at the head of the Gallic nations. The Aedui were in possession of the hostages whom Caesar had placed in their country, and they terrified the wavering Galli with the threat of massacring them. They invited Vercingetorix to visit them and deliberate on the plan of operations, but when he came, they claimed the general conduct of the war, and as the claim was resisted, a meeting of deputies from all Gallia was summoned to Bibracte. The meeting was large, the question was put to the vote of the assembly and Vercingetorix was unanimously elected commander of the united Gallic forces. The Remi, Lingones and Treviri were not present, for the Remi and Lingones were faithful to the Romans, and the Treviri, who were a long way off, were hard pressed by the Germans, which was the reason of their taking no part in the war on either side. The Aedui were greatly annoyed at losing the supremacy, and began to regret the favour of Caesar which they had enjoyed, but they did not venture now to desert the confederation, and Eporedorix and Viridumarus, those two ambitious young men unwillingly submitted to Vercingetorix. The Gallic commander-in-chief required hostages from the several states to be brought on a fixed day, and he commanded all the horsemen 15,000 in number to come immediately to Bibracte. He declared that he had sufficient infantry and did not intend to fight battles, but to employ his numerous cavalry in preventing the Romans

---

[3] This short campaign is well explained by the author of the "Histoire," and also previously by M. de Saulcy in his "Campagnes de Jules César" (pp. 3—61). Dion (40, c. 38) despatches this campaign in one sentence, which is unintelligible.

from getting food and forage: he recommended the Galli to destroy their own corn and burn their buildings, a loss which would be small compared with the certain recovery of their liberty. Next he required the Aedui and the Segusiani[1] who bordered on the Provincia to furnish ten thousand infantry and he sent eight hundred horsemen to join them. This force was placed under the command of a brother of Epordorix, who was ordered to attack the Allobroges. In another quarter Vercingetorix sent the Gabali and the bordering cantons of the Arverni to attack the Helvii, and the Ruteni and Cadurci to waste the country of the Volcae Arecomici, who occupied that part of the Provincia south of the Helvii, which extended along the west bank of the Rhone and corresponded nearly to the French departments of Hérault and Gard. At the same time Vercingetorix tried to gain the Allobroges by secret emissaries, for he hoped that they had not yet forgotten their last struggle against the Romans (vol. iii. 890). He promised money to the chiefs of the Allobroges, and the dominion over the whole Provincia. To meet this danger there were two and twenty cohorts, raised in the Provincia and under the command of L. Caesar, consul in B.C. 64, who was now serving as legatus under his kinsman C. Caesar. The Helvii without having received any orders fought a battle with the invaders, in which they were defeated with the loss of C. Valerius Donotaurus, the son of Caburus (B. G. i. 47), one of their chief men, and many others, and after the defeat they shut themselves up in their towns. The Allobroges placed numerous posts along the Rhone and carefully protected their territory against invasion. Seeing the superiority of the enemy in cavalry and that all the roads being closed he could get no help from the Provincia and Italy, Caesar sent over the Rhine to the German states which in past years he had reduced to submission, and got cavalry and light infantry who were trained to fight among the cavalry (B. G. i. 48). These men not being well mounted, Caesar took the horses of the military tribunes, of the Roman equites in the

[1] The Segusiani (B. G. i. 10) were north of the Rhone and in the angle between the Saône and Rhone; some of them were also west of the Saône.

army and of the Evocati*, and distributed them among the
Germans.

Labienus, as we have seen, returned to his camp at Agendicum, and then marching from Agendicum joined Caesar, who
had crossed the Loire, but it is impossible to determine in
the absence of all evidence where the two armies met. As
Caesar's object was to leave the territory of the Aedui, who
were in arms against him, and to reach the Provincia by the
safest road, he marched from the Loire towards the territory

---

* The Evocati were either Roman citizens or allies, horsemen or infantry,
who were called or invited (II. C. iii. 20), after their time of service was over,
to join some commander. They were in fact veterans, who volunteered for
fresh service.

The author of the "Histoire" has (p. 292) some remarks on the amount of
Caesar's forces at this time. In B.C. 58 Caesar had six legions, and in B.C. 57 he
raised two more in Italy (p. 44). In B.C. 54, the second expedition to Britain,
he took five legions with him and left three in Gallia under Labienus. But
after his return from Britain he enumerates eight legions and five cohorts
(B. G. v. 24, and p. 216), and of these legions one was a legion which he had
last raised north of the Po. This appears to be a legion which he has never
mentioned before. If he had lost no men in Britain, he would have had nine
complete legions to put into winter quarters in B.C. 54. A legion and five
cohorts were destroyed at Aduatuca (B. G. v. 37), and thus Caesar's eight
legions and a half legion were reduced to seven. In B.C. 53 he obtained three
more legions (B. G. vi. 1) from Italy, one of which named the first was sent to
Caesar by Cn. Pompeius (B. G. viii. 54): another was the fourteenth (B. G.
vi. 32). Thus his troops were raised to ten legions; but there was also a
"supplementum," which arrived from Italy in B.C. 52 (B. G. vii. 7, 57). After
the capture of Alesia Caesar mentions the winter quarters of only nine legions
(B. G. vii. 90), but we may assume that he had one with him at Bibracte.
These ten legions were the 1st, 6th, 7th, 8th, 9th, 10th, 11th, 12th, 13th,
14th, and again in B.C. 51, we find that he had ten legions (B. G. viii. 46) in
Gallia Transalpina. Caesar (viii. 24) sent Labienus into Gallia Togata with a
legion, which in some editions is named the twelfth and in other editions the
fifteenth. This is the legion mentioned in viii. 54. It appears that Caesar had
in B.C. 51 eleven legions (viii. 24, 46) after the capture of Uxellodunum, but
one of them was in North Italy. I cannot discover that he had eleven legions
in B.C. 52. The author of the "Histoire" (ii. 315) assigns two legions to M.
Antonius in his winter quarters after the capture of Alesia, and thus he makes
eleven legions even in B.C. 52; but I do not see the proof of this assertion.
Caesar's legions must have suffered in his campaigns and they were recruited,
but as already observed (p. 1) we do not know the average force of his legions,
and we cannot accept the French writer's estimate of them at 50,000 legionary
soldiers at the siege of Alesia. Caesar had also light-armed men, bowmen, and
slingers, cavalry Gallic, Spanish, and German, and a large body of camp-
servants.

of the Lingones, who were faithful to him, with the intention
as he tells us of passing along the borders of these people into
the country of the Sequani, in order to reach and to protect the
Provincia. Labienus may have marched south-east from Sens
to join Caesar. But in the mean time Vercingetorix, with
the infantry raised in the country of the Arverni and the
cavalry from all parts of Gallia, had followed Caesar, with the
intention of cutting off his retreat, and he planted his force
in three separate camps about ten miles from Caesar's camp.
As Caesar tells us the Gaul had changed his intention about
not fighting a battle, for he summoned the commanders of the
cavalry and told them that now there was an opportunity of
gaining a victory, for the enemy was retreating to the Provincia; but this would only give the Galli security for the present,
as the Romans would certainly return with a larger force.
Though we do not know what authority Caesar had for report-
ing the words of Vercingetorix, we may believe that the intentions which the Gallic chief is supposed to have imputed to
Caesar were his real intentions: he was only retreating in
order to return in greater force. Vercingetorix recommended
an attack on the Romans during their march when they were
encumbered with baggage, for he argued that if the infantry
attempted to protect their long train, they could not continue
the march; or if, as he rather expected, they abandoned the
baggage to save themselves, they would lose all that they had
and their honour too. As to the enemy's cavalry, they might
be sure that these horsemen would never venture to move one
step out of the column. To encourage his own cavalry, Vercingetorix promised that he would place his infantry in front
of the camps, to intimidate the Romans. The Gallic cavalry
responded to their general by crying out that every man must
take a solemn oath never to return home to children, parents
and wife unless he rode through the line of the enemy and rode
back again. The oath was taken, and after this Gallic brag,
which was characteristic of the nation, Vercingetorix prepared
for battle.

On the following day he divided his cavalry into three parts
and advanced to meet the Romans, who were coming from the
north in a long line, each legion followed by the baggage.

As soon as the Romans were in sight, a division of the enemy's
cavalry appeared on each flank, and a third division stopped
the Roman march in front. Caesar divided his cavalry also
into three parts, and ordered each part to move against the
enemy. The battle began at once on these several lines: the
legions halted and received the baggage among them. Wherever the Roman cavalry was hard pressed, Caesar ordered
some of the infantry to advance to support them, which movement checked the pursuit of the enemy and encouraged his
own cavalry. At last the German horsemen on Caesar's right
got possession of a hill, drove the enemy from it and pursued
the fugitives to a stream, on the opposite side of which Vercingetorix had placed himself with the Gallic infantry. Many
of the Gallic horsemen were killed in the pursuit, and the rest
fled in terror from the field. The slaughter was now general.
Three Aedui of the highest rank were captured and brought to
Caesar; Cotus, the rival of Convictolitanis, who commanded
the Aeduan cavalry; Cavarillus, who after the defection of
Litavicus commanded the infantry, and a man named Eporedorix, who commanded the Aedui against the Sequani before
Caesar's arrival in Gallia. All his cavalry being routed, Vercingetorix, who had placed his infantry in front of his camps,
led them off towards Alesia, a town of the Mandubii, without
waiting for his baggage, which he ordered to be taken immediately from the camps and to follow him. Caesar placed his
own baggage on the nearest hill, and leaving two legions to
look after it followed the enemy as long as it was daylight,
killed about three thousand of those in the rear, and on the
next[4] day reached Alesia. We must conclude that the

[4] "Altero die" is explained by the author of the "Histoire" (iL 209) to be
"le surlendemain," not "le lendemain." In a note (p. 216) he contends that
"altero die," employed with reference to any event, signifies the second day
which follows that of the event mentioned. In the passages which he cites,
"alter" certainly means the "second," and so he thinks that he has proved
what he undertakes to prove. But in all these passages there is a word which
expresses directly or indirectly "first," and so "alter" of course means
"second." In this passage "first" is implied in the narrative of the battle
and "altero" is the next to the "first." Here he assumes the site of the
battle to be ascertained, and then the distance from the field to Alesia confirms
his interpretation of "altero die;" and again, having fixed this meaning of
"altero die," he thus confirms his conjecture about the site of the battle-field.

enemy's baggage did not follow in the line of the flying Galli, for it would have been directly in the way of Caesar, who says nothing about it. If the baggage went by a circuitous road, it could never have joined Vercingetorix, for Caesar would be at Alesia long before the Gallic baggage. It is a just conclusion that the Gallic commander lost all that he had, and that his men escaped only with their lives. As soon as Caesar arrived at Alesia, in which the enemy had taken refuge, he saw that it could only be taken by blockade, and he encouraged his men to prepare for a difficult siege (c. 68).

The site of Alesia is certain. It is Alise-Sainte-Reine on Mont Auxois in the department of the Côte-d'Or near Flavigny. If a man will approach Alise from the railway-station Les Laumes on the line from Paris to Dijon, and if he has read Caesar's description, he will recognize the place as soon as he sees it. The site of Alesia determines within certain limits the battle-field in which Vercingetorix was defeated. The author of the "Histoire" follows the opinion of M. H. Delay of Langres, who supposes the river mentioned in Caesar to be the Vingeanne, which joins the right bank of the Saône a little higher up than Pontailler, and that the battle was fought in the angle formed by the junction of a small stream named the Badin with the Vingeanne [1]. If the site of this battle-field is truly determined, it is certain that Caesar could not reach Alise on the day after the battle, for the field is 65 kilomètres from Alise, and the intervening country is hilly. If the Romans pursued the enemy on the day of battle 15 kilomètres [2], there would be a distance of 50 kilomètres to march on the two following days before arriving at Alise, or 25 kilomètres each day, rather more than 15½ miles. Consequently, if the author is mistaken in his interpretation of "altero die," and he certainly is, he must by the force of his own argument look for some other site of this battle-field.

The town of Alesia, says Caesar, was on the summit of a hill, which was so high that the place could only be taken by blockade. Two streams on opposite sides flowed along the base of the hill. In front of the town there was a level tract

---

[1] "Hist. de César," ii. p. 296, note, and Planche, 24.
[2] "Hist. de César," ii. p. 299, note.

about three miles wide: on all other sides the town was surrounded by hills of about the same height as the hill of Alesia, and separated from it by a moderate interval. This description is correct [*]. Alesia was on the plateau of Mont Auxois, on the west slope of which are now the village and hospital of Alise. This isolated hill is about 540 feet above the valleys which surround it. The two streams are the Ose and Oserain, the Oserain on the south side of Mont Auxois, and the Ose on the north side. Both of them join the Brenne, which runs from south to north through the Plaine des Laumes. This plain, the width of which is three Roman miles or about 14,400 feet, is west of Mont Auxois and immediately below it. On all other sides Mont Auxois is surrounded by flat-topped hills covered with short grass, and about the same height as Mont Auxois. On the north-west is Réa, on the north-east is Bussy, on the south-east Pennevelle, and on the south the hill of Flavigny; in a depression and near the Oserain is the town of Flavigny. The length from east to west of the plateau of Mont Auxois, which was occupied by the Gallic town is near 7000 feet, and the greatest width is about 2600 feet. The narrowest part is the west end and it is a little higher than the east end of the plateau. The summit is generally level, and the sides of the hill immediately below the summit are steep and abrupt, like some other hills to the east on the road to Dijon. At the east end of the plateau is a small spring, the water of which is now conveyed to supply the hospital at the west end of the hill. It is stated ("Histoire de César", ii. 300) that there are two abundant springs at the west end of the plateau near the summit [1]. All the eastern part of the hill beneath the town wall and between the two rivers was occupied by the Gallic troops, who were protected by a ditch and a wall of dry stones six feet high. A great quantity of

[*] "Hist. de César," Planche, 23.

[1] It is also said that there are traces of many wells on the plateau. Such wells might be made in the lower parts of the summit. "The old Gallic wall on the plateau of Mont Auxois has been laid bare in places all along the escarpments; from which we must conclude that the town occupied all the plateau. A remarkable specimen of this wall is visible at the point of Mont Auxois, near the spot where the statue of Vercingetorix has recently been placed."—("Hist. de César," ii. 323.)

loose fragments of rock lie on the slopes of the hill; and there are some on the east slope where Vercingetorix constructed his dry stone wall. The rest may have been using in building the village of Alise. Caesar formed camps in convenient positions and made twenty-three castella (redoutes), in which during the day men were posted to prevent any sudden sally of the enemy, and they were occupied in the night by the men on watch. These redoutes were placed at intervals between the camps. The position of the camps and the redoutes would determine the line of investment, which was eleven Roman miles. (Compare the blockade of Numantia, vol. i. p. 94; and " Histoire de César," Pl. 25.)

As soon as the works were commenced, there was a fierce cavalry fight in the plain of Les Laumes. Vercingetorix was at the east end of the plateau of Alesia, and his cavalry would advance to the plain, where alone there is room for a cavalry fight. The Gallic cavalry would leave their fortified post under the east end of the plateau and move along a secondary and lower plateau on the south side of the mountain by the site of the modern Alise and the hospital at the west end of the plateau, which they could do easily and without risk of being attacked, for there is a descent by this lower plateau to the bed of the Oserain and the plain. Caesar's cavalry being hard pressed in the fight, he sent the German cavalry to support them, and placed his legions in front of the camps to prevent any sally of the enemy's infantry. The Roman cavalry encouraged by the support of the legions put the enemy to flight, who escaped by the way by which they came, but being embarrassed by their own numbers they crowded in the narrow openings which were left in the stone wall which formed their camp at the east end. The Germans pursued them up to the defences and made a great slaughter: some of the Galli leaving their horses attempted to cross the ditch and climb the wall. At this moment Caesar ordered the legions who were in front of the camps to advance a little, a movement which caused alarm within the enemy's lines. The Galli thought that the Romans were coming to attack them; there was a cry to arms, and some of the terrified men broke into Alesia, upon which Vercingetorix ordered the town gates to be closed for fear that the Gallic camp should be deserted. The Germans retired after killing many men and taking many horses.

Before the Roman works were completed Vercingetorix determined to send away all his cavalry by night. On taking leave of them he recommended the men to visit their several states and to bring together all who were able to bear arms: he entreated them to remember his services and not to let him fall into the hands of the Romans; if they neglected what he said, they would cause the loss of eighty thousand[1] picked men and himself too; after examination he had ascertained that he had barely provisions for thirty days, but by great care he might be able to make them last a little longer. With these instructions he sent off the cavalry silently during the second watch of the night; and they made their escape by a part where the Roman line of investment allowed a passage. Vercingetorix now ordered under pain of death all the grain that was in Alesia to be brought to him. He took the cattle, of which a great quantity had been driven into the town by the Mandubii, and distributed the beasts among his men[2]. He gave out the grain in small quantities and at short intervals: and he received into the town all the troops which he had originally placed outside at the east end of Mont Auxois. With these preparations he waited for the arrival of aid from the Galli.

As soon as this was communicated to Caesar by deserters and prisoners, he began his contravallation. He first made a ditch twenty feet wide with perpendicular sides, for the purpose of preventing the extensive lines, which he was going to form, from being suddenly attacked during the night and the workers in the daytime from being annoyed with the enemy's missiles. The author of the "Histoire" says that Caesar began by digging in the Plaine des Laumes a ditch twenty feet wide, and he supposes, as his plan shows, that this great ditch was dug in no other part, though this interpretation perhaps con-

---

[1] So it is in Caesar's text, but the number may be incorrect. It is not credible that 80,000 men shut themselves up in Alesia.

[2] These beasts would be fed on the high grounds round Alesia which do not seem to have been disturbed by the plough. The grass is short like that on the Sussex downs.

tradicts the Latin text, for Caesar says that he placed all his line of contrevallation at the distance of four hundred feet from this ditch. He then made two other ditches fifteen feet wide, and of the same depth⁴, and he filled the inner ditch in the level and low parts with water from a stream. Behind these ditches he constructed a rampart and palisade together twelve feet high, and he added to the palisade a crenelated parapet (loricam pinnasque). At the parts where the breastwork formed by the vallum and lorica was attached to the rampart, he placed large forked branches projecting horizontally, called "cervi," "stags," to check the attack of the enemy; and along the whole line of contrevallation he built towers at intervals of eighty feet. The Romans were compelled to go a great distance from the camps to get timber and corn, and at the same time to work at the lines with diminished numbers; and sometimes the Galli attacked the works by vigorous sallies from the town at several gates. Caesar accordingly resolved to make additions to his works that the lines might be defended by a smaller number of men. For this purpose he took trunks of trees or very strong branches, the extremities of which were stripped of bark, and pointed. The thick ends being then planted in trenches five feet deep and securely fixed, the pointed branches rose above the ground⁵.

⁴ The author of the "Histoire" (ii. 319) supposes that in cc. 72, 73 Caesar is describing the works in the Plaine des Laumes. "The traces of the two ditches exist in all the extent of the plain from one river to the other."—"The depth of the two ditches is the same, but it is not fifteen feet, as the translators have incorrectly taken it. To dig a ditch fifteen feet deep is so great a work, considering that it requires two stages of workers, that perhaps it has never been executed as a temporary fortification. Besides, the result of the excavations allows no doubt about the matter: the two ditches are only from eight to nine feet deep each." Caesar's text says that the ditches were fifteen feet wide, "and of the same depth;" which is ambiguous. It may mean that one ditch was the same depth as the other; and the real depth is not stated. The writer in the "Revue des Deux Mondes" (hereafter referred to) supposes the two ditches to be each fifteen feet deep. But how would the Romans make a ditch fifteen feet deep, and what would be the use of so deep a ditch?

⁵ These trenches were continuous (perpetuae), but it is not said how many there were, and it seems probable that they were only made in certain parts. As the fossae were "quinos pedes altae," we must conclude that there were more than one fossa. From the words "quini erant ordines" the author of the "Histoire" seems to have concluded that there were five trenches, and so he has

There were five of these rows connected with one another and interlaced, so that those who ventured among them came on the sharp points of the branches. Caesar's men named these things "cippi." In front of these cippi there were dug holes three feet deep, growing narrower from top to bottom, and so placed with respect to one another as to form what the Romans called a quincunx or V. In these holes[6] were planted smooth stakes, as thick as a man's thigh, pointed at the top which was hardened by fire, and rising four fingers' breadth above the level of the ground. Each stake was secured in its place by a foot deep of earth trampled down: the remainder of the hole was covered with brushwood for the purpose of hiding the snare. There were eight rows of these holes, and each row was three feet distant from the row on each side of it. The soldiers called each hole with its stake a lily from the resemblance to that flower. Still in front of these lilies, pieces of wood a foot long with iron hooks fastened to them were buried in the earth. They were planted all over the ground at small distances. These caltrops were named stimuli, or goads[7].

Finally the line of circumvallation was formed for the purpose of protecting the Romans against external attacks (c. 74). This line, which was fourteen Roman miles in circuit, enclosed all the works, and the camps and castella. It was carried along the most level parts which the nature of the ground allowed the Romans to choose; not only the level parts in the valleys, but the level parts on the high lands which surround Alise on three sides. The line of circumvallation was constructed like the line of contrevallation, but turned in the contrary direction.

represented them in the plan (Planche 27). I am not certain about the meaning of "quini ordines." The author of the "Histoire" (p. 303) reads "dolabratis" instead of "delibratis."

[6] "In the Plains des Laumes close to the outer border of the ditch of circonvallation there have been counted more than fifty of these holes (trous de loup) in five rows. Others have been opened on the heights; they were formed in the rock and their state of preservation is such that they seem to have been just made. All these holes are three feet deep, two feet in diameter at the top, and a little less than one foot at the bottom" ("Hist. de César," ii. 322).

[7] There have been found in the excavations at Alise five stimuli ("Hist. de César," ii. 304, Planche 27).

That the men might not be compelled to leave the camps to get forage and food, Caesar gave orders that all the army should bring in a supply for thirty days. The Romans would get water from the rivers. It is said that there is a good source of water on the hill named Pennevelle, which is connected with the east end of Alesia by a small neck of land, which separates the basins of the two rivers. This neck is the only part by which the hill of Alesia is connected with the surrounding heights, and it is the only place where the plateau is easily accessible; a fact which explains why Vercingetorix occupied it*.

These prodigious works were made by the continuous labour of many thousand men for several weeks, and they are evidence of the daring genius of the Roman commander, of the endurance of the men and the ability of the engineers. The time occupied in these works was more than thirty days (c. 77). The difficulty of finding food for so large a body of men in an enemy's country must have been great, and we know that the army suffered privations (B. C. iii. 47).

While Caesar was thus employed, the Gallic states called a meeting of their chiefs in which it was determined not to summon all the men who were able to bear arms, as Vercingetorix advised, but to require certain contingents from the several states. They were afraid, if they summoned all the Galli, that they would not be able to maintain discipline in so large and mixed a multitude nor to supply them with food. Caesar names the several states from which troops were demanded, and the number of men required from them. It is not his fashion to say how he got his information. The list of names comprehends the greatest part of the Gallic states, but it certainly contains errors in the names, and probably in the numbers. The Lingones, Treviri, and Remi are not in the list. The Bellovaci, who were asked to send ten thousand men, refused; they said that they would determine for themselves whether they should make war on the Romans, and they would not submit to any orders. However at the request of their friend Comm they sent two thousand. Comm was the man

---

* The people name a spot on the south slope of Pennevelle " La cuisine de César."

who had been useful to Caesar in Britain (B. G. iv. 21), and in return for his services Caesar had freed the Atrebates, his countrymen, from all demands, restored them to independence and made the Morini dependent on them. In fact the Atrebates were placed in the condition of a free community (libera civitas) in Roman political language; and by Caesar's own act, as it seems. But such was the passion of the Galli for the recovery of their liberty and warlike reputation, that benefits and friendship were forgotten, and all of them eagerly engaged in the war. The force which was actually collected was eight thousand horse and about 240,000 foot. The troops were reviewed and numbered in the territory of the Aedui, and officers were appointed. The general command was given to Comm, Virdumarus, and Eporedorix the Aedui, and to Vergasillaunus, a cousin of Vercingetorix. But commissioners were selected from the different states to accompany the army and direct or watch these commanders; such commissioners as the French Convention used to send to the republican armies to watch the generals and report. The confederate forces marched to Alesia full of confidence. They believed that the bare sight of such an army would terrify the Romans, and still more the consideration that they were exposed to attack from the Galli in Alesia on one side and from such a mighty force on the outside at the same time.

The day was now passed when the besieged in Alesia expected the aid of the Galli. The provisions were consumed, they did not know what was passing in the country of the Aedui, and they were in despair. The leaders met to deliberate. Some advised a surrender, others proposed to make a sally while they had still strength left. Critognatus an Arvernian of high birth and great influence made a strange and abominable speech, as Caesar names it. He treated with contempt the proposal to surrender: he would only argue with those who advised a sally, but he said it was weakness not to be able to endure hunger for a short time, and it was easier to find men ready to expose themselves to death than to endure pain. They must not think of themselves only: they must think of the Galli whom they had summoned to their aid; and what courage could their allies have, if they came and found eighty thousand soldiers massacred in one spot instead of being ready to help them against the Romans? They must not doubt about the fidelity of their friends because they had not come at the time fixed; and they ought to consider the activity of the Romans, who were working day and night on their external lines, as evidence that they expected the arrival of the Gallic army. What then did he recommend? Why, to follow the example of their ancestors who, when the Cimbri and Teutones invaded the country and shut them up in the towns, supported life by eating those who were too young or too old to fight, and refused to surrender (vol. ii. p. 47). If they had not such an example to follow, they ought for the sake of liberty to establish such a glorious precedent and to transmit it to posterity.

When all the opinions had been given, it was agreed that those who from feeble health or by reason of their age were useless must leave the town: they ought to endure every thing before accepting the desperate proposal of Critognatus, though even that must be adopted, if circumstances made it necessary, in preference to surrendering or accepting terms of peace. Accordingly the Mandubii, who had received the Galli in their town, were compelled to leave it with their wives and children. They came up to the Roman lines and earnestly entreated to be taken as slaves, and fed; but Caesar placed men along the rampart with orders not to receive them. The necessary conclusion is that these unfortunate people died of hunger in the sight of both armies[b]. When Comm and the other generals arrived, they occupied a hill not more than a mile from the Roman lines. On the following day they brought out the cavalry and filled with it the Plaine des Laumes. The infantry was posted at a small distance from the plain on higher ground. The hill which the enemy occupied was Mussy-la-Fosse on the south-west side of the Plaine

---

[b] Dion (40, c. 40) states this as a fact. Worse things were done at the siege of Pistoia by the Florentines in 1800. The besieged turned the poor and most of the women and children out of the town, who coming into the camp of the besiegers were shamefully treated, and many of them being first mutilated were carried back to the foot of the town walls, where they died. At the siege of Mainz in the Revolutionary war the French behaved better to those whom they had turned out.—Michelet, "Hist. de la Révol. Française," vi. 249.

des Laumes, and separated from Mont Auxois by the river Ibrance[1]. The west end of the plateau of Alesia commands a view of the plain and the heights which border it. On the appearance of their countrymen who had come to relieve them, the besieged crowded together, congratulated one another, and full of joy came out of the town, filled up the nearest ditch with earth and fascines and made ready for a desperate sally. Caesar placed all his forces on the two opposite lines of his fortifications that, if the occasion should arise, every man might know and defend his position; and he ordered the cavalry to quit their camps and begin the battle. All the camps (c. 80) which occupied the heights round Alesia commanded a view of the Plaine des Laumes, and the Roman soldiers looked on and waited with anxiety for the result of the fight. The Galli had intermingled bowmen and light-armed troops among their cavalry to support the horsemen and to check the Romans, many of whom were wounded by the enemy's missiles coming unexpectedly on them and were compelled to retire from the field. When it was plain that the Galli had the advantage and the Roman cavalry was hard pressed, both the men shut in by Caesar's lines and the relieving army set up loud shouts. The struggle was in the presence of both armies: no act of courage nor of cowardice could pass unnoticed; the combatants on both sides were animated by the desire of glory and the fear of shame. The battle had raged from midday nearly to sunset and the victory was still doubtful, when the German cavalry forming in close masses and falling on one part of the enemy routed them and killed the bowmen. Caesar's own cavalry followed the rest of the Galli up to their camp without giving them time to rally. The besieged who had come out of Alesia retired within the town almost in despair.

After resting one day and preparing a great number of fascines, ladders, and poles with hooks at the end, the Galli of the relieving army silently left the camp at midnight and approached the Roman lines in the Plaine des Laumes. Suddenly raising a shout, which was intended to be a signal to

---

[1] "Hist. de César," Planche 25.

the besieged, they began to throw their fascines into the ditch, to drive the Romans from the rampart with slings, arrows, and stones, and to make all the preparations for an assault. At the same time Vercingetorix hearing the shouts gave the signal to his men by trumpet, and led them out of the town. The Romans manned the lines and took the places already assigned to them. With slings, stones, stakes of wood previously placed on the lines, and balls of lead, they threw the assailants into confusion. Numerous missiles were also discharged from the engines. As it was dark, many wounds were received on both sides. M. Antonius, who was quaestor in this year, and C. Trebonius, legati under Caesar, had been appointed to defend this part of the fortifications, and whenever they knew that the Romans were hard pressed in any place, they sent up men from the remoter forts to support them. So long as the Galli remained at some distance from the lines, they had the advantage by the multitude of their missiles, but when they came nearer, they either stepped on the caltrops or fell into the holes (scrobes) where they were impaled, or were transfixed by the pikes thrown from the rampart and the towers. Many were wounded on both sides, but the lines were not forced in any part, and when the day was dawning, the enemy retired for fear of being attacked on the flanks by a sally of the Romans from the camps on the higher grounds. These were the camps on Mont Réa to the north-west, and the hill of Flavigny south of Mont Auxois. The besieged spent too much time in bringing out the material that was prepared for the attack on the lines and in filling up the nearest ditch, and hearing of the retreat of their friends before they had reached the Roman lines, they retired to the town.

Twice had the Galli been repelled with great loss. From the inhabitants of the country who were well acquainted with the localities, they now got information about the positions and defences of the camps which were placed on the higher grounds. On the north side of Alesia there was the hill of Réa, which was so large that the Romans had not been enabled to enclose it within their lines, and they had been compelled to plant the camp which they made there in a disadvantageous position and on ground which had a gentle downward slope.

The camp was placed on the south-east side of Réa near the Ose. East of Mont Réa and separated from it by the small valley of the Rabutin is the Montagne de Bussy. The camp on Mont Réa was occupied by the legati C. Antistius Reginus and C. Caninius Rebilus with two legions. Having sent scouts to examine the position of this camp, the generals of the relieving army selected out of all the troops 60,000 of the best men, and keeping their plans secret they gave orders that the camp on Réa should be attacked at midday. Vergasillaunus being appointed to command this force left the Gallic camp during the first watch, and having nearly accomplished his march by daybreak, he concealed his troops on the north side of Mont Réa and allowed them to take rest. About midday he led his men against the camp on Mont Réa, and at the same time the enemy's cavalry began to approach the lines in the Plaine des Laumes and the rest of the Gallic army showed themselves in front of their camp. From the plateau of Alesia Vercingetorix saw these movements, and came down with his men. He brought with him poles hooked at the end, strong covered sheds (musculi) to protect the men who should attempt to destroy the enemy's breastworks, and whatever else he had got ready to assist in breaking through the lines. The battle began all round, and the greatest efforts of the enemy were directed against the weakest parts. Caesar's forces being thus engaged at all points were hardly able to resist the numerous assailants; and as both the outer and inner lines were attacked at the same time, the Romans on each line had the enemy in front and the tumult of battle in the rear, and they knew that their safety depended not only on themselves but on those who were fighting behind them. This circumstance tended to discourage the Romans, for, as Caesar observes, that which is unseen generally disturbs us most. Caesar chose a convenient position from which he could see what was going on in all directions, and wherever his men were hard pressed, he sent aid. He had placed himself on the north-west side of the hill of Flavigny, from which he could see the whole plain and the camp on Mont Réa. Both the Galli and the Romans knew that the time for the final struggle was come. If the Galli did not break through the Roman lines, they had no hope left; and if the Romans successfully resisted, they expected to see the end of their toils. The great struggle was at the lines on Mont Réa, to which Vergasillaunus had led his men, and the enemy who assailed these lines had the advantage of higher ground. "A small inclination downwards," says Caesar, "has a great effect;" a military maxim which is exemplified in the warfare of the Romans and their selection of battle-fields. Some of the Galli hurled their missiles within the Roman lines, others formed the tortoise (p. 49) and approached close to the rampart, and those who were exhausted were relieved by fresh men. The Galli threw earth and other materials into the ditch, and thus at the same time they enabled the men to climb upwards and buried the Roman "lilies" and "cippi." The Romans began to fall short of missiles and to be exhausted. At this moment Caesar sent Labienus with six cohorts to support the troops on Mont Réa, and gave him orders to sally out on the enemy, if he should be unable to resist them; but not to do so, unless it was necessary. Labienus, it is conjectured, brought his six cohorts from the camp on the Montagne de Bussy. Caesar visited the combatants on other parts of the line, and encouraged them to persevere in the hope of a victory which would repay them for all their labours. The besieged, who now despaired of breaking through the strong lines in the Plaine des Laumes, attempted to scale the steep sides of the hill of Flavigny, where Caesar stood, and hither they brought all their means of attack. They drove the Romans from their towers by a shower of missiles, filled up the ditch with earth and fascines, and tore down the vallum and parapet with their hooked poles. Caesar at first sent young Brutus, as he names him (B. G. iii. 11 and in another passage) with six cohorts, then the legatus C. Fabius with seven other cohorts, and finally, as the struggle became desperate, he himself brought fresh men to oppose the assailants. The enemy being repulsed, Caesar hurried towards the camp on Réa to which he had sent Labienus. He took four cohorts from the nearest fort (castellum), and ordered part of the cavalry to follow him and part to go round the external lines and attack the enemy on the rear. Labienus finding that neither the rampart nor the ditch could stop the enemy, got together thirty-nine cohorts which he was fortunately able to draw from the nearest forts, and sent a message to inform Caesar of his intention to sally out on the enemy. Conspicuous by the scarlet cloak which he wore in battle, the man whose presence brought victory hurried between the lines down the slopes of the hill of Flavigny and across the Plaine des Laumes to the camp on Réa, followed by his cavalry and cohorts. The decisive struggle was begun, for the sally had been made. The Galli in Alesia and the Gallic army outside raise a shout, which is answered by the Romans along the rampart and the lines. Caesar is impatient to finish the contest and his narrative, which becomes more rapid and abrupt. "The Romans drop their pila and use the sword. All at once the cavalry appear on the enemy's rear: other cohorts come up: the enemy turn their backs: the cavalry meet the fugitives: the slaughter is great." Sedulius, the commander of the Lemovices was killed: Vergasillaunus was taken prisoner in the flight: seventy-four military standards were brought to Caesar. Few out of so great a number escaped to the Gallic camp. The men in Alesia seeing the massacre and flight of the relieving army withdrew in despair from the Roman lines. As soon as this was known in the Gallic camp, they took to flight, and if the Roman soldiers had not been exhausted by their labours through the day, it would have been possible to destroy all the enemy. Immediately after midnight the cavalry being sent in pursuit overtook the rear, made many prisoners and killed a great number. The rest fled to their several homes.

This last battle was fought on the north side of Mont Auxois in the valley between Réa and Bussy, between the Ose and the village of Grésigny. The day after Vercingetorix (c. 89) called a meeting, in which he said that he had not begun the war for his own interests, but for the liberty of all, and as they must yield to fortune, he gave himself up to them either to satisfy the Romans by putting him to death or by surrendering him alive. Caesar being informed of this proposal by commissioners ordered the arms to be given up and the chiefs to be brought forward. He was seated before one of the camps within the entrenchments, when the chiefs appeared before him, and Vercingetorix was surrendered. All the arms of the

Galli were laid down. The prisoners who were of the nation of the Aedui and the Arverni were excepted from the fate of the rest, in the hope that Caesar might thus bring back these states to the Roman alliance. The rest of the prisoners were distributed among the army at the rate of one prisoner to a soldier, as booty or prize-money. The soldier would get the value of his man by selling him to the dealers who followed the camp.

The surrender of Vercingetorix requires no embellishment; but Plutarch (Caesar, c. 27) cannot let such an opportunity pass without decorating the simple and affecting story, and we cannot tell whether he had any authority for what he wrote. He certainly did not find it in Caesar. Dion Cassius (40, c. 41), who wrote much later than Plutarch, has also a romantic description of the surrender. He says that Vercingetorix, trusting to his former friendship with Caesar and hoping for pardon, suddenly appeared before the proconsul, fell on his knees and clasped his hands as a suppliant. Caesar's narrative rather leads to the conclusion that Vercingetorix was made of sterner stuff. Whether he humbled himself or not, he did not move the compassion of the Roman, who kept him in chains for six years, when he appeared in Caesar's four days' triumph (B.C. 46) and was then put to death.

The capture of Alesia was a great feat of arms, and the consequences were great. Gallia never recovered from the blow. In this blockade Caesar displayed his genius and the fertility of his resources. His description of the siege is nearly free from all difficulty even now. His veracity "is justified by the unerring evidence of the localities, and those who have ignorantly found fault with the Commentaries of this incomparable writer, may learn a lesson of modesty and self-distrust from the siege of Alesia⁸."

[8] There is a long and valuable essay in the "Revue des Deux Mondes," Mai, 1858, on the siege of Alesia. At the head of this essay there is a list of eight recent works on the site of Alesia. The narrative of the siege in the "Histoire de César" (ii. pp. 298—315) is well written and has been useful to me; but I have deviated very little here from what I wrote in my second edition of the Commentaries (1860, p. 417). The maps and plans which accompany the "Histoire de César" are very valuable; and the work contains an account of the excavations made at Alise and of the objects which were found (ii. p. 316—323). There

Caesar now entered the country of the Aedui, who returned to their former alliance. Commissioners were also sent to Caesar from the Arverni, who professed their readiness to obey his orders. He required from them a large number of hostages. About twenty thousand prisoners were restored to the Aedui and Arverni. The legions were placed in winter quarters. T. Labienus was sent with two legions and cavalry to the Sequani; and M. Sempronius Rutilus was placed under his orders. C. Fabius and L. Minucius Basilus were placed among the Remi, with two legions to protect them against their neighbours the Bellovaci. C. Antistius Reginus was sent among the Ambivareti[5], T. Sextius among the Bituriges, and C. Caninius Rebilus among the Ruteni, each with a legion. Q. Tullius Cicero was placed at Cabillonum (Chalon) and P. Sulpicius at Matisco (Mâcon), both of which places were in the country of the Aedui on the Saône, for the purpose of looking after supplies; and each commander had a legion (B. G. viii. 4). Caesar fixed his quarters at Bibracte (Autun) in the territory of the Aedui, and not far from Chalon and

---

were discovered in the ditches of the camp under Mont Réa, and perhaps in other places, 619 coins, some Roman and others Gallic (Appendice C. p. 535). All the Roman coins belong to the Republican period, and the most recent of them to the year 54 B.C. Consequently all these Roman coins were struck before the siege of Alesia in B.C. 52. The Gallic coins belong to twenty-four different states or peoples. Of 487 Gallic coins 103 belong to the Arverni. One of them has the name VERCINGETORIXS. Sixty-one of the Arvernian pieces bear the name Epasnactus, for it is assumed that the EPAD of the coins represents the Epasnactus of B. G. viii. 44. All these coins have pure Gallic types; but there are coins of Epasnactus, perhaps the same man, of a Romanized type, and therefore of a date subsequent to his surrender to the Romans.

The people of Allise find coins and various articles by grubbing on the plateau. The coins found there, as far as I have seen them, belong to the Imperial period, and seem to prove that there was then a town there. A fine gold medal of Nero has been dug up, a steelyard, keys, and various other things.

Some French writers think that they have discovered the site of Alesia in a place named Alaise east of the Saône. The "Revue des Deux Mondes" contains a plan of Allise and also of Alaise, and those who are curious may compare them.

[5] The Ambivareti, if that is the true form of the name, were within or on the borders of the Aedui, west of Bibracte and east of the Loire. They were clients or dependents of the Aedui.

Mâcon. But he has only mentioned the quarters of nine legions, and he does not say what force he had at Bibracte. If he had a legion there, the ten legions will be accounted for. When Caesar's despatches reached Rome, a thanksgiving for twenty days was proclaimed.

CHAPTER XX.

MILO AND CLODIUS.

B.C. 52.

At the beginning of B.C. 52 Rome was without the superior magistrates (p. 287). Before the end of January an event happened which gave a new turn to affairs. The chief authority for this chapter is the Argumentum of Asconius to Cicero's oration for Milo, and the oration itself; and the chief authorities of Asconius were Cicero's oration and the Acta.

On the 10th of January in the morning Cicero and P. Clodius went to witness the will of the architect Cyrus, who was dying, and had named Cicero and Clodius his "heredes" or testamentary successors (Cic. Pro Milone, c. 18). Clodius then left Rome for Aricia on the Appian road, where he had some business to transact with the Decuriones or town-council, and from Aricia he turned aside to his Alban villa, with the intention, it was said, of staying there on the twentieth; but in the afternoon of that day, on the news arriving of the death of Cyrus, he set out for Rome. On the twentieth Milo left Rome to visit his native town Lanuvium, where he held the office of dictator, and to assist at the appointment of a priest of Juno. Clodius and Milo met on the road at the ninth hour near Bovillae and near a chapel dedicated to the Bona Dea, whose mysteries Clodius had formerly violated. Milo was in a carriage with his wife Fausta, the daughter of the Dictator Sulla, followed by a great number of slaves and some gladiators, two of whom were noted fighters. Clodius was on horseback, accompanied by about thirty slaves, armed with swords, as it was the fashion for men who were travelling, and by a few friends.

The meeting appears to have been accidental. The men of Milo who brought up the rear of his train began a quarrel with the other party, and when Clodius turned round on hearing the noise he was pierced through the shoulder by Milo's gladiator Birria. More of Milo's men now joined in the fray, and Clodius was carried by his slaves into an inn at Bovillae. Milo seeing what had happened ordered the house to be broken open, and Clodius was dragged out and despatched with numerous wounds. As it is probable, perhaps certain, that Milo had no intention of seeking a quarrel with Clodius when they met, it seems strange that after his enemy was wounded and had taken shelter in the inn, he should proceed to such extremities. Asconius says, and Appian and Dion, either following him or some other authority, wrote nearly to the same effect, that Milo thought that he ran still greater risk if Clodius was allowed to live after he was wounded, and that if Clodius was killed, he would have this consolation at least, even if he was punished for his enemy's death. Cicero, whose statements however (Pro Milone, c. 10) may always be doubted, says that Clodius' men attacked Milo and killed his coachman, and that in the fray which followed Milo's slaves killed Clodius without any command from Milo and without his knowledge. As Milo's men were the stronger party, they only did, as Cicero says, what every man under like circumstances would wish his slaves to do. Eleven of Clodius' men were left dead on the road with the body of their master. Milo went on his way to Lanuvium.

A senator Sextus Tedius, who happened to be returning to the city, picked up the corpse of Clodius and carried it to Rome in his "lectica" before the first hour of the evening was passed. The corpse was placed in the hall of Clodius' house, where it was surrounded by a great number of persons of the common sort and slaves. His wife Fulvia with passionate lamentations pointed out to the crowd the wounds on the body of her husband. Early the following morning there was again a great concourse of people about the house of Clodius, and among them T. Munatius Plancus, and Q. Pompeius Rufus a grandson of the Dictator Sulla, both of them tribunes. In their presence the furious crowd carried the body of Clodius uncovered to the Forum and placed it on the Rostra that all

Rome might see the wounds. The two tribunes, who were opposed to Milo's candidature for the consulship addressed the people, and to such effect that led by Sextus Clodius they carried the body into the Curia Hostilia, where they made a funeral pile of benches, tribunalia or wooden seats, where magistrates used to sit, tables, and books perhaps taken from the booksellers' stalls, and set fire to the heap. The Curia was burnt; and the Porcia Basilica, which was built by Cato the Censor, and stood close to the Curia, was also destroyed by the flames.

M. Lepidus was now appointed Interrex. It was not the usage for the first Interrex to hold the Comitia; and, when the partisans of Hypsaeus and Scipio urged Lepidus to proceed to an election and he refused, they blockaded his house during his five days of office, broke in the door, threw down the ancestral busts, destroyed his wife's bed and the looms, which according to antient usage were in the hall. Then came Milo's men also calling out for the election, and the rabble of Hypsaeus and Scipio turning from the house of Lepidus came to blows with them. An attack was also made on Milo's house, but it was repulsed. The rabble now seized the fasces[1] and after offering the consular office to Hypsaeus and Scipio they went to the gardens of Pompeius to proclaim him consul or dictator.

The indignation of the citizens was roused more by the burning of the Curia than by the death of Clodius, and Milo encouraged by this circumstance returned to Rome on the evening of the day on which the Curia was burnt. But as he returned so soon, it is more probable that he came back to look after his election, for if he secured the consulship, he would be safe against his enemies for a year at least. Cicero (Pro Milone, c. 23), who declares that Milo entered the Forum while the Curia was still blazing, urges the fact as an argument of the man's confidence in his innocence. Milo, who was protected by a band of slaves and men from the country, resumed his canvas and distributed money among the electors. A friendly

---

[1] "Fasces ex lecto Libitinae raptos," Asconius says, but I have not been able to ascertain the meaning of the passage. We might make a guess.

tribune, M. Caelius, in a few days gave him an opportunity of addressing the people, and both Caelius and Milo endeavoured to convince the assembly that Clodius had laid an ambuscade; and this was the defence which Cicero afterwards adopted. While Milo was still speaking the other party armed made an attack. Caelius and Milo escaped in the disguise of slaves, but many of their followers were massacred, and not only Milo's friends, but any man better dressed than usual who came in the rioters' way. Under the pretext of looking for Milo's partisans they broke into houses, but their real object was plunder. For several days Rome was like a city taken by storm (Appian, B. C. ii. 22).

The Interreges, who were successively appointed, could not hold the Comitia in this disturbed state of affairs, and the Senate at last were driven to the necessity of issuing in the usual form the commission with extraordinary powers to save the State (p. 287).

Pompeius was empowered to raise troops all through Italy, and this is the conscription to which Caesar alludes (B. G. vii. 1). When Pompeius returned to Rome, the Senate assembled near the theatre in the Campus Martius that he might be present, for as he still held his proconsular authority he could not enter the city. It was resolved to take up the bones of Clodius, and that the Curia should be restored by Faustus, the son of the dictator Sulla (Dion, 40, c. 50).

Pompeius was afraid or pretended to fear that Milo had designs against his life, and when Milo on the 24th of January proposed to pay him a visit in his gardens, Pompeius let him know that he would not be received. During the time between the death of Clodius and the appointment of Pompeius as sole consul, the tribunes Q. Pompeius Rufus, C. Sallustius Crispus, the historian, and T. Munatius Plancus kept up the popular hostility to Milo by daily public speeches. Sallustius had particular reasons for disliking Milo. M. Varro (Gellius, xvii. 18), an honest man, wrote in a book that Sallustius had been detected by Milo in adultery with his wife Fausta, and that Sallustius was well flogged, and only allowed to go away on paying a sum of money. These tribunes brought Pompeius before the people, and asked him if he had not evidence of Milo's designs; and Pompeius then told a lame story of one Licinius, a man employed about the sacrifices, bringing him information of designs by Milo's slaves against his life. On this occasion Pompeius advised with his friends, and Cicero among them, what should be done (Pro Milone, c. 24). Cicero was surprised that any credit was given to such evidence, but he says that Pompeius was not so much afraid as acting from extreme caution. This appearance of Pompeius before the people preceded the granting of the commission under which he raised troops. When the meeting of the Senate was held after Pompeius' return to Rome, and Milo was present, Pompeius ordered him to be searched before he was allowed to enter the house, because it had been said that he was armed (Asconius, p. 52).

During the intercalary month, which fell in this year, two Appii Claudii, the nephews of P. Clodius, the sons of his brother C. Appius, appeared before Pompeius to demand the production of the slaves of Milo and Fausta for the purpose of getting evidence from them. Three other persons also made the same demand. Caelius at the same time demanded the slaves of P. Clodius and his companions; and some person, whose name is omitted in the text of Asconius, demanded the slaves of Hypsaeus and Q. Pompeius. Q. Hortensius, Cicero and others were present to look after the interests of Milo. Hortensius in a few words replied that those who were demanded as slaves were now free men, for Milo had manumitted them after the death of Clodius because they had protected him. About thirty days after Clodius' death Q. Metellus Scipio made an attack on Milo in the Senate and charged him with beginning the attack on Clodius, and with other acts of violence after Clodius' death. It was reported that, for the purpose of conciliating Pompeius, Milo offered to renounce his canvas for the consulship in favour of Hypsaeus, and that Pompeius replied, he would have nothing to do with such matters.

It was now the general opinion that a dictatorship alone could settle the disturbed affairs of Rome, and that Pompeius must be the dictator; but after some discussion in the Senate, a resolution was passed on the motion of M. Bibulus that Pompeius should be appointed sole consul, and even M. Cato assented. While Servius Sulpicius was Interrex and on the fifth day before the Calends of March, and in the intercalary month, Pompeius was made sole consul. This measure, as Velleius remarks (ii. 47), reconciled Pompeius to the Optimates, but drew him farther from his connexion with Caesar, who was however too busy this year with his own affairs in Gallia to attend much to those of Rome. Pompeius immediately promulgated two bills, pursuant to a resolution of the Senate, one on disturbances of the public peace (de vi), which had special reference to the death of Clodius, the burning of the Curia and the attack on M. Lepidus' house; the other on bribery at elections. By this second law he proposed to bring to trial all who had been guilty of bribery since his own first consulship[*] (B.C. 70). It was observed that this period would comprehend even Caesar's consulship and M. Cato (Plut. c. 48) advised Pompeius not to care about the past, but to look to the future, and he said that it was not just to punish men under a law which they had not violated. The penalties for bribery were increased by the proposed law (Asconius), but it is not said what the new penalties were. Dion states (40, c. 52) that under the new law if any man, who had been convicted of bribery, prosecuted to conviction either two persons charged with the like offences with himself or with smaller, or one man guilty of a greater offence, such person obtained his pardon. But it may be suspected that Dion has fallen into some error in this statement, to which it is easy to make some objections. Both of the bills of Pompeius proposed that in the trials the witnesses should be examined first, and for this purpose three days were allowed, and on the fourth day the prosecutor and the defendant should make their speeches, the prosecutor being allowed two hours, and the defendant three (Asconius, p. 37). Formerly it was the practice to hear the evidence after the speeches were made, as it is said; but sometimes written evidence at least was put in during the

---

[*] This is the statement of Appian (B. C. ii. 23), who also observes that the law would comprise a past period of near twenty years and even Caesar's consulship. Neither Appian nor Plutarch states that this objection prevailed. Drumann (ii. 351) assumes that the law only went back to B.C. 55 the year of Pompeius' second consulship, but I cannot find the evidence for this assertion.

speeches. By these laws or one of them persons were not allowed to deliver speeches in favour of the accused (Plut. Cato, c. 48; Dion, 40, c. 52). Dion states that Pompeius himself chose all the persons from whom the juries should be taken by lot, and limited the number of advocates whom the prosecutor and defendant might employ; but he means, I think, that these matters were contained in the Lex which was doubtless drawn up under the direction of Pompeius. The law also (Dion, 40, c. 55) allowed the prosecutor and defendant each to challenge five jurymen, or as Asconius states it, five out of each class, which would make fifteen. It was also proposed that the quaesitor or presiding judge should be elected by the people out of those who had been consuls (Asconius, p. 39). These restrictions on the advocates were considered by the author of the Dialogue on Orators (c. 38) as checks on eloquence; but they were checks on long speeches.

On the day before the first of March Pompeius proposed his bills to the Senate, who made a resolution (senatus consultum) that the death of Clodius and the other violent acts which followed were attacks on the authority of the state (contra rem publicam), a usual Roman formula, by which it was implied that those who were guilty should be punished. Cicero (Pro Milone, c. 5) attempts to reduce this resolution of the Senate to a mere expression of opinion that every act of violence in a free state is "contra rem publicam;" a truth which cannot be disputed, but the enunciation of this truth without any further meaning would have been a useless declaration. Asconius (In Mil. p. 44) says that he found in the journals (acta) of the Senate of the day before the calends of March, nothing more than the resolution just mentioned; but that the tribune T. Munatius Plancus on the next day informed the people of what took place in the Senate, and he reports the tribune's words literally (ad verbum) as he says. The passage of Asconius is intended to explain Cicero's words (Pro Milone, c. 6, "divisa sententia est"). The full meaning of the reported speech of Plancus is not clear; but we can collect from Cicero and Asconius, that Q. Hortensius attempted to prevent the acceptance of Pompeius' bills on the ground that the existing laws were sufficient for the occasion; and that Fufius Calenus and the tribunes T. Munatius Plancus and Sallustius frustrated Hortensius, and accordingly as nothing was done on this motion, there was no record of the attempt in the journals of the house. The Senate at last gave their assent to the proposed bills of Pompeius. When they were brought before the popular assembly, the tribune M. Caelius opposed them: the measure directed against Milo was a Privilegium, he said, a bill of pains and penalties. As he persisted in his opposition, Pompeius declared that if he were driven to it he would defend the state by force of arms; and the two bills were enacted.

Pompeius still pretended that he was afraid of Milo. During a sitting of the Senate in the Capitol when Milo was present, P. Cornificius declared that Milo had a dagger under his clothes. Milo answered the charge by showing that he had nothing concealed, and this fact afterwards furnished Cicero with an argument for his client's innocence (Pro Milone, c. 24).

The tribunes by their public meetings kept up the popular hostility to Milo (Asconius, p. 38). Plancus produced before the people a freedman of M. Lepidus, who declared that he and four others, free men, happened to be travelling on the Appian road and reached the spot just when Clodius was being murdered; and that they were seized and shut up for two months in one of Milo's villas. Nothing is said about any evidence being given by the four free men. One of the "triumviri capitales" was also produced and asked whether he had detected Galata, a slave of Milo, in the act of committing murder. The triumvir answered that Galata had been arrested as a runaway slave while he was asleep in a tavern and brought to him. The tribunes gave the triumvir notice to keep the man, but the next day the tribunes Caelius and Q. Manilius took Galata out of custody and gave him up to Milo. Asconius observes that Cicero said nothing of these matters, but as he had found them recorded, probably in the Acta, he thought them worth mentioning. The tribunes Q. Pompeius, Sallustius, and Plancus continued their attacks on Milo, and roused the popular indignation against Cicero who had undertaken Milo's defence, and he was charged with planning Clodius' death (Pro Milone, c. 18). Plancus even threatened to bring Cicero to trial; but says Asconius, Cicero was unmoved by the hostility of the people and his own danger, though he might have escaped this unpopularity and secured the favour of Pompeius, if he had shown less zeal in his defence of Milo. Cicero indeed affirms, B.C. 50, in a letter to Appius Pulcher (Ad Div. iii. 10. 10), that Cn. Pompeius showed the greatest forbearance towards him on this occasion, and though Cicero was sometimes opposed to his measures, Pompeius protected him against his enemies. Perhaps Pompeius practised a little double-dealing.

As soon as the Lex Pompeia was enacted, the comitia were held and L. Domitius Ahenobarbus, consul B.C. 54, was elected Quaesitor (quaestor) or presiding judge under the new act for the trial de vi. A. Torquatus was elected to preside at the trials for bribery. The jurymen whom Pompeius named, as Asconius expresses it, were men of the highest character, selected from the Senators, Equites and Tribuni Aerarii, 360 in number as Velleius (ii. 76) and Plutarch state[3]. The prosecution before L. Domitius was immediately commenced by the two Appii Claudii, who had already demanded Milo's slaves, but only the elder is mentioned as taking part in the prosecution, and he was supported by M. Antonius[4] and P. Valerius Nepos. Milo was also charged with bribery before Torquatus by the same Appii, assisted by P. Valerius Leo and Cn. Domitius, the son. He was also prosecuted under the Lex de sodalitiis by P. Fulvius Neratus before the quaesitor Favonius; and a second prosecution de vi awaited him. Milo's enemies were determined to drive him from Rome.

Torquatus and Domitius summoned Milo to appear before them severally on the fourth of April. Milo appeared before Domitius, and sent his friends to represent him before Torquatus, who at the request of M. Marcellus consented to hear

[3] See Cic. ad Att. viii. 16, 2, and ad Div. viii. 8, 5, and the commentators. I have followed Asconius (p. 39) in stating that Pompeius named the jurymen. If it was so, this extraordinary authority must have been given to him by the Lex Pompeia. See what Dion says on the matter (p. 358).

[4] M. Antonius must be the quaestor who in this year joined Caesar in Gallia.

the case about Ambitus (bribery) after the trial de vi. The man could not of course be tried in two separate courts at the same time. The elder Appius repeated his demand for the production of Milo's slaves to the number of fifty-four, and though Milo affirmed that those who were named were no longer in his power, Domitius after consulting with the jury (ex sententia judicum) allowed the prosecutor to select out of these slaves for examination as many as he chose without, as it seems, taking any notice of the fact whether they were still Milo's slaves or not[a]. Appius also put to the torture the slaves of P. Clodius to ascertain the facts of the fray at Bovillae. Cicero says that these slaves of P. Clodius had been a hundred days in the custody of Appius. He also observes that it was not lawful to put a man's slaves to the torture to obtain evidence against the master except in the case of incestus, as Cicero says (Pro Milone, c. 22), if that passage is genuine; and he also argues that the truth cannot be obtained by examining the slaves of the prosecutor against the accused, but he does not say that it was illegal. There was a rule of law at a later time certainly that the witnesses whom a prosecutor produced out of his own house could not be examined (Dig. 22. 5. 24). If the slaves of P. Clodius were put to the torture, it is certain that their evidence would not be against their late master.

The trial began on the fifth of April and ended on the eighth. It is not easy to understand Asconius here (p. 40). He says that the law enacted that the witnesses should be examined on the first three days and the judices (jury) "should confirm what they said," which may mean that they should accept what they approved[b], and see that it was committed to writing.

---

[a] Cicero (Pro Milone, c. 21, 22) speaks of Milo manumitting those slaves who were faithful to him in the fray with Clodius, and he says nothing of this order of Domitius. There is no absolute inconsistency between Asconius and Cicero.

[b] "Confirmarent" in Orelli's text of Asconius should probably be "consignarent." The evidence was no doubt taken down in writing and signed or in some way marked to show that it was taken correctly. The words "quarta die ... in diem posterum," and "dein rursus postera die" confuse the explanation. But we know that there were only four days. The meaning of "pilae aequarentur" is not certain. The "pilae" are not the voting-tablets or ballots, for the votes of the several jurymen were not known.

On the fourth day all the jurymen were required to be present, and the balls on which their names were written must be verified (acquarentur) in the presence of the prosecutor and the accused; then 81 judices or jurymen must be selected by lot and take their seats, but before they voted the prosecutor must reject or challenge five jurymen out of each class, and the accused as many, and so there would remain fifty-one to vote.

According to this statement the jurymen heard the evidence, or some jurymen heard it: on the fourth day "all" were required to be present, "all" we may suppose who had heard the evidence, and their names must be verified; then the appointment of 81 by lot must be made, which implies an appointment out of a larger number than 81, and then this number would be reduced to 51 by the challenges. The first body of jurymen who heard the evidence must therefore have been more than 81.

On the first day Cassinius Schola, who said that he was with Clodius when he was killed, gave evidence, and he made the case as strong as he could against Milo. M. Marcellus, when he began to cross-examine Schola, was so terrified by the numerous partisans of Clodius that he feared for his life, and Domitius allowed him to take refuge on his tribunal or seat. Marcellus and Milo also implored Domitius to give them protection. Pompeius at this time was sitting at the Treasury, where he heard the tumult and he promised Domitius that he would come down the next day with an armed force, and he did so. The faction of Clodius was kept in order by this display of force, and during the two days they allowed the evidence of the witnesses to be taken quietly. Many of the persons who lived about Bovillae gave evidence to the effect that the tavern-keeper was killed, the tavern was broken open, and the body of Clodius was dragged out on the road. Other evidence is mentioned by Asconius, but it was of no value. The court adjourned about the tenth hour on the third day, and then Plancus addressed the people, whom he exhorted to meet next day in full force to prevent Milo's acquittal, and to let the jurymen who were going to vote know their opinion. On the next day, which was the eighth of

April¹, all the shops in Rome were shut, armed men were placed by Pompeius in the Forum and in all the approaches. Pompeius took his station, as he had done the day before, in front of the Treasury, protected by a picked body of men. At the beginning of the first hour the appointment by lot (sortitio) of the jurymen was made. There was deep silence all through the Forum, and the prosecutors, Appius Major, M. Antonius and P. Valerius Nepos made their speeches.

After the prosecutors had spoken two hours, Cicero rose for the defence, and in a state of great trepidation (Plutarch, Cicero, c. 35). Pompeius had come to the court with an armed force, the sight of which caused a great clamour among some of the crowd. Pompeius ordered his men to strike the disturbers with the flat of their swords and drive them out of the Forum. As the men refused to move and even made a joke of the blows, some were wounded and killed. According to Dion this disturbance took place before the court sat. Asconius, whose evidence we may trust, reports that when Cicero rose to speak, he was received with loud clamours by the party of Clodius who were not restrained even by fear of the soldiers. Whether it was from fear or any other cause, Cicero did not speak as well as usual. His speech was taken down in writing, and Asconius and Quintilian (iv. 3. 16) read it. Some persons thought that Cicero ought to have maintained that it was for the public interest that Clodius should be killed, and that this would be a sufficient defence of Milo. Indeed M. Brutus afterwards wrote an oration, as a rhetorical exercise, in which this defence was adopted. But Cicero knew that he could not maintain that a man might be put to death without trial because it would be advantageous to the public that he should die. The prosecutors had endeavoured to prove that Milo formed a design against the life of Clodius, and as this was certainly false, for the meeting was accidental, Cicero main-

---

¹ The MSS. in this passage of Asconius (p. 41) have iii. Id. April; but in the introduction Asconius has vi. Id. April, and he also says that Milo was summoned to appear before Domitius and Torquatus prid. Non. April. Cicero says (c. 35) it is now the 102nd day since Milo's death. This result is obtained by reckoning from the 20th of January to the 8th of April, the intercalary month of twenty-eight days included, and the twenty-three days of February.

tained that Clodius formed a design against Milo; and this, says Asconius, was the whole of his argument (see Pro Milone, c. 11). If he could have persuaded the jury of this fact, Milo would have been easily justified by the natural law, as Cicero calls it, of self-defence (Pro Milone, c. 4).

When Cicero's speech was finished and the 81 "judices" had been reduced to 51 by the challenges, the votes were taken. There were thirteen votes for Milo, and thirty-eight against him, and consequently he was condemned[*]. The jury knew that Clodius was wounded without the knowledge of Milo, but they also knew that after he was wounded, he was killed by Milo's order. It was reported that M. Cato, who was on the jury, voted for an acquittal. But as the jury voted by ballot, Cato's vote could only be known from his own declaration. Indeed Velleius (ii. 47) says that he gave his vote openly, but if he did choose to say which way he voted, he must still have deposited his ballot in the urn. One condemnation did not satisfy Milo's enemies. Though he did not appear at the subsequent trials, he was convicted of bribery at elections, and also under the Lex de sodalitiis, and lastly, as we are told, on some other charge of Vis. Milo went to Massilia in exile. His property was sold, but it produced only a nominal sum, for Milo's debts were enormous.

This is the remark of Asconius, which we can only understand by supposing that the purchasers took the property with the debts secured on it; and if the debts were nearly equal to the value of the property, the purchasers would give very little more than the amount of the debts.

Drumann (i. 49) observes that Cicero fell under strong suspicion of having taken advantage of Milo's misfortune and having bought part of his property by the agency and in the name of Philotimus, a freedman of Cicero's wife. On his journey from Rome to his province Cicero informed Atticus (v. 8) that he heard by letters that his friend Milo had written to complain of him, because Philotimus was a partner with others in buying Milo's property. Cicero's answer is that he

[*] Asconius reports the votes of the Senatorian judices, the Equites and the Tribuni Aerarii separately, from which we conclude that the three classes of the jury placed their ballots in separate boxes.

did what he had done, upon the advice of C. Duronius a most intimate friend of Milo, and that the purpose of himself and Duronius was that the property might be under Cicero's control and that an unfriendly purchaser might not deprive Milo of his slaves, many of whom he had with him; further the purpose was to secure the interests of Fausta, Milo's wife, for if any thing could be saved, Cicero could do it best. However if Milo really complained, and Fausta was of the same mind, Cicero tells Atticus not to let Philotimus retain any share in the purchase contrary to Milo's wish, as Cicero had already told Philotimus, who had promised to do as he desired. The explanation seems sufficient. If Philotimus acted knavishly, that was not Cicero's fault. There are two other letters to Atticus in B.C. 50 (vi. 4, 5), in which Cicero writes of this matter in Greek, but it is impossible to ascertain his meaning exactly, though Drumann does not seem to doubt about it. There is also the letter to Atticus (vi. 7) and that from Caelius to Cicero (Ad Div. viii. 3) which speak of this affair. Middleton can see nothing in Cicero's conduct except a wish to befriend Milo, and such an opinion is quite consistent with all that Cicero has said. Drumann has forced the meaning of the letters to support his bad opinion of Cicero[*].

The extant speech in defence of Milo is a rhetorical exercise, which Asconius considered to be one of Cicero's best orations. The argument (c. 12, etc.) as to the probability of Clodius having formed a design on Milo's life is well handled; but there is much in the speech which is in bad taste. In fact Cicero had a difficult case, and he failed. It is said (Dion, 40, c. 54) that Cicero sent to Milo to Massilia a copy of the extant speech, to which Milo returned an answer that it was lucky Cicero had not made the speech at his trial, for if he had,

---

[*] Mongault in his French translation has done the same. He has translated the Greek, which a better scholar would leave untouched. Melmoth in his translation of the letters (1. 298) affirms that "it appears very evidently from Cicero's letters to Atticus upon this subject that he shared with Philotimus in the advantages of the purchase." I cannot see the evidence for this, because I cannot understand the letters. If there was any dishonest dealing in the matter, Heberden conjectures that Cicero's wife might have used her authority over Philotimus to make some profit out of Milo's property. There was certainly something which Cicero wished to be kept secret.

Milo would not have been eating such fine mullets. Dion has added his own explanation of Milo's answer.

M. Saufeius, who had been most active in breaking open the tavern at Bovillae and killing Clodius was tried under the Lex Pompeia, and acquitted by a single vote. He was defended by Cicero and M. Caelius. He was tried again under the Lex Plautia de vi, and again acquitted. Cicero and another defended him. Sex. Clodius, who had been the leader in taking the corpse of Clodius into the Curia, was tried and convicted by a great majority. Many others who appeared, and others who did not appear, were convicted under the Lex Pompeia. The greater part were of the faction of Clodius, which is apparently evidence of the impartiality of Pompeius and the Roman juries.

Plautius Hypsaeus, who had accompanied Pompeius in the Mithridatic war and now entreated for his protection, was also convicted of bribery; but Scipio, the father-in-law of Pompeius escaped trial through the influence of his son-in-law, who (Plutarch, Pomp. c. 55) sent for the three hundred and sixty judices to his house and obtained their support for him, and the prosecutor gave up the prosecution when he saw Scipio conducted from the Forum by the "judices" (the body from which the juries were taken). The prosecutor, according to Appian (B. C. ii. 24), was Memmius, one of the four bribing candidates (p. 270) of B.C. 54, for though Memmius had been convicted of bribery himself, he prosecuted under the provisions of the Lex Pompeia, mentioned by Dion (p. 357). M. Aemilius Scaurus was also tried for bribery. The common sort interceded with Pompeius in his behalf, but he told them by a public notice that they must let the trial take its course; and when they were attempting to disturb the prosecutors, Pompeius' soldiers fell on the rabble and killed some of them. Cicero defended Scaurus (Quintil. Inst. iv. 1. 69), but he was convicted and went into exile.

On the first of August Pompeius made his father-in-law Scipio his colleague in the consulship for the rest of the year. Our authorities say that the appointment of Scipio was the act of Pompeius. If that was so, the act proved that the Roman constitution no longer existed. Pompeius also (Dion, 40, c. 56) caused to be re-enacted a law, which had been neglected, as the historian says, and to the following effect, that the candidates for a magistracy must be present at the Comitia, and consequently no man could be elected in his absence. There was as Dion says also a confirmation of the Senatus consultum, which declared that those who had held magistracies in the city should not be entitled to hold a provincial government before the lapse of five years. But Dion (40, c. 46; p. 284) had already stated that a Senatus consultum was made in B.C. 53, that no praetor or consul should take a provincial government before the lapse of five years. There is a difference, as it will be observed, in the terms of these Senatus consulta, as Dion reports them, but it appears from another passage (40, c. 30) that the Senatus consulta were the same. No reason is given why the Senatus consultum was confirmed. Notwithstanding this rule Pompeius shortly after accepted for five years more the government of Spain with an allowance of a thousand talents yearly for his troops, and when Caesar's friends complained that the law about absent candidates would exclude Caesar from being a candidate for a second consulship in his absence, Pompeius consented that Caesar should be excepted. Suetonius (Caesar, c. 28) reports this exception of Caesar in a somewhat different way. Cicero, in a letter to Atticus (viii. 3. 3, written in B.C. 49), says that Pompeius used his influence to persuade the ten tribuni plebis to propose that Caesar should be a candidate for the consulship in his absence and that it was ratified by his own law. About Cicero's behaviour in this matter we have his own statement (Ad Div. vi. 6. 5; Ad. Att. vii. 1. 4), that he used his influence to secure Caesar against the operation of the law, and yet he afterwards denied that he had done so (Phil. ii. 10).

After the tenth of December the tribunes Q. Pompeius Rufus and T. Munatius Plancus were tried on the charge of burning the Curia. Rufus was convicted, and retired to Bauli in Campania, where he lived in great poverty. Plancus was prosecuted by Cicero, the only instance, it is said, except the case of Verres in which he acted as prosecutor. Plancus was convicted, though Pompeius, contrary to his own law, attempted to save him by sending to be read before the jury a manuscript which contained a eulogium of Plancus and an entreaty that he might be acquitted. Plancus retired to Ravenna, where he received money from Caesar, by whom he was afterwards restored. Cicero was delighted with the conviction of Plancus, whom he hated, he says, more than Clodius himself (Ad Div. vii. 2).

Scipio proposed no enactment during the five months of his consulship except one for the restoration of the censorian authority, which had been limited in B.C. 58 in the tribuneship of Clodius (vol. iii. p. 448). The consuls elected for the next year were Servius Sulpicius Rufus, the great lawyer, a friend of Cicero, and M. Claudius Marcellus. M. Cato was a candidate for the consulship, not, it is said, because he wished for the office, but that he might destroy the influence of Caesar and Pompeius, and prevent either of them from seizing the supreme power. Plutarch says (Cato, c. 49) that Cato persuaded the Senate to pass a resolution that the candidates for the office should canvas the electors themselves, and not through others, which the people did not like, because they were deprived of the opportunity of receiving money, and even of conferring a favour; by which Plutarch means probably that the electors did not like to lose the importance which the possession of a vote gives to a man when he is solicited; and the new rule would diminish solicitation, for the candidates could not pay their respects personally to all the voters. Cato's manners were not agreeable, and he would not descend to the usual trick of shaking hands with the electors of Rome; and so he lost the office.

Pliny (33. 1. 5.) records the fact, without further remark, that in the third consulship of Pompeius two thousand pounds of gold disappeared from the seat of Jupiter Capitolinus [1].

---

[1] See Harduin's text, and Emendations.

CHAPTER XXI.

THE STATE OF GALLIA.

B.C. 51.

THE history of the two years (B.C. 51, 50) is contained in the eighth book of the Commentaries, but this book was not written by Caesar, as the Preface shows, and as any person may see who reads it. This book is assigned by one antient authority (Suetonius, Caesar, c. 56) to Aulus Hirtius.

During the winter Caesar was informed that several of the Gallic states were planning an insurrection, for though the Galli knew that with all their forces combined they could not resist the Romans, they also believed that if many states rose at the same time, the Romans would not be able to deal with all of them. Caesar determined not to allow such a plan to be realized. Placing his quaestor M. Antonius over his winter-quarters, he went on the last day of the year (52 B.C.) from Bibracte to the thirteenth legion, which he had placed in the country of the Bituriges not far from the borders of the Aedui, and he joined to it the eleventh legion, which was nearer than any other. He left two cohorts of each legion to protect the baggage, and with the rest of the two legions he marched into the most fertile parts of the territory of the Bituriges, which being very extensive and containing many towns could not be kept in check by a single legion. In consequence of Caesar's unexpected arrival the people were surprised by the cavalry before they could escape into the towns, for Caesar had forbidden any of the buildings to be set on fire, which was the usual signal of the approach of an enemy, and he wished to

secure a supply of forage and corn, if he should advance
farther, and not to terrify the enemy by burning their property. Many thousand prisoners were taken, and those who
escaped from the first attack of the Romans fled to neighbouring states, either because they had friends there or because
they expected support from communities which had also determined to rise against the Romans. But Caesar by making
forced marches showed himself every where, and did not allow
any state time to think of the interests of others more than of
their own. By this activity he maintained the allegiance of
those who were faithful to him and terrified into submission
those who were hesitating. The Bituriges seeing that Caesar's
clemency gave them the opportunity of recovering his favour
and that the neighbouring states were only required to give
hostages, followed their example. To reward his soldiers for
their endurance during the short days of this winter season
and for the difficult marches which they had made in very
severe weather, Caesar promised to every soldier two hundred
sestertii and two thousand to every centurion, if the text is
right. The two legions were sent back to their quarters, and
Caesar returned to Bibracte on the thirtieth day, which would
be at the end of January B.C. 51, according to the Roman
calendar. While he was holding his courts in that city, the
Bituriges sent to ask for his aid against the Carnutes who were
attacking them. Though Caesar had been only eighteen days
at Bibracte, he drew the fourteenth and sixth legions from
their quarters on the Saône (B. G. vii. 90, and p. 350), and
went against the Carnutes. On the news of his approach the
Carnutes, warned by what others had suffered, deserted the
villages and towns in which they had hastily constructed huts
to protect them during the winter, for many of their towns were
ruined in the last campaign, and fled. Caesar being unwilling
to expose his men to the severe weather at this time of the
year placed them in Genabum (Orléans), in the huts of the Galli,
or in tents which were hastily roofed with straw. The cavalry
and the auxiliary infantry were sent after the enemy, and they
generally returned loaded with booty. The Carnutes being
surprised in the midst of the winter, driven from their homes,
and unable to stay long in any place, or to shelter themselves

in the forests in the extreme cold, were dispersed with great loss of life among the neighbouring states (c. 5).

At this inclement season Caesar was satisfied with scattering the bands of men which assembled; and as far as he was able to judge, when the fine weather came there was no probability of any great rising of the Galli. Accordingly he placed his two legions in quarters at Genabum under C. Trebonius. In the meantime he received frequent messages from the Remi, to the effect that the Bellovaci, who had the highest military reputation of all the Galli and Belgae, and the states bordering on them, were collecting their forces at one spot under Correus, a Bellovacan, and Comm in order to attack the Suessiones, who were now dependents of the Remi. Considering it necessary both for his reputation and his safety to protect faithful allies, Caesar again summoned the eleventh legion from winter-quarters, and wrote to C. Fabius to lead his two legions into the country of the Suessiones, and he also sent for one of the two legions which were with Labienus. Thus without taking any rest himself he imposed on the legions in turns the labour of these several expeditions, as far as the position of the winter-quarters and the necessities of the campaign required. Having got together these forces he advanced against the Bellovaci and fixing his camp in their territory he sent his cavalry out to take prisoners who could inform him of the enemy's designs. The cavalry reported that few persons were found in the houses, and that even these few had not remained to look after their lands, for there was a general departure of the people, but had been sent back to watch the Romans. Caesar learned from these prisoners where the chief body of the Bellovaci was, and what was their purpose; he also learned that all who were able to bear arms had assembled in one place, and that the Ambiani, Aulerci, Caleti, Velliocasses, and Atrebates had joined them. These forces were collected from the country between the Isara (Oise) a branch of the Seine and the Ocean, and between the borders of the Morini and the Lower Seine. The Aulerci were probably the Aulerci-Eburovices on the south bank of the Seine opposite to the Velliocasses. The prisoners also reported that the enemy had chosen for their camp an elevated place in a thick forest surrounded by a swamp, and had placed their baggage in some woods still farther off; that several chiefs were active in promoting the war, but the multitude most readily obeyed Correus because of his extreme hatred of the Romans; that Comm had left the camp a few days before to bring auxiliaries from the numerous Germans who lived near; that the Bellovaci had unanimously determined, if Caesar should come with three legions, as it was reported, to fight a battle that they might not be compelled to fight afterwards on more unfavourable terms with all his army: if he should attack them with a larger force, they would remain where they had placed themselves, and by laying ambuscades they would prevent the Romans from getting forage, which was scarce at that season, and cut them off from corn and other supplies. Caesar convinced of the truth of what he heard by the agreement among his prisoners, and seeing that the enemy's plans were prudent and very different from the rash resolves of barbarians, determined to bring them to a battle by leading them to despise the small force of the Romans. He had with him the seventh, eighth, and ninth legions, all veterans and of tried courage; also the eleventh, consisting of promising young men, who were now serving their eighth campaign and yet had not equal reputation with the men of the three veteran legions. With the view of drawing out the enemy to fight he made the following order of march: the seventh, eighth, and ninth legions preceded the baggage, which was small, and was followed by the eleventh legion. In this order, which nearly formed the "agmon quadratum," Caesar came in sight of the enemy before he was expected. The place where they had fixed themselves is supposed by the author of the "Histoire de César'" to be Mont St. Marc in the forest of Compiègne above the junction of the Aisne and

[1] Planche 20. M. de Saulcy ("Les Campagnes de Jules César," 1862) had previously fixed the position of the Gallic camp at Mont St. Marc. The narrative of Hirtius leads us to place the campaign in the country of the Bellovaci and near the borders of the Suessiones and the forests at the junction of the Aisne and Oise, where now are the forests of Cuise, Compiègne and Laigue. "I have often traversed," says M. de Saulcy, "and in all directions, these magnificent forests, and have found only one point that agrees with Hirtius' description." But this one point, he observes, completely corresponds with the description.

THE STATE OF GALLIA. 373

the Oise. When the enemy (c. 9) saw the Romans approaching with steady step and almost in battle-order, either moved by the imminence of a fight or by the sudden arrival of the Romans or by a resolution to wait for their movements, they drew up in front of their camp, but did not leave the higher ground. Though Caesar wished to fight, yet as the numbers of the enemy were greater than he expected, he pitched his camp[1] opposite to them with a valley between, which was rather deep than wide. He fortified his camp with a vallum twelve foot high and a breastwork in proportion to the height of the rampart[2]. The camp had two ditches each fifteen feet wide (so we must understand the passage) with vertical sides. Numerous towers were built three stories high, and united by covered galleries, the front of which was protected by a breastwork of osiers, so that the enemy would be repelled by a double line of men; one line fighting from the galleries would be protected by the elevation and would discharge their missiles with more confidence and to a greater distance; the other nearer to the enemy and standing on the vallum would be protected by the galleries against missiles falling on them. The gates were defended by doors and higher towers.

The object of these defences was double. It was assumed that the magnitude of the works and the fear thus shown by the Romans would give the barbarians confidence; and since it was necessary for Caesar's men to go a great distance for forage and corn, the camp being so strongly fortified might be protected by a small number of men. There were frequent skirmishes in the marshy plain between small parties sallying out from both camps: sometimes the auxiliary Galli and Germans on the Roman side crossed the marsh and pursued the enemy vigorously; and sometimes the enemy would cross and drive back the Roman troops. In the daily forages, as

---

[1] The author of the "Histoire" (ii. 328) supposes the site of Caesar's camp to be "St. Pierre-en-Chatre (in Castris)." He states that the camp has been found; and that the ditches, as appears from the sections (Planche 30), could not have vertical sides, and that Hirtius by the expression "lateribus directis" means that a section would not be triangular, but as the French say "à fond de cuve" or flat-bottomed. See also M. de Saulcy, p. 400.

[2] "Coronique loriculam," etc., the reading is not certain.

it was necessary to get supplies from the farmhouses which were few and scattered about the country, it happened that the foragers being in small parties were surrounded by the enemy, and though the loss of beasts and slaves was no great damage to the Romans, it encouraged the foolish expectations of the enemy, which were increased by the return of Comm who brought with him five hundred German horsemen. Caesar seeing that the enemy continued to keep within their camp, which was protected by the marsh and the position, and that it could not be assaulted without great hazard nor invested without a larger force, wrote to C. Trebonius to summon the thirteenth legion, which was wintering among the Bituriges with the legatus T. Sextius, and to come with this legion and the two which he had at Genabum as soon as he could. He also sent in turns detachments of the cavalry of the Remi and Lingones and of other states, of which he had a large amount with him, to protect the foragers and prevent surprise. These foraging parties going out daily and as is usual in like cases, growing less careful, the Bellovaci, who were acquainted with their places of resort, made an ambuscade in the woods with a picked body of infantry, and on the following day sent cavalry to the spot with instructions to draw on the foragers to the place and then fall upon them. The Remi on their day of service suddenly coming in sight of the enemy's cavalry and despising their inferior numbers pursued them eagerly till they were surrounded by the infantry in ambuscade. Being thrown into confusion they made a hurried retreat with the loss of Vertiscus, the chief man of the state and commander of the cavalry, who, though so old that he could hardly sit on his horse, yet following Gallic usage would neither make his age an excuse for not taking the command, nor allow his men to fight without him. The enemy's spirits were raised by this success, and the Romans were warned by their loss to examine the ground more carefully, to place bodies of men in various positions, and to be more cautious in pursuit.

In the mean time there was daily skirmishing in sight of both camps where the marsh was fordable. On one occasion the Germans, whom Caesar had sent for from the east side of the Rhine to fight among the cavalry, according to German fashion, boldly crossed the marsh and killing the few who made resistance pursued the rest. The Galli fled in terror, not only those on whom the Germans fell, and those who were wounded by missiles, but also those who were accustomed to act as a reserve at some distance in the rear, and they did not stop their flight after being driven successively from several higher positions until they found refuge in the camp, and some being ashamed to appear there fled still farther. This defeat threw all the enemy's men into such disorder that it was hard to say whether they were made more arrogant by slight success or more depressed by a reverse.

After several days the leaders of the Bellovaci, being informed of the arrival of C. Trebonius and the three legions, and fearing a blockade like that of Alesia, sent off by night the aged, the feeble and those who were unarmed, and with them "the rest of the baggage[1]." While this multitude was retiring in great disorder, for it is the Gallic fashion to have a large number of waggons following the troops even when they are in light marching order, the morning surprised them, and the Galli occupied with their forces all the roads in front of their camp that the Romans might not pursue the retreating column before it had advanced some distance. But Caesar saw that he ought not to attack the enemy, if they kept their ground, since the ascent of the hill was so steep, and yet he ought to bring his legions so near that the enemy could not leave their position without some danger if the Roman soldiers pressed hard upon them. Accordingly as the two camps were separated by a marsh, the crossing of which would delay the pursuit, and a ridge beyond the marsh extended almost to the enemy's camp, from which it was divided by a small depression, Caesar took his army over the marsh by bridges which he ordered to be made, and quickly reached the level summit of this ridge, which was protected on the right and left by sloping sides. The legions

---

[1] "Reliqua Impedimenta:" perhaps he means all the baggage except what was left in the camp; but Hirtius, or whoever wrote this book, is often obscure; or "all the remaining baggage" may mean all that they then had.

were drawn up at the extremity of the ridge, and placed in such a position that missiles from an engine could reach the enemy[a].

The barbarians (c. 15) remained on their ground trusting to the advantage of position, being ready to fight if the Romans should attempt to ascend the hill, and not daring to send off their troops in small divisions lest they should fall into disorder. Caesar observing their obstinate resolution kept twenty cohorts under arms, and determined to make a camp on the spot which he had occupied. When the works were completed, he drew up his legions in front of the rampart and placed the cavalry at the outposts. The Bellovaci seeing that the Romans were ready to pursue them, and that they could neither pass the night without danger nor stay longer for want of food, used the following stratagem. Passing from hand to hand the bundles of straw and sticks, of which there was great plenty in the camp, they placed them in front of their line and at nightfall on a given signal set them on fire. A long line of flame suddenly hid the enemy from the Romans, and they began a hurried retreat. Though Caesar could not see the flight of the barbarians, he suspected that the fire was made to cover a retreat, and he ordered his legions to advance and sent the cavalry in pursuit. However he himself moved on slowly for fear that the enemy might draw the Romans on unfavourable ground. The cavalry also were afraid to enter the dense smoke, and if any of them ventured to do so, they could scarcely see the horses' heads, and thus the Bellovaci had the opportunity of retreating without any loss about ten miles. They fixed their new camp in a strong position[b], from which they sent out cavalry and infantry to lie in ambuscade and did great damage to the Roman foragers.

Caesar (c. 17) at last learned from a prisoner that Correus had sent six thousand picked men and a thousand horsemen to form an ambuscade in a place which he expected that the

---

[a] This ridge is supposed to be Mont Collet. "Histoire," Planche 29; and the plate in De Saulcy.

[b] Mont Ganelon ("Histoire," II. 332), which is in a bend of the Oise on the west side and a little above the junction of the Aisne and Oise. Compiègne is on the Oise below the junction of the two rivers.

Romans would visit for the abundance of corn[1] and forage. Upon receiving this information Caesar marched forward with a greater number of legions than usual, and sent the cavalry before him, according to his practice, to protect the foragers. The auxiliary light-armed troops were mixed with the cavalry. The enemy had laid their ambuscade in a plain about a mile wide in all directions, surrounded by thick forests or a very deep river, which was either the Aisne or the Oise[2]. The design of the Bellovaci being ascertained, the cavalry knowing that they would be supported by the infantry advanced to this spot in companies. Correus seeing them approach and thinking that the opportunity was favourable, appeared with a small force and attacked the nearest companies of cavalry. Caesar's cavalry boldly resisted the enemy and did not crowd together on one spot, which, as the author remarks, happens often in cavalry fights through fear, and then the men suffer loss through their own numbers. While the Roman cavalry so placed themselves that a few companies in turns came forward to fight, and those in the rear prevented the enemy from turning the flanks, the rest of the horsemen of Correus burst out of the woods. The fight was then continued on various lines with great fury and with equal advantage on both sides, until the enemy's infantry in battle order came out of the forest and compelled the Roman cavalry to retire. But they were soon supported by the light-armed men who had been sent forward in advance of the legions, and now resolutely fought intermixed with the cavalry. The fight had continued some time, when the speedy arrival of the commander-in-chief was announced to both sides by numerous scouts. The Roman cavalry being now sure of support fought with still greater energy that they might secure for themselves the honour of the victory, and the enemy being discouraged fled

---

[1] "Propter copiam frumenti ac pabuli" (c. 17). If "frumenti" means "standing corn," as it may, for it is followed by "pabuli" and "pabulatum," the author means "green corn" for the year was still young (c. 11). Among other defects in the narrative of Hirtius, it is deficient in indications of the season.

[2] The Aisne, as the author of the "Histoire" (ii. 332) supposes. A careful reader of Caesar may discover that the scene of this campaign was the country on the Aisne and Oise, and about the junction of the rivers.

in various directions. But their flight was impeded by the
very obstacles which they had intended to oppose to the
Romans, and after great loss they fled in terror wherever
chance led them, some to the woods, others to the river, followed and cut to pieces by the pursuing Romans. Correus
who resolutely refused to leave the battle-field or to surrender fell beneath the Roman missiles[1]. Caesar followed
on the track of the fugitives expecting that the news of the
defeat would make the enemy leave their camp, which was
not more than eight miles from the battle-field, and though
the river was in his way he crossed it and went on with his
army.

The Bellovaci and their allies learned from a few wounded
men, who escaped under shelter of the woods, the calamity
that had befallen their troops, and expecting the immediate
arrival of the Romans they summoned a general meeting by
sound of trumpet and decided by acclamation to send commissioners and hostages to Caesar. As soon as this was
resolved, Comm made his escape to the Germans from whom
he had got help for the war. A message was immediately
sent to Caesar to implore his clemency and to inform him of
the great loss which the Bellovaci had sustained: they had
however one consolation in the death of Correus, who was the
cause of the war, and the leader of the common sort, and so
long as he lived, the Senate had not so much power as the
ignorant mob. Caesar replied that the Bellovaci and the
rest of the Gallic states had risen the year before, and that
the Bellovaci had persisted most obstinately in the rebellion:
it was very easy to throw all the blame on the dead; but no
single man was powerful enough, in spite of the chiefs, the
Senate, and all well-disposed people, to excite and conduct a
war with the support only of a weak rabble: however he was
well satisfied with the punishment which they had brought
on themselves. On the following night the commissioners
carried back Caesar's answer, and made up the number of
hostages. Commissioners assembled from the other states

---

[1] M. de Saulcy believes that the battle in which Correus fell, was fought on the banks of the Aisne in the little plain which is opposite to Choisy.

which were waiting for the answers of the Bellovaci; they gave hostages, and submitted to Caesar's orders with the exception of Comm, who was afraid to trust his life to any person. The year before while Caesar was in Gallia Cisalpina T. Labienus having discovered that Comm was conspiring against Caesar, thought that he might punish him for his faithlessness without being guilty of any perfidy. As he supposed that Comm would not come to the camp if he was summoned, and that a summons would only make him more cautious, he sent C. Volusenus Quadratus to draw him to a conference and then to kill him. Volusenus was accompanied by some centurions. When they met, Volusenus took Comm's hand, which was the signal agreed on, and a centurion attempted to kill Comm, but either through want of presence of mind or being prevented by Comm's friends, he only inflicted a severe wound, and Comm escaped. After this attempt on his life Comm is said to have determined that he would never again come in sight of a Roman.

The most warlike nations of Gallia were now defeated (c. 24) and there was no further resistance; but some of the people were leaving the towns and others were flying from the country to avoid the Roman dominion. To prevent this migration Caesar sent troops in several directions. He summoned the quaestor M. Antonius to him with the eleventh (twelfth, in some texts) legion, and sent C. Fabius with twenty-five cohorts to the south-west of Gallia, where he heard that some states were in arms, and that C. Caninius Rebilus, who commanded in those parts, was not strong enough with his two[1] legions. He also summoned T. Labienus to join him. The twelfth[2] legion, which had been with Labienus in winter-quarters, was sent into Gallia Cisalpina to protect the Roman colonies and to prevent any mischief from the invasion of barbarians, such as had happened the year before to the people of Tergeste (Trieste). Caesar himself set out to

---

[1] Rebilus (vii. 90) had at first only one legion, and he was sent to the country of the Ruteni (Rouergue). Orosius (vi. 11) says that Caninius "found war among the Pictones" (Poitou), and that C. Fabius joined him there.

[2] In some editions the "fifteenth legion," perhaps the right reading. See B. G. viii. 54.

ravage the territory of Ambiorix, and as he had no hope of getting possession of the fugitive king he considered that the next best thing for his credit, as Hirtius expresses it, was to destroy the people, buildings, and cattle, so that the hatred of his own subjects, if any happened to survive, might prevent Ambiorix from returning. Accordingly the legionary and auxiliary soldiers were spread all over the country, where they burnt the houses, robbed the people, and killed or captured a large part of the population. Labienus with two legions was sent to the Treviri, a people, who were almost as savage as their German neighbours and always at war with them, and were never kept in obedience to the Romans except by the presence of an army.

In the mean time C. Caninius (c. 20) advanced towards Lemonum (Poitiers) on the Clain, a branch of the Vienne, having received information from Duratius by letters and messengers that a large hostile force had invaded the territory of the Pictones. Duratius had always been faithful to the Romans, though part of his people had fallen off. When Caninius was approaching Lemonum, he learned from some prisoners that Duratius was blockaded in the town by many thousand men under Dumnacus, the commander of the Andes, and as Caninius did not venture to risk a battle with his legions, he fixed his camp in a strong position. Dumnacus hearing of the approach of Caninius moved off with all his forces to attack the Roman camp, but after several days' fruitless attempt on the lines of Caninius and a great loss of men he returned to the siege of Lemonum.

At the same time C. Fabius received the submission of several states, and secured their fidelity by exacting hostages. Being informed by letter of the events among the Pictones, Fabius marched thither to relieve Duratius. Dumnacus hearing of the approach of Fabius, and seeing no possibility of resisting the Romans and the men in Lemonum at the same time, suddenly left the town, nor did he think that he would be safe unless he carried his troops across the river by a bridge which existed over the lower Loire. As there was a bridge at Genabum, there may have been one also at Caesarodunum (Tours), which is one of the nearest points on the Loire to

Poitiers[a]. Though Fabius was not yet in sight of the enemy
and had not joined Caninius, he concluded from the information that he had from those who were well acquainted with
the country, that Dumnacus was retreating towards this
bridge. Accordingly he marched in that direction, but sent
the cavalry ahead with orders to proceed only so far that they
could without exhausting their horses retire to the camp which
would be made. The cavalry came up with Dumnacus while
his men were marching under their burdens, attacked them
while they were flying in terror, killed a great number and
retired with a large booty to the camp of Fabius.

On the following night Fabius sent forward his cavalry to
attack the enemy and stop their march till he should be able
to come up with them. Varus the commander of the Roman
cavalry, a brave and skilful officer, overtook the Galli, placed
some of his squadrons in convenient positions and with the
rest attacked the enemy's cavalry, who boldly stood their
ground being supported by the infantry intermingled among
them. The men on both sides fought desperately. The
Romans despising the enemy whom they had defeated the day
before and knowing that the legions were following up, bravely
resisted the enemy's combined cavalry and infantry; and the
enemy expecting no more troops to come up, as it had happened
the day before, thought that they had a good opportunity of
destroying the Roman cavalry. The struggle had continued
for some time when Dumnacus placed his infantry in order of
battle to support the cavalry in turns. All at once the Roman
legions came in sight, the enemy's cavalry and infantry were
struck with terror, the disorder spread among the files of baggage, and a general flight followed. The Roman cavalry
pursued the fugitives, of whom twelve thousand were killed,
and all the baggage was taken. About two thousand men
or five thousand (for the readings vary) who escaped from the
battle directed their course towards the Roman Provincia under
Drappes a Senon. This Drappes had got together a number

---

[a] In the "Hist. de César" (II. 336) it is suggested that the bridge was at Saumur, lower down the river. If there was a bridge at Saumur, that place would
be nearer Poitiers than Tours, which Dumnacus could not reach without crossing the Vienne before he came to the Loire.

of desperate men, slaves, exiles, and robbers at the time when Gallia revolted (B.C. 52), and with them he intercepted the supplies and baggage of the Romans. He was now joined by Lucterius, who the year before attempted to invade the Provincia (p. 290). Caninius set out with two legions in pursuit of Drappes and Lucterius to prevent the Provincia from being plundered by a band of scoundrels.

C. Fabius (c. 31) with the rest of the army marched against the Carnutes and other states whose forces had been reduced by the battle with Dumnacus. He knew that they would readily submit after their recent losses, but if time were allowed, they would rally again under Dumnacus. The Carnutes, who though often harassed by the Romans had never proposed peace, gave hostages and surrendered[*]; and the other states, called Armoric, which bordered on the Ocean, following the example of the Carnutes, submitted on the approach of Fabius and the legions. Dumnacus driven from his own country, a solitary wanderer, hiding himself from pursuit, sought refuge in the remotest parts of Gallia.

Drappes and Lucterius (c. 32) knowing that they were followed by Caninius, and that, if they entered the Provincia, they would certainly perish, and having no longer an opportunity of subsisting by plunder, stopped their march in the country of the Cadurci and occupied Uxellodunum where they were received by the townsmen. Lucterius had great influence among these people in the days of their independence, as he was an active agitator, and the town had been in a kind of dependence on him. When Caninius reached this strong place, he saw that it was protected on all sides by abrupt precipices, which it would be difficult for armed men to ascend even if they were not resisted. He knew also that if the townsmen attempted to carry off secretly the great quantity of movables which they had, it would be impossible for them to escape from the cavalry or even from the infantry. Accordingly he divided his forces into three parts, and making

---

[*] They had given hostages before (B. G. vi. 4). Perhaps the writer means that they had not submitted since they sent a force to the relief of Alesia (vii. 75). Such facts as these show the difficulty that Caesar had in reducing to obedience this extensive country named Gallia.

three camps on the highest points round the town, he began to form a line of contrevallation as quick as he could with the small force that he possessed[1]. The townsmen remembered the wretched fate of Alesia, and Lucterius who had been present at that siege advised them to secure a supply of provisions. On the following night Drappes and Lucterius leaving two thousand men to guard the place went out with the rest of the troops. In a few days they collected a great quantity of provisions from the country of the Cadurci, for some of the inhabitants supplied them readily, and others gave because they could not help it. In their absence the men in the town sometimes attacked the Roman forts by night[2], for which reason Caninius was compelled to suspend the works of contrevallation for fear that he should not be able to defend the line, if it was completed, or that the outposts, if distributed in a great number of places, would be too weak. Drappes and Lucterius were now about ten miles from the town, into which they intended to introduce their supplies gradually. Drappes remained with part of the troops to protect the camp, and Lucterius led a file of beasts with their loads towards the town. Having posted troops to protect the convoy, he made an attempt when the night was far spent, to carry the corn into the place by narrow and wooded paths, but the sentinels heard the noise and scouts reported what was going on. Just upon daybreak Caninius with some cohorts from the nearest forts fell upon the men who were leading the beasts, and they being terrified by the sudden attack fled to those whose business it was to protect them. As soon as the Romans spied this escort, they put them all to the sword. Lucterius escaped with a few men, but he did not rejoin Drappes. Caninius hearing from his prisoners where Drappes was, concluded that it would be easy to surprise him, as not a single person had escaped from the massacre to tell him what had happened, and probably therefore he knew nothing about it, and there

---

[1] "Hist. de César" Planche, 31.

[2] According to the text of Hirtius, the troops of Drappes and Lucterius attacked the forts at night. The author of the "Histoire" (ii. p. 338) supposes that the men in the town made the attacks. Either the text is defective, or Hirtius, as usual, has written badly.

could be no danger in making the attempt. Caninius sent
forward all the cavalry and the active German infantry. He
left one legion to guard the three camps, and followed with
the other legion unencumbered. As he came near the enemy,
he was informed by his scouts that the barbarians, according
to their practice had not occupied the higher grounds, but had
made their camp on the bank of the river, and that the Germans had attacked them by surprise. Caninius with his
legion occupied the heights, and when the cavalry and the
Germans saw the legionary standards they fell on the enemy
with great fury. The cohorts joined in the battle, the enemy's
men were all killed or taken, and an immense booty was
made. Drappes was made prisoner. Caninius who had sustained no loss returned to Uxellodunum and carried on his
siege works. On the next day Fabius arrived with his troops
and undertook the blockade of part of the town.

During this time Caesar left the quaestor M. Antonius with
fifteen cohorts in the country of the Bellovaci to prevent any
rising. He visited the other states himself, demanded more
hostages and endeavoured to soothe the fears of the population. He then came to the Carnutes, who began the rebellion of the preceding year, and in order to free the people
from their alarm on this account, he demanded of them
Gutruatus[7] the chief mover in the insurrection. Gutruatus,
who would not trust himself to his own citizens, tried to
escape, but he was hunted, taken, and brought to Caesar,
who contrary to his natural disposition towards clemency was
compelled to punish him by the loud clamour of the soldiers,
for they threw on Gutruatus the blame of all their dangers
and sufferings. The man was almost flogged to death and
then beheaded.

Here we may observe two things. When Caesar punished
Acco the same way (vi. 44), he makes no apology; but here
Hirtius makes one for him, and the apology is not creditable
to the proconsul. Again, the Carnutes sacrificed Gutruatus
when fortune turned against him. Caesar well knew the dis-

[7] The name Gutruatus is not certain. He may be the man named Cotuatus (vii. 3).

position of the Galli: they would follow a leader without reflection, and when reverses surprised them, they would immediately desert and betray the man whom they had followed and obeyed. This national characteristic still exists.

When Caesar was among the Carnutes he was informed of the siege of Uxellodunum by the letters of Caninius, and though the townsmen were contemptible in numbers, it was his opinion that their obstinacy must be severely punished, lest all the Galli should suppose that it was not for want of strength but through want of resolution that they failed in their resistance to the Romans, and lest other states taking advantage of strong positions should assert their freedom. He further considered that it was well known to all the Galli "that there remained only one summer for his administration," as Hirtius says; and if they could hold out so long, they would have nothing more to fear. Accordingly he ordered Q. Calenus with two legions to follow him by regular marches, while he with all the cavalry hurried to Caninius.

As soon as Caesar came, he saw that the town was completely shut in by the Roman lines, and as the siege could not be given up, and deserters informed him that there was plenty of provisions in the place, he made an attempt to cut off the water. A river flowed through the lowest part of the depression which surrounded almost the whole of the steep heights on which Uxellodunum was situated. The nature of the ground did not allow the stream to be diverted, for it flowed so close to the base of the heights that it could not be drawn off in any direction by digging ditches; nor could the townsmen go down to the river without risk of wounds or life, if the Romans attempted to prevent them, and they could not return up the steep slope without the same danger. Caesar therefore by placing archers and slingers, and even engines in some places where the descent to the river was easiest, prevented the townsmen from getting water from the river, and they were obliged to draw it from a large spring which issued from the ground close under the wall at that part where the river did not surround the town, which was a distance of about three hundred feet. In order to prevent the people from using this spring Caesar brought covered

galleries against the heights at a point right opposite to the
spring, and began to construct earthworks with great labour
and amidst continual attacks from the enemy, who fought
from the higher ground without any danger and wounded
many of the Romans. Yet Caesar's men were not deterred
from pushing on the galleries and overcoming by their exertions the difficulties of the ground. At the same time they
drove subterraneous galleries towards the source without any
risk and without being perceived by the enemy. The earthworks were raised to the height of nine[*] feet, and a tower ten
storeys high was placed on it, which was not indeed high
enough to reach the elevation of the walls, for that could not
have been accomplished by any labour, but high enough to be
above the level of the source. From this tower missiles were
discharged from engines which made it dangerous for the townsmen to approach the spring, and many animals and men
within the place died of thirst.

The townsmen (c. 42) now filled casks with fat, pitch, and
chips of wood, and sent them blazing down, at the same time
using all their efforts to prevent the Romans from extinguishing the flames. All at once there was a great conflagration
in the Roman works, for the burning materials being stopped
by the covered galleries and the earthworks set on fire all that
was combustible. In the midst of this danger the Roman
soldiers showed the greatest fortitude, for the struggle was in
an elevated position and in sight of the army. Caesar seeing
that many of his men were wounded, ordered the cohorts to
climb the hill on all sides and to raise a loud shout while they
made a feint of assaulting the walls. This movement alarmed
the townsmen, who recalled their men from the attack on the
works and placed them along the walls. Thus the Romans
had the opportunity of quickly extinguishing the fire or stopping it by cutting their works. The place still resisted obstinately though a great part of the townsmen died of thirst, but
at last the subterraneous galleries were driven up to the sources
of the water, which were diverted in another direction. The
people of Uxellodunum seeing this perennial spring suddenly

[*] "Sixty feet," as some editions have it. But "sixty" is a bad emendation
founded on Orosius (vi. 11).

become dry were seized with despair: they thought that it was the work of the gods, and they surrendered. Caesar saw that his purpose of subjugating Gallia would never be accomplished, if such risings took place in other parts of the country, and as he knew that his clemency was notorious, he was under no fear that his behaviour would be imputed to a cruel temper. This is the apology of Hirtius for what he did. It would be consistent with Caesar's character to have made no apology if he had written the eighth book. He cut off the hands of all the men who had fought in defence of the town, that they might be living examples of the punishment which awaited all villains. But these poor wretches probably did not long survive this barbarous punishment which other Romans had inflicted on other occasions (vol. i. 97). Drappes, either through vexation at being put in chains or fearing a worse punishment refused to take food and died in a few days. At the same time Lucterius, who had rambled about the country and consequently was compelled to trust himself to many persons, fell into the hands of Epasnactus, an Arvernian, a partisan of the Romans, who put him in chains and delivered him up to Caesar (comp. p. 350, note 2). It is not said what became of him, but we may guess.

The site of Uxellodunum is placed by the author of the "Histoire de César" (ii. 343) at Puy d'Issolu, an eminence between Vayrac and Martel, not far from the right bank of the Dordogne. It stands completely isolated except on the north, where it is connected by a neck of high land about 1300 feet wide with an elevation named Pech Demont. The summit of Puy d'Issolu is an undulating plateau 650 feet above the surrounding valleys, and the sides of the hill are a steep escarpment of rock, some parts of which are above 130 feet high on the south-east side, which looks towards Vayrac and the Dordogne. On the west side the slopes are abrupt enough to justify the description in the Commentaries of the difficulty of the ascent, and on this side at the base of the slope there flows nearly in a direct line from north to south the Tourmente, a small stream about 30 feet wide sunk in a deep bed between Puy d'Issolu and the high land on the opposite side. (See "Histoire," etc. Planche 31.) The ground at Puy d'Issolu agrees with the description of Hirtius, but the river does not nearly surround the hill, as Hirtius says. There is no spring on the plateau of Puy d'Issolu, but there are several on the sides of the hill, though only one is copious enough to supply a large population, and this is on the west side of the hill 80 feet below the walls of the town and about 300 mètres or 1000 feet from the Tourmente. These 300 mètres, as the author of the " Histoire de César " remarks, are equivalent to 200 Roman passus, whence he concludes that in the text of Hirtius (viii. 41) we must read 200 passus, and that " fluminis circuitu " must mean the " course of the river '." The author places two of the Roman camps on the heights opposite to Puy d'Issolu, and the third on Pech Demont, where excavations have been made, which show a double line of parallel ditches which barred the passage along the neck of land. The subterraneous gallery has also been discovered, which the Romans constructed for the purpose of reaching the source, and it has been opened to the extent of forty mètres². It was cut in a thick bed of tufa. The upper part of the gallery is semicircular and the sides are perpendicular. The mean height is 1m. 80, and the mean breadth 1m. 50. The mud which has been brought down by the water had almost filled up the gallery, leaving only a little space near the top through which the water was flowing when the excavations were made. The gallery is particularly described by the author of the " Histoire." It is stated that under the earth, which has fallen down since the siege, traces have been discovered of the conflagration described by Hirtius. " Planche 32 represents the side of the hill which was the scene of the struggle: on this plate is also represented the earth terrace, the tower and the covered galleries, as well as the subterranean gallery, according to a very exact plan made on the spot '."

[1] The texts of Caesar have 300 feet, not 200. We cannot translate "circuitu," as the author does. Hirtius also says (viii. 40), "flumen infimam vallem dividebat, quae totum paene montem cingebat." Orosius (vi. 11), who has followed Hirtius, says, "oppidum .. duabus partibus per abrupta latera non parvo flumine cingebatur."

[1] " Hist. de César," Planche 32, and vol. ii. 315.

[2] The discovery of the subterranean gallery is due to the persevering labours of M. J. B. Cessac, who was assisted at a later time by the departmental commission of the Lot.

THE STATE OF GALLIA.

The description of Hirtius does not agree with the locality of Puy d'Issolu as to the river, but the discovery of the subterranean gallery must be accepted as decisive evidence. If Hirtius received his information from others, and never saw Uxellodunum, the discrepancy between the reality and his description may be explained.

During this time Labienus in a cavalry fight defeated the Treviri and the Germans, who were always ready to aid against the Romans. He made prisoners of the chiefs, and among them of Surus, an Aeduan, a man of merit and rank, the only one of his countrymen who remained in arms.

Caesar now considered Gallia reduced to submission, but as he had never seen Aquitania, part of which P. Crassus had subdued (B. G. iii. 20), he visited that country with two legions in the latter part of the summer season. He accomplished his object, as he usually did, speedily and successfully: all the states of Aquitania sent commissioners to him and delivered hostages. He then went to Narbo with an escort of cavalry, and made arrangements for the winter-quarters of the army. He placed four legions in Belgium under the legati M. Antonius, C. Trebonius, P. Vatinius, and Q. Tullius Cicero. P. Vatinius was Cicero's old enemy, to whom he had become reconciled (p. 273). Two legions were placed in the country of the Aedui, a people whose influence was very great all over Gallia. Two other legions were stationed among the Turoni on the Loire close upon the territory of the Carnutes, for the purpose of keeping in check all the country bordering on the ocean. The two remaining legions were placed among the Lemovices (the Limousin) not far from the Arverni (Auvergne), that no part of Gallia might be without an army of occupation. He stayed a few days in the Provincia, quickly visited all the circuits (conventus), settled matters in dispute among the several communities, and rewarded those who had served him well, for he had good opportunities of knowing the disposition of the people to the Roman state during the insurrection of the previous year, which he had been enabled to resist successfully through the fidelity of the Provincia and the aid which he received from it. He then joined his legions in Belgium at Nemetocenna (Arras), where he spent the winter.

It seems that he was still afraid that the warlike Bellovaci
might give trouble.

At Nemetocenna he heard that Comm had been fighting
with the Roman cavalry. When Antonius had gone to his
quarters, the Atrebates, in whose country he was stationed,
were quiet, but Comm, who had not forgotten the attempt to
assassinate him, was still active in annoying the Romans.
He and his horsemen supported themselves by plundering,
and frequently intercepted the supplies which were carried to
the Roman camp. Antonius had for his commander of cavalry
C. Volusenus Quadratus whom he sent in pursuit of Comm.
Volusenus, who hated Comm, undertook the business with
great pleasure, and placing his men in ambuscade obtained
several advantages over the enemy. On the last occasion
there was a furious contest, and Volusenus being eager to
take Comm, obstinately pursued him with a few horsemen,
while Comm by a rapid flight drew Volusenus away from his
men. All at once Comm cried out to his cavalry to support
him, and turning his horse round rode right against Volusenus. All Comm's horsemen followed his example, put the
few Roman cavalry to flight and pursued them. Comm spur-
ring his horse up to the horse of Volusenus drove his spear
through the thigh of the Roman commander. Upon this the
Roman cavalry were roused to greater exertions; they turned
round, fell on the enemy furiously, wounded some, trampled
down others, and made some prisoners. Comm escaped by
the swiftness of his horse, and Volusenus was carried back to
the camp dangerously wounded. Comm being either satisfied
with the vengeance he had taken or having lost many of his
men sent a message to Antonius to inform him that he would
stay in any place where he was ordered to remain and would
give hostages as security for his obedience. He had only one
request to make, which was this, that he might never see a
Roman again : he was afraid of them. Antonius, who thought
that he had good reason to be afraid of the Romans, granted
his request and accepted the hostages. Frontinus (Strat. ii.
13. 11) reports that Comm retired to Britannia. If that was
so, he may have fled on this occasion.

CHAPTER XXII.

CAESAR AND THE SENATE.

B.C. 51.

EARLY in May Cicero left Rome to take the government of Cilicia, which had been assigned to him. He went unwillingly, and in the hope that he should not stay in his province more than a year, as he says to Atticus (v. 2). He wrote many letters to Atticus on his journey, and during his absence from Rome (lib. v. vi. vii.). Cicero's friend M. Caelius also corresponded with him and sent him the news (Ad. Div. lib. viii.). Bibulus, Caesar's colleague in the consulship, went at the same time to take the province of Syria, which was threatened by the Parthians. If there was any real danger in the east, the two men who were sent to those parts, were little qualified to meet it. In Spain, where there was no danger, so far as we know, Pompeius had four legions, and two in Italy, which was tranquil. But there was danger from another quarter.

While Caesar was carrying on the war against the Bellovaci, there were rumours at Rome, as Caelius informed Cicero, that he was blockaded by these Galli and cut off from the rest of his army. Caelius also told Cicero that the great question of the appointment of a successor to Caesar in the Gallic provinces was deferred to the first of June. Pompeius at this time was at Tarentum, and Cicero paid him a visit there before he embarked at Brundisium. He stayed three days with his great friend, and left him with the conviction that he was an excellent citizen and quite ready to protect the state against the danger that was feared from a quarrel with Caesar. Caelius wrote to Cicero that he should like to know in what disposition he found Pompeius and what he said: the man, he observed, was used to think one thing and say another, but he was not clever enough to conceal his real wishes. Cicero replied (Ad Div. ii. 8. 2) that he had spent several days in talking with Pompeius about public affairs, but it was not possible to write down what was said, and indeed it ought not to be committed to writing. But he gave Caelius the same assurance that he had given to Atticus, and advised him to attach himself to Pompeius. Cicero thought that Pompeius intended to go to Spain, which Cicero did not approve, and he easily persuaded Theophanes, who had great influence with Pompeius, that the best thing was for Pompeius not to leave Italy (Ad Att. v. 11. 3).

Nothing was done on the first of June about Caesar. At the consular comitia in July C. Claudius Marcellus and L. Aemilius Paulus, both of the senatorian party were elected. Young C. Scribonius Curio was also elected one of the tribunes, and Cicero wrote to congratulate Curio on his election (Ad Div. ii. 7) and to say how much was expected from him. M. Caelius was elected curule aedile. On the twenty-second of July, when the Senate met about the pay for the troops of Pompeius, and something was said about the legion which Pompeius had put down to Caesar's account[1], it was asked what was the number of the legion, and why Caesar had asked for it. Pompeius could not avoid saying that the legion was in Gallia and that he would recall it, but not immediately after the matter had been thus spoken of, nor would he do it simply because his enemies reproached him for his conduct. He was then questioned about Caesar being superseded, and it was settled that the Senate should debate about the provinces when Pompeius returned to Rome, for he was going to Ariminum to the Italian army; and he went immediately. Pompeius said at this sitting that the orders of the Senate ought to be obeyed. This army had been raised for a particular purpose (p. 287), and there was no reason for keeping it together at great cost; nor is it explained why it was at Ariminum on the borders of Caesar's Cisalpine province.

[1] The Latin text (Ad Div. viii. 4. 4) is not clear, and probably it is corrupt.

On the second of September Caelius informed Cicero that nothing was done about the provinces on the thirteenth of August, on which day he had told Cicero that the business would be settled. But the trial of C. Marcellus, the consul elect, for bribery stood in the way. Marcellus was acquitted, for he was consul next year. As far as Caelius could see at the date of this letter, all this affair about the provinces would be put off to the next year. Caelius reminds Cicero that he had written to him in nearly every letter about sending him some panthers for the exhibitions, for which Caelius expected that he would be obliged to provide without the assistance of his colleague. If Cicero, he says, would only give notice to the Cibyratae in Lycia and would write to Pamphylia, where panthers were caught in abundance, Caelius would send men to bring the beasts to Rome, when they were taken.

Finally, after all this delay, when it was fully ascertained that Pompeius intended that Caesar should leave his provinces after the first of March of the next year, a resolution of the Senate was made to the following effect on the motion of the consul M. Marcellus, and on the twenty-ninth of September (Ad Div. viii. 8) it was resolved that the consuls of the following year should bring before the Senate the question of the consular provinces on the first of March, before any thing else and unconnected with any thing else; that for this purpose the Senate might be held during the comitial days (on which a senate could not regularly be held), and that those senators, who formed a Decuria[a] of the judices, might be present at the discussion; and if any Lex or Plebiscitum should be necessary to give effect to this resolution, the consuls Servius Sulpicius and M. Marcellus, or the praetors and tribunes, or if none of them should do it, then their successors should bring the matter before the Populus or Plebs. There was no veto interposed; and some of the senators testified, in the usual way, by the superscription of their names, that they were present when the resolution was reduced to writing[b].

---

[a] The text is corrupt.

[b] This letter of Caelius contains several examples of the form in which such resolutions were drawn up. They began thus: "Pridie Kal. Oct. in aede Apollinis scribendo adfuerunt"; then come the names of the superscribing senators;

A second resolution was made to the effect that no person
who had the legal authority to interpose his veto on a resolution of the Senate about the provinces should do so, under
pain of being declared an enemy to the state; and if any veto
was interposed against this second resolution, it was the
pleasure of the Senate that the resolution should still be
formally drawn up and referred to the Senate and the people.
Four tribunes interposed their veto on this resolution. A
third resolution was to the effect that the Senate should
inquire what soldiers of Caesar had served their time or had
other claims for being released from service. The tribunes
C. Caelius and C. Pansa put their veto on this resolution.
Further, it was resolved that Cilicia and the eight* remaining provinces, which for the future were to be held by praetorians, should be governed by praetorians chosen by lot from
those praetorians who had never governed a province and
according to a previous Senatus consultum were bound to discharge this duty; if there was not a sufficient number of
such praetorians to satisfy the terms of the previous Senatus
consultum, then the praetors of a previous year should be
taken, and if they were not sufficient, then those of a year
previous to the last mentioned and so on, till the number was
made up. C. Caelius and C. Pansa interposed their veto.
At this sitting Pompeius declared that he could not give his
opinion about Caesar's provinces before the first of March of
the next year (B.C. 50) without doing wrong, but that after
that date he would not hesitate. On being asked, what if
a veto was then interposed? he replied it was all the same
whether C. Caesar refused to obey the Senate or prompted

and these are followed by the terms of the resolution, headed by the name
of the consul who proposed it.

* At this time there were fifteen provinces. The two Hispaniae were consular
and held by Pompeius. Bibulus had Syria; and Caesar had Gallia Ulterior,
Gallia Cisalpina, and Illyricum. Thus there were six consular provinces.
Cilicia was to be converted into a praetorian province, though in this year it
was held by Cicero. Cilicia, and the eight remaining provinces, added to the
six consular provinces make up the number fifteen. The eight remaining provinces were Sicily, Sardinia with Corsica, Macedonia, Achaea, Africa, Asia,
Bithynia, Cyrene and Creta. If Macedonia and Achaea were one province, and
Creta and Cyrene were separate provinces, the result is also eight.

any one to prevent the Senate from coming to a decision.
Again, when he was asked, what if Caesar shall resolve to be
consul and keep his army too? What, replied Pompeius, if
my son shall attempt to thrash me with a stick? In another
letter written the next year (Ad Div. viii. 14. 2) Caelius
says that the nearer the unavoidable quarrel approaches, the
more manifest is the danger: Pompeius is resolved not to
allow Caesar to be elected consul unless he gives up his army
and his provinces, and Caesar is convinced that he cannot be
safe without his army, but he will be content if both Pompeius
and himself gave up their armies.

The consul M. Marcellus showed his pitiful spite to Caesar
by his behaviour to a man of Novum Comum. For some
reason, as Appian (B. C. ii. 26) states it, Marcellus flogged
a man of Novum Comum in Gallia Transpadana, who had
held a magistracy in his own city and consequently had
become a Roman citizen, and as such was not liable to be
flogged. The story adds that the consul told the man that
the stripes were intended as a proof that he was not a Roman
citizen, and he bade him show them to Caesar. Plutarch
(Caesar, c. 29) states that M. Marcellus the consul of this year
and Lentulus had deprived the inhabitants of Novum Comum of
the citizenship and that the man whom M. Marcellus punished
was a senator of Novum Comum, who had come to Rome,
and that Marcellus declared that the stripes were for the
purpose of showing that the man was not a Roman. Suetonius, who says nothing of a man being punished, only
informs us that Marcellus made a motion for depriving the
people of Novum Comum of their citizenship. Cicero, who
heard of this affair at Athens on his road to Cilicia remarks
that the man had not been a magistrate at Novum Comum,
but still he was a Transpadane, therefore one of those who
enjoyed the benefit of the law of Pompeius Strabo, the father
of Cn. Pompeius, and that it was therefore an insult to the
son as well as to Caesar, who is said to have given the Roman
citizenship to the people of Novum Comum (vol. iii. p. 438).
The story then is reduced to this that some man of Novum
Comum was punished at Rome by M. Marcellus, and probably for acting as if he were a Roman citizen, but whether

he claimed citizenship as having been a magistrate at Novum
Comum, or under a law made in Caesar's consulship, is uncertain. The purpose of the consul was to annoy Caesar
through his connexion with the town of Novum Comum.

While Caesar was in his quarters in Belgium (B. G. viii.
40), during the winter of B.C. 51 and 50, he employed himself in establishing friendly relations with the Gallic states,
in showing them they had nothing to expect from rising
against him, and in taking care that they had no ground for
doing so. The time was approaching when he must quit
the country, and there was nothing that he wished to avoid
more than leaving a war behind him. Accordingly he
treated the several states with great respect, gave large sums
of money to the chief men, made no fresh requisitions, and
by imposing easy terms of submission he easily kept quiet a
country which was exhausted by so many defeats. After an
eight years' struggle, Gallia was humbled, and did not rise
again. When the conqueror turned his back on her to invade
Italy, she remained quiet. The warlike nations of the extensive country between the Pyrenees and the Rhine had resisted
with desperate courage, but the courage of a distracted and
divided people is useless. There was no political organization
which could enable Gallia to resist Caesar, and the state of
affairs when he entered the country was favourable to the
accomplishment of his ambitious design[4].

Suetonius says (Caesar, 25) that Caesar reduced Gallia to
the form of a province, and imposed on the country an annual
payment of forty millions of sesterces; but this statement is
inconsistent with other facts which we know. We may admit
that he imposed the annual payment of a sum of money, and

[4] Orosius (vi. 12) has described the condition of conquered Gallia in his
peculiar way. Plutarch (Caesar, c. 15) has given in very exaggerated terms
the result of Caesar's campaigns; but the plain truth leaves a deeper impression. Thousands were slaughtered in battle, massacred after surrender, mutilated, or sold into slavery. Cities were destroyed, villages, houses, and farm-
buildings burnt, heavy requisitions were laid on the people, cultivated lands
laid waste, and those who escaped the sword would die of cold and hunger in
the severe winters. Gallia has often suffered from invading armies since
Caesar's time, and not least in this very year (1870-1). Yet Gallia is strong
enough, if ever she shall become wise enough, to repel any invader.

made the country stipendiary as the Romans termed it. He must also have made some arrangements for the collection of the money, and we cannot doubt that he received large sums from Gallia before he invaded Italy. The sums which he paid to the Gallic chiefs would come out of the requisitions made on the people, who in all ages since Caesar's time have been pillaged for the benefit of invaders and their own governors. But Caesar had neither time to establish a regular provincial government nor would he attempt to do it without the authority of the Senate. The country was held as a conquered province in B.C. 49 and 46 by D. Drutus.

For the present Caesar governed Gallia in another way. The Romans first entered central France by their alliance with the Aedui (B.C. 121), and when Caesar began his Gallic campaigns in B.C. 58, he relied on the aid of the Aedui. This people, who were very useful to him, received great favours. The smaller states, which had been dependent on the Aedui, were again put under them, and their power was increased by new dependencies placed in subjection to them by Caesar. The power of the Sequani was broken, who on Caesar's arrival in Gallia had humbled the Aedui by calling in the Germans to help them. By securing the alliance of a large power in the centre of Gallia Caesar prepared the way for the conquest of the whole country. He also gained the Remi, who inhabited the plains of Champagne, and the Remi were always faithful to him. Those dependent states, who did not like the Aedui, were attached to the Remi, the Carnutes for instance, and thus after the downfall of the Sequani the Remi held the next place to the Aedui among the Gallic states. In B.C. 52 the Aedui joined the general rising against Caesar, but after the defeat of the confederates before Alesia, he gave back their prisoners to the Aedui and Arverni in the hope of again establishing friendly relations with these two powerful peoples. Before the year 52 he had named Comm, who was useful to him in Britannia, king of his native state, the Atrebates, under whose dependence he also placed the Morini, or people of the Boulonnois. Comm, as we have seen, afterwards became his enemy. Caesar also gave the Carnutes a king, a man of royal descent who had been useful to him;

and also a king to the Senones. The commentaries are military memoirs, and we only learn something of Caesar's policy towards the Gauls when it is connected with his military operations. But we see enough to learn that he dealt with communities as he did with men: he never allowed passion or resentment to prevail over his interest, and he pursued his way steadily to the end that he had before him.

When he had brought a large part of Gallia to submission, it was his practice to convoke annually in spring the representatives of the states at Lutetia (Paris) or some other central situation. If any of them refused to attend, it would be a sign that they were meditating rebellion. At these meetings public affairs were discussed, the contingents of cavalry were fixed, and we may assume that requisitions of other kinds were made. After bringing the Galli to submission Caesar had the most fertile part of Europe at his command and the means of feeding his army and obtaining all necessary supplies. If he levied money contributions, he would receive large sums from the Galli, and the plunder of captured places and the sale of prisoners would enrich the general and his men. He had built at great cost a villa near Aricia when he was still poor, and he demolished it because he was not altogether satisfied with it (Sueton. Caesar, 46). We may infer from one of Cicero's letters (Ad Att. vi. 1, 25) that in B.C. 50 he was rebuilding the house, at the very time when his enemies at Rome were plotting against him. When Cicero was in Cilicia he heard some odious reports about the tribune Curio and the consul Paulus (Ad Att. vi. 3, 4; Sueton. Caesar, 29). There is little doubt that the reports were about Caesar paying Curio's heavy debts, and giving Paulus a large sum of money with which he built his Basilica. The tribune and the consul of course were bound after such acts of generosity to support Caesar's interests. Cicero also was kept in good humour while he was in Cilicia by letters of congratulation from Caesar (Ad Att. vii, 2, 7) on his exploits in those parts.

CHAPTER XXIII.

CICERO IN CILICIA.

B.C. 50.

In the early part of B.C. 50, Cicero who was then in Cilicia was informed by M. Caelius (Ad Div. viii. 0. 1) that Appius Claudius, Cicero's predecessor in the government of Cilicia, was under prosecution at Rome, and the prosecutor was P. Dolabella, who shortly afterwards married Cicero's daughter Tullia. The charge against Appius was Majestas, a term which comprehended treason against the state and any acts which exceeded the powers of a governor. The precise charge against Appius is not stated, but he was acquitted, as he informed Cicero in a letter written on the fifth of April (Ad Div. iii. 11). He was again prosecuted on the charge of bribery at the election for the Censorship, and again he was acquitted (Ad Div. iii. 12). Appius had been elected Censor, and he had for his colleague L. Piso, Caesar's father-in-law, and consul B.C. 58. Piso undertook the office unwillingly and at Caesar's request. If Cicero's judgment of Piso is true, he was a very unfit man to exercise the office of censor, and a fit object for censorian judgment himself. The censors had been restored to their full powers in B.C. 52 by the repeal of the law of P. Clodius (vol. iii. 448), but the office was not one which a man could desire to hold at this time when so many senators deserved censure (Dion, 40, c. 57). Piso served his son-in-law by acting with great moderation, but his colleague exercised his powers with great severity, and Piso did not interfere except to protect the tribune Curio, whom Caesar, as it is said, had already bought. Appius in his censorship, as Caelius wrote to Cicero, was doing wondrous things; exerting himself most actively against the practice of getting together of statues and paintings from the provincials, about the limits to the occupation of land (de agri modo), and about debts (Ad Div. viii. 14, 4). He is convinced, Caelius adds, that the censorship is like a lye for washing and scouring; "but in my judgment, he is mistaken: he intends to scrub off his own dirt, but he is laying his veins and viscera bare." This active censor ejected from the Senate all the freedmen, who had obtained admission and also some senators of the class of nobles, and among them the historian Sallustius (Dion, 40, c. 63). Appius, who belonged to the party of Pompeius, did damage to his own side by the severity which he showed in his office.

Curio, who was a pontifex, proposed early in the year that a month should be intercalated, that is, added to the calendar to set the reckoning right. This was no unusual thing, for the calendar was in disorder, but the intercalation was now generally made for political purposes [1]. Curio's proposal was rejected, upon which, as Caelius says (Ad Div. viii. 6, 5), with the greatest levity he passed over to the popular party and began to speak in favour of Caesar. It seems probable that Curio in proposing the intercalation only sought an excuse for changing sides and hiding his corrupt bargain with Caesar. Next, he brought in a bill about roads, not unlike the Agrarian proposal of Rullus (vol. iii. chap. xiii.), and he impudently proposed that he himself should be the commissioner and hold the office for five years. He also proposed a bill (lex alimentaria) to empower the aediles to give allowances of corn to the people. Both these bills were rejected.

Cicero writing from Cilicia to Atticus (vi. 2. 6) informs

---

[1] Censorinus de die natali, c. 20. The correction of the error caused by the difference between the civil and the natural year was at some time, but it is not said when, put in the hands of the Pontifices an ecclesiastical body. But, as Censorinus says, the majority moved either by dislike to some public personages, or by a desire to favour others, and in order that a man might sooner give up his office or hold it longer, or a farmer of the taxes might gain or lose according to the length of the year, intercalated more or less according to their pleasure. Curio's proposal about the intercalation was therefore made to the College of Pontifices.

him that he had news (acta urbana) from Rome to the seventh of March (B.C. 50), from which he learned that through Curio's firmness nothing would be settled about the provinces. It appears probable then that the Senate met on the first of March pursuant to the resolution of the twenty-ninth of September of B.C. 51, and the meeting described by Appian (B. C. ii. c. 27) seems to refer to this day. The consul C. Marcellus proposed that Caesar should leave his provinces on the thirteenth of November (B.C. 50), and this was the wish of the majority of the Senate and of Pompeius, who was afraid of Caesar being elected consul before he had given up his army and his provinces. The consul Paulus said nothing on the motion of C. Marcellus, but Curio expressed his approbation of it, and made this addition, that Pompeius also should give up his province and his army, and thus the state would be secured. Many of the senators objected that this would not be fair because the time of Pompeius had not expired. It would have been an answer to this objection that Caesar's time also had not expired; and Curio declared that Caesar ought not to be superseded unless Pompeius also was superseded, and he knew that Pompeius would not consent. Pompeius was not present at this meeting of the Senate. When Curio's proposal was discussed, M. Marcellus who had been consul in B.C. 51, was of opinion that they ought to treat with the tribunes about Curio withdrawing his proposal, which amounted to a veto on that of the consul C. Marcellus, but the Senate rejected the advice of M. Marcellus, and the consequence was that nothing was done, and Caesar was not superseded (Ad Attic. vii. 7. 5), and could be a candidate for the consulship without giving up his army or his provinces, and without being present at the election. Plutarch (Pompeius, c. 58) gives a somewhat different version of this matter. He says that Curio first divided the Senate on the question whether Caesar alone should lay down his arms and Pompeius should retain his command; and there was a majority in favour of Caesar alone laying down his arms. He next put the question whether both should lay down their arms, and all the Senate except two and twenty voted that they should. Curio considered that he had gained a victory,

and when he came out of the senate-house the people received
him with clapping of hands, and threw on him chaplets and
flowers. Plutarch's narrative is inconsistent with what we
know of this meeting from other authorities. Plutarch then
tells a story of the Senate putting on mourning and of
Marcellus advancing through the Forum with the Senate
following him and giving a sword to Pompeius with an
injunction to defend his country; though he had just said
that Pompeius was not in the Senate when these votes were
taken, because those who are in command of an army do
not enter the city. The Senate too, as he says, who had just
voted for Curio's second motion, now accompanied Marcellus
when he told Pompeius to take up arms. The events of this
year are told in a confused way both by Plutarch and Appian,
who do not trouble themselves about chronology; and Plutarch
has perhaps confounded two meetings.

Sometime in March Q. Hortensius, the great orator died,
and Caesar's quaestor M. Antonius came to Rome to be a
candidate for the place in the college of Augurs which was
vacant by the death of Hortensius[*]. After inspecting all the
winter-quarters Caesar visited Cisalpine Gallia to recommend
Antonius to the Municipia and Coloniae, and though he heard
of the election of his quaestor before he reached Italy, he still
determined to visit these towns to thank them for their services to Antonius, and to secure their votes for his own election
in the following year (B.C. 49). The consuls for that year
were already elected, L. Lentulus and C. Marcellus, both of
them Caesar's enemies, and their faction were exulting in
having two men who would strip Caesar of all his honours,
and had gained a victory over Servius Galba, one of Caesar's
legati, who had been a candidate for the consulship.

This was Caesar's first visit to Cisalpine Gallia after the
great victories of B.C. 52 and the complete subjugation of the

---

[*] Caesar himself was Pontifex Maximus, head of religion at Rome and commander-in-chief in Gallia at the same time. One of his successors in the
priestly title, an old man, Pope Julius II., led his army to attack Mirandola in a
very cold winter and exposed himself to the dangers of war. Antonius was
ambitious to imitate his master, who discovered that the man had talents and
could be made useful.

Transalpine nations. The conqueror was received by all the towns of his province with unbounded demonstrations of honour and affection. Wherever he went, preparations were made to greet him, and the gates of the towns through which he passed were decorated. Men, women, and children came out to see the great soldier who in eight hard campaigns had tamed the warlike people that had so often threatened Italy. Victims were sacrificed, the market-places and temples were ornamented for religious celebrations. It was an anticipation of Caesar's triumph at Rome. The rich contributed their wealth; the poor showed their devotion[3]. After visiting all parts of Cisalpine Gallia, Caesar returned with his usual rapidity to his army at Nemetocenna and summoned all the legions from their quarters to meet him in the country of the Treviri. His departure from Gallia was drawing nigh, and he gave all his old companions in arms the opportunity of seeing one another and their victorious general near the borders of the great river which he had twice crossed. The Germans, who had felt the power of the Roman arms on the Rhine, would hear of this mustering of their terrible enemy. The meeting of the army was celebrated by a solemn religious ceremony. Caesar set T. Labienus over Cisalpine Gallia that he might be useful in securing the votes of that province at Caesar's election. Caesar himself, as Hirtius says, only moved about for change of place and enough to keep in health. He had nothing to do except to put the affairs of Gallia in order, but we may conclude that he did not move about alone, and change of encampment, as Vegetius observes (iii. 2) is necessary in summer and autumn to preserve the soldiers in health. We may wonder how so active a man passed the summer in Gallia, but he would find something to do in setting things in order, and as he was always busy, he would have time for writing, which was his great amusement. When Caesar was north of the Alps he heard many reports of his

[3] Bonaparte, after receiving the imperial title in France, visited Cisalpine Gallia and was crowned King of Italy at Milan. He made a progress through his new dominions, and received the homage of his people, not so sincere, we may suppose, as the respect paid to the Proconsul of Gallia, though some of the Italian towns struck medals on the occasion.

enemies attempting to seduce Labienus, and he was informed
that a small party designed by means of a resolution of the Senate
to deprive him of part of his army; but he would not believe
what was said about Labienus, nor could he be induced to do
any thing against the authority of the Senate, as he was confident that if the Senate should be allowed to vote freely, his
claims would be maintained. He knew that Curio, who had
undertaken the care of his interests, had often proposed to the
Senate that both Caesar and Pompeius should give up their
armies; and, as Hirtius says (B. G. viii. 52), Curio had not
only made this proposal, but had attempted to bring the
Senate to a vote upon it, and only failed through the influence of the consuls and the friends of Pompeius. Hirtius
then alludes (c. 53) to what the consul Marcellus had done in
the preceding year (B.C. 51) when he made a motion, in violation of the law of Pompeius and Crassus, before the proper time
about Caesar's provinces, and brought the Senate to a vote
upon his motion which was negatived. This appears to refer
to the proceedings of the twenty-ninth of September B.C. 51.
Drumann assumes that Hirtius is mistaken in referring what
he says about M. Marcellus (B. G. viii. 53) to B.C. 51, but the
mistake, I think, is with Drumann. The law passed in the
second consulship of Pompeius and Crassus B.C. 55, which
Hirtius names the law of Pompeius and Crassus, is the Lex
Trebonia which gave to Caesar his second term of five years.
In B.C. 52 an enactment was made and Cicero supported it, by
which Caesar was allowed to be a candidate in his absence.
Cicero (Ad Attic. vii. 1. 5) alludes to the attempts made to
supersede Caesar during the consulships of the two Marcelli[4].

---

[4] Compare Ad Attic. vii. 1. 4, where he says that he aided in the matter of
Caesar being allowed to be a candidate in his absence; and Ad Div. vi. 6. 5,
where he says, if we understand him right, that he only recommended that
Caesar should have this privilege after the people had voted for it. Again (Ad
Attic. viii. 3. 3), he speaks of M. Marcellus (B.C. 51) attempting to determine
Caesar's command on the first of March (B.C. 50).

CHAPTER XXIV.

CICERO IN CILICIA.

B.C. 51, 50.

SOME time during this year (B.C. 50) Pompeius being in Campania, where he went probably to be out of the way during the discussions at Rome, addressed a letter to the Senate, in which he extolled Caesar's services, and recapitulated his own. He spoke of the third consulship which had been conferred on him, and of the provinces and army which he had afterwards received without asking for them, and had accepted only for the interest of the commonwealth; and he added that he was willing to give up the provinces and the army before the appointed time. His subsequent conduct shows that he did not mean what he said. When he wrote this letter, he was dangerously ill at Naples, or he may have fallen sick after writing it. The people of Naples offered sacrifices for his recovery, and when his health was restored there was general rejoicing in Italy. The Neapolitans and people of Puteoli wore crowns, and deputations came from many towns to congratulate him. On his return to Rome he was received on the road by crowds who threw flowers over him and accompanied him with torches. Such a demonstration was likely enough to turn a vain man's head, and make him believe that he was popular; but Cicero at a later time wrote to Atticus (viii. 10. 1; ix. 5, 3), when he was in a spiteful mood, that all this show was only pretence, and was done through fear. On his return to Rome Pompeius spoke to the same effect as he had written to the Senate, and again offered to give up his provinces and army, saying that his friend Caesar would also be glad to do the same and to repose after his laborious campaigns. Appian (B.C. ii. 28) who is in some respects a careless compiler, often shows good sense in his judgments, and it was his opinion that Pompeius wished Caesar to be superseded immediately, but himself to go no farther than promising; and the behaviour of Pompeius is consistent with this conclusion of the historian. But Curio who saw through his trickery, declared that he ought not to promise only; he ought to surrender his power and not to disarm Caesar before he had himself descended to the condition of a private person: Caesar had enemies, and it was not consistent with his safety to be stripped of his army, nor was it the interest of Rome that a single man should hold so much power; it would be better that each should retain his legions and employ them against the other, if any violence against the state was designed by either of them. Curio charged Pompeius with aiming at the supreme authority, and declared that, if Pompeius did not surrender his commission now when he was afraid of Caesar, he would never do it. He proposed that, if Pompeius and Caesar did not give up their provinces and armies, the Senate should declare them enemies and raise a force against them. Curio must have felt quite certain that his proposal would not be accepted, but it served to conceal his alleged corrupt bargain with Caesar. The proposal to raise an army against the conqueror of Gallia and the man who held both the Spains with his legions must have seemed ridiculous. Pompeius withdrew to his villa in the suburbs after this bold attack. He now understood what he had done in restoring the full authority of the tribunes (vol. iii. 51), which Sulla had reduced within narrow limits.

L. Cassius after the defeat of Crassus in Mesopotamia (B.C. 53) crossed the Euphrates and prepared to defend Syria against the Parthians. In B.C. 52 the enemy passed the river with a small force, for they did not expect to meet with any resistance. But Cassius, who had been the quaestor of Crassus and now acted as governor of Syria, easily repelled the invaders (Dion Cassius, 40. c. 28). In the next year the Parthians came again in greater numbers, nominally under the command of Pacorus, the youthful son of Orodes, but the real commander was Osaces. The enemy took all the places which lay on their route, and advanced as far as Antiocheia, in which Cassius shut himself up. Cicero received a letter from Atticus, written on the nineteenth of July, in answer to which he informed Atticus that he was with his army at Cybistra near the range of Taurus, at which time he had no news of Bibulus having arrived in Syria, and Cassius, as he says, was in Antiocheia with his forces, and the Parthians were in that part of Syria named Cyrrhestica, which was nearest to Cicero's province of Cilicia (Ad Attic. v. 18. 1). The Parthians being unable to besiege Antiocheia moved off to Antigonia on the Orontes, the suburbs of which town were covered with plantations of trees, which the enemy intended to clear away in order to make an approach to the place (Dion Cassius, 40, c. 29). But the labour was too much for them; and Cassius cut off all their stragglers. After this check the Parthians left this place also, and Cassius lying in wait for them on the road destroyed part of the army. Osaces was wounded and died. Pacorus quitted Syria with his troops, and did not return.

Cicero with his army crossed the Taurus and advanced to the Amanus, the range which, as he says, forms the watershed between Syria and Cilicia. He was at Tarsus on the fifth of October B.C. 51, and on the thirteenth he "killed a great number of the mountaineers," took and burnt some strong hill-forts, and was greeted with the title of Imperator by his army. He occupied for four days the site of the camp which Alexander occupied before his battle with Darius at Issus. After this great exploit he undertook the siege of Pindenissus, a strong place of the Eleutherocilices or free Cilicians, who had never submitted even to the kings. He speaks of the investment of this hill-fort, of the vallum, the ditch, the huge agger, or mound of earth, the lofty towers, the engines for discharging missiles, the archers; but his description is more in the style of Sallust, who perhaps never saw a siege, than in Caesar's style. The town was knocked down or burnt and the people surrendered on the seventeenth day of December, the first day of the Saturnalia, on the forty-seventh day of the siege, as Cicero states to Atticus (v. 20. 1) or the fifty-seventh, as it is in a letter to Cato (Ad Div. xv. 4. 10). If the town was battered down and burnt, the surrender was a matter of necessity. The booty, except the horses, was given to the soldiers; and the inhabitants after seeing their houses burnt were sold as slaves on the third day of the Saturnalia; and, as Cicero was writing his letter, he reports that the amount realized by the sale was twelve millions of sesterces. Perhaps it was more humane to sell the people after they had lost every thing than to leave them to perish by hunger and cold. Cicero's brother Quintus led the victorious army to winter-quarters; and Cicero went to Laodicea. When he was at Tarsus again in June of the following year, there was war in Syria, and Cilicia was full of robbers, which means it was full of starving people.

It was the report of Cicero's approach to Cilicia through Cappadocia, as he says (Ad Att. v. 20. 3), which encouraged Cassius, who was shut up in Antiocheia, and alarmed the Parthians, so that Cassius was enabled to defeat the flying enemy, and Cicero's name was in favour in Syria. Soon after the victory, when Cassius was leaving his province or was on his way to Rome, Cicero wrote to congratulate him on his recent victory, and to express a hope that their old friendship might be continued (Ad Div. xv. 14). In a letter to Atticus (v. 21. 2) Cicero says that Cassius made a report to the Senate in which he declared that he had finished the Parthian war not a very modest declaration, as Cicero observes, for the enemy had left Antiocheia before Bibulus arrived in Syria, not through any good fortune of the Roman arms, and they were wintering in Cyrrhestica. This report of Cassius was read as Cicero says in the Senate on the seventh of October, on the same day in which Cicero's letters were read announcing disturbance in the east. Cicero's friend Axius had informed him that the report of Cassius was not believed, and that his own was received with great respect : no letters from Bibulus had then reached Rome, but Cicero says that he knows they will certainly shew great alarm. Thus Cicero's two letters contradict one another. The report of Cassius' victory was received at Rome on the seventh of October, and Cicero did not reach Tarsus until the fifth of October, only two days before the news of Cassius' victory arrived at Rome. Consequently Cassius gained his victory some time in September or earlier, and before Cicero crossed the Taurus, and several weeks before Cicero was saluted Imperator; and yet he ascribes the success of Cassius to the rumour of his approach. Cicero was at Cybistra north of the Taurus on the twenty-first of September (Ad Attic. vi. 1. 1). In his letter to Cato (Ad Div. xv. 4. 7) Cicero says that when he reached the Amanus he learned that the enemy had left Antiocheia and that Bibulus was there; and he then describes his victory of the thirteenth of October. When he wrote this letter to the Roman Stoic he had found out how the facts were and he did not venture on the impudent assertion that his defeat of a few poor mountaineers had contributed to a victory over the Parthians which Cassius had gained probably a month earlier. In a letter to Caelius also (Ad Div. ii. 10) Cicero says that when he reached the Amanus, Cassius to Cicero's great delight had driven the enemy from Antiocheia and Bibulus had taken possession of the province. This letter to Cato is that in which Cicero intreats him to use all his interest to secure a triumph for his old friend. Cato's answer (Ad Div. xv. 5), which he calls a longer letter than he usually wrote,—it is about twenty lines —is an honourable testimonial to his character. He tells the conqueror of the Amanus, the burner of the little towns of the mountaineers, and the devastator of their poor fields, that a triumph was not necessarily granted after a supplicatio or thanksgiving had been decreed, and it was a greater honour than a triumph for the Senate to declare that the province had been saved by the mild administration and integrity of the governor rather than by military force or the favour of the immortal gods; and this, Cato said, he had declared in the Senate. We do not know what Cicero wrote in reply to Cato, but we know what he wrote to Atticus (vii. 2). He said that he never wished for a triumph until Bibulus sent his impudent despatches to the Senate and obtained a twenty days' supplicatio for doing nothing, and that Cato voted for it. Cato was shamefully spiteful to him. He bore testimony to Cicero's integrity, justice and honour, which Cicero did not ask for; and he refused what Cicero did ask. Caesar, he said, who by letter congratulated him and proffered his services, exulted in Cato's most ungrateful behaviour. "Excuse me," he says to Atticus, "I cannot endure this nor will I endure it."

In July of B.C. 50 Cicero learned that the Parthians had retired, and he had the welcome certainty that he should not be detained much longer in his province. It was a great piece of good luck he says that the enemy went away, and he adds with a sneer that they left Bibulus half alive; so much alarmed was the governor of Syria as we must suppose. The enemies of Caesar saw an opportunity in the state of affairs in Syria to deal a side-blow at him. Caelius wrote to Cicero that, if either Caesar or Pompeius did not go to the Parthian war, he saw that a great quarrel was imminent which would be decided by the sword; for both the rivals were prepared for the contest (Ad Div. viii. 14. 4). In order to strengthen Pompeius a resolution of the Senate was made that two legions should be sent to Bibulus for the Parthian war, though the war really ended in B.C. 51; one legion from the forces of Pompeius, and one from the forces of Caesar (D. G. viii. 54). It was plain that this was only a scheme for depriving Caesar of two legions; for Pompeius asked Caesar to send back the legion, the first, which had been raised in Gallia Cisalpina and lent by him to Caesar, and Caesar was required to send one of his own legions also. Pompeius gave the legion, which Caesar sent back to him, as his contribution to the troops for the Parthian war, and Caesar gave as his contribution the fifteenth legion which was in Gallia Cisalpina. The thirteenth legion was sent into Gallia Cisalpina to take the place of the fifteenth. Caesar placed his remaining eight legions in winter-quarters, and then went into Italy. C. Trebonius was in Belgium with four legions, and C. Fabius with the remaining four legions in the country of the Aedui. Caesar thought the peace of Gallia would be thus best secured by placing half of his force among the Belgae who were the bravest of the Galli, and the other half among the Aedui, whose influence was the greatest.

When Caesar sent back the legion of Pompeius, he gave each man 250 denarii (Plutarch, Caesar, c. 29; Appian, B. C. ii. 29). Appius Claudius, not the censor of this year, was sent to bring the legion of Pompeius from Gallia, and he had thus the opportunity of seeing the troops of Caesar. Appius and others also, as it is said, reported that Caesar's army, worn out by the long wars, desired to return home, and would pass over to Pompeius as soon as they had crossed the Alps. This report was entirely false, but whether it was made through ignorance and prejudice or from some other cause, we do not know. For Caesar's men, as Appian observes, were inured to ready obedience and toil by long service and by the profit which war brings to victorious soldiers, as well as by the bounty of their commander, for he gave without stint, having a view to future designs, of which his men were not ignorant, and yet they continued faithful to him. When Caesar reached Italy, he learned that the consul C. Marcellus had kept at home the two legions, which according to the resolution of the Senate ought to have been sent to the Parthian war, and had given them to Pompeius (B. G. viii. 55). The two legions wintered at Capua.

Pompeius relying on the reports about the disposition of Caesar's soldiers remained inactive; and Curio made no opposition to the proposal for granting money for the payment of Pompeius' troops. The consul C. Claudius proposed the question to the Senate if Caesar should be superseded, and another question separately if Pompeius should be deprived of his power. The Senate rejected the second proposal, but the majority were in favour of superseding Caesar. Curio then proposed that both Caesar and Pompeius should lay down their power, and only two and twenty voted against this proposal. Three hundred and seventy voted for it, upon which Claudius dissolved the meeting, crying out, "Have it your own way, and take Caesar for your master" (Appian, B.C. ii. 30).

A report now reached Rome that Caesar had crossed the Alps and was marching on the city. On the fifteenth of October Cicero was at Athens on his return from Cilicia, and on this very day, as Atticus wrote, Caesar would reach Placentia with four legions. "What will become of us?" he says (Ad Attic. vi. 9. 5). There was great alarm at Rome, and the consul C. Marcellus proposed that the legions in Capua should be led against Caesar. Curio opposed the motion, and declared the report to be false; and it was at this time[1] (Appian,

---
[1] See the narrative of Plutarch, Pompeius, 58, and p. 401.

B. C. ii. 31), that the consul C. Marcellus with his colleague went to Pompeius, who was outside the walls and presenting a sword to him said, we empower you to march against Caesar, and for this purpose we give you all the troops in Italy and empower you to raise more. Pompeius expressed his willingness to obey the consuls' commands, but added "unless something better can be done." Curio complained to the people of the proceedings of the consul, but he could do nothing, and when his term of office expired on the tenth of December, not feeling himself safe in Rome he went to Caesar, who was at Ravenna with five thousand soldiers and three hundred horsemen, as Appian states (B. C. ii. 32).

On the twenty-fourth of November Cicero arrived at Brundisium, where he was met by his wife Terentia (Ad Attic. vii. 2. 2). On the ninth of December he wrote to Atticus (vii. 3) from the villa of Pontius near Trebula in Campania. He tells Atticus that he is quite right when he says that Caesar has not been as liberal to him as he ought to have been, considering Cicero's good offices and Caesar's profuse gifts to others, and that Atticus gives the true reason for Caesar's behaviour: Caesar was now become so powerful that there was no hope of resisting him except through Pompeius, and since matters were come to such a state, Cicero will not ask "where is the vessel of the Atridae[2]?" but there will be only one vessel for him, and that will be the vessel which Pompeius steers. On his road towards Rome and on the tenth of December he saw Pompeius, and was with him about two hours (Ad Attic. vii. 4. 2). It does not appear why Pompeius now left Rome, but he was blamed for quitting the city at so critical a time. He expressed great pleasure at seeing Cicero, urged him to claim a triumph and offered his support, but advised him not to enter the Senate before the matter was settled, that he might not offend any of the tribunes by what he might say. Pompeius spoke as if war was certain: he knew that Caesar had no friendly feeling towards him, and his opinion was con-

[2] Cicero quotes part of a verse from the Troades of Euripides (v. 455) ποῦ σκάφος τὸ τοῦ στρατηγοῦ; ποῖ ποτ' ἐμβαίνειν μὲ χρή; but he has written τῶν Ἀτρειδῶν for τοῦ στρατηγοῦ.

firmed by the fact that Hirtius, one of Caesar's greatest
friends had come to Rome from Caesar on the evening of the
sixth of December without visiting him, and though Balbus
appointed a meeting with Scipio about the state of affairs on
the seventh before day-break, yet Hirtius returned to Caesar
at a late hour of the night.

Cicero heard a report (Ad Attic. vii. 7. 4) that Pompeius and
his advisers had determined to send him into Sicily, because
he still held the Imperium; but neither the Senate nor the
people had made any order on this matter, as he says, and if
the Senate should empower Pompeius to send him, why
"should he be sent rather than any other person." If this
Imperium should cause him trouble, he will enter the City by
the first gate that he can find. If he entered the city, he
of course gave up all hope of a triumph, which, as he says, he
regards with indifference; but if he did not care for it now,
he had changed his mind. He was in a state of great perplexity
at this time, as his letters to Atticus show. He had said in
a previous letter (vii. 3. 5) that he should put himself in the
same boat with Pompeius, but that he would still urge him to
peace: affairs were in a critical state, and they had to deal
with a most audacious man, who was well prepared and had
on his side all the rogues and villains.

Velleius (ii. 48) and Plutarch speak of Cicero attempting
to mediate between Caesar and Pompeius, or they use words
which appear to have this meaning; but there is no evidence
to this effect in Cicero's letters, though we cannot doubt that
he would have gladly reconciled these two leaders. Neither
of these men however wanted his mediation; both were resolved to push the quarrel to extremities, but each thought
that Cicero's tongue might be useful to him. It was Cicero's
opinion that it would be better to grant what Caesar demanded
than to go to war, and that it was too late to resist a man
whom during ten years they had been strengthening against
themselves (Ad Attic. vii. 5. 5). He says, when he was at
Athens in October on his road to Italy, that both Caesar and
Pompeius were writing to him in such terms as if they esteemed
no man more: both of them reckoned him among their friends,
unless perchance one of them was only pretending. Again,

after his arrival in Italy (vii. 3. 11) Caesar wrote a flattering letter to him and Balbus did the same on Caesar's behalf; but Cicero was resolved not to move a finger's breadth from the line of duty. There was however a difficulty. Cicero owed Caesar money, and it was possible that if Cicero acted with little vigour, some one might charge him with the fact of being in debt to Caesar, or Caesar might demand his money, if Cicero made any opposition to him. In that case, says Cicero to Atticus, I suppose you will say we must pay; and Cicero answers his own question by adding: well we will borrow from Caelius (some money-lender); I wish you to reflect on this; for I think that if ever I shall speak nobly in the Senate about the state, your friend from Tartessus (Balbus) will say to me as I am going out, "I wish you would look after that money being paid" (Ad. Att. vii. 3. 11). There are other allusions to this debt in the letters to Atticus (v. 1. 2, 5. 2, 10. 3; vii. 8. 5). In the last passage Cicero says that he is very much annoyed that he must pay his debt to Caesar and apply to this purpose the money that would be useful in his triumph; from which we see that he is still thinking about it near the end of December, when the war was now imminent.

On the twenty-fifth of December Cicero and Pompeius happened to meet at Lavernium, and went together to Formiae. They were talking on public affairs all the afternoon (Ad. Attic. vii. 8. 4). As far as Cicero could collect from the conversation, Pompeius did not wish for peace. He thought that even if Caesar gave up his army, there would be a revolution, if he was elected consul. It was the opinion of Pompeius, that when Caesar heard of the active opposition preparing against him, he would not be a candidate for the consulship in the coming year, and would rather keep his army and province. But if Caesar should be resolved on violent measures, Pompeius expressed the greatest contempt for him and full confidence in the troops at his own disposal. Though Cicero thought of the saying (Ευνός 'Ενυάλιος) that the fortune of war belongs to both sides, he says that he was relieved of anxiety when he heard a brave, experienced man, of the highest reputation talking like a statesman of the dangers of a fictitious peace. Cicero and Pompeius had with them a copy of a speech delivered before the popular assembly on the twenty-first of December by the tribune M. Antonius, formerly Caesar's quaestor, in which Antonius inveighed against all that Pompeius had done since he entered on public life, against the condemnation of citizens under his laws about bribery at elections, and against his striking terror into the citizens by the employment of an armed force. "What do you think," said Pompeius to Cicero, "will Caesar do if he obtains the power, when his feeble, needy quaestor dares to talk in this way?" Cicero at last appeared before the city on the fourth of January, B.C. 49, but he did not enter, because he expected to have his triumph. People came out to meet the conqueror of the Amanus, who was satisfied with his reception; but he says, "I have fallen amidst the very flames of civil discord or rather of war" (Ad. Div. xvi. 11. 2).

Caesar was now at Ravenna, near the southern boundary of his province of Gallia Cisalpina with only the thirteenth legion, or three hundred horse and five thousand legionary soldiers, as both Plutarch and Appian estimate his force; but if he had only this legion, the estimate is in excess. Curio is said to have advised Caesar to draw all his legions from Gallia Transalpina and to march right upon Rome, but Caesar had his own plans. He sent Curio on the twenty-ninth of December with a letter to the Senate and the new Consuls, which was delivered on the first of January, B.C. 49. It was a threatening letter, as Cicero says. Caesar in this letter enumerated what he had done for the state, and declared that he was ready to lay down his authority if Pompeius would do the same, but if Pompeius would not give up his power, neither would he, for by doing so, he would be at the mercy of his enemies. Plutarch and Appian speak of Caesar proposing that he should retain Gallia Cisalpina and Illyricum with two legions till he was elected Consul a second time; or as Suetonius affirms he would be content with one legion and Illyricum (Sueton. Caesar, c. 29). If these proposals were made, we must assume that it was in the letter which Curio delivered. Caesar himself says that his demands were most moderate (B. C. i. 5).

CHAPTER XXV.

CICERO IN CILICIA.

B.C. 51, 50.

A SHORT sketch of Cicero's administration in Cilicia will complete the view of the Roman provincial administration. (Vol. ii. p. 169 ; iii. c. 4.)

Cicero sailed from Brundisium (p. 391) to Corcyra, where he was well entertained by the people of Atticus, and also at the islands Sybota, where he put in. He landed at Actium on the fourteenth of June, from which place he went by land to Patrae near the entrance of the Corinthian gulf. He reached Athens on the twenty-fourth of June. So far, he says to Atticus, neither community nor private person had been put to any cost on his account, nor on account of any person who accompanied him: nothing had been received under the provisions of the Lex Julia (vol. iii. p. 410), and nothing from any person who furnished him with lodgings. He was much pleased with Athens, and the citizens' affectionate remembrance of Atticus, and their kindness to himself. Cicero lodged with the academician Aristus, and his brother Quintus, with the Epicurean Xeno, a friend of Atticus. Cicero and his companions left Athens in some vessels of Rhodes, of Mitylene, and others on the sixth of July, and they did not reach Ephesus until the twenty-second of July. At Samos, where he had called, and also at Ephesus he was met by deputations, private persons, and a great number of people. The Roman Publicani paid their respects to him just as if he had arrived with authority in the province of Asia, and the Greeks received him as they would have

received the praetor of Ephesus. Atticus had money affairs at
Ephesus, and Cicero recommended the interests of his friend to
Q. Minucius Thermus, the governor of Asia. It was a hot and
dusty journey to Tralles, where Cicero arrived on the twenty-
seventh of July, and all his train with him except the legatus
Tullius. Here he heard that the Parthians were quiet, that the
agreements between the publicani and the taxpayers were settled
in his province, and that a mutiny among the soldiers had been
suppressed by his predecessor Appius Pulcher, who had paid his
men up to the fifteenth of July. Cicero reached Laodicea in
Phrygia on the thirty-first of July, and he was now in his own
province. From this date Cicero reckoned the commencement
of his year of government, which he anxiously wished not to
be prolonged.

The province Cilicia at this time comprehended the level
Cilicia, the mountainous Cilicia, Pamphylia, and Pisidia, all which
divisions were south of the range of Taurus. It comprehended
also north of the Taurus the divisions Isauria, Lycaonia, and the
three dioceses of Laodicea, Apamea, and Synnada, which were
in Phrygia[1]; and also the island Cyprus, which was annexed
in B.C. 58 (p. 70). This province Cilicia was governed by P.
Lentulus Spinther[2] from B.C. 56 to 53, by Appius Claudius
Pulcher from B.C. 53 to 51, and by Cicero from July B.C. 51
to July 50. It was divided into Conventus or circuits: the
conventus of the level Cilicia contained Tarsus, the governor's
residence. Cicero had four legati, his brother Quintus, C.
Pomptinus, who had been praetor in B.C. 63 and arrested the
ambassadors of the Allobroges, M. Annoius, and L. Tullius. It
was usual for governors of provinces to name also Praefecti, of
whom there will be occasion to speak again. Those who
managed the affairs of the great Roman money-lenders or their
own business sometimes obtained from a governor this office of
Praefectus and the command of soldiers, with whose aid they
compelled private persons or town communities to pay what
they owed to their Roman creditors. Cicero, who wished to

---

[1] Cicero (Ad Div. xiii. 67) says that three Asiatic dioceses were attached to his province Cilicia. It seems that these were the three dioceses mentioned here.
[2] The first nine letters of the first book of Cicero's Epistles (Ad Fam. L 1—9) are addressed to this Lentulus.

conduct his administration in an honourable manner, declared that he would name no man a Praefectus who had money transactions in the province. Cicero also had with him in the province his favourite slave Tiro, and three Greeks, Dionysius, Nicanor, and Chrysippus, who seem to have been tutors and guardians of Cicero's son Marcus and his nephew Quintus, both of whom accompanied him to Cilicia.

The letters of Cicero to Appius Claudius Pulcher, which are contained in the third book of his Epistles (Ad Div. iii.), show Cicero's great anxiety to continue on friendly terms with Appius since their reconciliation, for they had not always been friends. Appius, who was the eldest brother of Cicero's great enemy P. Clodius, did nothing when he was praetor (B.C. 57) for Cicero's restoration from exile; and when Cicero asked permission to address the people on the subject of conferring on Pompeius the office of supplying Rome with corn, Appius and two tribunes alone refused their consent (Ad Att. iv. 1. 6). In B.C. 54 Appius was consul, and as Claudia, one of Appius' daughters, was married to a son of Cicero's great friend Pompeius, Cicero prudently was reconciled to Appius, and, as he says, supported him steadily in his consulship (Ad Div. iii. 10. 8). When Appius left Rome for his province Cilicia (B.C. 53), Cicero accompanied him as far as Puteoli in Campania, and during the absence of Appius looked faithfully after his interests at Rome. Cicero accordingly expected that Appius would show his gratitude by delivering up the province in the best condition to one who was his dearest friend, and would never forget such a valuable service. He particularly requested Appius (Ad Div. iii. 3) not to dismiss any of his soldiers, for the Parthians were threatening Cilicia, which required more men to defend it, and Cicero did not conceal his fear of the enemy. When Cicero was at Brundisium, he inquired of Phanias, a freedman of Appius, at what place he supposed that Appius desired his successor to enter the province, and Phanias replied at the port of Sida in Pamphylia. Though Cicero did not think Sida a convenient place to land at, he said that he would do so. At Corcyra Cicero saw L. Clodius, the head of the engineers of Appius, who advised him to go direct to Laodicea, where the late governor wished to meet him. Accordingly Cicero wrote to Appius from Tralles on the twenty-seventh of July to say that he expected to be at Laodicea on the thirty-first and stay a few days there to receive the money which would be paid to him on account of the Roman treasury[1]. He would then proceed to join the army at Iconium (Konieh), where he expected to arrive about the fifteenth of August. He promised to inform Appius of his progress by every opportunity. He did not presume, he said, nor ought he to impose any trouble on Appius, but if it was convenient to him, it would be for the advantage of both that they should meet before Appius left the province. But they did not meet; and Cicero (Ad Div. iii. 6) wrote a very humble letter of complaint to Appius, in which he says that Appius not only did not come to the place where he might have seen Cicero, but even went off to so remote a part of the province that Cicero could not have reached him within the thirty days, which a Lex Cornelia allowed a retiring governor for leaving his province after the arrival of his successor. In fact Appius went off to Tarsus, the farthest part of the province, where he held courts, and transacted public business, though, as Cicero tells him, he had reason to believe that his successor had arrived, and though he knew that he was doing what it was unusual for a governor to do who was even expecting to be soon superseded. In a letter

---

[1] "Dum pecunia accipitur, quae mihi ex publica permutatione debetur?" (Ad Div. III. 5. 4). Compare Paulus, Dig. 19. 5. 5. 4, and Forcellini, Permutatio; and Ad Att. v. 13. 2, "ego praeterea rationem Philogeni permutationis ejus quam tecum feci reddidi." See Permutare, Forcellini, and Cicero ad Att. xii. 24 and 27. The words of Paulus are: "nam si pacti sumus ut tu a meo debitore Carthagine exigas, ego a tuo Romae," etc. Cicero had probably received an order on the Publicani from the Roman treasury, which order when paid would be equivalent to a receipt to the Publicani for so much money due to the treasury (aerarium). The Roman "permutatio" was in the nature of a bill of exchange, which is a written order or request addressed by one man to another. The order or request directs the man to whom it is addressed to pay on the account of him who writes the order a sum of money at a fixed time to a third person or to his order, or to the order of the man who writes the request. The form in use among the Romans, and the simplest form of such a bill, was an order addressed by one man to another, which order directed the second person to pay a sum of money to a third who was named in the order. The modern practice of empowering this third person to transfer the order to a fourth, who is thereby entitled to receive the money or to transfer the power of receiving it to a fifth person, and so on, was not in use, we may assume, among the Romans.

to Atticus (v. 16. 4) Cicero says plainly that as soon as Appius heard of his coming, he removed to Tarsus. However Cicero (Ad Div. iii. 6. 6) informed Appius that he had left Iconium on the last day of August, and was advancing through Cappadocia to Cilicia, and if Appius wished to see him, he could determine when and where they should meet. Appius sent a messenger to inform Cicero that he would see him at Iconium; but there were two ways by which Appius could reach Iconium, and he did not say which way he would take. Cicero sent Varro, an intimate friend of Appius, by one way to meet the late governor, and Lepta his head of engineers by the other way, and both had instructions to return to Cicero and inform him which road he should take to meet Appius. Lepta came back in a hurry and reported that Appius had passed by the camp of Cicero, who then immediately went to Iconium. Appius in fact slipped past Cicero apparently in the night, and then had the impudence to complain that Cicero had not advanced to meet him. He did not wish to see Cicero.

Again Cicero wrote to Appius (Ad Div. iii. 8) when he was on the way to Rome, in answer to his complaints about certain reports that had reached him from the province. Some of these complaints were vague, and amounted to no more than that Cicero by the expression of his countenance and by silent reserve had indicated that he was no friend to Appius. On the contrary Cicero declares that both in court and out of it he had spoken in the highest terms of Appius, and shown the utmost solicitude about expressing the friendly relations between them. One complaint of Appius was very specific, and Cicero answered it. He says, "With respect to the deputies (legati), what could I do more appropriate or just than limit the expenditure of the impoverished town communities without any disparagement to you, especially when the towns themselves asked me?" These deputies were the men who were sent to Rome, according to a bad practice, to thank the Senate for having sent them the governor who had just retired. This ceremony was very expensive, and Cicero says that when he was at Apamea, the chief men of many towns complained that large sums of money were appropriated for these missions, though the towns were really insolvent. Cicero says that he did not suppose that so wise a man as Appius could be pleased with such missions; and further, he had observed that such missions had often gone to Rome without obtaining permission to appear before the Senate[4]. Appius had said that some persons thought that Cicero's Edictum, or general rules for the administration of the province, was framed with a view to prevent these missions. Cicero replies that he drew up his Edictum before leaving Rome, and that the chapter about diminishing the costs of town communities was drawn up with very great care, and contained some useful regulations; but those regulations which gave rise to the suspicion that Cicero designed to annoy Appius were really taken from former Edicta. In all the towns north of the Taurus, in which such missions had been arranged, Cicero made no orders about diminishing the cost of them or not allowing it at all until he was urged by the chief persons, who wished to save the towns from grievous exactions, for the money necessary for these missions would be advanced by the Roman money-lenders, who would be empowered to reimburse themselves with profit by a poll-tax and a tax on every door, which, says Cicero to Appius, you are not unacquainted with.

When Appius had reached Rome, Cicero at length received a letter from him, which was quite satisfactory, and gave him the greatest pleasure, for the letter announced the certainty that Appius would have a triumph (Ad Div. iii. 9. 2). Appius had during his government dedicated and sent to Cicero his treatise on augury (Liber Auguralis, Ad Div. iii. 4. 1), and Cicero now professes his great wish to become acquainted with this branch of ecclesiastical law. He entreats Appius out of regard to their old friendship to secure for him a thanksgiving (supplicatio) as soon as possible for his military success in the Amanus. Again (Ad Div. iii. 11) Cicero wrote to say how much he was grieved at the troubles which the enemies of Appius were causing him by the threatened prosecutions, which had deprived him of the triumph which was

---

[4] He speaks ambiguously (Ad Div. iii. 8. 3); does he mean to say that no such missions were allowed a hearing before the Senate?

most justly due. But this disappointment will only redound
to the credit and honour of Appius, and Cicero renews his
declarations of affection and respect; he tells Appius to ask
and expect every thing from him, and promises that his acts
shall go beyond every thing that Appius can expect. These
letters to Appius prove Cicero's great anxiety to keep on good
terms with his predecessor, and they are written in a tone of
humility and almost servility, which may raise a suspicion
that it was fear of some kind and regard to his own interests
rather than affection and respect which prompted him to
make such protestations of friendship. But we certainly
could not discover from these letters that Appius had scan-
dalously abused his power in Cilicia, though we learn that
some of his subordinates were charged with damaging his
character by misconduct.

From the letters to Atticus (v. 16. 2) we learn something
more. Cicero's arrival was most agreeable to the provincials.
The country, he says, was in a deplorable state, from which it
could never recover. At Laodicea, at Apamea, at Synnada
he heard of nothing but heavy requisitions which the people
could not pay; there was universal lamentation and complaint, all caused by one who did not deserve the name of a
man, but rather of a savage beast. These requisitions, or
some of them, are those spoken of in the letter to Appius
(Ad Div. iii. 8), and were made by the magistrates themselves
to raise the money for the cost of the deputations to Rome,
and probably they were used as a pretext for getting more
out of the people than the costs of the missions; for Cicero,
as he tells us in another place, compelled the Greek magistrates to repay money which they had extorted from the
people (Ad Attic. vi. 2. 5). The real object of the missions to
Rome was to protect Appius against charges of maladministration by the lying evidence of the very people whom he had
plundered. Cicero relieved the towns through which he
passed by making no requisitions for himself nor for any of
his staff and attendants. He did not accept fodder for the
cattle or any thing which the Lex Julia allowed; not even
fire-wood; he paid for every thing. For himself he only
accepted at each place the use of four beds, and he often slept

under tents. We have only his own authority for his liberal and just behaviour during his government, but we may accept his statements. Again Cicero says (Ad Attic. vi. 1. 2) that Appius on his road to Rome wrote several letters in which he complained that Cicero was altering some of his regulations; but a physician from whom a sick man has been taken and handed over to another, might just as well complain that the second physician follows a different mode of treatment. Appius treated the province by the method of depletion; he let blood, took from the patient all that he could, and delivered up the sick man completely exhausted. He did not like to see Cicero using a generous diet, and he was offended at the contrast between his own treatment and that of his successor. Under his administration the province was exhausted by heavy requisitions and wasteful expenditure. Cicero demanded nothing either for himself or on the public account. The Praefecti, the staff, the legati of Appius were guilty of rapacity and brutal behaviour; but under Cicero the whole province was administered like a well-managed family.

It might be said that Cicero's remarks about the maladministration of Cilicia are too vague to justify the severe condemnation of his predecessor; but he has left other evidence, which confirms his general statement and proves the greediness and rapacity of the Roman nobility. This evidence is contained in four letters (Ad Attic. v. 21; vi. 1, 2, 3)[5].

In B.C. 50 there came to Rome from Salamis in Cyprus certain deputies to borrow money for their town. Two Romans, M. Scaptius and P. Matinius, were ready to lend the money at 48 per cent., but there was a Lex Gabinia[6] which caused a difficulty. Scaptius and Matinius however had a powerful friend M. Brutus, the son of the Brutus whom Cn. Pompeius put to death in B.C. 77, the son-in-law of Appius Pulcher,

[5] This matter is discussed by Savigny in his Vermischte Schriften, Ueber den Zinswucher des M. Brutus. He has stated the case very clearly, and I have followed his statement with small additions and variations.

[6] Ernesti assumes that this Lex was enacted in B.C. 67, when Gabinius was tribune; but Asconius ad Cornel. p. 58 states that the tribune C. Cornelius in B.C. 67 proposed to the Senate a Lex to this effect, and that the Senate refused to accept it (vol. iii. p. 108). The law then was probably enacted in the consulship of Gabinius B.C. 58.

governor of Cilicia B.C. 53—51, and afterwards one of the
assassins of the Dictator Caesar. Brutus contrived to procure
two Senatusconsulta, the object of which was to protect the
lenders against the penalties of the Lex Gabinia, and Scaptius
and Matinius then lent the money. The purpose of this Lex
Gabinia will be explained hereafter.

During the government of Appius Pulcher, one of these
creditors, Scaptius, obtained from Appius the office of a praefectus and fifty horsemen to enable him to enforce the
payment of the money and the interest. There is no doubt
that Savigny correctly supposes the praefectura, which Scaptius
obtained from Appius, to be a military praefectura, or command
of a body of horse, and not a " praefectura juri dicundo " or a
judicial office, as P. Manutius supposed (Ad Cic. ad Div. ii.
17). Scaptius took his force to Salamis, and on one occasion
blockaded the Senate so long in the Senate-house that five of
the members died of starvation. (Ad. Attic. vi. 1. 6.) It is
not said whether Scaptius got any money out of the Salaminians by this unusual proceeding.

When Cicero arrived in Cilicia, Brutus by letter strongly
recommended Scaptius and Matinius to him, but Cicero only
knew Scaptius, who came to the governor's camp, and asked
for a renewal of the praefectura. Cicero refused his request, but
promised for Brutus' sake that he would see that the money
was paid to Scaptius, who thanked him and went away. The
deputies of Salamis had met Cicero as soon as he landed at
Ephesus to complain about these troops being in the island,
and as soon as Cicero was within his province he sent orders
to the troops to quit Cyprus (Ad Attic. vi. 1. 6). The soldiers
had doubtless been living by making requisitions on the people. It was usual, as Cicero says (Ad Attic. v. 21. 7), for the
rich towns to pay large sums of money to avoid having soldiers
quartered on them in winter: the Cypriots used to pay two
hundred talents, but Cicero declares to Atticus that during
his government not a single coin should be demanded from
them. Scaptius was displeased at the troops being withdrawn
from Cyprus, but he met the deputies from Salamis at Tarsus,
and Cicero there ordered them to pay the money. A good
deal was said by the Salaminians about the written engage-

ment (syngrapha¹), and a good deal about the bad behaviour of Scaptius, which Cicero refused to listen to. He urged the men to pay in consideration of what he had done for the island, and finally he said that he would compel them to pay. The men replied that they were ready, and would pay "by Cicero himself" (solvere a me), a Roman expression which signified payment to a creditor by an order of the debtor on some debtor to himself. For they said that, since Cicero had not received what they had been accustomed to give to the governor, they would be making him in a manner the payer, and they observed that the debt due to Scaptius was something less than what was paid to the governor. Cicero's Edictum allowed 12 per cent. as the interest of money, and also allowed the interest in arrear of each year to be added to the principal so as to bear interest (fenus cum anatocismo). Accordingly Cicero ordered the interest to be thus computed, and the Salaminii to pay what should be found due. Scaptius insisted on the 48 per cent., and as we may assume with the anatocismus or compound interest. Cicero replied that he could not consent to this demand, for his own Edictum only allowed 12 per cent. Scaptius appealed to the two Senatusconsulta, but Cicero showed that they did not help his case. Scaptius then proposed to take 200 talents, and asked Cicero to induce his debtors to pay this amount. The Salaminii maintained that the amount was only 106 talents, and upon taking the account this appeared to be the truth, and the Salaminians were ready to pay. Scaptius would not consent to settle on these terms, and asked Cicero to leave the matter unsettled, which he did; nor would he allow the Salaminians at their request to deposit in a temple the amount which was found due². Thus the

¹ "Syngrapha" is described by Gaius (III. 134) as a written acknowledgment of a debt, and as peculiar to Peregrini, that is, those who were not Roman citizens. The Romans found "syngraphas" in use in their Greek provinces and the rule of law established that a man might sue on them. "Syngrapha" in fact is a general name for any written evidence of an agreement. The remarks of the so-called Pseudo-Asconius (Cicero, In Verr. ii. 1. 181, ed. Orelli) show that he did not understand the matter.

² In the expression (Ad Attic. vi. 1. 7) "consistere usura debuit quae erat in edicto meo," "consistere" has been explained incorrectly as equivalent to "cessare;" but it plainly means as Savigny states, and the context shows

matter was left unsettled, and we know no more about it. Cicero asks, however, what will happen to the Salaminians, if Paulus should come to Cilicia as governor? Paulus was one of the consuls of B.C. 50, the man who is said to have been bought by Caesar.

The Lex Gabinia had forbidden such loans as that which the Salaminians wished to contract at Rome, and it was therefore necessary for the security of the lenders to obtain a dispensation from this Lex, which dispensation was effected by the two Senatusconsulta (Ad Attic. v. 21. 11, etc.). The first Senatusconsultum merely relieved the lenders from the penalties of the Lex Gabinia; but as the Lex also deprived them of the right of action for the recovery of the money lent, the lenders sought and obtained a second Senatusconsultum, the effect of which was that they could sue on this debt just as on any other debt. Scaptius claimed his 48 per cent. under the Senatusconsultum, but Cicero declared that the Senatusconsultum merely made the debt like other debts as to the right of action, and that the rate of interest was fixed by his Edictum.

We now come to the strangest part of this affair. Cicero, who had already (v. 21) reported this matter to Atticus, speaks of it again (vi. 1. 5). He says it is as surprising to him as it is to Atticus to learn that this money belongs to Brutus, of which however Brutus had never informed him. In fact, he says, I have his own letter in which he writes, "the Salaminians are indebted to M. Scaptius and P. Matinius, my intimate friends," whom he recommends to me, and he adds by way of moving me to greater activity, that he had become security for them to a large amount. The meaning of this may be that Scaptius and Matinius had been employed to borrow the money which they lent at 48 per cent., and Brutus was their security to the men who furnished the money. Further, at the time when Cicero had brought the Salaminians to consent to pay the six years' interest at 12 per cent. with compound interest, Scaptius tried to clench the matter in his own favour by producing a letter from Brutus

that Cicero means that the rate of interest fixed by his Edictum must be maintained.

in which he said that this affair was at his own risk, "which," says Cicero, "he had never told me before nor you: at the same time he urged me to give Scaptius a praefectura." Cicero adds that if Brutus shall not be satisfied with what he has done, he will be sorry, but much more sorry to find that he is not the man that he supposed him to be.

But this is not all. Ariobarzanes III., king of Cappadocia, and grandson*, as some suppose, of the Ariobarzanes whom Cn. Pompeius (vol. iii. p. 193) restored to the throne of Cappadocia, was a debtor both to Cn. Pompeius and M. Brutus. The debt to Pompeius may have been contracted by the grandfather; but we do not know how M. Brutus became the creditor of this poor king, for Cicero tells us that Ariobarzanes had nothing. Brutus had given Cicero instructions to look after Ariobarzanes and try to make him pay; but the king was also pressed by the agents of Pompeius, and when Cicero wrote (Ad Attic. vi. 1. 3), Pompeius was receiving every month thirty-three Attic talents raised by requisitions, which the king levied on his people, and yet these thirty-three talents did not cover the interest of the debt. But the king paid no one else, though he promised Cicero to pay Brutus. Again (Ad Attic. vi. 3. 5) Cicero says that in proportion to the amount of his debt Brutus had been treated better than Pompeius, for Brutus had received in the year (B.C. 50) about one hundred talents, and Pompeius had been promised two hundred in six months. It is not necessary to attempt to reconcile any contradictions that may appear between these two statements. We have the fact of Cicero being employed by Brutus to dun this beggarly king, and the evidence of the shameless greediness of two men not the worst of the Romans.

After the campaign of B.C. 51 Cicero placed his brother Quintus over Cilicia, and sent Q. Volusius for a few days to Cyprus that the Roman citizens, who carried on business in

* "Grandson." Drumann (vi. 130) says that he was the son of the Ariobarzanes whom Pompeius restored (B.C. 60), and that the restored king soon after gave the kingdom to his son. "In Cappadocia trvs Ariobarzanes regnasse, postea redactam in provinciae formam a Strabone didicimus."—P. Manutii in Epist. ad Atticum Commentarius, p. 208.

the island, might not say that justice was denied them; for
the Cypriots could not be summoned to any place out of their
island. Cicero left Tarsus on the fifth of January for the
Asiatic dioceses, as he calls them (p. 417), which for six
months of his administration had received from him none of
the usual letters of requisition, and had not seen a single guest
quartered on them. The people were amazed at this unusual
honesty in a governor, who also refused the statues, temples,
and other honours which were often given by the provincials
to their unworthy proconsuls and propraetors. There was a
famine in the early part of B.C. 50 in these dioceses, for the
harvest had totally failed the year before; but Cicero without
any exercise of authority prevailed on the Greeks and Romans
who had stocks of corn which they kept back to supply
the people's wants. He made his circuits in these parts in
February and March; and during the month of June he
intended to be at Tarsus, and he arrived there on the fifth of
June. He had entered his province on the thirty-first of
July, B.C. 51 at Laodicea, and he must quit the province on
the thirtieth of July B.C. 50. But it was necessary to leave
some fit person in charge of the province, for no successor had
been appointed at Rome. C. Pomptinus had, according to
agreement when he accepted the office of legatus, returned to
Italy, and Quintus, the governor's brother, hated the province,
and, it was supposed, could not be persuaded to stay. Cicero
did not consider his quaestor Mescinius a fit man to be trusted
with the government of Cilicia. In conformity with the Lex
Julia Cicero left in two towns of his province, Apamea and
Laodicea, a statement of the provincial accounts during his
year of office, and he ordered Mescinius to wait at Laodicea
until this business was done. No man, says Cicero, except the
quaestores urbani, that is, the Roman people has ever touched
or ever will touch a farthing of my booty (p. 408). In order
to secure himself and the Roman people against the risk of
carrying this money to Rome, he intended to leave it at Laodicea,
where he would receive an order or bill, as we say, for the payment of an equivalent sum at Rome. This business would
probably be managed by the agents of the Publicani. Cicero
was at last relieved of his difficulties by the arrival of the

quaestor C. Caelius Caldus, who took the place of Mescinius, and Cicero delivered up the province to Caelius. On the third of August he had advanced by sea as far as Sida in Pamphylia, and thence he sailed to Rhodes to please the two boys, his son and nephew. It was eight-and-twenty years since his former visit to the island, where he would find few of his old friends alive. Here, as he says (Brutus, 1), he received the news of the death of the orator Hortensius, his friend and in a manner his rival[1]. From Rhodes he sailed to Ephesus, and from Ephesus to Athens, which he only reached on the fourteenth of October. He sailed from Patrae (Patras) on the second of November, where he left his faithful servant Tiro, who was sick, to the care of two friends, Lyson and Manius Curius. While he was on the voyage to Italy he wrote many most affectionate letters to Tiro[2]. He sailed along the coast of Acarnania and reached Corcyra on the ninth of November, where he was kept by bad weather to the twenty-second, when he sailed in the evening and had a good voyage to Hydruntum (Otranto) in Italy, from which place he reached Brundisium on the twenty-fourth of November. A letter to Tiro (Ad Fam. xvi. 9) gives Cicero's journal till his arrival at Brundisium, where he informs Tiro that he has left a horse and a mule for him; and at the same time he expresses his opinion that there will be great uneasiness at Rome on and after the first day of the next January.

[1] Drumann (vI. 181) quotes Tunstall's opinion (Ep. ad Middlet. p. 66) that Cicero invented this statement in order to have a good introduction to his essay entitled "Brutus," and that a letter to Atticus (vI. 6) written while he was in Cilicia proves that he then heard of the death of Hortensius. But the passage in the letter to Atticus certainly does not prove that Cicero had then heard of the death of Hortensius, though Caelius (Ad Fam. viii. 13) had written to say that he was dying. Drumann's answer to Tunstall is sufficient.

[2] The twenty-seven letters of the sixteenth book of the Epistolae ad Diversos or ad Familiares are addressed to Tiro, who preserved them.

NOTE.—The story (p. 420) about Appius not meeting Cicero is not clear. Compare Ad Div. iii. 6 and 7.

APPENDIX I.

ON THE TWO INVASIONS OF BRITANNIA.

MUCH has been written on Caesar's expeditions to Britain, and there is still great difference of opinion on the matter. I have endeavoured to give the meaning of Caesar's text (chaps. ix. xii.), and I will now state what are the difficulties in his narrative.

The problem is to determine from what place on the French coast Caesar sailed, and at what part of the English coast he landed. If names of places were the same now as they were in Caesar's time, of course there would be no occasion for this inquiry, if he had named the place of embarkation and the place of landing. But he has only given a name to the place of embarkation, and it is not certain what modern position corresponds to it; and he has not given a name to his landing-place. We must therefore attempt to solve the problem from his narrative, and from a consideration of the tides and stream in the English Channel. Every solution of the problem ought to be consistent with Caesar's text, and also consistent with the state of the tide and the direction of the Channel stream at the times of embarkation, anchoring, and landing. A solution which fails in any one of these conditions is not satisfactory, if we assume that Caesar's narrative is true.

The only contemporary evidence is the Commentaries. The statements of compilers, if they contain only what is in Caesar, add nothing to the evidence: if they contradict Caesar, we cannot accept the statements; and if the compilers tell us any thing which is not in Caesar, it cannot be accepted absolutely. Strabo, Plutarch, Appian, and Dion must have had some authority for what they have written, but we do not know what authorities they had except Caesar himself. Dion certainly used the Commentaries, but he has often perverted the meaning, and he has added circumstances which are false and manifestly his own invention. I have given in this volume sufficient proofs of Dion's carelessness, ignorance, and incapacity. Yet some writers who have discussed Caesar's British expeditions use Caesar, Plutarch, Dion, Florus as if they were all of nearly equal value with the Commentaries as evidence of a fact, and as if we may trust any of them for a fact which is found nowhere else. Even the adventure of Scaeva (Valerius, iii. 2. 23) is used as evidence in the matter of the landing. The story may be true, though Caesar says nothing of him. Lucan (vi. 144, x. 544) has preserved the centurion's name[1]. We have in Polyaenus (p. 210) a story about Caesar having an elephant with him which is certainly false, though we may suppose that a writer on military stratagems found this statement somewhere. It is probable that much was written in the imperial period about Caesar's expeditions, and that most of it was as worthless as the great mass of writings of that age[2].

The first question is, from what port did Caesar sail? The majority of opinions is now on the side of Boulogne: a few still maintain that he sailed from Wissant. If we take the evidence of the name, it is in favour of Wissant, a word which resembles in some degree Caesar's Itius or Itium; but it is not certain whether Caesar wrote Itium or Iccium. Wissant was a usual place of embarkation and landing between France and England for many centuries, from A.D. 686 to A.D. 1327, as the learned Dufresne (Ducange) proves in his dissertation De Portu Iccio, translated into Latin by Gibson,

---

[1] Scaeva's exploits in the civil war are recorded by Caesar (B. C. III. 53), by Suetonius (Caesar, 68), by Florus (iv. 2. 40), and by Valerius Maximus (iii. 2. 23) also in the same chapter in which he speaks of Scaeva's great deeds in Britain, where he was so roughly handled, according to the story, that it is a wonder that he ever fought again.

[2] There were traditions about Caesar's invasion of Britain, which would be the foundation of stories. Aper says in the Dialogus de Oratoribus of Tacitus (c. 17), "Nam ipse ego in Britannia vidi senem qui se fateretur ei pugnae interfuisse qua Caesarem inferentem arma Britannis arcere litoribus et pellere adgressi sunt." I wish Aper had told us in what year he was in Britain.

Oxford, 1004. Dufresne also proves from two chroniclers, Gulielmus Gemeticensis and Gulielmus Pictavensis, that one of them names the port Witsand, and the other names it Itium, and both writers are speaking of the same voyage of Alured to England. We have therefore proof, that whether Wissant was used by Caesar or not, it was a well-frequented port many centuries after his time, and that one writer has named it Itium. Wissant is now sanded up, and it is very difficult to form an opinion of the capabilities of this port nineteen hundred years ago. Boulogne was used as a port in and after the time of the Emperor Claudius, and the Gallic name was Gesoriacum, a word which contains one of the usual Gallo-Roman terminations—*acum*. The place afterwards received the Roman name Bononia. Now if it was named Gesoriacum in Caesar's time, why did he name it Itium? It is not easy to answer this question. Some critics indeed find the name Iccius, which they assume to be the true name, in the village of Isques, " which stood in ancient times at the head of the aestuary of the Liane, the river of Boulogne, and thus Isques would naturally give its name to the port below." As Napoleon placed himself at Isques when he was preparing the invasion of England, " what more probable than that Caesar also should have pitched the Praetorian tent at Isques, and then have spoken of the port below as Portus Iccius?" (Lewin, Invasion of Britain by Julius Caesar, p. 24.) Mr. Lewin does not say that the port was named Iccius by the Galli, but that Caesar spoke of it as Portus Iccius; nor does Mr. Lewin say what the Gallic name was. If in Caesar's time it was named Gesoriacum, we may assume that Caesar would have named it so. If it had then no name, which is not probable, Mr. Lewin allows us to infer that he affirms that Caesar gave it the name Iccius. Whether it had no name or was named Iccius, when did it take the name Gesoriacum?

The question between Wissant and Boulogne cannot be decided by assuming or even proving, if it were possible, that Boulogne was the better port in Caesar's time. Caesar sailed from some French port on the English Channel, which he names the most convenient, and the passage was the shortest. The passage to Britain is shorter from Wissant than from Boulogne. Caesar estimates the passage from Itium at thirty Roman miles, but this estimate exceeds the distance from Wissant to the nearest part of the English coast, and it is about the true distance from Boulogne to the same part of the English coast. The conclusion is that it will never be settled whether Caesar sailed from Wissant or from Boulogne.

As to Caesar's landing-place, I have said (p. 106) that if his ships anchored off Dover and he continued his course from Dover in the direction in which he moved thither, after sailing seven miles farther he would come to the open shore about Deal. But it is said that he could not continue his voyage in this northern direction, because on that day from half-past eleven to half-past six the stream was flowing down the Channel, and he must therefore have gone towards Hythe, and landed about those parts. If we ask whether he could not have gone up the Channel with a fair wind, the answer now is that he could not. Caesar was at anchor from about half-past eight A.M. to about three or half-past three P.M., when the tide had been rising some time. He then set sail, and he had the wind as he says. If he did not go forward, his statement is false.

Mr. Lewin says that Caesar sailed from Boulogne and came to anchor off Dover, where he remained until three in the afternoon of the 27th of August. Then having the wind and the tide in his favour, he sailed to the west, and "rounding the precipitous cliffs which had so long defied him, came to the creek of Limne" (p. 41). The map in the book does not represent Caesar as sailing to Dover, but as moving in a direct line from Boulogne towards Folkstone, and when he was some miles short of Folkstone, turning due west to Limne. But it is a common thing for a book and a map not to agree. As the stream would be running to the west of Dover at three P.M. on the 27th of August, Mr. Lewin concludes that Caesar sailed from Dover in the same direction as the stream, and went towards Romney Marsh. He remarks (p. 38, note) that the place of debarkation depends altogether on the direction of the tide at three P.M. on the 27th of August, B.C. 55; which is not true, for the wind also must be taken into the account.

However, notwithstanding this remark, he does take the wind into the account, and in this way. If Caesar, he says, had the wind in his favour on the voyage from Boulogne to Dover, it must have been south or west; and if the wind continued in that quarter and Caesar sailed before it, he must have steered to the east. But, if the wind was south, "it would have been favourable to a movement either to the east or west from a point opposite to Dover" (p. 39). Having admitted so much, Mr. Lewin sees that it will be better for his theory to suppose that the wind was not from the south or west when Caesar set sail at three in the afternoon, and accordingly he supposes that the wind had changed, and he further supposes that this change is implied in the Latin word "nactus." But this is not a certain conclusion (see B. G. v. 9, and other passages).

It is difficult to say whether this inference from the word "nactus" is even probable. I think that it is not probable unless Caesar had already determined to sail to Limne, and that when he saw the stream setting in that direction and the wind also, he took advantage of both. But Caesar could know nothing of the stream, for he now felt it for the first time, but there was something else that he could understand better. He saw that the tide had been rising for some hours, for "aestus" ought to be translated "tide" and not "stream," and at the time when he was ready to sail, he had also, as he says, the wind favourable, which means favourable for his purpose, whatever it was; and he went on his course, and therefore northward, as he means by the word "progressus."

This interpretation is more consistent with the text than Mr. Lewin's. If the objection is made that it was impossible to sail northward against the stream, then the certain conclusion is that if Caesar's anchorage was off Dover, his narrative is not true. If Mr. Lewin's interpretation is true, it contradicts Caesar's text, and as long as the word "progressus" stands, we cannot reconcile Caesar's statement with Mr. Lewin's conclusion.

On the second voyage the wind dropped in the night, and Caesar's ships drifted from their course up the Channel. Mr. Lewin (p. 81) supposes that they were carried beyond or at least up to the South Foreland, and when the tide turned west "by dint of rowing with the current in their favour the whole fleet gained the familiar level shore just opposite Limne" (p. 81)*.

Mr. Lewin does not explain Caesar's statement that in the early morning after the night voyage he saw Britannia on the left hand "left behind" (relicta); a statement which cannot be reconciled with the supposition of his being no farther north than the South Foreland, and can only be explained by the assumption that he had been carried as far as the North Foreland, and so had left Britannia behind. Here are two instances in which Mr. Lewin's theory of the voyages directly contradicts Caesar's text.

Mr. Lewin (p. 44) thus explains the words "planum," "apertum," and "molle" (B. G. iv. 23; v. 9), by which words Caesar describes the nature of his landing-place: "Caesar had reached the creek of Limne, and on the western side of it was the shore where the debarkation was to be made; it was 'planum' or flat, as he describes it, for there was not a single elevation in the whole marsh, and it was also 'apertum' or open, for the heights to the north were at least a mile distant. The sea-beach was also 'molle' or soft, not with mud or ooze, but it consisted of shingle, than which nothing can be more favourable to the security of vessels."

Mr. Lewin supposes Romney Marsh to have been then as it is now or nearly so, but there was a creek, as he says, at Limne, and Caesar landed on the shore west of this creek. It is certain that there was a port of some kind at Limne during the Roman occupation of Britain; but that is all that we know from direct evidence. He explains the word "apertum" by affirming without any evidence that the heights to the north were at least a mile distant; but even if this could be proved, it would not justify the statement that the shore was open (apertum). The true conclusion would be that the shore was not open, and that the Romans could not look into the interior of the island.

* He says (p. 81) that the sun rose at four A.M., and he supposes (p. 79) that Caesar sailed on the eighteenth of July at full moon (p. 81); or as he says in another place (p. 85), "we may infer with the highest probability that Caesar sailed from Boulogne either on the very 18th of July, B.C. 54, or at all events within a day or two either before or after it."

When we are endeavouring to support an opinion, all of us are blind to some objections. If any person can read Caesar without a preconceived opinion, and if he wishes to find the truth, let him say after reading the description of the landing (B. G. iv. 24—26), whether Caesar landed near a creek or on an open sea-shore. I think that the description of the landing shows that it could not have been made near a creek. Mr. Lewin is obscure. Perhaps he means that on reaching this creek Caesar landed on the shore immediately west of the creek.

The title of Mr. Appach's book is "Caius Julius Caesar's British Expeditions from Boulogne to the Bay of Apuldore, and the subsequent formation geologically of Romney Marsh, 1868." Mr. Appach began his inquiries by assuming that in Caesar's time "the sea filled the whole of the Bay of Apuldore, and on testing this assumption with the Commentaries, I found it," he says, "in every respect consistent with the narrative." Mr. Appach's theory therefore requires the establishment of the fact that Romney Marsh has been formed since Caesar's time, and he attempts to prove this fact by a careful examination of the marsh, of the manner in which it has grown, and in which it was finally shut in and made what it is. Few readers will take the pains to examine his argument, and very few will be able to say whether he has proved his case. If he has not done this, his theory about Caesar's landing cannot be accepted; and if it be admitted that he has proved the recent formation of Romney Marsh, his theory must still be tested by its conformity to Caesar's text. There can be no doubt at all that in Caesar's time and long after Romney Marsh did not exist as it now is; and it may be granted that the sea filled up the Bay of Apuldore; but we cannot grant that this sea was navigable by the Roman ships, and of course it cannot be proved that it was navigable. It may however be assumed as an hypothesis, and if this assumption is the only thing requisite to explain Caesar's two voyages, and no other explanation can be given, the assumption may be allowed.

Mr. Appach (p. 12) concludes from the fact of Limne or Lympne being the ancient Portus Lemanis, and being long used by the Romans, that the Bay of Apuldore was not at that time completely closed by the growth of the marsh and shingle: and this conclusion is just. He also affirms (p. 47) that the coast from Sandgate to the west of Hythe being sheltered from the "force of the sea and stream in the Channel must therefore have been the principal British port on this part of the coast in the time of Caesar" (p. 48).

He maintains that Caesar's first voyage was from Boulogne (p. 8—11); and he concludes (p. 11) that in B.C. 55 "the cliffs [along the French coast at Boulogne] extended farther seaward than they do now, and there was no blown sand or much less than at present. The salient portions of the coast therefore, such as Cape Alprech, were then comparatively more prominent than they now are. With these exceptions, the French coast presented much the same appearance in the time of Caesar as it does at the present day." He says in his preface that "Boulogne as it must have been in ancient days, completely answers the description which Caesar gives of the port from which he sailed." But Caesar gives no description of the port from which he sailed, except that he says "that he had found it the most convenient for the voyage to Britain, a passage of thirty miles from the continent (B. G. v. 2).

Mr. Appach (p. 59) supposes that in the first voyage Caesar sailed from Boulogne to Hythe, and he applies the words (B. G. iv. 23) "in omnibus collibus" to the appearance of the heights about Hythe, where he says Caesar "would have seen no less than five separate and distinct hills lying nearly in a line from east to west." He further says, "In fine, if full force be given to Caesar's expressions, his description alone, independently of any other considerations, is sufficient to identify Hythe as the place at which he arrived on first reaching the shores of Britain" (p. 70). Caesar often uses "collis" as we use the word "hill;" for instance (B.G. vii. 69), when he is describing the flat-topped heights which surround the hill on which Alesia stood. But I understand "in omnibus collibus" (B. G. iv. 23) to mean simply "on all the heights," and I do not suppose that the notion of "separate and distinct hills" is a correct interpretation. When Caesar further says (iv. 23) that the place was hemmed in by heights (montibus *) so close to the sea that a missile

---

* Mr. Appach says, (p. 69) "Here it will be observed that in the first sentence

could be easily thrown upon the shore from the parts above, I think that his description does not correspond at all to the heights about Hythe. This is a matter of fact, of which any person can judge who has seen this part of the Kentish coast.

When Caesar saw all the heights covered with armed men, he could not land at Hythe, and "he must needs go either to Deal or Bonnington, at both of which places he knew from Volusenus' report that the ground was practicable for his intended operations" (p. 71). This assertion is much more than Caesar's words will justify (B. G. iv. 21).

Mr. Appach assumes (p. 71) that the officers assembled (B. G. iv. 23) in Caesar's ship about 9.30. A.M. "The tide was falling, the stream was running up channel at about 2¾ miles an hour, and the wind was about N.W. ¼ N.; a state of circumstances which was of course evident to the Romans as they lay at anchor." I do not see how we can infer from Caesar's words at what time he assembled his officers. Perhaps the correct conclusion would be that it was later than Mr. Appach supposes. Caesar, as he truly observes, was ignorant of the turn of the stream in the Channel, and as far as he could tell, therefore, it was utterly impossible to go to Bonnington. He could sail, as Mr. Appach says, as far as the South Foreland with ease; "and then they could row the rest of the distance with the aid of the stream, if they kept well under the shelter of the cliff." Mr. Appach then assumes that "Caesar gave orders for a landing at Deal, but when the stream turned down channel at 11.32 A.M. these arrangements had to be altered. The wind still remaining N.W. ¼ N., the ships might possibly be able to sail to

---

Caesar uses the word *all* (in *omnibus collibus*), and applies it to hills in the plural; and that in the second sentence he again speaks of the mountains (*montibus*) in the plural, thus pointedly implying, if not in fact asserting that there were more than two hills, in which case the expression *both* or *on each side*, instead of *all*, would be more appropriate." I do not understand the latter part of the sentence, in which he suggests that Caesar might have written better. The use of Roman plural nouns, "colles," "montes," "fossae," "funi," and other plurals, may be learned from Caesar and other Roman writers. The plurals are often used to indicate all or many or various parts of the same thing. "Fossae" often signifies every part of a "fossa" which surrounds a camp, and "funi" all the flames in every part of a wide conflagration (B. G. v. 48; iii. 18).

the South Foreland, but it would be quite impossible to row from that point to Deal against the stream. He must row with it, and therefore go to Bonnington, which he would be able to reach by keeping under the shelter of the high ground between Hythe and Aldington Knoll. Fresh orders were given accordingly a little after 11.32 A.M." Mr. Appach adds that all the ships "joined before 2.18 P.M., a little after the wind had changed to E.N.E."

Mr. Appach in his details of the first voyage, Section xxiv., makes the wind change several times, and here he makes it change again. This section on the voyage is very ingenious. The changes of the wind are assumed, I suppose, as necessary to explain the time occupied in the transit, and to make the voyage conformable to the tides and stream in the Channel. The last change of the wind to E.N.E. is very useful for the voyage from Hythe to Bonnington, where Caesar brought up his ships "on an open and flat coast," the flat ground to the west of Aldington Knoll, a distance of about seven Roman miles from Hythe. From Aldington Knoll, as Mr. Appach observes, westward to the end of the promontory of Apuldore, "the ground is perfectly open and so nearly level that it is almost impossible in many places to distinguish the line of junction of the upland with the marsh" (p. 73). Mr. Appach also observes, that his explanation of the voyage from Hythe to Bonnington is consistent with Caesar's word "progressus" (B. G. iv. 23).

In the second voyage (Section xxxvi.) Mr. Appach states that on the morning of the day after the evening on which Caesar set sail, his fleet was off the South Foreland (p. 106). "It was now daylight, as the sun rose at 4.19 A.M., and Caesar saw that he had left Britain behind." The author then explains how the fleet reached the former landing-place "at 11.51 A.M., or a little before noon, as Caesar says that it did."

If Caesar was off the South Foreland, he might have said that he had left his former landing-place behind, but he could not say that he had left Britain behind, for it was right in front of him. Caesar's position at daybreak must have been farther north to enable him to say that he had left Britain behind; and such a more northern position would make his remark consistent with his notion of the figure of the island (chapter xi. of this volume, p. 193).

Mr. Appach thus explains Caesar's words (B. G. v. 8), "orta luce sub sinistra Britanniam relictam conspexit;" "The words 'on the left' are an unmeaning expression, if the configuration of the coast had been the same in his day as it is at the present time, for Britain could not by any possibility have been in any other position. The expression, however, is peculiarly appropriate if the sea then filled the Bay of Apuldore; for Caesar sailing, as he thought, from Boulogne to Kennardlington (a little east of Apuldore), of course expected to see Britain on his right when daylight appeared, and being very much surprised to find it on his left, naturally mentioned the circumstance in his narrative" (p. 103).

To this I reply that there is no reason for supposing that "sub sinistra" is not a genuine part of Caesar's text, and if it is, the words cannot be unmeaning, for Caesar's words always mean something. Nor, as I think, does the meaning of these words depend in any degree on the fact whether the configuration of the coast is the same that it was in Caesar's time or different. The words express a fact, that Caesar had left the island behind: he had been carried so far that he could see no part of the island except what he saw on his left; and he uses the word "left" to express this fact. This passage presents an insuperable difficulty to all those who conduct Caesar's fleet to Hythe or any place west of Hythe.

There is still another passage in Caesar which is worth notice. On the first voyage eighteen ships with cavalry on board sailed from what Caesar names the upper port on the French coast (B. G. iv. 28). They sailed on the fourth day after Caesar's landing in Britain, and came near enough to be seen from the Roman camp. But a furious storm rose so suddenly that not a single vessel could keep its course: some were carried back to the place from which they came, and others with great risk of loss were driven to the lower part of the island which is nearer towards sunset. The "lower part" is the south (B. G. v. 13). The probable conclusion from this passage is, that the Roman camp was on what Caesar might call the upper (superior) or north part of the Kentish coast.

I have given the purport of these two essays as correctly as I can; but it is not easy to give another man's meaning in fewer words than he has used himself. Mr. Appach's work is a book of 149 pages. It is the most laborious attempt that I have seen to explain the Roman invasions of Britain, and it is a work of real value.

I still retain the opinion which I have stated (chapters ix. xii.), that Caesar landed at Deal; and I have nothing to add to the Note on Caesar's British expeditions in my second edition of the Commentaries on the Gallic War, 1860. I have already stated the objection made to this theory, and the objection cannot be answered, if it is true that under the circumstances Caesar on his first voyage could not sail from Dover to Deal. I have collected information from various persons who are acquainted with the tides at Dover, who think that Caesar under the circumstances could reach Deal, if he had a fair wind. Lieutenant Burstal, to whom I submitted many years ago the facts contained in Caesar's text without any remarks of my own, says "it is very possible that there was sufficient wind for Caesar to make good head-way against the stream, as at that period of the moon, four days before the full, the stream would not exceed $1\frac{1}{2}$ mile an hour." As to the second voyage Lieutenant Burstal observes, "It is probable that the stream would not carry Caesar farther to the east than this position (some miles off the North Foreland), from which the indraught towards the Thames and w.s.w. direction of the Gull stream materially assisted him in his progress towards Deal."

I have now done with this subject. If any man can prove by experiment that the voyage from Dover to Deal can be made under the circumstances in which Caesar was, he will settle a long-disputed question.

APPENDIX II

CAESAR'S PROVINCES.

Hirtius remarks (p. 385) that in B.C. 51 Caesar knew that it was well known to all the Galli that there remained only one year more of his provincial government. If this was so, his government terminated at the latest at the end of B.C. 50. But if his first term of five years began on the first of January, B.C. 58, it terminated at the end of B.C. 54; and his second term of five years would terminate at the end of B.C. 49. Hirtius also says (B. G. viii. 50), when he is speaking of Caesar going to Italy in B.C. 50, that one object of his visit was to recommend himself to the electors of Cisalpine Gallia for his election to the consulship in the following year (B.C. 49). L. Lentulus and C. Marcellus were already elected consuls for 49. It appears then from this second passage that Hirtius supposed that Caesar would hold his provincial government to the end of B.C. 49, or if it really ended with B.C. 50, he would be a candidate in B.C. 49 as a private person. But he knew that Caesar did not intend to part with his troops before his second election, and his narrative proves it; for he says, when Caesar gave up two legions in obedience to the Senatusconsultum, he sent into Italy the thirteenth legion to take the place of the fifteenth, one of the two legions which he had given up. He then placed his troops in winter-quarters at the end of B.C. 50, four legions in North Gallia, and the other four among the Aedui to secure the tranquillity of the country. The eight legions were under the command of his two legati, C. Trebonius and C. Fabius, and therefore under Caesar's orders. Caesar then went to Italy.

Perhaps it is not easy to reconcile the two passages in Hirtius, but the meaning of the first passage may be that Caesar would have no time for a campaign in Gallia in B.C. 49, for he would be in Cisalpine Gallia and communicating with his friends at Rome about his election in that year.

If the beginning and end of his first five years' commission were not clearly defined, it is not likely that the termination of his second five years was left uncertain in the Lex Trebonia, for Caesar well knew that he had enemies at Rome who wished to deprive him of his provincial government, and his friends at Rome, who secured for him his second term of five years, were able to make the Lex Trebonia so clear that there should be no doubt. I think it is certain that the first term of five years was reckoned from the beginning of B.C. 58. Caesar, we may assume, could have left Rome for Gallia on the first of January, B.C. 58, and though he did not go thither till about three months later, there was a reason for it. He was waiting till the affair of Cicero was decided (vol. iii. p. 457).

There was so much irregularity at this time that we hardly know what were the rules which determined the ordinary duration of a provincial government, or perhaps we may say more correctly, the time at which a man's provincial government began. Cicero, when he was in Cilicia (Ad Att. v. 16, 4), says of Bibulus, who was sent to Syria, that he was not thinking even then of entering his province, and it was said that he did this because he wished to leave it later; which evidently means that his term of office would be reckoned from the day when he entered his province. Cicero entered his province of Cilicia on the thirty-first of July, B.C. 51, and he intended to leave it on the thirtieth of July, B.C. 50, and so complete his proconsular year (Ad Att. v. 21, 0). But both Bibulus and Cicero were sent out as governors under a new regulation, and were not entering on a provincial government immediately after a consulship.

The author of the "Histoire de César" (ii. 472) says that in his opinion, A. W. Zumpt (Studia Romana, Berlin, 1859) is the only person who has cleared up this question, and accordingly he says that he borrows most of Zumpt's arguments.

He states that the month of March was usually the time when the consuls who had last gone out of office took possession of their provincial governments; and it is therefore probable that the law of Vatinius, which gave Caesar his Cisalpine province for five years, was enacted in the last days of February B.C. 59, and that Caesar's proconsulship must be dated from the day when this law was enacted; but that nothing would have prevented Caesar "from abridging the time of his consular office before the expiration of it, and seizing the military command or the imperium, as Crassus did in B.C. 55, who set out for Syria without waiting for the end of his consulship." He then says, if we suppose, which is not impossible, that the whole year of Caesar's consulship was comprised in his proconsulship, the first term of five years would terminate at the end of B.C. 55, and consequently the second at the end of B.C. 50. He adds, " Such was the system of the Senate, who were naturally much disposed to shorten the duration of the proconsulship of the Gallic provinces."

I think that this explanation cannot be accepted. The supposition that the whole year of Caesar's consulship was comprised in his proconsulship appears to me a most absurd conjecture. That the Senate were naturally much disposed to shorten Caesar's term, if they could, is true, for the evidence proves it. The author of the "Histoire" has a note which is founded on his own experience: he says, "In all ages it has been seen that assemblies (assemblées: he means of course such bodies as the Roman Senate and the English Parliament) attempt to diminish the duration of the powers given by the people to a man who did not sympathize with them. This is an example: the constitution of 1848 declared that the President of the French Republic should be named for four years. Prince Louis Napoleon was elected on the 10th of December, 1848, and proclaimed on the 20th of the same month. His powers would properly have ended on the 20th of December, 1852. Now the Constituent Assembly, who foresaw the election of Prince Louis Napoleon, fixed the limit of the presidency on the second Monday of May 1852, thus taking from him seven months."

Dion (40, c. 59), when he is speaking of the attempt of the consul M. Marcellus in B.C. 51 to supersede Caesar before the proper time, remarks that Caesar's term ended in the next year, B.C. 50. Appian (B. C. ii. 27) states that C. Claudius, one of the consuls of B.C. 50, proposed in that year, but it is not said at what time of the year, to supersede Caesar, for his time was near an end; an expression which probably means that Appian understood the close of B.C. 50 to be the limit of Caesar's proconsular government. In a letter to Atticus (vii. 7. 6) written at the end of B.C. 50, Cicero says, "Should we then allow a man in his absence to be a candidate for the consulship, when he retains his army, though the day fixed by the law is past?" Here he affirms indirectly that the legal authority of Caesar was terminated, but it is not certain what he means by the law, though perhaps he means the law which gave him a second term of five years. In another letter (Ad Att. vii. 9. 4) Cicero supposes himself to say to Caesar, "You have held a province for ten years, a term given to you not by the Senate, but by yourself through violence and a faction. The time is past, not the time fixed by law, but by your own pleasure. But suppose that it was granted by law: a decree has been made for the purpose of superseding you. You put a difficulty in the way, and you say, Have respect to my claims. I reply, Have respect to our wishes. Would you keep your army longer than the term for which the people granted it, and against the will of the Senate? You must fight it out then, he would reply, unless you allow it." These two passages do not seem to enable us to determine the question between Caesar and the Senate. The real question was whether Caesar should be a candidate for the consulship without coming to Rome, and as this had been allowed by a law which was supported by Pompeius and Cicero, it seems to be implied that he should keep his army and his provinces at least until he was elected. It is certain that he did not intend to give them up until he had secured the consulship; and it appears that his enemies attempted to strip him of his power even before his term expired according to their own reckoning. The Epitome of Livy (108), an authority of no great value, states that Caesar was entitled under a law to hold his provinces to the time of his consulship. This law seems to be the law which allowed him to be a candidate for the consulship without coming to Rome; and the statement in the Epitome may be true. Caesar certainly did not intend to give up his provinces until he had the consular power in his hands. Cicero (Ad Att. vii. 7. 6) admits that when Caesar was empowered to be a candidate for the consulship without appearing at Rome, the power of keeping his army was also allowed, not directly, I suppose, for he does not say that, but he means the power of keeping his army was a necessary consequence of or involved in the permission to be a candidate in his absence.

APPENDIX III.

CATO AND MARCIA.

DRUMANN (Porcii, 198) says of Marcia, the second wife of Cato Uticensis, "she bare several children, and then after B.C. 56, in which year she reconciled Cato with Munatius Rufus, and with the consent of Cato, she lived with Hortensius, after whose death in the year 50 she returned into her former condition." He should have said that she lived with Hortensius as his wife, and that Cato married her again as a widow, as Plutarch says (Cato, c. 52). The death of Hortensius made the vacancy in the College of Augurs which was filled by the election of M. Antonius.

It is not easy to see how Drumann understood this transaction about Marcia, nor will his readers easily understand what he has written. Perhaps he viewed the affair as an instance of a man lending his wife or granting a lease of her for the life of the grantee. So Cato would have the reversion of her, which would become an estate in possession when the estate of Hortensius was determined by his death. It is wonderful that this matter has been so much misunderstood.

Plutarch (Cato, cc. 25, 52) has told the story on the authority of Thrasea, who used as his authority Munatius Rufus, an intimate friend of Cato who accompanied him to Cyprus in B.C. 58 (p. 81). Q. Hortensius wishing to be more intimately connected with Cato asked for Cato's daughter Porcia as a wife, though Porcia was then the wife of Bibulus and had brought him two sons. Hortensius said "that according to men's opinions such a thing was strange, but that according to nature it was good and for the advantage of states that a woman who was in her youth and perfection should neither be idle and check her procreative power, nor yet should by breeding more children than enough cause trouble to her husband and impoverish him, when he wanted no more children; but that if there was a community of offspring among worthy men, it would make virtue abundant and widely diffused among families, and would mingle the State with itself by these family relationships. If Bibulus, he said, was greatly attached to his wife, he would return her as soon as she had borne a child, and he had become more closely united with Bibulus and Cato by a community of children." It is plain from the story that it was quite possible for Bibulus to part with his wife and for Hortensius then to marry her, for in whatever form Porcia had been married to Bibulus, a divorce was possible according to Roman usages, and then Porcia could marry Hortensius.

Cato replied that he loved and esteemed Hortensius, but he thought it strange that he should propose to marry Porcia, who was the wife of another man. Upon this Hortensius asked for Cato's wife Marcia, who was still young enough to have children, and Cato had children enough. It was said, as Plutarch adds, that Marcia was then with child. Cato seeing the eagerness of Hortensius did not refuse, but he said that L. Marcius Philippus, the father of Marcia, must consent. Philippus did consent, and he gave Marcia in marriage to Hortensius in the presence of Cato, and Cato joined in giving her away. Now it is an elementary principle of Roman law that a woman could not have two husbands at the same time, nor a man two wives. Marcia therefore was divorced, and then she was married, as Plutarch says, to Hortensius. If she was with child at the time, the child would be Cato's, as we see in the case of Octavius, afterwards the Emperor Augustus, who married Livia when she was with child by her husband Tiberius Claudius Nero. Nero surrendered Livia to Octavius, who married her, and on the birth of the child sent it to Nero, the former husband of Livia. Octavius, who was a very methodical man and kept a journal, made an entry in it that he sent to the father the child that Livia, then his own wife, had produced (Dion, 48, c. 44). The object of Hortensius was to have legitimate children by Marcia, who must therefore have become his wife, for a Roman could not have children who should be in his power, as the phrase was, unless the woman was capable of becoming his wife, and therefore, as it has been stated, Marcia was divorced before she could marry Hortensius.

Strabo (p. 515) says it is reported that it is the custom among the Tapyri for husbands to give up their wives to other men when they have had two or three children from them: as in our time according to an old Roman custom Cato gave up his wife Marcia to Hortensius who asked for her. It is not certain whether Strabo understood the real nature of the transaction; but perhaps he did.

When Hortensius died, Cato, who wanted a person to look after his household and daughters, took Marcia again, who was a widow with a large estate, which Hortensius had left to her. This was the ground on which Caesar in his discourse against Cato (Anticato, or Anticatones, for there were two books) charged Cato with covetousness and making a traffic of his marriage, "for why should he give up his wife," said Caesar, "if he still wanted one, or why should he take her back, if he did not want one, if it was not that from the first the woman was put as a bait in the way of Hortensius, and Cato gave her up when she was young that he might have her back when she was rich?" Plutarch replies that "to accuse Cato of filthy lucre is like upbraiding Hercules with cowardice: but whether the matter of the marriage was not well in other respects is a thing for inquiry. However Cato did espouse Marcia, and entrusting to her his family and daughters hurried after Pompeius" (c. 52).

END OF VOL. IV.

www.ingramcontent.com/pod-product-compliance
Lightning Source LLC
Chambersburg PA
CBHW051851300426
44117CB00006B/353